Exile and Identity

Pitt Series in Russian and East European Studies

JONATHAN HARRIS, EDITOR

Exile and Identity

POLISH WOMEN IN
THE SOVIET UNION
DURING WORLD WAR II

Katherine R. Jolluck

UNIVERSITY OF PITTSBURGH PRESS

Published by the University of Pittsburgh Press, Pittsburgh, Pa., 15260
Copyright © 2002, University of Pittsburgh Press
All rights reserved
Manufactured in the United States of America
Printed on acid-free paper
10 9 8 7 6 5 4 3 2 1

All illustrations are reproduced courtesy of the
Hoover Institution Archives, Stanford, California.

Portions of chapters 6 and 8 appeared in "You Can't Even Call Them
Women: Poles and 'Others' in Soviet Exile during the Second World War,"
Contemporary European History 10, no. 3 (November 2001): 463–80.

Library of Congress Cataloging-in-Publication Data

Jolluck, Katherine R.
  Exile and identity : Polish women in the Soviet Union during World War
II / Katherine R. Jolluck.
    p. cm. — (Pitt series in Russian and East European studies)
  Includes bibliographical references and index.
  ISBN 0-8229-4185-6
  1. World War, 1939–1945—Women—Poland. 2. World War,
1939–1945—Women—Soviet Union. 3. World War, 1939–1945—Personal
narratives, Polish. 4. Exiles—Soviet Union. 5. Poles—Soviet Union.
I. Title. II. Series in Russian and East European studies.
  D810.W7 J65 2002
  940.53'082'09438—dc21

                                                              2002000568

To my mother, Helen,
and in memory of my father,
John M. Jolluck

Contents

Illustrations following page 182

Acknowledgments

In the course of writing this book, I have incurred many institutional, intellectual, and emotional debts. I would like to thank the kind and knowledgeable staff at the Hoover Institution Archives who aided me throughout the research process, particularly Irena Czernichowska and Zbyszek Stanczyk. Wojciech Zalewski of the Stanford University Libraries also provided valuable assistance. My colleagues and friends at Stanford gave invaluable insight and support; Lou Roberts pushed me in new directions and helped me develop my theoretical approach, and I would like to reiterate my undying appreciation and affection to Jeff Fear, Lynne Hirsch, Tom Jackson, Allison Katsev, and Wendy Wall.

I received research and writing grants and fellowships from the MacArthur Foundation, the American Association of University Women, the Kosciuszko Foundation, the American Council of Learned Societies/Social Science Research Council Joint Committee on Eastern Europe, the Hoover Institution, and the History Departments at the University of North Carolina, Chapel Hill, and Stanford University. I am extremely grateful to these institutions, and the individuals behind them, for the generous support that made this book possible.

During the revision process, Don Raleigh, my former colleague at the University of North Carolina, provided encouragement and thoughtful feedback on my manuscript. More than that, he made invaluable contributions to my intellectual and professional development. Thanks to Robert Blobaum and an anonymous reader for their very helpful comments on the manuscript. I would also like to express my gratitude to several anonymous readers who commented on draft versions of articles drawn from this material. Special thanks to Stewart Walker, Greg Madejski, and Helen Wang.

No one has helped me more than Norman Naimark—my model of a historian, my friend, and my husband. His advice, insights, and criticisms have continually strengthened my work, while his warmth and encouragement have sustained me.

Introduction

In the fall of 1997, I was working at the Hoover Institution Archives, completing the research for this book. Among the archives of the wartime Polish government-in-exile, I came across a personal statement, written in 1943, by Józef Ptak. I immediately recalled that name from my childhood, hearing my father, an immigrant from Poland, talk about his friends in the local Polish community in Cleveland. Although Józef Ptak is as common a name in Poland as Joe Brown is in the United States, a phone call to my father established that his friend had indeed been deported from eastern Poland, with his wife and children, to a settlement in the Gor'kii *oblast'* of Soviet Russia; the birthdate, hometown, and occupation recorded on the document confirmed that these men were one and the same.

A photocopy of the document, intended for my father to read and then pass on to Mr. Ptak, lay on my desk when I received a phone call several weeks later informing me of my father's death. A veteran of the Korean War, my father had been active in the Polish League of American Veterans, which sent a delegation to the funeral home to honor him. In uniform, the elderly men held a brief ceremony that ended with one of them speaking, in Polish, about my father and his military service. That man was Józef Ptak. When he finished, I approached him as he stood with his wife and told them that in California I read the document he had written more than fifty years ago in Iran, in which he described his ordeals under the Soviet regime. He replied that he had long forgotten about it and would like to read it once again and show it to his children. The fact that I, a young American, knew somewhat of his wartime trials created an unspoken yet immediate connection, for few in his adopted country had even an inkling of what had happened in eastern Poland in the early years of World War II. Only the 1943 discovery of 4,400 murdered Polish army officers in mass graves in the forests of Katyń is widely known.[1] But how many are aware that these officers were among hundreds of thousands of individuals forcibly transported from Poland to the USSR in 1939–1941? That the majority were administratively exiled, without being charged with any crime? That women and children, as well as men, were taken?

Several factors caused the events, and the stories of the lives they disrupted, to be left in obscurity. The enormity and barbarity of the Holocaust that had taken place on Polish soil overshadowed the crimes that the other wartime occupier—the USSR—committed there. The wartime alliance between the Western Allies and the USSR quieted discussion about the Soviet invasion and annexation of eastern Poland in 1939 and the subsequent treatment of its inhabitants. And the Soviet-backed Communist government installed in Poland at the close of WWII silenced public discussion of the topic there for decades; the imperatives of the much-glorified Polish-Soviet friendship placed the entire historical episode out of bounds for scholars.[2]

Researchers in the West, particularly Polish émigrés, devoted attention to the invasion of eastern Poland beginning in the early postwar years. Lack of access to Soviet and Communist Polish archives hampered the historiography, which tended to follow traditional historical biases. Preoccupied with the military, foreign relations, the economy, and high politics, the scholarly literature left society and culture out of the academic inquiry.[3] The murder of the officers at Katyń received by far the most sustained attention.[4] The fate of Polish citizens arrested and sent to forced labor camps was used to illustrate the character of the Soviet Gulag.[5] Civilian deportations did not receive sustained analysis. Stories of individuals such as Józef Ptak and his wife, Janina, a forester and a homemaker, if told at all, came out in the form of memoirs.[6]

In the 1980s, Jan Gross and Irena Grudzińska-Gross brought the plight of Poles under Soviet occupation to the attention of Western scholars with a collection of children's accounts of the episode.[7] Jan Gross subsequently published an important study of the Soviet invasion and administration of eastern Poland. He discussed the circumstances of the deportations and their effects on the Polish population in the region but did not follow the subjects into the USSR.[8] Several other works also focused on the occupation, and one traced the fate of Poles who ended up in the USSR, through arrest, deportation, and border changes, over a period of nearly fifty years, beginning in 1939.[9] The scholarly literature has largely focused on Soviet policies, not on the way they affected and were interpreted by those to whom they were applied. It may have been inevitable that while the Soviet Union existed and denied its brutal treatment of the Poles, emphasis in the research would fall on bringing the extent of these wrongs to light. Nevertheless, the consequences of Soviet actions, particularly the deportations, demand exploration from the perspective of the victims.

The collapse of the Communist regimes in both Poland and the USSR lifted the taboos on the history of Polish-Soviet relations, and scholars have since received access to some archives. The 1990s saw an explosion of publications in Poland on the occupation and subsequent deportations, filling the hunger for information and the need to air long-suppressed wrongs. Firsthand accounts, previously publishable only in the West, filled the pages of Polish journals and books.[10] The massacre at Katyń continued to receive attention, since scholars had located the initial orders for these executions and for those of approximately ten thousand other missing Polish prisoners.[11] Polish scholarship also began wrestling with the question of numbers: of internees, arrestees, and deportees, and of those who died as a direct result of Soviet policies toward the Poles. Historians are now trying to reconcile earlier estimates with statistics contained in documents examined from NKVD (Soviet security police) archives.[12] Finally, monographs on the living conditions in exile, addressing one of the neglected aspects of the Soviet domination of eastern Poland, have started to appear.[13]

Still, something is missing. At my father's funeral I also met Janina Ptak. I knew, from her husband's testimony, that she had also been deported. His document told me that she had been forced to perform heavy physical labor and that he worried about her weak health. It stated that she led clandestine Easter celebrations in the forest and that they lost two small children while in exile. Thin and frail, Janina was quiet at our meeting. Though I had not found any document written by her in the archives, I knew she had her own story. The intensity and warmth with which she clasped my hands, as she thanked me profusely and wished me well, struck me as a hallmark of many such women who survive the hell of war: soft-spoken, even self-effacing, yet possessed of a remarkable strength and endurance.

Women's experiences of major historical events have long suffered neglect. Though this myopia has undergone some correction, it particularly affects accounts of war. With the spotlight trained on battles and treaties, on politicians, on diplomats and fighters, the involvement of women falls into the shadows, for they are not typically the decision makers or the armed combatants. The persistent myth of war as largely a struggle between two military forces, relegates women to the sidelines. And yet, as the wars of the twentieth century dramatically demonstrate, women are centrally involved in the violence of war in diverse capacities: as members of the military services, the backbone of underground movements, mothers of soldiers, and subjects and supporters of war aims and propaganda. Above all, they have been objects of wartime destruction and dislocation, in general, and of sexual violation, in particular. As the wars in Bosnia and Kosovo made clear in the 1990s, targeting women is a central aspect of warfare, equal in import to battles and bombings. The experiences of deportation, forced labor, rape, struggling to keep children alive, and maintaining one's identity in the face of attempts to erase it are not incidental to war, but as integral to its full story as the soldier's varied travails. We need not only to understand the aims and mechanisms of policies directed at women but also how the women themselves reacted.

This book focuses on the women who were forcibly transported from eastern Poland to the interior of the USSR and endeavors to explain not only the ways these women were victimized but also how they responded: how they interpreted what was happening to them and the strategies they used to cope with their daily traumas. It uses the women's own words from descriptions of their exile written immediately upon their release. Though Janina Ptak did not write such a document, several thousand other women did.

Sources

These unique documents resulted from a complicated series of events. After the German army invaded the USSR on 22 June 1941, the official Soviet attitude toward the Poles changed drastically. Seeking in them an ally, Soviet officials negotiated an agreement with the exiled Polish government, located in London. Besides restoring diplomatic relations between the two governments, the Sikorski-Maiskii Pact of 30 July 1941 had two major provisions. First, it called for the formation of a Polish army in the USSR to fight the Nazis, set up under the command of General Władysław Anders, who was released for this purpose from a Moscow prison. Second, a protocol attached to the pact promised "amnesty to all Polish citizens who are at present deprived of their freedom on the territory of the USSR either as prisoners of war or on other adequate grounds."[14] Although amnesty implied pardon for guilt that the civilian deportees did not feel they bore, they nonetheless received the news of their release as a miracle. Some Poles received no notification of the amnesty, while others were barred from leaving their places of exile because local authorities denied them the documents necessary for departure and travel. Additionally, Soviet officials routinely diverted trains of Polish citizens in search of Polish delegations, routing them to collective farms in Kirghizia and Uzbekistan for continued forced labor. Despite the Soviet side's reluctance to consistently uphold the terms of the amnesty, in the late summer of 1941, waves of Poles started flowing from all over the country to the southern portions of the USSR in search of outposts of the newly formed Anders army. Polish citizens traveled for months in extremely dismal conditions seeking the care and protection of their own government.

The rapprochement between the Soviet and Polish governments soon began to erode, and by the spring of 1942, General Sikorski, prime minister of the Polish government-in-exile, sought the removal of the Anders army from Soviet territory. With Stalin's agreement, two evacuations of Polish citizens took place, the first in March–April 1942 and the second in August. The evacuations included military personnel, their surviving family members, and orphaned children, and altogether rescued approximately 115,000 Polish citizens, only part of those initially exiled from their homeland.[15] Although more evacuations were promised, they did not materialize, as increasingly troubled relations between the Polish and Soviet governments climaxed in a complete break in April 1943 after the German discovery of the graves at Katyń.

Shortly after the evacuees traveled across the Caspian Sea to Iran, Polish authorities asked them to write about their experiences under the Soviet regime. The initiative for gathering such documents came from Stanisław Kot, a historian who was appointed Polish ambassador to the USSR after the Sikorski-Maiskii Pact restored diplomatic relations. Kot had two motives in this undertaking. First, he hoped that evidence from exiled Poles might establish the fate of the 15,000 missing Polish officers, some of whose bodies were later found at Katyń. Second, he thought that information collected on the invasion and occupation would help Poland, at the war's end, achieve the nullification of the annexation of the eastern Polish territories to the USSR.[16] Although he began collecting documents immediately after the amnesty, it proved a difficult task while still on Soviet territory, and he renewed his efforts in Iran.[17] Soon afterwards, General Anders agreed that the army would carry on the work Kot began and oversaw the creation of the Bureau of Documents to work with the material.[18] Report gathering continued even after the tragic fate of the missing officers had been revealed, because Polish authorities believed that the information their citizens possessed about life in the USSR could prove useful in negotiating a peace settlement at the close of the war. The following excerpt of a note, written late in 1943 by one of the individuals assigned to analyze the documents, explains this expectation:

> Polish citizens who went through Russia are the first large group of people in about twenty years who were exposed to life in the Soviet Union, who know from experience the nature of the Soviet regime, and who were then allowed to leave Russia's borders. The testimonies may constitute a precious source enabling us to reveal to world opinion the truth about Russia.[19]

Polish authorities collected tens of thousands of handwritten reports from the evacuees, written from late 1942 through 1944, soon after their departure from the USSR. Approximately 20,000 are located in the Hoover Institution Archives at Stanford University.[20] These descriptions of recently experienced events, written from memories still fresh, retain an immediacy and an often extraordinary recollection of detail. Their authors represent a cross section of Polish society in terms of class, education, occupation, and place of origin. While some documents are comprehensive and eloquent, others are barely literate, written almost as stream of consciousness, sometimes rendered phonetically. Children too young to write drew pictures. Evacuated Poles recorded their experiences in a variety of forms. The army circulated several questionnaires, to which many respondents provided brief, straightforward answers; some used these forms as a jumping board, filling composition books with expanded replies and descriptions. Still others offered detailed narratives and lengthy memoirs, numbering several hundred pages long. Content ranges from the briefly factual to the intensely personal.

Several points must be made regarding the reliability of these documents that were written under the auspices of a government institution. First, the authorities overseeing the documentation process encouraged the authors to write freely and expansively of their ordeals. An order written by General Anders in 1943 states: "The development of each topic and its presentation in the form of a free-flowing narrative is highly desirable."[21] One man involved in this work remarked on its spontaneity, caused by the fierce desire of the exiles to unload their experiences once in contact with representatives of Poland.[22] Many of the statements do not address the topics of the questionnaires, following their own course completely. Second, in the process of preparing the documents for possible use with representatives of the American and British governments, members of the Bureau of Documents of the Polish Army in the East marked parts of the originals—recollections or sentiments that the government apparently feared might prove detrimental to its case—to be omitted in typed versions. The need to edit suggests that the authors, for the most part, felt unrestricted in recording their stories. As Jan Gross stressed, "that the Polish authorities were uncomfortable with the answers to their questionnaires is an important confirmation of their worthiness."[23] Third, the accounts seem more often to be understated rather than exaggerated. Events that are chilling to the reader are often told in a matter-of-fact way, thus suggesting their commonness. The basic similarity between experiences of individuals from various walks of life, who were sent to a wide range of places in the USSR, also provides authenticity. Indeed, the very repetitiveness of the stories points to a common ground of shared misery. The experiences speak for themselves; these individuals did not need to be coaxed into writing denunciations of the Soviet system. Certainly the testimonies constitute effective propaganda for the Polish government-in-exile, which desired to show the Western allies the exploitative nature of the Soviet government. But, with few exceptions, the recollections and assessments are not consciously propagandistic, nor do they dwell on overtly political issues. It is precisely the myriad ways that the Poles felt wronged by the Soviet regime in their daily and intimate lives that reveal the brutal use of power and the lack of boundaries between the personal and the political. Simple accounts of their daily lives and losses are more effective and expressive than mere propaganda.

Since the evacuations centered on the Anders army, men were overrepresented on the ships traveling to Iran and, consequently, in the documents collected there. Because of the focus of my research, I read 1,864 testimonies by women and several hundred by men. I also used a collection of letters that the Anders army received from women and children stranded in Soviet Central Asia. Writing primarily in 1942–1943, the authors describe their deplorable conditions and plead for help, anticipating imminent death.

These letters were addressed mainly to husbands, sons, and fathers presumed to have joined the Anders army and, therefore, in a position, it was hoped, to rescue the authors. Many of the letters never reached the addressees and remained sealed until a researcher opened them in 1989.[24] Additionally, I used Polish government communiqués and reports on the conditions of its citizens in the USSR found in various collections of the Hoover Institution Archives.[25] Finally, recently released documents of the NKVD provided insight into Soviet intentions and operations.[26] These documents form the central sources for this book.

The aggregation of accounts provides a clear and detailed picture of the conditions in which the women lived. It also tells us much more. In reading the documents, I look for shared anxieties and coping strategies, characterizations and metaphors. I examine what they chose to comment on and in what terms they did so. Equally telling are the silences, particularly on issues such as rape, that appear in the official documents. Inaccuracies and biases in the testimonies are revealing: a collective pattern of meanings, which illuminates how the authors perceived themselves and their new environment, can be discerned. Thus, what interests me is both "what really happened," and how it was interpreted and remembered.

Since memories, sensibilities, and interpretations are constantly changing, I considered it necessary to focus on accounts written soon after the experiences and decided not to interview survivors or rely on recently written memoirs. While the outlines of the stories would be the same, changes in the survivors' lives and the world around them would undoubtedly alter their coloration. Instead, I wanted to examine how the Poles understood and responded to the events as close as possible to their occurrence. I approached these documents as a window on mid-twentieth century Polish identity.

Traumas of Exile

On the heels of the German invasion from the west, the Soviet incursion into eastern Poland and the subsequent arrest and deportation of hundreds of thousands of its citizens subverted many of the conventional categories that had seemed to provide order to the world, even during moments of great chaos. No formal declaration of war was made, yet the Poles lost their territory and sovereignty. Despite assurances by the Soviet government that it only intended to give the Polish people "the opportunity to live a peaceful life," army units were routed and officers taken prisoner.[27] Though the Poles quickly understood that they were at war with the USSR, the categories traditionally expected to organize this reality did not hold true. The binary opposites commonly associated with wartime, of front and home front, combatant and civilian, were completely overrun.[28] While Red Army troops disarmed Polish soldiers and arrested government officials, NKVD agents, banging on doors in the middle of the night, invaded the privacy of the home and shattered its peace. Women, children, elderly, and infirm individuals were subject to treatment usually reserved for male belligerents: they were crowded into prison cells, loaded into cattle cars, and punitively exiled from their homeland. Handled as dangerous criminals, many were never told what transgression put them in this category.

The crossing and blurring of boundaries—the physical ones dividing states and the mental ones separating categories of people and activities—profoundly destabilized the people of eastern Poland, especially those forcibly transported eastward. Locked in the transports, Poles screamed with anguish and fainted from grief when they crossed the border of their country. They dreaded what they would encounter once they had passed the border, for it seemed they were leaving behind their entire civilization. These individuals were taken deep into the Soviet Union and deposited in prisons, labor camps, special settlements, or collective farms. Polish women found that little in exile resembled their former homes—not the geography and climate, material conditions, ethnic and demographic composition, social relations, or the daily routine. Countless certainties of their previous lives collapsed. In exile, the Poles faced unaccustomed mixes of peoples and encountered daily attacks on their national identity. They endured insults, efforts at "reeducation," and the prohibition of the practice and transmission of their religious and national customs. Maintaining one's "Polishness" became a constant struggle.

So, too, was daily existence. Women endured physically debilitating conditions and treatment. More insidiously, the altered shape of their lives threatened both their sense of self and of belonging to a community. Mothers saw the corpses of their children crudely discarded. Some women faced sexual abuse or the prospect of forced prostitution for survival—a circumstance seen as destroying one's overlapping honor as a Pole and as a woman. They spent eighteen-hour days logging or mining in ruined health, while their children sat at home, hungry and unattended. Often separated from their families, husbands and fathers no longer served as sources of protection and support, so women suddenly became the sole providers for themselves and their families. Given the meager payment they received, even this role was often beyond their capacity to fulfill, forcing some mothers to give their children up to Soviet orphanages or watch them die. Nearly all of the women were deprived of the opportunity to spend their days with their children; to teach them Polish language, history, and traditions; or to impart their Catholicism. They grieved for their families and their nation.

The experience of Polish women in Soviet exile can be seen as the story of how they adapted and preserved themselves in this foreign and hostile environment. In other words, how they strove to recreate home. The desire for home, for their private and familiar world, translated into the search for a stable and unified identity, for in being taken from their homes, they suffered much more than the loss of property, family, and routine. In its more abstract sense, home signifies safety and stability and a coherence and unity that implies boundaries separating out those who do not fit. It also embraces the knowledge of who one is and where one belongs—even if unarticulated. Therefore, the physical uprooting of the women critically affected their definition of self and of order in the surrounding world. Both men and women were subjected to the Soviet policy of arrest and deportation, and the loss of home and community, concretely and metaphorically speaking, struck both sexes. The loss of home, however, dealt a compounded injury to women because the home in Polish society, as in many others, was traditionally perceived as female space. And women were defined by this space that they occupied. Consequently, the loss of home—the functions women performed there and the family members to whom they were tied—threatened their very identity. In the words of Biddy Martin and Chandra Talpade Mohanty, "To the extent that identity is collapsed with home and community, and based on homogeneity and comfort, on skin, blood, and heart, the giving up of home will necessarily mean the giving up of self."[29]

The problem of identity constitutes a central aspect of Polish women's experience of Soviet exile. In response to the chaos and trauma of total dislocation, nationality emerges as one of their foremost concerns. The concept of nationality cannot be separated from the category of gender, an equally important and complicating preoccupation of the exiled women. Polish females struggled against the loss of identity in a foreign land by trying to impose the coherence of home and community, in the image of the traditional family, on themselves and their collective. Their accounts of life in exile demonstrate a complex process of identity construction, in which notions of "proper" womanhood and loyalty to the Polish nation are inextricably bound. They apply traditional social norms to their relations and functions in their small communities, microcosms of the nation; threatening behaviors or identities are attached to "others," defined on the basis of nationality. Through exclusion and the erection of borders, Polish women delineate the boundaries and configuration of their own community, their own selves. In this process, they essentialize and intertwine these elements of identity, gender, and nationality. The women continually link the configuration of gender roles that they regard as proper, civilized, and natural to their own particular national group.

Examining fiction from the postcolonial African nationalist movement, Rhonda Cobham found a similar effort "to recuperate some semblance of national dignity from the horrifying chaos and decay . . . by asserting the stability of gender identities."[30] For the women forcibly removed from Poland, this effort not only helped to recapture a feeling of national dignity but also restored a sense of order and offered hope for the future. The process of differentiation from the numerous others enabled them to remain apart from the society into which they were so unwillingly thrust and served to maintain a connection to home—to that which they perceived as familiar, Polish, and civilized. Here as elsewhere, the female tends to be the focus and the symbol of ethnic difference in, to use the term of Benedict Anderson, "imagining" the nation.

Nation and Gender

Even the slightest acquaintance with modern Polish history would lead one to expect a preoccupation with nationality among the exiles, for the issue of the nation has constituted a major concern of Polish society since the partitions at the end of the eighteenth century eliminated the state of Poland for 123 years. The historiography traces the struggle to preserve national identity in the face of foreign domination, but historians of Poland, like Polish nationalists, long operated from an ahistorical view of nationality, according it "the attributes of a force of nature rather than a product of history."[31] From the days of the romantic nationalists of the early nineteenth century, particularly Adam Mickiewicz and Maurycy Mochnacki, poets, politicians, and historians have treated the Polish nation as an enduring individuality.[32] Although the precise definition of the Polish nation—whether a political, cultural, linguistic, or ethnographic unit—was long debated, its existence as transhistorical, something above and beyond the attributes of its individual members, was not questioned. Privileging continuities, the traditional view has long treated the nation as a reified category. Some historians continue to talk of Polishness (*polskość*) as "something elusive," simply "the very essence of being a Pole."[33]

Scholars have begun to analyze the fluid nature and political character of nationality. In a recent book, Brian Porter traced the development of Polish nationalism in the nineteenth century from a moral principle to a closed and disciplined community.[34] As his work shows, nationality, like class and gender, is not an identity that simply exists but is constantly in the making in response to external influences and both individual and collective needs.[35] Additionally, it means different things to different persons, depending on the historical context and the circumstances of their lives. Histories of the Polish nation and nationalism, Porter's included, have consistently focused on the ideas and aspirations of men, typically elite ones, analyzing the thoughts and writings of Poland's famous writers, politicians, and insurrectionists.[36] While such inquiry represents a critical aspect in understanding how the nation is conceived, it has preempted attention to other manifestations of the nation, particularly among the general populace.

One consequence of this approach is the consistent assumption of the unity of the Polish nation. The romantic poet Kazimierz Brodziński voiced an idea in 1831 that has lingered through various incarnations of Polish nationalism: "The nation is an inborn idea, which its members, fused into one, strive to realize."[37] Polish writing, from the era of the partitions through the period of Solidarity, is suffused with invocations of this unity.[38] Polishness continues to be treated by many as a homogeneous and overriding identity, cutting across divisions within society and overshadowing all other aspects of identity. This assumption of the unity of the nation precludes investigation of the intersections of nationality with other categories, such as gender and class. Such a starting point also results in a failure to problematize differing relationships individuals and groups have to the nation. The historiography tends to assume that all individuals share the same experience of the nation and have the same thing in mind when they invoke it, reproducing the division denounced by the nineteenth-century poet Cyprian Norwid, between "Poland as a society" and "Poland as a nation."[39] The spotlight must be turned on the question of how an individual comes to know her- or himself as a Pole, or on the construction, organization, and functioning of those elements of self-perception and national identity throughout society as a whole.

A period of great trauma, as the experience of Soviet occupation and exile was for the Poles, represents a critical moment in the development of national identity and, therefore, offers a prime opportunity for investigating such issues. During this crisis, the lives of the Poles were completely uprooted and their nationality directly assaulted. Under these pressures their notions of Polishness were continually tested, developed, and rearticulated. Examining the experiences of women, particularly "determining precisely what notions of female identity were available to [them],"[40] does much more than fill gaps in the historical knowledge about the experiences of half of a society's population. It offers insight into the organization of a society or nation and the maintenance of hierarchies of power and subordination. It also reveals the ways women figure in and relate to the nation, exposing both differences and commonalities between women's and men's Polishness. Finally, such inquiry deepens our understanding of the cultural meaning ascribed to historical events by the given collective.

This book shifts the focus of inquiry into the Soviet domination of eastern Poland to the women, examining this episode from their perspective. It looks at the background and context of their adaptation and articulation of national identity. In this respect, *Exile and Identity* offers a ground-level view of Polish nationalism and seeks to show the centrality of gender to conceptions of nationality. This undertaking, I hope, will expand the notion of Polishness, for the experience of the Polish nation cannot be comprehended solely through the concept of nationality as traditionally understood. Gender emerges from the documents as an equally important and a complicating factor both in how these women were affected by what was happening to them and how they interpreted it. Gender also determined what aspects of women's experiences became part of the story of the victimized nation.

Part One of this book sets up the background for the analysis of women's experiences in exile, following the women from their homes in the summer of 1939 across the Polish-Soviet border in 1940–1941. Chapter 1 provides the context for the displacement of Poles, explaining the events, beginning in September 1939, that disrupted the lives of millions of Polish citizens. It discusses the mechanism of the deportations, including when they occurred, who was affected, and why. The next chapter presents a picture of the women whose interpretations of the experience of Soviet exile form the basis of this study. Based on the information they provide about themselves, it analyzes their socioeconomic background, as well as the reasons for and final destinations of their forced journeys to the USSR.

The main sections of the book, Parts Two and Three, explore the women's lives in exile, particularly how they interpreted and coped with profound changes in their existence. Part Two focuses on the conditions and routine of their lives in Soviet prisons, labor camps, and special settlements, and analyzes how the altered shape of their existence affected their identity as Poles and as women. At the same time, it examines the ways that their previous identities and ideals shaped both their interpretations of the experience and their coping strategies, revealing that conceptions of proper gender roles are inextricably bound to their ideals of patriotism and expressions of attachment to the nation. Together, chapters 3 through 5 seek to demonstrate that the experience of exile in the USSR entailed the articulation of a traditional, homogeneous identity for Polish females.

Part Three explores another mechanism in that process of identity consolidation and articulation, which occurred not merely through the interplay of historical legacy, past experiences, and the realities of daily life under the Soviet regime. An equally important component of self-definition was differentiation from others, isolated on the basis of nationality. This part focuses on relations between ethnic Polish females and women of other nationalities with whom they were forced to live. On the whole, the exiled Polish women do not feel solidarity with females of other nationalities, regardless of the fact that they, too, were victims of the Stalinist regime. Perceiving a multifold threat to their own identity, women use gender to construct nationality—their own and others', erecting sharp boundaries between themselves and these others. In this way, the women affirm that they do not belong in the alien world of the USSR and maintain a connection to home, to what they understand as Polish, European, and civilized.

I

"Thus Began the Wandering of the Polish People"

The Background to Exile

I

"We Were Seized by Utter Despair"

From Invasion to Exile

Like most civilians, Maria Wojnilowiczówna, a high school student from a village near Baranowicze in the Nowogród province of Poland, dismissed the talk of war that began in the spring of 1939. Poland was strong, she believed, and in the event of war it would "show" the Germans. Wojnilowiczówna, along with many other Poles, fondly recalls the summer of 1939 as a beautiful and happy time. Even her father's mobilization in August was a sanguine event. "I myself don't know what kind of impression the knowledge of war made on me. War! War! What does it look like?" she reminisces. "What will it bring?" For those of the older generations who had lived through World War I and the subsequent border wars, the idea of war was more concrete and frightening, and women agonized over what might lay in store for the men in their lives. "I wondered why the women at the station who had come to see their husbands off so frightfully despaired," admits Wojnilowiczówna. "Why cry? Was it possible that every one had to perish and not return?" In the first days of September 1939, she was far removed from the war. "At home it was peaceful and quiet," she notes. "Several times I thought to myself: this is supposed to be war? And I couldn't believe in it, I could not imagine, that far away in the west a dogged struggle seethed, that people were shedding blood and dying an honorable death."[1]

The separation of the battle front and the home was not to last long; Wojnilowiczówna and millions of her fellow citizens—civilian as well as military—were soon engulfed by the Second World War in a way none of them had foreseen or could have imagined possible. As the German army, which had invaded on 1 September without having declared war, advanced eastward, villages and towns that lay in its path endured bombings and floods of refugees fleeing from the Nazis. Overwhelmed by a superior foe, the Polish government, army detachments, and the high command fell back to the southeastern regions of Poland, from which they gradually withdrew to Romania.[2] Reeling from the German offensive, Poles in the east were surprised by the arrival of Soviet tanks and troop columns on 17 September. As the USSR had not declared war, many Poles initially assumed that the Red Army had come to help the Poles fight against the Nazis. The Polish-Soviet Non-Aggression Treaty of 1932 had been renewed in March 1934 for ten years, a fact lending credence to this interpretation. In some places, Soviet soldiers themselves encouraged this idea by announcing such assistance as their purpose, sometimes even waving white flags. Furthermore, the Polish high command, also uncertain about Soviet intentions, ordered Polish troops not to fight the Red Army unless it attacked or attempted to disarm them.[3]

What none of the Poles knew was that the Nazi-Soviet Pact, also known as the Molotov-Ribbentrop Pact, signed on 23 August 1939, included secret protocols to divide the Polish state between the two powers. This aspect of the treaty only became known in the West in 1945, at war's end; the Soviet government denied its existence until 1989.[4] The secret protocols spelled Poland's doom: "In the case of a territorial and political transformation of the territories belonging to the Polish State, the spheres of interest of Germany and the USSR will be delimited approximately along the line of the rivers Narew, Vistula and San."[5] The Soviet government considered that, in light of the German invasion and the flight of the Polish government, the Polish state ceased to exist. At 3 AM on 17 September, Vladimir Potemkin, deputy people's commissar for foreign affairs of the USSR, delivered a note to this effect to the Polish ambassador in Moscow, Wacław Grzybowski. The note further announced the nullification of all previous agreements between the Soviet and Polish governments. Two hours later, the Red Army crossed into Polish territory.[6]

The civilians realized quickly that the Soviets had not arrived in a friendly capacity. Poles reacted with shock and despair. Many women found the gravity of the situation reflected in the effect the news had on their fathers and husbands coming back from the German front. Maria Wojnilowiczówna watched her father return after the defense against the Nazis collapsed. "His eyes burned hotly, and it seemed that two tears shone on his cheeks," she recalls. "He did not greet us. He stood for a moment, and from faltering lips fell only one word, full of tragedy and threat: 'Bolsheviks.' I understood everything." A woman from Łomża describes a similar moment: "On the morning of 2 October I saw my father crying for the first time in my life. He came from town and said, 'Children, we are finished.' The Bolsheviks were in town."[7] To women unaccustomed to male tears, this sight was extremely disturbing, representing a break in the male protection and control that they had come to expect—just one rupture of the normal order, promising more to come.

By 1 October, virtually all armed resistance had been defeated; Warsaw surrendered to the Germans; Wilno, Grodno, and Lwów fell to the Soviets. Confident of their conquests, the invading powers had negotiated a new pact on 28 September, the German-Soviet Boundary and Friendship Treaty, which adjusted and sanctioned the new border between Germany and the USSR, effectively removing Poland from the map of Europe. In an oft-quoted speech at a session of the Supreme Soviet on 31 October, the Soviet Minister of Foreign Affairs, Viacheslav Molotov, pronounced, "But a brief blow by the German army, and then the Red Army, turned out to be enough to reduce the deformed offspring of the Treaty of Versailles, which had been living off the oppression of non-Polish nationalities, to nothing."[8] The Soviet Union thus acquired 52 percent of the Polish state, along with 13.5 million of its inhabitants.

Soviet representatives moved quickly to establish their authority. They took approximately 200,000 prisoners of war, interning them in camps in Poland, Lithuania, and Latvia, subsequently transporting some to the USSR.[9] On 22 October, after several weeks of propagandizing, cajoling, and threatening, Soviet authorities held compulsory and predetermined elections throughout the territories of eastern Poland. These elections sanctioned delegates to national assemblies in what were now called Western Belorussia and Western Ukraine. Several days later, these assemblies met and voted to request incorporation into the USSR, which the Supreme Soviet in Moscow quickly granted.

With the same speed and determination with which they accomplished the submission and incorporation of eastern Poland, the new rulers set out to Sovietize these lands. Large-scale arrests began soon after the invasion, robbing the population of its national and local leaders in the military, political, economic, religious, and cultural spheres. The initial targets were Polish army officers and reservists, government officials, police officers, political activists, landowners, businessmen, administrative elites, and the clergy. Village committees and local militias, formed under Soviet guidance, overturned previously established lines of authority and often carried out acts of revenge for past grievances. When the ruble replaced the *złoty* as legal tender, prewar savings were wiped out and businesses devastated. The economy was further disrupted as land and personal property were confiscated, redistributed, and, in the case of factories and goods, shipped eastward into Soviet Russia. In the spring of 1940, a campaign to force the population to renounce Polish citizenship and accept Soviet passports began; the occupiers made compliance imperative by attaching the privilege of a job or housing to acceptance or threatening arrest or deportation in the event of refusal.[10]

The new regime went beyond reorganizing the military, central and local governments, and the economy. It touched civilians deep in their homes, disrupting families and altering personal relationships. Even one's bed at night was no longer a private and secure space. Just as it did in the USSR, the NKVD conducted most of its business with Polish citizens during the night. "No one could ever be sure that he would sleep through a peaceful night," recalls Jadwiga Niemiec.[11] Security officers routinely barged in on sleeping families in the dead of night, ostensibly to check documents or search for weapons. As part of this procedure, they would often shine flashlights into the eyes of sleeping inhabitants, "as if to drive home the point that they could enter everywhere and could always do what they pleased."[12] And indeed they did. During their searches, Soviet security agents ransacked people's homes, confiscating or destroying what they considered desirable for themselves or subversive to the government. Private property seemingly ceased to exist.

Soviet officers and officials, and later their families, took up residence in the homes of Polish citizens. With little notice, the latter were forced to confine themselves to one room within their own houses and apartments. They watched the newcomers appropriate whatever they desired, including food, livestock, and firewood.[13] In many cases, the occupiers soon threw the Poles out of their homes altogether, requisitioning Polish domiciles for their own use.[14] Evicted families had to seek refuge in the already crowded homes of relatives and acquaintances.

Little of daily life remained as it had been previously. Many men never returned home after the organized armed resistance ceased because they either died fighting or were taken prisoner. Some men, particularly those with officer's rank, hid in the woods to avoid certain arrest should they arrive at their homes. Many women write of the terror of waiting for news of fathers and husbands and sons who had gone off to fight. Others recall furtive trips to the woods to see a loved one, to bring him food and clothing. Regina Ostaszkiewicz remembers how her father, the local post office director, would leave his hiding place to see his children briefly, to kiss them. On one such visit the Bolsheviks arrested him.[15]

Many night visits by the NKVD in the early months of the occupation resulted in the arrest of the men of the household. Frequently, security agents lied about the purpose of their visit, saying they were merely taking the relative for questioning; he would return the next day, they promised. Barbara Sokolowska, who lived in Lwów, notes, "The 9th of December is a memorable day for me." On that day the NKVD arrested her father, an army reserve officer; they told her he was only going for a brief interrogation, but he never returned. "Even now, three years later," she adds, "the memory of that nightmarish night makes me shiver and my hatred for the enemy grows." By the end of the year, writes Zofia Sicińska, "there was not a home in town in which they were not crying for someone, from which they had not taken the father, brother, or husband."[16]

Besides the toll of mass arrests, some families were separated simply by chance. With no forewarning that Poland was about to be split within, individuals who happened to be located—on a vacation, a business trip, or even at school—in the western half of Poland, which quickly fell to the Germans, were suddenly severed from their homes and relatives in the eastern part, now under Soviet occupation.[17] The same held true in the reverse direction. A large number of people arrested for so-called border infractions were caught trying to cross from one side of Poland to the other.

As a result of the severe and sudden disruption of families and social networks, females unexpectedly became the sole providers for themselves and their families. In many cases the women had never worked outside the home. They now spent their time scrounging for jobs and adapting their skills to the new economic conditions. One popular source of income in urban areas was from sewing clothing, often for Soviet officers and their families; other women survived by giving Russian lessons to Poles trying to find a place for themselves under the new regime. Frequently, women could not earn enough to provide food, shelter, and heat for their families, so they began selling their possessions to get by—a preview of their future existence in the USSR.[18]

Another new feature of life in eastern Poland was the interminable and ubiquitous lines, which appeared as a shocking marker of the changed conditions. People queued for everything.[19] Buying bread, in particular, required long waits each day. In addition to trying to purchase necessary goods, women now stood in lines to gather information about the whereabouts and health of arrested husbands and fathers. Families generally received no notice of the location of arrested members; many women, therefore, devoted large amounts of time and energy simply trying to find this out. If they did learn something, they stood in lines outside the prisons day after day, hoping that the guards would permit them to pass a parcel of food or clothing to imprisoned loved ones. Many women recall the desperate and humiliating ordeal of waiting outside these prisons, subjected to the abuse of guards, the ill humor of wardens, and the cold indifference of the weather. Teodozia Gołowczyńska writes that after the arrest of her husband, she divided her time between the school, where she worked, and prison lines, in which she waited in hope of passing food and underwear to her husband. Another woman went every day, from December through March, to try to deliver a package to her husband in a prison in Brześć-nad-Bugiem; her attempts ended with her deportation in April.[20]

Other women describe painful instances of walking down a street or standing in a line and suddenly catching a glimpse of a family member in a convoy of prisoners under guard and dog escort. The convicts were forbidden to speak and generally prohibited from even raising their heads. Relatives had to watch them being led away, not knowing where they were being taken. "Thus we saw Papa for the last time," recalls one young woman, "and we still don't know if we will see him again, if he survived it all, if they tortured him."[21]

By late 1939, terror, fear, and secrecy pervaded the atmosphere in eastern Poland. In the initial days after the entry of the Red Army, the invaders inflamed tensions among Ukrainians, Belorussians, and ethnic Poles, which often resulted in bloody conflicts and the seizure of property. Individuals were prompted to denounce neighbors and coworkers. Many people lost their jobs, others had to accommodate to the new conditions to keep their positions by learning the Ukrainian, Belorussian, or Russian languages. Teachers, in particular, had to make significant adjustments in their work, including removing all mention of God or Poland from their lessons.[22] The Soviet regime disbanded social, charitable, and cultural organizations; it viewed even scout leaders as politically dangerous and, therefore, targets for arrest. Informal groups disintegrated, relationships between neighbors and friends became constrained.

After the new year began, Soviet officials commenced procedures for a more chilling and catastrophic upheaval of civilian life—mass deportations to the interior of the USSR. Many Poles grew suspicious at the sight of increasing numbers of trains at the railway stations in the early months of 1940. Initially, at least, no one expected what was to subsequently transpire: the forced resettlement of hundreds of thousands, perhaps even one million, Polish citizens.

Until its final days, the Soviet government neither publicized data on the forced deportations nor allowed researchers access to the relevant archives; therefore, all calculations came from the wartime Polish government and the underground and, subsequently, émigré historians.[23] Their estimations stemmed largely from material gathered and analyzed by the Polish Army in the East, which was formed in the USSR in 1941. In addition to the testimonies of Polish citizens released from Soviet detention, the army used information collected by the Polish Embassy and social welfare delegates who provided relief to the amnestied Poles from February 1942 until January 1943. These estimates of the total number of Polish citizens forcibly transported from eastern Poland to the interior of the USSR range from 1 to 2 million (see table 1.1).[24] The total includes four categories of people.[25] The first and largest is that of civilian deportees, a group thought to include 980,000 to 1,080,000 individuals. The second category consists of Polish citizens arrested and imprisoned, numbering approximately 250,000. Additionally, between 180,000 and 240,000 men were taken as prisoners of war after the September 1939 campaign. Men forced into the Red Army and work battalions, numbering from 200,000 to 250,000, compose the final category. In the ensuing decades, historians tended to work from these wartime data,

Table 1.1

Early estimates of the total number of Polish citizens forcibly
removed from Poland to the USSR, 1939–1941

Source	Total	Deported	Arrested	Mobilized to Red Army	P.O.W.
Polish Embassy 1943	1,442,000	1,050,000	—	200,000	192,000
Polish Army 1944	1,692,000	990,000	250,000	210,000	242,000
Ministry of Justice 1949	1,660,000	980,000	250,000	250,000	180,000

Sources: Polish Government in London, *Polish-Soviet Relations: 1918–1943. Official Documents. Confidential.* (Washington, D.C.: 1943), 17–21; AC, box 68, no. 62c, Bohdan Podoski, "Polskie Wschodnie w 1939–1940," 29; Bronisław Kuśnierz, *Stalin and the Poles. An Indictment of the Soviet Leaders* (London: Hollis & Carter, 1949), 80.

arriving at estimates of 1.6 to 1.8 million as the total number of individuals transported against their will from Polish territory into the USSR.[26]

The collapse of the Communist regimes in Poland and the USSR opened new avenues of investigation and discussion, particularly into the so-called blank spots in Polish-Soviet relations. The opening of some Soviet archives has produced new research and dramatically revised—and contested —estimates of the number of deportees. Using documents of the NKVD's convoy troops, those responsible for transporting the individuals from Poland, and of the department charged with overseeing their receipt and placement, Aleksander Gurjanow concludes that the number of deportees reached only 315,000.[27] Similarly basing his work on post-Soviet archives, Albin Głowacki asserts that "the mass deportations of the years 1940–41 encompassed approximately 325,000 Polish citizens."[28] The similarity between these researchers' calculations and the figure given to the Polish ambassador by Deputy Commissar of Foreign Affairs Andrei Vyshinsky in 1941, has led several scholars to revise their assessments to a minimum of 320,000 deportees and a maximum of 400,000.[29] These figures amount to approximately one-third of the long-accepted total.

The revised data have prompted considerable debate among historians. Some question the reliability of the NKVD statistics and point out that since all figures come from the same basic source—the NKVD—the concurrence of documents means little.[30] Given the likelihood of discrepancies in interpreting and executing directives from the center at the local level, it may be that the NKVD documents simply do not tell the whole story.[31] While deportations were carried out methodically and from precise instructions, the testimonies of eyewitnesses confirm an inevitable level of chaos and arbitrariness not accounted for in the central documents.[32] No information exists in the NKVD documents thus far examined either on deaths or escapes from the transports, throwing into question the reliability of statistics from authorities at the receiving end of the journeys.[33] Some NKVD documents, including ones signed by its head, Lavrenti Beria, present different figures, leading one researcher to conclude that "the NKVD registers were not at all precise or unambiguous, so the information in them cannot finally solve the question of the number of deportees."[34]

A critical problem for interpreting Soviet statistics centers on the national minorities: since the regime sought to deny Polish citizenship to Ukrainians, Belorussians, and Jews taken from the occupied territory, it is unclear precisely who is included in the Soviet figures.[35] One final reason the conclusions of Gurjanow and Głowacki have met with resistance is that complete access has not yet been given to all Soviet archives.[36] Using statistics from later repatriations and demographic studies, some scholars continue to assert that the total number of deportees reached nearly one million.[37] While the early estimates, based on imprecise information, may well be inflated, work on the Soviet documents remains in its early stages, so a complete revision of the data is not yet possible. In the ensuing discussion, both minimum and maximum numbers of deportees will be provided, with the assumption that the real figure lies somewhere in between.

Two categories of individuals taken eastward, prisoners of war and conscripts to the Red Army, were exclusively male.[38] They were military men of all ranks and men of active service age. This book focuses solely on the other two categories: those transported to the USSR as deportees or under arrest —largely a civilian population, including individuals of both sexes. According to early estimates, 10 percent of Polish citizens arrested and sent to Soviet prisons and labor camps were female, numbering approximately 25,000.[39] Based on new research of NKVD documents for Western Belorussia—roughly half of the occupied territory—Krzysztof Jasiewicz estimates that 5 percent of all arrested persons were female.[40] His data, extrapolated to cover the entire area annexed by the USSR, yields an approximate total of 4,500

Table 1.2

Polish citizens forcibly removed to the USSR by sex and age
(based on early estimates)

	Total	Deported	Arrested	Mobilized to Red Army	P.O.W.
Men	1,121,000	434,000	235,000	210,000	242,000
Women	571,000	556,000	15,000	—	—
Age: 15–49	1,128,500	462,500	216,000	210,000	240,000
<15	379,500	379,500	—	—	—
>50	184,000	148,000	34,000	—	2,000

Source: AC, box 68, no. 62c, Bohdan Podoski, "Polskie Wschodnie w 1939–1940," 31–33.

arrested women. Other scholars, however, stress that the total number of in-dividuals imprisoned in the annexed territories has not yet been established.[41]

While most arrested persons were adult males, the majority of deportees were women and children.[42] For decades, scholars have reported that women constituted 52–57 percent of the total, numbering approximately 560,000 (see table 1.2).[43] The revisionist literature generally lacks information on the sex of the deportees. The new figure given for the deportations (320,000) and the old estimate of the percentage of females (55%) yields a total of 176,000. Combining both deportees and arrestees, the number of women who were removed from their homes and forced into Soviet exile ranges from a min-imum of 180,500 to a maximum of 585,000.

Several points require emphasis. Those Polish citizens arrested and imprisoned by Soviet authorities were charged, investigated, and sentenced ostensibly according to Soviet law. The charges were routinely fabricated, and many accusations referred to actions not considered criminal in Polish law. The Soviet regime regarded many individuals guilty simply because of their class origins, occupation, political allegiance, or national identity and convicted them for alleged counterrevolutionary activities or as "enemies of the people." In contrast, the civilian deportees, the largest group of ex-iled Poles, were never charged with any crime. Their social origins or rela-tionships to other Polish citizens sufficed to render them suspicious or dangerous in the eyes of Soviet authorities who exiled them by administra-tive decree. In the present discussion, this group is distinguished from those arrested and imprisoned—"prisoners"—by the term "deportees," and "ex-iles" refers to both groups as a whole.

Table 1.3
Estimates of the four deportations, 1940–1941

Deportation date	Traditional estimate	Revised estimates Gurjanow	Głowacki
1. February 1940	220,000	143,000	140,000
2. April 1940	320,000	61,000	61,000
3. June/July 1940	240,000	75,267	78,000
4. May/June 1941	200,000	36,000	40,000
Total	980,000	315,267	319,000

Deportations occurred in four waves, executed in an astonishingly short time.[44] In the first two cases, over the course of one to two nights, tens or hundreds of thousands of people were disturbed in their sleep, forced to undergo extensive searches, allowed to gather a few belongings, conveyed to train stations, locked inside cargo cars, and then transported eastward, across the Polish border. The first deportation commenced on the night of 10–11 February 1940, involving 220,000 people according to traditional (trad.) estimates or 140,000 according to revised (rev.) estimates, as shown in table 1.3. The next episode occurred the night of 12–13 April 1940 and affected 320,000 individuals (trad.) or 61,000 (rev.). Two months later, on 29 June 1940, another deportation began, involving 240,000 people (trad.) or 78,000 (rev.). The fourth deportation occurred one year later, from late May to mid-June 1941. It was still in progress when the German army invaded the USSR on 22 June, disrupting all Soviet administrative activity in its western territories and prompting the hasty eastward evacuation of Soviet authorities and their prisoners. Estimates of the number of persons transported at this time are 200,000 (trad.) and 40,000 (rev.).

The deportations resulted from the occupying power's desire to rid the territory of eastern Poland of all elements it suspected would be disloyal to the new regime or counterrevolutionary. This meant individuals whose national identity, class origins, political orientation, or level of social activism did not conform to the dictates of the Communist Soviet government, which proclaimed itself the leading force in society. Individuals with relatives abroad or in Soviet prisons and labor camps also became undesirables.[45] Soviet authorities meticulously gathered information on persons of targeted social groups. The nighttime seizures went smoothly and efficiently partly because of the surprise and terror of the population but largely because the authorities operated from lists drawn up in advance.

Each of the four deportations had a specific character in terms of the people affected. The first one targeted the military colonists known as *osadnicy*. Mostly privates and noncommissioned officers who fought in World War I and the Polish-Soviet war of 1920–21, they had received free plots of land in the eastern portions of the state under the Polish government's land redistribution program. Almost from the moment the Red Army entered Polish territory, the *osadnicy* were singled out in an extensive propaganda campaign as enemies of the Soviet system. Part of the antagonism stemmed from the policing and Polonizing function that these men and their families had been expected to serve in the borderlands. Additionally, Soviet authorities manipulated the resentment Ukrainian and Belorussian peasants with little land felt toward the colonizers.[46] The Soviet press in the occupied area blasted the *osadnicy* as "servants of the Polish government" who "brutally exploited the peasantry," exaggerating their numbers to 70,000—though the total did not surpass 8,000.[47]

On 5 December 1939, the Soviet Council of People's Commissars (Sovnarkom) adopted a resolution calling for the deportation of the military colonists; detailed regulations for carrying out the operation were issued several weeks later in a resolution entitled, "Instructions for deporting the Polish colonists (*osadniki*) from the western regions of the USSR and BSSR."[48] These documents, until recently secret, reveal the extensive procedures set into motion by the top echelons of Soviet power, directed by Lavrenti Beria.[49] He appointed L. Tsanava as chief of operations for the deportation in so-called Western Belorussia and I. Serov to the corresponding position in Western Ukraine, with instructions to have lists of individuals and families to be deported by early January. Besides the *osadnicy*, this deportation included civil servants, local government officials, police officers, forest workers, and small farmers.[50] Beria's assistant, Vsevolod Merkulov, personally supervised the operation.

The NKVD designated these individuals "special settlers" (*spetspereselentsy-osadniki*) and ordered that they be sent to special settlements of 100–500 families, far from populated areas.[51] Their status thus mirrored that of the kulaks, Soviet peasants deported as part of the collectivization campaign in 1930–1931. Like the kulaks, special settlers lived under the supervision of the NKVD, from which they had to obtain permission to leave the settlement for more than twenty-four hours or even to change barracks.

The April deportation removed the families of persons who had previously been arrested or taken as prisoners of war—in Soviet parlance, "individuals subjected to repressive measures"—and families of those who fled abroad or went into hiding. Employing the notion of collective responsibility, the Sovnarkom made the decision to deport these families, mostly women and children, on 2 March 1940.[52] Three days later, the Politburo of the Communist Party decided the fate of 14,700 Polish officers interned in Kozel'sk, Ostashkov, and Starobel'sk, as well as that of 11,000 others imprisoned in Ukraine and Belorussia; at the instigation of Beria, these men received "the supreme penalty—execution."[53] Many of these men were the fathers, sons, and husbands of the April deportees, who remained uninformed about the fate of their relatives for several years. The April group also included tradespeople and more small farmers, as well as prostitutes, who were considered "a foreign and dangerous element."[54] Not slated to live in special settlements, these deportees were administratively exiled (administrativno-vysslanye) for a period of ten years. Though they lived among the locals and not under NKVD supervision, they could not change their location in exile.

Soviet authorities initially planned to include another group in the April transports, the so-called refugees (bezhentsy), but had to postpone their deportation until June.[55] An estimated 300,000 individuals fled western Poland in the wake of the Nazi invasion, ending up under Soviet occupation. In December 1939, the German and Soviet governments agreed to repatriate refugees from their respective partitions. A total of 14,000 Ukrainians and Belorussians left the General-Gouvernement for the eastern part of Poland in the spring of 1940. At the same time, German evacuation committees, under Otto von Wächter, went to work in the Soviet zone, registering those who wished to return to western Poland. Prepared to accept up to 70,000 individuals, they had 164,000 petitioners and began evacuations in April. A total of 66,000 individuals, including some Jews, thus returned to the German partition.[56] When the operation ended in June, the NKVD ordered the deportation "of refugees who desired to go to Germany, but were not accepted by German authorities." Jews formed the majority of this group. This deportation also included small merchants, professionals, and individuals who refused to accept Soviet passports. The NKVD referred to them as "special settlers-refugees" (spetspereselentsy-bezhentsy) and sent them, like the February deportees, to live in NKVD-supervised settlements.

The final deportation, one year later, seemed to be a roundup of persons in the targeted groups who had earlier escaped capture. On 14 May 1941, the Central Committee of the Communist Party and the Sovnarkom adopted Joint Resolution No. 1299–526ss, calling for a cleansing of the regions incorporated into the USSR in 1939–40.[57] This episode also affected the Baltic republics, Northern Bukovina, and Bessarabia, which had been incorporated into the USSR in August 1940.[58] The first transports left Western Ukraine on 22 May; the operations in the Baltic republics took place on 14 June and in Western Belorussia began on the night of 19–20 June. Cut short by the German attack on the USSR, this last deportation took place under Nazi bombing.[59] Termed "exiled settlers" (ssyl'no-poselentsy), the June 1941 group was sentenced to outlying places of exile under NKVD supervision for twenty years.[60] Unlike the other deportees, Grzegorz Hryciuk explains, they were given the rights of free Soviet citizens, including a choice of job and place to live, and thus occupied a status between that of special settler and administratively exiled.[61]

The odyssey began for all deportees in the dead of night, as it had for most of those who were arrested. It started as an invasion of the home, no longer a safe and private space. Banging on the door, the NKVD roused the targeted family from sleep. The visit usually commenced with a call to surrender all weapons, followed by a meticulous search of the premises. Females report that the men of their families, if they were still free and at home, were immobilized by the officers, who held them at gunpoint throughout the search, ordering them to keep their arms raised.[62] For most families, this was not the first of such visits. But this time, relates one victim, it "was not really a search but rather an attempt to disorient us in our own home."[63] The screaming, crying, and fainting that resulted testify to the effectiveness of this tactic.

Following the search came the order to dress and pack; they would be leaving their homes. While some officers told the families they were being deported to Russia, others lied. Frequently, they said the family would be resettled in a nearby region where they would join previously seized husbands and fathers.[64] The amount of time agents gave the deportees to pack varied. While on average, families had half an hour to prepare to leave their homes for a journey to an unknown destination, some report being given as little as ten minutes.[65] Though Beria's instructions for carrying out the operation included a list of items the deportees be permitted to bring, up to 500 kilograms per family, some of the officers did not allow them to take anything, stating that they would find all they needed in Russia.[66] One woman, whose husband had been arrested, was told that she could take only what she was able to carry; since she had to carry her smallest child and hold the other by the hand, that meant nothing.[67]

Women write of the panic, disbelief, and grief that they experienced at the sound of the deportation order. They describe a nightmarish scene, dominated by cries and screams. Recalls one woman: "Father, who never in his life sang even the simplest melody, starts to sing. Mother faints and the baby cries. We simply don't know what to do." "They didn't let my husband or brother move anywhere my brothers kids started to cry a lot and I just didn't know what was happening around me," writes Stanisława Gwanczuk. Some women screamed and refused to go; the officers merely dragged them out. So shocked was Jadwiga Woźniak that she fell into a kind of trance. Similarly, another woman states that the information struck her "like a bolt from the clear blue sky." Although for those taken in the first rounds of deportation the order came as a shock, many of those apprehended later report knowing exactly what would happen once they heard the knock on the door. Some even report a measure of relief when the moment finally came, feeling that they could not withstand the nervous tension caused by the fear of deportation.[68]

Regardless of their level of expectation, the night of their seizure was one of pain and grief for the deportees, who describe an unforgettably horrible experience. "That freezing and gloomy day 10 February 1940," notes Maria Kielan, "when we left our family home and with tears in our eyes bade farewell to our beloved town, is engraved in my memory."[69] Forced removal from their homes constituted the first step in their total uprooting. Like the former borders of Poland, the boundaries of home and private life were quickly obliterated; the Soviet government regarded as enemies not only soldiers but noncombatants, as well. Jadwiga Wolańska explains: "They took us by force, like some kind of criminals, people dangerous to society, whom it was necessary to remove from their homes, to destroy, to turn into beggars without a roof over their heads."[70]

What they encountered at the train stations did nothing to lessen the trauma of leaving their homes. Upon arrival at the stations, they were locked into cargo trains unequipped for human beings. Even the NKVD, checking several days before the first operation that Beria's instructions for preparing the trains had been carried out, reported a dismal situation.[71] Lacking seats, toilets, windows, and heat, these trains quickly grew hellish for their passengers, who generally were not allowed out until they had crossed from Polish territory into the USSR proper. According to one woman, they were trains "that we Poles never even dreamed existed." Another deportee remarks that "there was none of that humanitarianism that the Soviets always speak of, for in our country pigs are exported in better conditions than they transport people."[72]

According to many eyewitnesses, the NKVD typically packed forty to sixty individuals into each cattle car; Beria's instructions called for thirty. "There were eighty-some people in the car, like sardines in a can, including several pregnant women and children," writes Aleksandra Wodzicka. The indiscriminate mixing caused considerable distress for the passengers, as a lawyer from Lwów relates: "Under guard, in locked cargo cars, were packed thirty to forty people, without regard to sex or age." The passengers experienced a complete loss of personal boundaries: they had to sleep in a cramped common space and relieve themselves there, either in a bucket or through a hole in the floor. "The journey lasted seventeen days in very difficult conditions," writes one woman, "in cargo cars women, men, children all together."[73] Many deportees include this detail in their descriptions of the transports, suggesting that this enforced intimacy rendered an already difficult situation much worse.

For those individuals deported in the summer months, the crowding of the cars intensified the unbearable heat and lack of ventilation. With only small slits at the top of the walls for air, deportees often fainted. Those transported in the winter found the severe cold similarly hard to endure. Józefa Nowakowska recalls waking up in the transport unable to move; she assumed someone was holding her down but discovered that her hair had frozen to the wall of the car.[74] Soviet authorities typically made only meager provision for the passengers' other needs, leaving them to suffer hunger and thirst. Food was given sporadically and in insufficient quantities; sometimes it was spoiled. At best, the guards distributed one bucket of water for an entire car each day.[75] Describing the typical food allotment, Aniela Kubicka notes that the passengers in her car received one bucket of soup and one of water daily; additionally, each person got a small piece of bread.[76] Some deportees received neither food nor water for several days at a time; they report catching rain or scraping snow off the roof of the car to quench their thirst.[77]

Women note that the cars rang with the tormented cries of hungry children and the moans of mothers who were powerless to do anything for their little ones. "The children cried to eat, the old people begged God for death," writes Zofia Misiak. The guards did little to alleviate their agony. One woman asked an NKVD guard for milk for her infant. He reportedly sneered, "What, do I have milk in my breasts?" Other Poles recount begging for a drink of water for their children, only to be told, "Let them croak."[78]

The deportees endured these conditions for several weeks, for they were taken far from their homes. Most journeys lasted two to four weeks. Not everyone survived. The mortality rate on the transports appears undocumented and constitutes a matter of dispute among historians. Many deportees report deaths, including suicides, in the course of their journeys.[79] Children and the elderly suffered worst. "Children died from hunger and cold in the arms of their parents, and the unhappy corpses were thrown onto the snow," writes one young woman.[80] Others report watching mothers lose their children, with no opportunity to bury them, which magnified their grief. "One of the infants died after a week and was taken away in a bag," writes Wanda Kulczycka, "without letting the mother take part in the burial of the remains." Powerlessness and despair overtook many. Anna Gimsewska, who was deported in February, remembers the hopelessness. After a three-week transport her group had to travel three more days on sleds in snow to their waists. "I saw stiff infants frozen to death, which mothers left along the road," she relates. "I saw men weakened and driven to despair, who sat down in the snow and sentenced themselves to voluntary death." In the words of one who had survived the transport, "The road was a streak of anguish."[81]

Maria Wojnilowiczówna, who wondered in the beginning of September 1939 what war would look like and how it might affect her, soon saw her world fall apart. Not long after the Red Army invasion, she watched as the NKVD arrested her father. She describes the scene as one of helpless rage and unbounded grief, feelings that, as she stood before the armed soldiers and observed the helplessness of her own father, could find no words, no outlet whatsoever. She writes: "I stood supported by the desk, I watched and it seemed to me that I didn't see anything that was going on around me. . . . They are taking my father from me, they want to separate us, they are vile, they are cruel. Grief, despair, hatred—I suppressed all that within me and had to stand helplessly, for where was I to await rescue and assistance from?"

As a member of a military family, she was included in the first deportation. On 10 February 1940, Soviet officers seized Wojnilowiczówna and locked her in a train car bound for Russia. Recalling her despair at leaving her homeland, she notes, "I wanted to go as far as possible, without stopping, without an end, for the end was terrifying." Hundreds of thousands of people like her were ripped apart from all that they loved and sent on a journey into the terrifying unknown. "Thus began the wandering of the Polish people from their familial homes," writes one of them, "in a direction unknown, hostile, and foreign to us."[82]

2

"The Element that Was Dangerous for 'Our Liberators'"

The Women of This Study

Józefa Telemajer-Dorobkowa recalls sitting in the closed train, feeling she must be "a wild animal, one that had to be locked behind bars in an iron cage. Am I really such a dangerous criminal?" she wondered.[1] What had she done to deserve such a fate? Who were these thousands and thousands of women transported eastward, and what criteria rendered them dangerous to the Soviet government, so much so that it would not let them remain in their homes? This chapter presents a picture of the 1,864 women whose interpretations of their experience of Soviet exile form the basis for this book. It examines the circumstances of their forced removal from Poland, profiles their socioeconomic backgrounds, and follows them across the border, charting the endpoints of their journeys to the USSR.

These women were not combatants; a mere handful worked in the underground resistance, and only a small minority took any action that violated Soviet law. Just as in the exiled population as a whole, the majority of the females studied here—82 percent—were deported as the result of an administrative decision, with no formal charges made against them. Only 17 percent were arrested and conveyed eastward as criminals.[2] Since administrative exile represents the most common experience of females, it is considered first.

Deportation

This study includes women from all four deportations, though the majority of them were transported during the first two, early in 1940. As the evacuations from the USSR occurred in April and August of 1942, these individuals spent a full two and one-half years deep in the USSR. Thirty-four percent of the women were taken from their homes in the dead of winter, in February 1940, and 35 percent were taken in April. Another 8 percent of the women were deported in June 1940 and an additional 8 percent in June 1941.[3] The underrepresentation of the June transports in the sample stems from the nature of the separate deportations and of the subsequent evacuations. The February and April deportations hit ethnic Poles the hardest, as the first to go were the families of arrested men, those who appeared to have the greatest stake in and identification with the Polish state—either through military, political, and civic service, cultural and economic leadership, or land ownership.[4] Many of the women portrayed in this book belong to these strata. The third deportation involved a large proportion of Jews and the final one, Lithuanians and other nationalities.[5] In 1942, females were evacuated by the Polish army—and thus able to write about their experiences—if they joined the Women's Auxiliary, had family members in the military, or were orphans. They tended to be ethnic Poles and to come from the families initially targeted by the invader.

Researchers agree that ethnic Poles made up well over half of the total number of exiles.[6] There are two reasons to assume that the majority of these women were ethnic Poles. First, the Soviet government blocked citizens of the former Polish state of non-Polish nationality (i.e., Jews, Belorussians, and Ukrainians) from leaving, announcing in December 1941 that it considered the latter to be Soviet citizens. Second, the Polish army seems to have given preference to individuals of Polish nationality in the evacuations.[7] In the documents examined for this book, ten women identify themselves as Belorussian, thirty-two as Jewish, and none as Ukrainian. Most of the women, more than 70 percent, record neither their ethnicity, presumably considering it self-evident, nor their religion.[8] When they supply such information they typically use both identifiers, as a unit. In such cases, women note "Polish Catholic" at the beginning of their testimonies, along with their names and other facts of their existence. The content of the women's writing often signals their Polish nationality. Clues include descriptions of religious beliefs and practices, the components of their loyalty and devotion to the Polish nation, and their attitudes toward peoples of other nationalities.

That most of the females who ended up in the USSR endured administrative exile rather than arrest suggests that they were less involved in the leadership and management of the Polish state, as well as in the ownership of its assets. They were not the military or political figures, the economic or social leaders automatically deemed enemies—ones that should be locked up —by the occupier. They were resettled not as a result of anything they did or a position that they held, but simply for belonging to certain social groups in the area annexed by Soviet forces. Most of these females were deported merely because of their relationship to a man whom Soviet authorities considered guilty or potentially guilty of disloyalty to the new regime. Thus, women and girls were considered dangerous not for anything inherent to their own identities but because of the identity or activity of their male relatives.

Nearly half (46%) of the deported females were told or understood the cause of their fate to be either an alleged act or the social position of a male family member.[9] Of those women offering this explanation, 37 percent were deported because their husbands, fathers, sons, or brothers had been arrested and 58 percent because of such relatives' occupation or social status. Occupations and social positions that led to the deportation of wives and children include: army officer, soldier, government official, administrative elite, forester, gamekeeper, railroad worker, policeman, large landowner, independent farmer, military settler, and legal expert. The reason the men had been arrested is not always clear, as some women merely note that their deportation followed an arrest in the family. The most common reasons for arrest given in the present sample, which correspond to research on the exiles as a whole, are a man's position as an army officer, soldier, reservist, military settler, or policeman. Soviet authorities deported some women for being relatives of prisoners of war, whether the latter had fallen captive to the Soviets or the Nazis.

Wives and daughters of such men thus did nothing out of the ordinary to exact the punishment of banishment from their homes. They neither committed an act nor held a position considered criminal or suspect by the Soviet occupiers. Only 6 percent of the women attribute their deportation to an act of their own, most commonly application to the German commission to be allowed to return to the western half of Poland, where they had lived before the invasions or had family members they wished to join. Since these women wanted to leave the Soviet-occupied zone, the new regime considered them disloyal and, therefore, deserving of deportation. Additionally, a few women declined Soviet passports, refused to vote in the plebiscite, or had jobs that put them in the category of "dangerous element."[10] One woman joined the transports headed eastward of her own accord; not wanting to be left alone after her family was taken, she begged the guards to let her on the train.[11] These cases, though, represent a small fraction of the deportees. The fact is that most females found themselves punished merely for living their daily lives, for maintaining relationships with individuals who, until recently, had simply been family members and ordinary citizens.

Polish women were not singled out for this treatment. In the 1930s, hundreds of women in the USSR were sent to the Gulag for being wives and daughters of prominent men purged by the NKVD. So commonly were women incarcerated because of their husbands that convicts referred to the relevant clause of article 58 of the criminal code, which called for the punishment of a "Member of the Family of a Traitor to the Fatherland," as the "Ladies' Paragraph."[12] Used predominantly against the wives of political prisoners during the purge of 1936–1937, this paragraph provided for a sentence of five to eight years imprisonment. The labor camp Karaganda, in Kazakhstan, earned the nickname "wives' camp" because of the large numbers of "wives of enemies of the people" confined there. The principle of collective responsibility had a gendered dimension. In applying it mostly to women, Soviet officials thus routinely collapsed their identity with that of male family members; during the Stalinist era relationships to men commonly rendered women criminal.

Arrest

Unlike Soviet wives, most Polish ones, though deported because of their relations, were spared incarceration. Other women, however, were not so fortunate. Seventeen percent of the women of this study were arrested, charged with a crime, and sentenced, ending up first in prisons and then in the forced labor camps of the infamous Gulag. In contrast to the deported females, these women faced punishment for jobs they held or actions they took that violated Soviet regulations. In most cases, though the women did not feel that their jobs or activities rendered them criminals, in the context of Soviet logic they could attribute their fate largely to their own identities and not to that of a relative. Three-quarters of the arrested women report that their misfortune arose from something they had done.[13] The link between their own actions and their fate may have mitigated their sense of powerlessness somewhat.

Some women took bold actions that knowingly put them at risk, and eventually landed them in Soviet prisons. The most common crime was attempting to cross the Polish borders, either to Lithuania, Romania, Hungary, or the General-Gouvernement—the other side of the new German-Soviet border, which cut through the middle of the recently defeated Polish state. Border transgressions account for 44 percent of the total arrests. In many cases, these women simply sought to join their parents or other relatives; under article 120 of the Soviet Criminal Code, they were convicted of spying.[14] Dorota Majewska received a sentence of five years of hard labor for attempting to travel from Warsaw to Grodno, which she wryly notes as, "Going from Poland to Poland."[15]

Membership in a resistance organization ranks as the second most frequent reason for the arrest of women, 14 percent of the total. One such woman writes that, feeling "the pain of the loss of Poland," she joined the underground to take action.[16] Many like her became members of the Z.W.Z. (Union of Armed Struggle) and engaged in active resistance, serving as typists, couriers, and guides, as well as hiding and providing care for Polish soldiers. Invoking articles 64, 66, 76, and 80 of the Criminal Code, the NKVD special tribunals (*Osoboe Soveshchanie)* sentenced them to either eight or ten years in a labor camp, followed by the loss of the rights of a citizen for five years and the confiscation of all possessions. These two crimes— border crossing and resistance activity—to which the women readily admit, account for more than half of the arrests. Other actions resulting in arrest include refusing to accept a Soviet passport or a job under the new regime and applying to relocate in the German-occupied part of Poland. These transgressions account for 4 percent of the total arrests.

Not all women could point to an action that would explain their incarceration. The authorities accused 8 percent of the women of the vague crimes of anti-Soviet agitation (art. 72) or of being a "socially dangerous element" (art. 74), designations that often indicated little about the reason for arrest to the victims. A few women sentenced for the latter (2% of the total im-

prisoned) report being arrested because they held positions of authority—
the most common reason for which Polish men ended up in Soviet prisons.
These women, though, did not occupy positions at the top of the social hierarchy; their jobs included school director, teacher, employee for the local
police, and scout leader.

The difference in their status vis-à-vis men is suggested by the time frame
of their seizure. The occupiers initially targeted for arrest the elements they
considered most dangerous: military and political figures, as well as foresters
and railway workers, who possessed knowledge useful for guerrilla warfare
—a predominantly male group. While large-scale arrests of Polish men occurred immediately after the Red Army invasion, as it strove to neutralize
the population, only 11 percent of the female prisoners were apprehended
in the first three months after the invasion. Their positions and offenses apparently had lower priority. Furthermore, only after armed resistance was
crushed and Soviet intelligence operations put in place could members of
the underground, which included many females, be rooted out.

Profile

Zofia Onakowa was taken from her home during the second wave of deportations, in April 1940, because her husband, a soldier in the Polish army,
had fallen into German captivity in the September campaign.[17] A thirty-
year-old teacher in a village in the Wołyń province of eastern Poland, she
represents a typical deportee. The information women writing about the
experience of exile provide about their origins and former lives in Poland is
uneven. While some offer details about their family, home, education, and
occupation, others merely describe their time in the USSR and sign their
names. Though the picture provided here is incomplete, it offers a sense of
the wide range of women who were forced to leave their homes, as well as
the features they shared in common.

Among the first observations to make about this group of exiles is its
relative youth. One of the youngest to write about the experience, Zofia
Stojak, was just eight years old when deported and eleven when evacuated
from the USSR. Onakowa's eleven-month-old son fell victim to the deportations, one of many such infants. At the opposite end stands Ada Dom-
ianewska, a secretary from Warsaw, age fifty-seven when her Soviet exile

ended.[18] Nearly all of those who recorded this information (approximately half of the total) are between the ages of fifteen and forty-nine.[19] In this regard, the sample group does not fully represent the exiled Polish population, for it does not reflect the large number of older individuals included in the deportations. Two factors explain this. First, the mortality rate among the exiles was high, and the elderly fared worst. Many deportees underscore this situation. Stating that two hundred Poles died in her settlement in northern Russia, Irena Gajewska adds: "Like others, I lost my dearest ones there, my mother and grandmother." Halina Gąsiorowska describes the period after the amnesty: "There were very many people terribly hot, kids and old people were dying twenty a day. There too my family mama and my sisters died."[20] Second, hampered by Soviet efforts to limit the numbers allowed to leave the USSR, the Polish army evacuated only men and women joining the armed services, their families, and orphans; older individuals did not have high priority and are underrepresented among the evacuees. Many young Poles in freedom bemoan their compatriots left behind. "But even here I have no peace," writes one young woman immediately after her evacuation to Iran, "as I left my mother in Russia."[21] Thus the women of this study are more youthful than the exiled population as a whole.

Some understanding of the area from which these women hailed can offer insight into the socioeconomic character of the group. The long subjugation of the Polish territories in the period of the partitions to three different empires, which governed and developed them differently, resulted in considerable heterogeneity across the country. The interwar Polish Republic comprised three zones. The western part was the most economically developed, while the east lagged far behind. The central section represented the middle ground for the country in economic and social development, as well as the geographic center.[22] Typically, it was joined with the western zone, constituting what journalists of the day referred to as "Poland A": the most industrialized, well-managed, and prosperous part of the country.

Slightly more than half of the women indicate where they lived before the outbreak of war. Of them, less than 8 percent had resided in the central provinces (*wojewódzstwa (woj.) centralne*) and a mere handful in the western ones (*woj. zachodnie*). In late 1939, these areas were either annexed directly by the German Reich or formed into the General-Gouvernement under draconian Nazi rule. Individuals from these provinces were largely deported to the USSR in the third wave, as refugees in the east. Some had, in fact, fled the Nazi occupation, while others sought to return to it. Halina Baczyńska was studying at an institute in the Stanisławów province when the Red Army invaded. Hoping to rejoin her parents in Kraków, now under Nazi control, she registered to return home. She reports that Soviet officials tried to get her to withdraw her request, scoffing: "What do you need your parents for, you'll marry a commander, have kids of your own, and forget about them." The militia came for her one night and escorted her to the station where others were waiting; she never doubted she would be transported to the German partition. The direction of the train, however, showed that she was mistaken; Baczyńska ended up in Siberia.[23]

Such cases represent a minority of the exiles. The majority of these women hailed from the eastern borderlands—the region invaded and annexed by the USSR. Forty-two percent of those identifying their homes came from the eastern provinces of Poland (*woj. wschodnie*), and another 40 percent from the southern ones (*woj. południowe*).[24] Together these provinces, often referred to as the *kresy*, formed the least economically developed zone of interwar Poland.[25] As the poorest areas of the country, these provinces constituted "Poland B," the second-class Poland. Populated predominantly by peasants living and working on small subsistence farms, its agriculture was characterized by low productivity and technological backwardness. Industry and commerce suffered even greater neglect in this region. According to Janusz Żarnowski, this part of Poland was the least developed socially, having a relatively undifferentiated social structure.[26] The eastern borderlands had the smallest working class and the lowest numbers of white-collar workers and members of the intelligentsia. Compared with the other regions of Poland, in the east and southeast health standards and consumption were lower, residential density greater, and education less valued. In 1931, the national illiteracy rate in Polish villages was 28 percent; the rate rose to 50 percent in the *kresy*. Rates of illiteracy reached even higher for women.[27]

This information suggests that a large number of the exiled individuals came from rural areas, many from peasant families, with a relatively low level of education. The documents reflect this. Many of the testimonies contain sketchy descriptions of the author's deportation and new life in the USSR, punctuated by emotional recollections and lamentations. Some are ungrammatical and semiliterate, rendering them extremely difficult to understand; these tend to provide the least amount of detail, particularly on the authors' background. Additionally, several sequences of statements in the archival collections are written in the same hand, suggesting that they were dictated, probably by individuals unable to write. At the same time, since Soviet authorities initially targeted political, economic, social, and cultural elites along with their families, white-collar workers and the intelligentsia are well represented. Owing to the unevenness of the autobiographical details provided by the women, it is difficult to establish a full picture of the socio-economic level of the women studied here, but the information given reveals that the group represents all walks of life.

The presence among the exiles of both peasants and the elite of a largely rural area is confirmed by the fact that the group contains representatives of the entire spectrum from tiny villages to the largest cities of Poland. Nearly one-third of the women who recorded the information resided in villages of less than one thousand inhabitants or outlying farms.[28] An additional 13 percent lived on *osady*, plots of land given to veterans of World War I and the ensuing border wars. Thus, more than 40 percent of the women were rural dwellers. Approximately 10 percent lived in small towns of less than 10,000 inhabitants, and 17 percent resided in medium-sized towns of 10,000 to 49,000 people. A small number (6%) came from large towns, such as Białystok and Stanisławów, whose populations ranged from 50,000 to 100,000. Finally, 23 percent of these women lived in Poland's cities, such as Warsaw, Wilno, and Lwów, whose populations exceeded 100,000.

The women's occupations also reveal the range of their socioeconomic status, as table 2.1 shows. Approximately one-third of the females of this study were students, either in grade schools or institutions of higher learning, which ranged from agricultural and technical schools to the prestigious Jagiellonian University in Kraków. This reflects both the presence of the elite stratum and the relative youth of the sample population. Eleven percent of the women had professional careers. Few, though, could be called the elites of their fields. The largest group of women in paid employment worked in the field of education (39%) as teachers and instructors; the group does contain three professors. The medical field embraced 16 percent of the employed women, mostly nurses and midwives but also eleven doctors. Several women note their profession as painter or musician.

After the field of education, the largest group of paid workers includes office workers of all types, most commonly: secretaries, bookkeepers, clerks, stenographers, typists, and switchboard operators. These low-level white-

Table 2.1

Occupations of the women of this study

Occupation	Number of women	Percentage of total
University professors and scientists	6	0.6
Lawyers	4	0.4
Journalists	2	0.2
Doctors	11	1.0
Nurses and other trained medical personnel	41	3.8
Schoolteachers	121	11.2
Directors of private and public enterprises	5	0.5
Clerical workers	97	8.9
Other white-collar workers	2	0.2
Artists and musicians	9	0.8
Small business owners	2	0.2
Shopkeepers	2	0.2
Factory workers	3	0.3
Other manual laborers	7	0.6
Artisans	5	0.5
Landowners (gentry)	5	0.5
Farmers	11	1.0
Housewives	56	5.2
Students	626	58.0
None	64	5.9

Note: The remaining 785 individuals do not provide this information.

collar positions account for 31 percent of the women reporting paid labor. The group also contains several artisans, mostly dressmakers. Only a few identify themselves as workers, employed as cashiers, cafeteria workers, and factory laborers.

While only a few women specifically record farming as their occupation (1%), it is likely that some of those who report nothing in this category lived and worked on small subsistence farms. Many of the females omitting information about their occupation note living in rural areas in the *kresy*.[29] Given the traditional and widespread undervaluation of women's work, they probably did not consider their occupations, particularly if on family farms, worthy of note. Unless asked, they presumably did not think to record such information. Furthermore, 6 percent of the women write

Table 2.2

Occupations of civilians deported from Poland

Type of work	Total (in thousands)	Percentage
Agriculture	522.4	56.8
Fishing and forestry	24.6	2.7
Industry and mining	84.0	9.1
Trade and insurance	30.2	3.3
Communication and transportation	81.3	8.8
Public service and church	104.1	11.3
School and culture	29.7	3.2
Medical and hygiene	8.3	1.0
Domestic service	3.6	0.4
Other	18.9	2.0
None	12.9	1.4

Source: AC, box 68, no. 62c, Bohdan Podoski, "Polskie Wschodnie w 1939–1940," 34–36.

specifically that they had no occupation, and 5 percent identify themselves as housewives (*przy męża*); several of them write, "Housewife (farmer)." Such labels obscure work done in the home, in small family enterprises, and on family farms. Far from being idle, these women may simply have not considered what they did on a daily basis as work. The actual number of women engaged in agricultural labor undoubtedly exceeds that explicitly stated in the documents.

General statistics on the population exiled from Poland reveal a predominance of peasant farmers. Data compiled by the Polish army suggests that over half of the deportees were engaged in farming—57 percent of the total. Table 2.2 shows the data for all branches of the economy. That sample contains a disproportionate number of males relative to the entire group of exiles. Nevertheless, since the wives and daughters of many of these men were deported, it offers some indication of their socioeconomic status in Poland. The data shows both the wide range of socioeconomic groups affected by punitive Soviet policies, as well as the high representation of those employed in agriculture.

Another Polish government report, calculated from files of the Polish Red Cross in Teheran, offers a more detailed breakdown of prewar employment. It covers only those exiles who had been evacuated, however. Presented in table 2.3, these statistics differ from those above, most notably

Table 2.3

Occupations of the exiled population as a whole

Profession	Percentage of population
Clergy of all denominations	0.5
University professors and scientists	0.6
Judges and public prosecutors	0.8
Journalists, writers, and artists	1.2
Defense attorneys	1.3
Doctors and trained medical personnel	3.1
White-collar workers, private sector	3.2
Workers	3.3
Foresters	3.7
Police and border guards	4.0
Schoolteachers	4.0
Merchants	4.4
Engineers, technicians, and agronomists	4.7
White-collar workers, state and local government	5.0
Professional military	8.0
Artisans	24.6
Peasants	27.6

Source: MID, box 91, folder 9, "Deportations from the Soviet-Occupied Polish Territories," July 1944, 16.

in the percentage of peasants among the exiles, who nonetheless constitute the largest group. Like the army data, these figures show that the majority of the exiled individuals did not come from the top of the social hierarchy: physical laborers compose 63 percent of the total. At the same time, the elites of society are well represented, as are members of the middle social strata.

The recent historiography does not contain detailed socioeconomic data on the deportees, though some has been found on those arrested. Analyzing the files of ethnic Poles arrested in the annexed territory, one researcher concluded that the majority (70%) were peasants, while 21 percent came from the working class and 5 percent from the intelligentsia.[30] This closely reflects the socioeconomic composition of interwar Poland: with 61 percent of the population employed in agriculture and 20 percent as workers, the majority engaged in physical labor. Only 7 percent of the population were white-collar workers and professionals. The exiles formed a microcosm of prewar Polish society, with no group left out.[31]

The Women of This Study

Like the data on the exiled population as a whole, the testimonies of the women of this study reveal that they came from all walks of life. They include some of the most highly educated, as well as the uneducated. They lived on small farms and in tiny villages, as well as in towns and cities. Some concentrated on caring for their families, others devoted their time to farming, while still others attended school or held jobs. They taught in schools, delivered babies, and worked in offices. Despite differences in socioeconomic status, they all became targets of the Soviet occupiers, who decided they must be exiled from their homeland. Though the farmer from Hawinowicz may have felt little connection to the teacher from Słonim with whom she first came into contact in the crowded cattle car, the authorities paid little heed to any distinctions, treating all of its so-called enemies as a monolithic group. According to Soviet logic, that dangerous status inhered in the family's socioeconomic position or a relative's political stance, but these women perceived only the bond of nationality, which seemed to render them all victims. While being taken across the Polish-Soviet border, the deportees, of various social strata, faced a kind of boundary erasure among themselves, something not common to their previous lives. The experience of exile would throw into relief what bound them, rather than what separated them, for these women, this microcosm of the Polish nation in the east, were thrown together on the transports, in prisons, in camps, and in settlements throughout the USSR where they struggled against a common foe.

Final Destinations

The trains that left eastern Poland finally stopped in far-flung regions of the USSR. The exiled females were deposited in three main areas: the Far North, Siberia, and Central Asia. In none of these regions did the Poles find the landscape or the climate familiar. Bemoaning the loss of her family home and her fatherland, Maria Kokoszówna writes, "They took us to Siberia. Wild taiga, unknown fields, mad winds and severe winters. It was terrifying for us, who came from the far west. And then those long days, monotonous and desperate." Disoriented and despairing, they found little comfort. According to one young woman, the locals looked at them with hatred in their eyes.[32] When deportees asked for assistance in coping with the harsh material conditions, the authorities merely sneered, "get used to it or drop dead."[33]

It was a tall order for the displaced individuals, for nothing about their new lives was stable, not even their place of residence. The deportees were initially deposited at a farm or a settlement, but frequently and arbitrarily moved, often on assignment to a harvesting or construction brigade, sometimes because no work or food was available for them, occasionally as a punitive measure. Most of the arrested women first went to prison, where they often languished for months, or more than a year, before being sentenced to a hard labor camp.[34] The prisoners found themselves shifted from one prison to another, first on Polish territory, then on Soviet; even after sentencing they rarely remained in one labor camp. The following sketch of the endpoints of the women's journeys from Poland uses their initial destinations, if deported, and their first camp, if arrested.

These women were scattered throughout the USSR. The largest portion ended up in Kazakhstan, in Central Asia (30%). Many transports deposited passengers in Russia's European North (18%), Siberia (16%), the Urals (6%), and the Volga region (6%). Smaller groups were sent to the Central Industrial Region of Russia, to Ukraine, Belorussia, Kirghizia, and Uzbekistan. Some of the women (8%) were moved among so many different prisons and labor camps that it is impossible to establish a primary location for them in the USSR.[35] A handful spent most of their time on Polish territory, where they remained in prisons until the German invasion of June 1941, after which they were evacuated to the USSR and soon released by the amnesty.[36]

The Poles were not resettled or incarcerated together in large concentrations but sprinkled through thousands of locales, some with already-existing camps and settlements, some basically empty. The regime apparently sought to isolate them to preclude communication and the formation of organized resistance. The individuals of this study were distributed predominantly in thirty-three *oblasti* (districts). The largest number (15%) were in the Arkhangel'sk *oblast'* in the northern part of European Russia. The second most frequent depositing place was the Semipalatynsk *oblast'* (7%) in the Kazakh Republic, followed by the Novosibirsk *oblast'* (6%) and the Altai *krai* (5%) in Siberia, and North Kazakhstan *oblast'* (5%) in the Kazakh Republic.

Arrested Polish women ended up in labor camps stretching from the Gor'kii *oblast'* of European Russia all the way to Kolyma in the Far East; they lived in Vorkuta, in the subpolar region, as well as Karaganda in Central Asia. Some women report being the only Pole in their camp. Others had the company of compatriots, particularly if sent to the Kar-lag cluster of camps in Kazakhstan, where nearly 30 percent of the incarcerated women ended up. Another 25 percent was confined in the Temnikov cluster in the Mordovian ASSR, especially in the camp Pot'ma.

Forbidden to live in urban areas, the deportees ended up in outlying settlements, either preexisting or set up by the exiles themselves. Frequently the populations of older settlements consisted of groups of Soviet citizens forcibly resettled by the Stalinist regime in the preceding decade.[37] Forty-five percent of the women lived in special settlements; others were taken to existing collective farms (*kolkhozy*) (17%) and state farms (*sovkhozy*) (12%).[38] In these cases, the deportees were added to the local communities, which often related with hostility to the newcomers. None of the women could choose where she lived in exile. Some deportees found their movement even more restricted: twenty of them were arrested while in exile and then confined in labor camps.

THE WOMEN portrayed in this book present a microcosm of the female half of the Polish population of the eastern borderlands. Few were social leaders, though many of their husbands and fathers were—precisely the reason they ended up on the eastbound transports. Some came from the middle ranks of society, teachers and nurses, students and office workers; others worked on the land. Some women had earned university degrees, while others could barely read or write. Most of these females found themselves punished simply for living what seemed to them as normal lives. They were wives, daughters, and mothers, who took care of their homes, worked on farms, went to their jobs, or attended school. Few had done anything considered criminal, and those who did suffered the harshest sentence— confinement in a forced labor camp. Though from varied backgrounds, these women were united by their nationality and by the actions of the occupying authorities, who threw them out of their homes and sent them far to the east, to some of the most inhospitable regions of the USSR. There they had only themselves and each other to count on for survival. Maria Andrzejewska, a deportee from the Wołyń province, was dumped at a collective farm in Northern Kazakhstan, given neither food, nor shelter, nor a job. She recalls: "I ask the *predsedatel'* [chairman] what happens to us now? 'Live, however you want.' That's his answer. Some kind of energy rises in me. I resolve to endure."[39]

II

"After All, I Am a Polish Woman"

Self-Definition through the Experience of Exile

Part Two discusses the conditions women faced in exile and the substance of their everyday existence. The situation on the transports from Poland was not an aberration from what the exiles were to experience in the USSR; rather, it offered a taste of what was to come. By all accounts, the living conditions of the exiles were abominable. Securing the most basic physical necessities—nourishment, warmth, shelter, and medical care—became nightmarish struggles. Whether male or female, incarcerated or resettled, the exiles lived in conditions that at very best betrayed on the part of the Soviet regime a lack of regard for the Poles' well-being, at worst, a calculated desire to make them suffer.

Living conditions ranged from uncomfortable to lethal. One of the first problems that women detail is the lack of space, which plagued the Poles beginning with the overpacked freight cars that transported them from their homeland. Prison cells, in particular, were grossly overcrowded. Women report twenty-two individuals being jammed into cells made for three or four, thirty in cells for six. Maria Cieciska was kept in a four-by-four-meter cell with fifty-five other people.[1] In such conditions inmates had to take turns sitting or lying down; at night they found it impossible to extend their legs. One after another, women fainted from the suffocating atmosphere; some report inhaling air through the cracks in the walls, if they could get the coveted spots in the cell. Maria Kosińska, a government clerk who served time in four different Soviet prisons, writes, "In all of the prisons there was an indescribable crush of people."[2]

The overcrowding of living space did not substantially improve outside prison walls. In labor camps, barracks housed several hundred women each. Individuals in "free exile" also experienced cramped living conditions and the accompanying discomfort, for despite instructions from the center, local authorities had often made no provision for accommodating the resettled population. When ordering the deportation of the Poles, Beria stipulated that each family should get its own room or a separate place in a barracks and that each individual was entitled to not less than three square meters of living space.[3] However, some of the deportees, such as Irena Sypniewska, were sent to the empty steppe. After several nights of sleeping under the open sky, her group of Poles built a primitive barracks, which housed 120 people.[4] Many of the resettled Poles report living in like structures, overfilled with bodies and lacking any accoutrements of home. A seamstress from Krzemieniec thus describes her new residence as "terrible buildings they called barracks terribly dirty old ruined without windows lots of vermin and that's how we lived just the memory is frightening." Jadzia Przybylówna notes living in stark barracks, "like animals in a cage."[5]

In more established settlements, deportees found shelter in small huts, usually already inhabited by locals. These dwellings, too, were overfilled. Stanisława Schrammowa was given a "hut" in which to live—without a door, a window, or an oven; three families shared it. "For my family—five people, there were exactly 2½ m²," explains a teacher and mother of three. "The children slept on a shelf above us, and my husband and I slept in a sitting position. We lived like that for a whole year." Often these structures had only wet clay walls, bare earth for a floor, and no furniture. Klara Sawicka, a doctor deported to a collective farm, voices outrage that eight families were quartered in four such huts: "They were neither interested nor asked how we lived. I went to the NKVD several times and asked that they check out the conditions in which we live. Nothing happened!"[6] We need not take the Poles' word alone on the subject of their living conditions. In follow-up reports, the NKVD stated that in the places of exile conditions fell far short of the ideal: even months later barracks remained undivided, with at best one or two meters allotted to each person. In the fall of 1940, Beria sent a note to Stalin and Molotov attesting to the complete lack of preparations for winter in barracks in Siberia.[7]

Some deportees recall that ice formed on the walls inside their abodes. Intense cold plagued the Poles, who received no additional clothing appropriate for the climate of the places to which they were taken. It must be remembered that the Poles were deposited predominantly in Central Asia, Siberia, and the White Sea region, areas characterized by a continental climate, experiencing wide ranges between winter and summer temperatures. The Siberian winters are infamous for their cold and snowfall; the White Sea region, in the north, has a subarctic climate. Central Asia, too, experiences severe cold in the winter, and summers that are extremely hot and dry. Often possessing only the clothes on their backs, the exiles found themselves unprepared to live and work in such places.

Like many others, Marta Baśkiewicz relates that she had to continue working in the forest even if the temperature fell to -70 degrees Celsius (-94° F). After demanding a trial for her unexplained arrest in exile, one woman was forced to walk many kilometers in a snowstorm to court; she had three toes amputated after ending up with frostbite. According to Weronika Dejnarowicz, people froze to death on the way to work during blizzards in Kazakhstan.[8] The statements from evacuated Poles and letters from those stranded in the USSR after the amnesty contain endless accounts of the struggle to find heating material to stave off the ferocious cold and its destruction. Local authorities made no attempt to help them obtain fuel and even hampered their efforts, as the following excerpt from a letter sent by a young girl in Siberia to her father illustrates: "Our situation is very difficult since we have to pay for everything, for the apartment and for water and even for wood . . . at first Mama and I stole boards but now they are putting even our people in jail. For one board you can get a year in prison so now we're afraid to take it and we have no wood."[9]

In Central Asia, deportees survived the winter by collecting cow dung and forming it into bricks called *kiziaki*. A woman deported to the state farm Myn-Bulak recalls how necessity made gathering manure a habit; she even grew accustomed to using her bare hands and feet to mix it with clay and then shape it into bricks:

> The skin of my hands and feet was corroded, but what did I care—I even recalled with some amusement that last year, when I had begun to gather "keezyaks" I had used a sort of nippers because I didn't want to touch the stuff. And that had been dry "keezyak," solid and not smelling, while now—I had learned a lot. I admit that the question of fuel provision became an obsession with me. We were not going to suffer this winter as we had suffered the last.[10]

Such women demonstrated notable resourcefulness in adapting to difficult conditions and enabling themselves and their families to survive.

The second obsession of the exiles was food. The food rations, provided to those who worked, were minimal. With only minor variations, labor camp inmates report receiving the following allotment: "two portions of bread, totaling 600 grams, and one-half liter of watery soup." A woman in a labor camp in the Middle Volga region states that initially no food was brought to prisoners while they labored all day in the fields; that changed only when women started fainting. Another woman recalls the horrible preoccupation of her life in the camp Pot'ma: "Hunger, which tore at the insides, plucked the heart, turned a person into an animal with dull eyes and a single thought—how to get a piece of bread, how to calm the eternally empty stomach."[11]

Deported women also report constant hunger. "I remember how my thirteen-year-old son more than once said Mommy will we last till the time when we can eat our fill of bread," writes a mother of two. Many deportees recall being tortured by hunger and obsessed with food. "It was depressing," writes one woman, "because we were supposed to be educated people with high aspirations and strong minds, but so it was." Irena Denasiewicz, from Brześć-nad-Bugiem, tries to convey this daily struggle to survive: "How we lived, it's hard to say. Once a day we got soup, sometimes bread. We stole carrots and that kept us alive. We sold our last sweater. . . . Oh, how hard it was. There were days of absolute hunger. . . . For days people had nothing in their mouths. We decided then to eat dogs, and that saved us from death."[12]

The hunger that consumed the deportees can perhaps best be grasped through the words of children, who in a matter-of-fact way relate their deplorable condition. One young girl writes to her father from Barnaul early in 1942: "We all still look good, except Mommy and Danusia completely changed from the food, we eat at most two times a day, first bread and then the second time some kind of soup and that's how we get by." Written in yellow chalk on a scrap of black paper, another letter begins as follows: "Dear Papa I'm sending you a photograph I look very bad because of the lack of bread." In a composition written in a school in Isfahan after the evacuations, another girl encapsulates her experiences in Siberia:

> people dying from hunger cold and my family met that fate that my brother got sick and in a week died from hunger we buried him in a hill on the Siberian steppe mama from worry also got sick from hunger swelled up and laid in the barrack for two months. they didn't want to take her to the hospital until it was the end then they took her mama laid in the hospital for two weeks then her life ended when we learned this we were seized by a great despair we went to the burial twenty-five kilometers away we went to the hill you could hear the sound of the siberian forest where two of my family were left.[13]

The exiles succumbed not only to the cold and hunger but also to various illnesses. Malnutrition and exhaustion were ubiquitous, and diseases ravaged the exiles: dysentery, typhus, tuberculosis, diphtheria, pneumonia, meningitis, and malaria.[14] Many women remark that they left the USSR with souvenirs—dark blue scars on their bodies, telltale signs of scurvy. Others contracted brucellosis from working with the dung and hides of cows and sheep.[15] The health crisis grew to alarming proportions after the amnesty, as typhus epidemics took many of the Poles who gathered in the southern regions of the USSR, hoping to come under the care of the Polish army. Reports of Polish relief workers continually draw attention to the health emergency. One declares: "Women already sick from avitaminosis, covered with abscesses, or burning with a fever of the mysterious illness 'brucellosis,' to which they are exposed grazing sheep, in the winter will start falling ill with influenza, pneumonia."[16]

A low level of medical care compounded the deleterious living conditions and the prevalence of disease. Often no medical facilities or personnel were available at all, particularly for Poles sent to remote settlements, from which they were forbidden to travel. Many describe helplessly watching loved ones perish, with no medical assistance whatsoever. Recalling the complete lack of care in her settlement, one woman writes: "I have before my eyes at this moment an image so painful to me that I am just not able to write. My father, who was gravely ill from pneumonia, was left with absolutely no medical care at all, and died."[17]

Sometimes doctors and nurses were available, but because they typically had no medicines, they could provide little relief. Labor camp infirmaries provided notoriously inadequate care. "There can be no talk of medical care or any kind of hygiene," writes one woman of her camp near Novosibirsk. "There was in fact a doctor, a well-known criminal, who performed an operation on a boil on one of my girlfriends with an ordinary piece of glass from a broken bottle." A midwife from Poland who worked as a nurse in a Soviet hospital describes abominable conditions, in which she lost her own son to typhus. "I recall my work in a Soviet hospital like a terrible nightmare," she writes, "and if my own child were to meet me once more in life, I would wish myself and him immediate death, rather than again encountering that hypocritical Soviet paradise."[18]

Thrust into these formidable conditions, women fought a daily battle for physical survival, while performing forced labor for the Soviet state. They also struggled to keep their families intact and maintain their own culture. Women sought support for their efforts in the group, the nation. At the same time, they turned to traditional notions of womanhood to define themselves individually and collectively, thereby providing a measure of order and certainty amidst overwhelming chaos. As the women perceived it, Soviet policies threatened to degender and denationalize them. Upholding a distinct identity as Polish women kept them from succumbing to the deadening pressures of life in the USSR, where the exiles counted for little more than sources of labor to be exploited at the whim of policy makers. Chapter 3 discusses women's labor in exile. Rejecting the definition of their social identity thrust upon them by their enemies, the women articulate their proper and natural one, their paramount role in the nation: mothers—the subject of chapter 4. Consensus on the meaning of the female body sets parameters for the behavior and treatment of women, as well as a framework for ordering the world. Chapter 5 examines hardships connected with the body and sexuality and their effect on female identity.

To uncover women's experience and understanding of exile, these chapters focus on policies toward women and their responses. They also examine men's reactions to the same issues, highlighting gender-based differences and similarities, for they are components of the same, larger story. Cultural notions of women and men act as complementary aspects of a system that articulates sex-based social roles, which together define the demands and desires of the nation.

3

"Women Were Treated the Same as Men"

Labor in Exile

While harsh material conditions formed an uncompromising background to life in Soviet exile, hard labor shaped its content. A homemaker from Białystok begins the story of her exile in Kazakhstan in a characteristic way, commenting, "And there began hard, very hard labor." Descriptions of work dominate most of the accounts of the exiled Poles, for work—typically hard physical labor—ruled their waking moments and depleted their energy. Many women write of being too tired and too hungry for life, considering their existence in the USSR as vegetation. "I walked at dawn with the other workers six kilometers deep into the forest, and returned at nine o'clock at night," writes Irena Król. "Our life was like vegetation. Work and sleep." Another woman recalls: "We worked like machines, unfit for thought and moving as if in a dream."[1]

The work not only sapped the strength and ruined the health of the women but was also psychologically debilitating. "Our exhaustion, both psychic and physical, was so terrible that were it not for the amnesty in July we would not long have survived that hell," writes a labor camp inmate.[2] The labor completely altered women's social roles and therefore challenged their individual and collective identities. Leaders of the Soviet state regarded the exiles as they did their own population—a resource to be exploited. Citizenship in the USSR during the Stalinist regime virtually defined individuals as laborers for the socialist state, a definition that superseded other loyalties and functions. This view of individual as laborer applied as well to the persons transported from eastern Poland, who were considered both subjects of the Soviet Union and its real or potential enemies. The latter notion was used to justify the assignment of Poles—whether arrested or deported—almost exclusively to hard physical labor, under a regimen that threatened to render them work animals.

Many women thus found themselves in a wholly unfamiliar position, forced to carry out unaccustomed tasks and roles. A group of women at the Buzhenovskii state farm in Kazakhstan sent a protocol to Polish government delegates late in 1941, protesting their living conditions and begging for intervention. They wrote: "We are people deprived of normal conditions of existence, without husbands, burdened with the support and raising of our children, overstrained with impaired health from nearly two years of being here."

The type of labor they were forced to perform, particularly that it was the same as work done by men, disturbed female deportees and prisoners. The latter circumstance violated notions about what they considered proper for them as women, precluded them from fulfilling the functions to which they were accustomed, and, therefore, threatened their very identity. One woman, a midwife in Poland, describes the effect the situation had on her: "I myself stopped being an angel among the sick, as I thought only about how to get something for myself to eat, and about my own son."[3] Others bemoan that they were unable to act as proper Polish mothers.

The most important determinant of the Polish attitude toward women and work was the female body, with its capacity to bear children. Soviet leaders seemed to view the labor pool as a mass of male bodies, each one capable of and obligated to perform heavy labor; femaleness held little meaning. Poles found it outrageous that the physical difference between male and female bodies—understood as integral to their respective natures and proper roles in society—was not the organizing factor of the labor force in the USSR. This situation undermined the Poles' sense of order and signaled the Soviet system's perverse nature.

Women and Work before World War II

The sexual division of labor was one of the underlying organizational elements of the Polish economic and social order before 1939. Sexual difference, located in the female body, was understood as fixed and indisputable; it, therefore, established and justified distinct spheres of activity and responsibility for males and females. To apply the framework of historian Joan Scott, productivity was equated with masculinity, and women and children were placed "in auxiliary and dependent positions."[4] The male and female spheres, though seemingly separate, were complementary as well, and defined the social order from the family level upwards. Though changes occurred in the scale and range of women's participation in socioeconomic activity outside the home throughout the interwar period, a basic division of tasks, along with differing values associated with them, remained constant.

Women in the Polish territories began entering the paid labor force in significant numbers in the late nineteenth century, as new forces began to change the socioeconomic landscape. Overpopulation in the villages drove daughters of peasant families to paid employment, and women of the developing working class also found it imperative to seek jobs. At the same time, in the Russian partition, many landowners lost their property or went bankrupt after the failed uprising of 1863, and women from the nobility likewise went to the industrializing cities in search of employment.

In Warsaw, nearly one-quarter of the total number of women of working age had paying jobs by the end of the century.[5] According to Maria Nietyksza, more than two-thirds of working women in Warsaw in 1897 were hired physical laborers. Domestic service, their most common occupation, was the only field dominated by women, who accounted for nearly 80 percent of these workers.[6] Second in frequency for women's employment was industry, particularly textiles.

On the eve of World War I, women constituted 35 percent of the working class in the Congress Kingdom of Poland (under Russian rule).[7] Daughters of nobles largely joined the growing urban intelligentsia, the white-collar workers (*pracowniki umysłowie*) of Polish society. Limited by their relative lack of education and also by tradition, such females found jobs as teachers, governesses, and medical assistants; they gradually entered the fields of administration and trade.[8] At the end of the nineteenth century, women also became more active in the artisan and petty bourgeois sectors, particularly in dressmaking and the production of artificial flowers, and helping in family-owned businesses.

In the Second Polish Republic (1918–1939), women remained less qualified workers than men and generally obtained only low-skill, low-paying jobs.[9] They thus occupied the lowest rungs of the proletariat. Typically, women were the first dismissed in periods of unemployment, such as that which followed the First World War. Women had entered industry in large numbers during the war—in Congress Poland they made up 53 percent of industrial workers in 1915—but were quickly dismissed when the men returned from the battlefields.[10] Although women's wartime contribution received note, the jobs were regarded as rightfully belonging to men. The same process occurred during the depression in the 1930s.[11] The fact that women consistently earned less than men, even for the same job, further demonstrates the undervaluing of female labor, a phenomenon that persisted throughout the interwar decades. In 1935, the average weekly wage for a woman was 48 percent less than that of male workers, including the female-dominated domestic service sector; in agricultural and white-collar work, women also earned less than men.[12] Despite growing acceptance of women's engagement in wage labor, they were not considered workers in the same way as men; society viewed their participation in the labor force as temporary or auxiliary and their productivity as innately lower than men's. Those who contributed to the family economy through agricultural or household labor tended to be disregarded completely, as such work was considered devoid of economic value.[13] Simply put, women were not primarily identified as active members of the economy.

These attitudes obscure the reality of women's involvement in wage labor. According to the 1931 census, 489,760 women worked as hired agricultural laborers (36% of the total persons in this sector), while 1,673,657 were employed outside agriculture (31% of the total).[14] Women actively engaged in independent agricultural production compose the final category necessary for calculating the total number of working women. Statisticians of the day, however, found it impossible to divide the population connected with independent agriculture into active and passive, for the prevalence of small family farms on which members of all ages contributed at varying levels rendered the division illusory. It is known only that 8,304,138 females were connected with independent agriculture (52% of the total). Assuming, for the sake of an estimate, that half of this group worked full-time at some aspect of family farming, the total number would then be 4,152,069. Combined with the above figures, an estimated 6,315,486 women—64 percent of females of working age in Poland—worked outside the home. This figure is only a rough estimate, probably a conservative one. A study of employment trends in Poland from 1930 to 1960 determined the number of gainfully employed women in 1931 to be 7,142,000. This figure raises the percentage of women of working age actually employed to nearly 73 percent. These preliminary estimates suggest that labor, even physical labor, was well known to Polish women.[15]

During the interwar period, the garment and textile industries became feminized. By 1938, women constituted 60 percent of workers in the clothing industry and 53 percent in textiles. They were barely represented, though, in the masculine fields of metallurgy, mining, and logging. The number of female white-collar workers also grew; in 1931 women accounted for nearly 30 percent of the total. They worked predominantly in schools, trade, and administration, representing approximately half of public school teachers (largely at the elementary level) and 53 percent of employees engaged in the latter sectors. A rise in women's education accompanied their increased employment: the interwar Polish Republic boasted the second highest rate of female enrollment in higher education in the world. At 28 percent, they nonetheless remained a minority and faced restricted opportunities. The most popular courses of study for females were dentistry and physical education. Law and medicine, both prestigious professions, employed only a handful of women: in 1936, Poland had 157 female lawyers (of approximately 8,000) and 7 female judges. Less than 16 percent of all doctors were women.[16]

Though an increasing number of women worked outside the home during the interwar period, 84 percent of working women were engaged in agriculture. The percentage remained even higher in the *kresy*, the lands invaded and annexed by the USSR. In Lwów and Wołyń *województwa*, the provinces from which the largest numbers of the women of this study hailed, the rates of women working in agriculture were 87 percent and 95 percent, respectively. Farming, too, maintained a traditional division of labor, which designated men's work and women's work. Women, typically in charge of animal husbandry, were regarded as auxiliary to the main work presided over by males, who remained the heads of households. The father and the older generation held undisputed authority over children, who, because of economic necessity, were burdened with work from a very early age, often from five or six, and by the age of fifteen, they bore full obligations. In the village, children working at home was considered not exploitation but "a hard and good school of life."[17]

The number of women working outside the home, along with the realities of life on family farms, attest to the wide participation of women in both the familial and national economies. Though harder to quantify, women's unpaid labor in the home contributed significantly to these economies. Numbers, however, tell little about the meaning of women's work, either in their own eyes or in society's understanding of their roles. Popular journals of the 1920s and 1930s, particularly women's magazines, reveal several important trends. First, women's employment was undergoing change and expansion. Second, society manifested considerable tension and controversy over the matter, with liberals encouraging the expansion of women's participation in the labor market and conservatives arguing for the need for women to remain in (or return to) the home. Finally, despite change and controversy in women's work lives, the widespread view of Polish women primarily as wives and mothers did not undergo alteration.

The most important magazine devoted to women's issues in the interwar period, *Moja Przyjaciółka* (*My Girlfriend*), espouses a relatively progressive attitude toward women and work in Poland. Speaking of a new generation of women, many articles tout their newly found freedom: since the war, the basic message reads, all roads and opportunities are open for women, who can now find independence and satisfaction through work. Some authors proclaim working a moral imperative for "today's woman," giving her authority, opening new horizons, and making her the "master of her own will and actions." Other writers stress the practical necessity of women's employment: since females predominate in the population, they can no longer count on finding males to provide for them and must be able to support themselves. And some articles point out that women had proven themselves capable and useful workers during the war and, therefore, should be allowed to continue at their jobs, for their own and the nation's benefit.[18]

A similar message comes from the second most popular women's journal, *Bluszcz* (*Ivy*). More political than *Moja Przyjaciółka*, this journal emphasizes the mobilization of women in the economic, political, and social life of the new country, putting forth demands for equality from the incipient state and for recognition of reciprocal duties on the part of women. In 1918, for example, *Bluszcz* published a petition to the State Council for civil and political rights for women: "The current participation of women in economic and social life is already so great and so useful, that only fanatics can still maintain that the task of a woman amounts solely to raising children and taking care of the home." Women's proven ability to fulfill difficult tasks and responsible positions in the labor force during the war frequently provides the basis for claiming equal political rights, paralleling what Joan Scott found in French debates in the upheavals of 1848: "the way to claim political rights for women was to insist on their identity as workers."[19] Thus, in the political language of the day, participation in the national economy as paid workers made women citizens and worthy of the same rights as men. This belief demonstrates the disproportionate value placed on the (male) labor realm as opposed to the (female) domestic one.

While such claims reveal the value placed on paid productive labor in Polish society, they do not prove that women incorporated work identities in the same way as men. Two important notions, popular after World War I, suggest qualifications to the identities of females as workers. First, while some women's advocates insisted that their paid labor rendered them deserving of political rights, others insisted that women's difference from men made them worthy of such rights. Granting political rights to women would benefit the entire nation, the argument went, because women, "more upright than men, bring an ethical element to political struggles." Such reasoning attributed to females an essential nature, morally pure, linked with spirituality, rejuvenation, and education. Sławomira Walczewska argues that Polish suffragettes did not demand equality but "political rights without differentiation according to sex."[20] They did not question the notion of women's difference from men but insisted that it should not bear on the right to vote. Second, despite acknowledgments of a woman's ability and her right to work outside the home, the belief that she nonetheless possessed a special duty, which she should not ignore, persisted. In a characteristic article in *Bluszcz*, a male doctor cautions: "In the broadest, fairest demands for rights as a person, a woman must, however, remember that she has obligations to fulfill so great and sacred, which in the division of labor nature has laid upon her." The very journals supporting the expansion of women's activity beyond the home continually emphasize their duty as mothers and caretakers of the family. Praising the accomplishments of women during the war, the above-quoted petition for political rights maintains that only women could manage the double burden of job and family because of their "strong maternal instincts." The association of women with domesticity did not wane throughout the interwar period. Grounded by the invocation of nature, it seemed an indisputable fact: the sexual difference of women's bodies implied the bestowal, by nature itself, of a special vocation.[21]

The world remained divided into two spheres. The binary view of male and female realms appeared consistently in a wide range of issues, all based on assumptions of a different female nature. This notion resulted in a normative view of women as the "pillar of familial-domestic life." Societal consensus held that only women were equipped to foster familial and patriotic love, to maintain the edifice of the family and, consequently, the social order itself. Four months before the Nazi and Soviet invasions of Poland in 1939, an article in *Moja Przyjaciółka* asserted that since nearly all areas of professional life were open to women, it was now possible to talk about their service to the fatherland on the same scale as men's. Women's first duty, though, should be fulfilled through the family, raising "sensible patriots."[22]

More conservative journals unremittingly propagated throughout the 1920s and 1930s the image of women exclusively as wives and mothers. The most widely read periodical of the era, *Rycerz Niepokalanej* (*The Knight of the Virgin Mary*), a Catholic monthly written for the masses, offers dutiful wives and self-sacrificing mothers as models for women.[23] A typical article describes one such mother (the word woman rarely occurs in this journal): "Mama, although still rather young, is however a woman of the 'old days,' in the positive sense. She doesn't follow the 'progressive' women, living only for themselves and their own pleasure. She is a loving wife and caring mother." Little value is placed on learning or industry outside the home for females. One man acclaims his own mother as the epitome of Polish motherhood. He describes her as:

> a typical peasant mother, like many, many, that we meet in Catholic families. She had no education, she had no idea at all about pedagogy, she had only faith in her soul and love in her heart—a simple, yet deep faith, a generous love, self-sacrificing. She believed that she had to fulfill the will of God and with love, devoted herself to that which God assigned. Love sweetened her heavy task—the nourishing, caring and raising of a numerous progeny.[24]

The message of women's true duty gained urgency and dominance in the journals as the threat from Nazi Germany increased.

Scholars have only recently begun to investigate the consequences paid employment had on women's social identity and on their relations within the family. Studying working-class families in the Congress Kingdom at the turn of the century, Anna Żarnowska concludes that working women's vocational qualifications bore minor importance in determining their social status within their own milieu. "Among the factors shaping the social status of proletarian women, having a family was undoubtedly the most important one," she writes. "The role of a wife and mother to a large extent determined their economic situation and the prestige they enjoyed in their own social class." Both then and later, the working class, as well as the Catholic Church and the national press, looked with disfavor on married women who regularly worked outside the home. Women, therefore, sought jobs that did not compromise the male's position as head of the household, that did not upset the patriarchal family system. A wife's earnings were regarded as an addition to the main, male contribution, and work outside the home neither accorded women prestige nor sparked egalitarian tendencies within the family. According to Żarnowska, in families in which females regularly worked outside the home, "the father retained the decisive voice in basic family affairs; the mother had a subordinate position, but it was she who strengthened the emotional ties binding the family."[25]

Despite changes in women's participation in the labor force during the interwar period, a sexual division of labor remained, both in the activities in which women were engaged and in society's valuation of them. Though much research still needs to be done on this topic, it seems clear that work served less as a source of identity for most Polish women than for men. Women themselves undervalued their own labor: as common practice (one that progressives criticized) women working in their homes and family farms did not identify themselves as workers at all. When asked what they did, they frequently replied, "Nothing," and noted their employment status on surveys as being supported by their husbands (*przy męża*). According to one commentator of the day, "some kind of voluntary self-abasement" led women to consider their own work inferior to men's.[26]

The final issue of individual and group identity to consider here is class. The role of social class in the patterns that Polish females used to understand the events and activities of their daily lives has yet to be systematically addressed. Most literature on interwar Poland deals with class as a universal category, in which women are either absent or assumed to share the general (male) experience; the spotlight is only now being turned on women as a subject in their own right. Researchers have traditionally ascribed the class identity of male family members to the women closely linked with them. The occupation of spouses and fathers generally did determine the material position of women not employed in wage labor and strongly influenced their social status in the minds of others. While some women might well have internalized the class identity attached to male family members, it cannot be assumed, Kathleen Canning points out, "that the shared interests of family and community superseded the divisions within them and, similarly, that shared class identities transcended the fissures of gender within family and household." A husband's class position, although important to a wife's class identity, does not provide a complete account of subjective class identification.[27]

Even barring the problem of specifically female identification, notions of class identity in the modern Western sense do not directly transfer to interwar Poland, particularly its eastern territories, where social differentiation was least developed and categories were in flux. The eastern borderlands lacked the solidified social structure found in Western Europe, and modern economic classes were only beginning to form. Furthermore, according to Janusz Żarnowski, groups in interwar Poland did not necessarily differentiate themselves in matters of lifestyle and outlook according to their place in production. Groups joined by a common position in the economy did not always share the same culture or lifestyle; conversely, a common culture could unite persons of varying socioeconomic positions.[28]

All socioeconomic groups experienced fluidity in composition and character during the 1920s and 1930s. The stratum of workers was small and disparate. Many unskilled laborers came fresh from the village and maintained strong economic and cultural ties with the peasantry; the working class also included artisans and déclassé members of the petty nobility (drobna szlachta). Similarly, the petite bourgeoisie was a highly differentiated group, ranging from those employed at cottage industry to owners of large stores. It operated as a transitional class, with many members recruited from the working class and the village, and with many subsequently moving into the intelligentsia or the bourgeoisie. The latter was neither numerous nor did it possess a distinctive culture; the bourgeoisie included a mix of nationalities, native and foreign, with only a small Polish element. The intelligentsia, too, contained divisions, with the "real intelligentsia"—experts and professionals—at one extreme and the mass of white-collar workers, many of whom were poorly educated functionaries, at the other. Some highly educated members of the intelligentsia respected skilled workers even more than they did lower-level white-collar workers. Yet this latter group tended to feel a sense of superiority vis-à-vis manual laborers, even if the laborers received higher wages.[29]

The traditional classes of Polish society—the peasantry and the gentry —remained in existence but in a process of change or dissolution. Even the peasantry, the largest class of interwar Poland, had little socioeconomic or cultural unity. The boundary between peasants and agricultural workers was especially unclear; the latter served as a transitional group between the peasantry and the working class. The gentry included a large number of impoverished individuals, forced to seek paid employment. Some impoverished provincial nobles or country squires (*szlachta zagrodowa* or *zaściankowa*), particularly in the east, differed little from the peasants.[30]

Nevertheless, the gentry remained at the top of the social hierarchy, enjoying prestige throughout society and maintaining its image as the leading class of the nation. Though the noble culture applied directly to only some tens of thousands of families, it had considerable influence on the rest of the country. The intelligentsia, which by the twentieth century had replaced the nobility as the bearer of national consciousness, had taken on many of its values. On the eve of World War II, the noble ethos remained synonymous with Polish culture in the eyes of many.[31] This accounts for the enduring dichotomy in Polish society between physical and nonphysical labor. Writing in 1939, Stanisław Rychliński concluded that "nowhere does the social distance between intellectual work, even of the most unimportant sort, and physical work, however constructive, loom so glaringly as in Poland."[32] The disdain for physical labor represented one of the most important determinants of socioeconomic relationships and status in interwar Poland. It not only split the nation into two camps, but it also served as a descriptor— however inaccurate (approximately 59% of the ethnic Polish population was engaged in agriculture at the end of the 1930s)[33]—of the Polish nation and an ideal for those striving to leave the village. This attitude remained a constant, one that Poles carried with them into exile.

Class, in the words of Patrick Joyce, is "only one of the ways in which people patterned and gave meaning to the social order."[34] For Poles in the eastern borderlands, regional, ethnic, and religious identities loomed especially important, as did gender. Work and social class do not seem to have been the primary determinants of the identities of women. Though opportunities and attitudes underwent some democratization in the 1920s and 1930s, a basic division of labor remained both in the economy and in social roles. Though they worked at paid and unpaid labor, women were seen primarily as mothers, with a duty to the nation and an obligation before God and nature, to carry out their roles as such. Outside a few small pockets of feminist-minded individuals, the ideal for Polish females remained traditional marriage and motherhood. Women's physical bodies were assumed to have natural consequences for social organization, and the division of labor in the family constituted the foundation for the division of labor in the economy and society.

"I Turned into a Draft Animal"

The majority of women taken from Poland, whether arrested or deported, were forced to engage in extremely demanding and often dangerous physical labor on behalf of the Soviet state. They were compelled to work by the often tandem threats of punishment and starvation. The small minority of deportees not assigned to jobs did not lead lives of leisure but struggled to obtain on their own the necessities of life that Soviet authorities doled out only to the deserving—those who worked for the state. To survive without participating in that system required other forms of toil, as well as resourcefulness and often humility. Whatever form it took, labor and economic survival dominated the lives of all the exiled women.

The Poles were absorbed into the campaign for rapid industrialization and modernization launched by Joseph Stalin in 1928. With the goal of overcoming economic and social backwardness at breakneck speed, the Stalinist regime mobilized all elements of the population into what was billed as an urgent move to overtake and surpass the advanced capitalist countries. Lacking readily available sources for industrial development, the state extracted resources from the agrarian sector, massively transforming it through forced collectivization. All segments of the population bore the burdens of industrialization as the state squeezed consumption—real wages and living standards fell. The USSR lacked not only investment capital but also the skilled labor needed for rapid industrial expansion, which resulted in what Hiroaki Kuromiya calls "a wager on quantity: a desperate attempt to compensate for the dire shortage of skilled workers by using much larger numbers of workers than planned."[35]

By 1930, Soviet society had experienced a transformation from the massive unemployment of the 1920s to a chronic labor shortage. While this circumstance created some benefits for laborers, particularly those previously unable to find jobs or wishing to change them, the state stepped in to curb the chaos it found in the seller's market for labor. In the early 1930s, a series of law-and-order decrees sought to instill "values of discipline, patriotism, conformism, authority and orderly careerism" by circumscribing movement in the countryside, stemming labor turnover, extending the work day and week, and harshly punishing breaches of discipline. Some historians refer to a "near militarization of labor" by the end of the decade, as police terror routinely controlled the labor force. Invoking the revolutionary ideal of "whoever does not work does not eat," economic administrators were "given the tool of starving people in order to obtain their presence in the factories," as well as other workplaces. One Polish deportee relates how the maxim was explained to the newcomers: "Whoever works eats, whoever doesn't drops dead."[36] The Poles thus joined Soviet citizens in an uncompromising system, one which demanded labor and obedience at minimal compensation.

Individuals confined in the camps were explicitly sentenced to hard labor and faced severe penalties if they did not report daily to their assigned jobs. The category of deportee actually comprised three groups: one was subjected to "special settlement," another to "administrative exile," and the final to "exile to settlements." Officially, at least, their labor obligations differed.

Special settlers, the February and June 1940 deportees, enjoyed a day or two of rest upon reaching the endpoint of their journey from Poland. By the third day, however, they had to report to compulsory work assignments, just as inmates in the camps did. Long before the lists of deportees were drawn up, Beria gave explicit instructions on how the exiles should be used. Resolution no. 2122-617ss of the Soviet of People's Commissars, dated 29 December 1939, states: "the *osadnicy* and their families deported by the NKVD of the USSR from the Western regions of the U[krainian]SSR and the B[elorussian] SSR are slated for useful labor in specially organized settlements for clearing forests in regions belonging to the People's Commissariat of Forestry of the USSR."[37] Detailed orders to the responsible agencies followed. In January 1940, the Central Committee, "in connection with the increase in number of the families of special settlers-*osadnicy* subject to deportation," commanded the Commissariat of Nonferrous Metallurgy to prepare to accept some of them. Local authorities typically gathered the Poles together upon their arrival, informing them that as special settlers they had no right to leave the area, were required to work, and would remain there until they died. They usually announced that all persons, female and male, aged sixteen and older, must work; in reality, the minimum age proved to be fifteen, fourteen, or twelve. In some cases, even ten-year-olds received mandatory work assignments.[38]

The April deportees, those administratively exiled, theoretically did not face compulsory labor. They lived with locals on state and collective farms and shared many of the rights of Soviet citizens. As Maria Ches relates, though, their situation did not effectively differ from that of the settlers: "We were not forced to work," she notes, "but they didn't give us the means to live so we had to work."[39] The group exiled to settlements in June 1941 lived under NKVD supervision and bore the obligation "to perform socially useful labor," but supposedly had more choice in where they worked.[40] The punitive nature of the deportations and restrictions on the freedom of the individual set a basic and consistent framework for the lives of Poles in exile, blurring the lines between the deportation categories.

Despite directives from the center, labor requirements frequently varied with the locality and the personalities of the men in charge. In many places, authorities told the deportees that they were free citizens but would get no bread unless they worked. For some deportees, work became compulsory only in mid-1941, after the beginning of the war with Germany; others were never forced to work.[41] In still other cases, deportees not explicitly required to work were pressured—through daily visits by the NKVD, frequent meetings at which they were insulted and harangued, and threats of arrest and separation from family members—until they assented to labor for the state. The three types of deportation, then, cannot be seen as rigidly distinct; arbitrariness in administration compounded the built-in ambiguity of the category of exile.

The work regimen in most cases of free exile did not differ from that imposed on those whose status as special settlers explicitly bound them to work; that, in turn, bore a significant resemblance to conditions imposed on camp inmates. Józef Ptak called these different labels "useless words" that could be encapsulated by one term alone—*katorżnik* (convict laborer). "You had to work and suffer everywhere just the same," he explains. Comparing life in free exile in the Novosibirsk *oblast'* to that of convicts, Wanda Baczyńska, formerly a student of the Academy of Fine Arts in Kraków, writes: "Indeed, the prisoners were in a better situation, they didn't worry about a roof over their heads, nor the suffering of their closest ones from hunger and difficulties. The deportees were slaves; whether they wanted to or not they had to work, to give their maximum strength—it was a question of life for himself and his family." According to a woman who served time in prison and a camp, then worked as a civilian in a Soviet factory after her release, "Soviet freedom differs little from the camp." The same picture comes from Stanisława Kowalska: "The first months after being freed from the labor camp didn't go any better than behind the barbed wire," she writes, "and sometimes it was even worse."[42] Hard labor, therefore, cannot be associated solely with the Gulag; it constituted the dominant factor of life for deportees as well as prisoners.

A few exceptions existed. While most local authorities, plagued by chronic labor shortages, zealously conscripted the newly arrived Poles into their labor force, some just as vehemently rejected them. At this extreme stood collective farms behind in their debts to the state; they refused to employ the newcomers, as they had neither enough money nor food to support permanent members. In some settlements, local inhabitants and authorities refused to provide anything at all, including jobs, food rations, heating materials, and shelter, to people they had been taught to consider enemies. Deportees in such situations were left to their own wits, though still proscribed from leaving the area.[43]

A small minority of the women managed to avoid taking a job. This generally required unusual courage and resilience before the pressure of local authorities to compel them to work. It also necessitated some independent means for securing food and lodgings, for those persons not working for the state had no right to buy food in the stores. Additionally, even though the Poles were taken from their homeland against their will, they had to pay rent for their new lodgings, be it a corner in the hut of a local family or a bunk in a barracks; some even had to pay taxes to the Soviet government.[44] Deportees who avoided laboring for the state managed to survive largely by selling their own possessions to the local inhabitants, particularly articles of clothing that were impossible to purchase in the USSR. These goods came from two sources. Some women had the foresight, and the good fortune of sufficient time, to pack extra items when NKVD agents came to take them from their homes. Later, deportees acquired goods to barter from parcels they received from relatives remaining in the annexed Polish territories.

Despite the punitive nature of their exile and the far-flung locations in which they lived, deportees did receive packages, some regularly, until the Nazi invasion of the USSR in June 1941. Barbara Kryżanowska, who survived by trading articles of clothing sent from home, illustrates the value of these goods. For a sweater from Poland she could buy two poods (1 pood equals 36 pounds) of flour or nine buckets of potatoes; a pair of slippers bought 1 ½ kilograms of butter.[45] Many Poles credit the parcels from relatives with saving their lives. In fact, a large number of exiles report that these two sources of goods and income—personal belongings and packages from home—accounted for their survival in the USSR even when they worked every day.[46]

Few other means existed for providing for one's self and one's family. Seeing how impressed and covetous Soviet citizens were of the finer articles of clothing and linen from Poland, some deportees used their sewing and embroidering skills to supply the local elites with such goods.[47] Without the necessary materials and skills for such enterprise, many deportees fought a daily battle to subsist. Families strove to keep starvation in abeyance by scrounging the forests for berries and mushrooms and making soups from nettles and grasses; some took to trapping and eating dogs and cats. "Hunger predominated to such an extent," writes one woman, "that whoever managed to catch a cat ate it, and ate even rats."[48] With the passage of time, many women turned to stealing to stay alive; some resorted to begging. A teacher from Kraków with two small children to support begged for food for the first time in her life: "This was the last break of human pride," she notes.[49]

Despite these exceptions, the majority of the women did work for the Soviet state. Few remained at the same job for the entire period of exile, as they were continually transferred from one job to another according to the demands of the seasons or the central economic plan, or the whim of local commanders. Such movement characterized labor through most of the

Stalinist period, for, as historian Moshe Lewin observed, "the government and managers acquired the habit of shuffling the labor force around like cattle, their eyes fixed on their targets, forgetful of elementary human needs."[50] Transfers sometimes were used for punishment, requiring the targeted individual to work at more difficult jobs, in harsher conditions, or at great distances from family members. Most Poles relate working at three to five different jobs during their exile.

By far the most common work Polish women performed, especially those relocated to Siberia and the north of European Russia, was clearing forests. Their tasks included felling trees, sawing branches, floating logs, hauling and loading wood, and operating sawmills. Second to logging ranked fieldwork. Most women resettled in Kazakhstan and Siberia engaged in planting and digging potatoes, clearing and weeding fields, and harvesting vegetables, grains, and cotton; those in Kazakhstan also herded and tended livestock, including cattle, sheep, and pigs. Many Poles, particularly teenagers, were sent away from their families for several months as part of hay-cutting missions or plowing and tractor brigades. The Soviet government also used Poles as labor for large developmental projects. In the summer of 1941, many females were drafted to help build the Akmolinsk-Kartaly railroad in Kazakhstan; others were put to work constructing roads, hydration and sewage systems, and barracks.

These work assignments account for the majority of exiles but do not exhaust the list of jobs at which Polish women toiled. Many of them worked at brickmaking, from digging the clay and forming and firing the bricks to carting and loading them into trucks. They dug peat and mined iron, coal, and gold. They worked in quarries and industrial plants. They built snow banks, dug ditches, and cleaned stables. Some exiles labored in factories where they dyed material or sewed uniforms for the Soviet military, the very army that overran their homeland.

When Soviet officials came to deport the Poles, they announced that after relocation they would be given jobs according to their previous specialties. Though many women had been employed in white-collar jobs or worked only in their homes, few managed to secure jobs that did not involve heavy physical labor. Complaints met with ridicule or the declaration that such privileges did not extend to exploiters and enemies. The rare light jobs open to exiles included hospital or office work, cooking duties, and child care in state nurseries. Only a handful of women report the good fortune of landing such employment, which they generally attribute to their knowledge of the Russian language. They had an extremely difficult time keeping these jobs, for infractions such as arriving late or granting too many medical exemptions from work or, after the Soviet-German war, simply being Polish usually resulted in transfer to manual labor.[51]

Long hours, high production quotas, and grim working conditions rendered the physical labor even more onerous. The shortest workday mentioned in the statements is ten hours, but most women toiled twelve to fourteen hours per day, some even longer, with generally only a short break for lunch.[52] In addition to long hours of labor, many women spent a great deal of time walking to and from the work site, typically located at considerable distances from their living quarters: they frequently report walking ten to twelve kilometers in each direction.[53] These distances had to be covered on foot, whether under the blistering sun of the Central Asian summer, during the fury of a Siberian snowstorm, or in the midst of a downpour. Few women possessed proper footwear; after several months of exile many went barefoot, as the authorities made no provision for outfitting workers once their own articles of clothing wore out. Irena Sypniewska walked four kilometers in her bare feet to the quarry where she dug lime, while Anna Zaboklicka marched six kilometers to work in the forest, also without shoes.[54] Individuals considered themselves fortunate if they could make shoes from old tires, even though this footwear made their feet bleed. Labor camp inmates faced the additional trauma of marching under escort of armed guards and trained dogs after undergoing a morning search.[55] Hungry and weak, many women collapsed on the road.

Once they arrived at the work site, the exiles were watched so that they neither escaped nor rested and were continually exhorted to work harder. Conditions ranged from dismal to dangerous. Women made and handled bricks bare-handed, and field workers, lacking shovels, dug with sticks or their hands. One woman, employed as a cook for a field crew, carried buckets of potatoes five kilometers each day. "I always cried then," she writes. "The metal handle of the bucket stuck into my hand. When that went on for a week, my hands swelled and cracked. . . . It got so bad that blood ran into the soup."[56] Mines filled with deadly gases, and individuals employed in dyeing plants contracted lung and skin diseases from working with harsh chemicals without ventilation or protective gear.[57] Outdoor work took place in Siberia even when the temperature dropped to -70 degrees Celsius (-94° F) and in Kazakhstan when it rose to 50 degrees (122° F). In winter, workers felled trees while standing in snow up to their waists; in summer, mosquito bites swelled their faces and rendered them unrecognizable.[58]

Work in the USSR, for virtually all jobs, and for both convict and free laborers, was organized according to the so-called norm. Each job had a quota that had to be met for the worker to receive full food rations and avoid punishment. Cecylia Czajkowska had to produce 500 bricks per day, a norm she considered hopeless, while another woman in a similar factory had to carry and load 1,000 bricks into the oven during each shift.[59] A seventeen-year-old employed at making *kiziaki* from cow dung was required to make 1,000 of these bricks each day. The norm for tying bundles of hay in some places was 500; Weronika Hołowak reports that at most she could do ninety. Aniela Pawliszak was sent to build snowbanks; each woman was supposed to make twenty embankments per day, fifteen meters long, one meter wide, one meter tall. With great exertion, she could complete four.[60]

The norms could at any time be raised and often were. Failure to fulfill the norm resulted in diminished food rations and fines or arrest for repeated shortfalls. In some labor camps, permission to write letters depended on fulfillment of the norm. Payment for a day's labor in the camps, if one fulfilled the quota, typically consisted of 500–600 grams of bread and a portion, sometimes two, of watery soup. Almost every account of norms in Polish women's documents describes them as impossibly high, far beyond the women's strength: some could reach 50 percent, but others routinely managed only 25 percent. They, therefore, received drastically reduced food rations. "The norm was so high that not one of us could fulfill it," writes a woman from Lida who ended up in the Gulag, "for which reason I received 300 grams of bread twice a day and half a liter of warm water, which they called soup, without any fat."[61]

Most deportees faced an identical situation. Zofia Górska worked eleven hours per day hauling timber with a horse and cart. When she approached the commandant for her pay, he informed her that since she had never fulfilled the norm and yet was given bread to eat, she owed the state. Many deportees explain that they worked merely for the right to buy bread. A typical day's food rations for a working deportee (fulfilling the norm) included a breakfast of 600 grams of bread and hot water, a lunch of barley soup with some fish in it, and the same soup for dinner. "I went to work for reasons of the 'pay' of 400 grams of bread, and so as not to go mad from despair and the gigantic longing for my country that I can't even describe," writes a forty-one-year-old obstetrician, who worked at logging in exile.[62]

Some deportees did receive a wage for their labor, albeit minimal. "The maximum I earned was seven to ten rubles a month, and often I had to pay some kind of government tax and so I received nothing," relates Janina Kuraszkiewicz. Lucyna Tarnamkiewicz worked in the forest, earning one to two rubles per day, while a kilogram of bread, the mainstay of the diet of civilians and convicts alike, cost one ruble and ten kopecks. Halina Chojecka received 120 rubles per month for tending pigs on a collective farm, where a pood of wheat cost 150–200 rubles. She supported her mother and younger brothers not from her salary but by selling the family's possessions and stealing.[63]

The payment women received, either directly in bread or in the form of money and the right to buy a ration of food, did not suffice for subsistence. In actuality, they worked merely to keep out of prison. A clerk resettled in Siberia elaborates: "We worked not for the pay, because even for the most strenuous work the pay was impossible, but so as not to be punished for *progul*."[64] Due to the campaigns for labor discipline in the 1930s, *progul*—unexcused absence from the job—became a term used with great frequency and serious import. One could receive permission to miss a day of work only by obtaining a doctor's certificate attesting to a temperature of at least 40 degrees Celsius (104° F). Countless women and men, in the Polish documents as well as memoirs of others, report being severely ill, barely able to move, yet denied permission to remain in bed because they did not have a sufficiently high temperature. Excuses were also denied simply because of the ill will of medical personnel or the indifference or cruelty of the commandant. Halina Urbańska was hampered at her job at a construction site by extremely bad eyesight, which left her prone to accidents. The doctor rebuffed her request for reassignment on medical grounds with the comment that she had not come to the Riviera. According to Aleksandra Wodzicka, some people resorted to drinking gas after being denied a medical excuse in order to become sick enough to obtain one. "Maybe this will be difficult to understand," relates another woman of her experience in a clothing factory, "but sewing through a finger was sometimes a blessing, as you would then be freed from work for two to three days."[65]

A person who did not obtain a doctor's certificate and yet failed to show up for work, regardless of the excuse, was reported for *progul*. Punishment varied. Typically, the first instance resulted in a 25 percent reduction of pay; a second infraction received three months in prison and a third—one-year imprisonment. These penalties were not consistently applied. When Irena

Król stayed home one day because of illness, the police hauled her to the commandant, who declared that she was not sick and ordered her to report to her job in the forest; crying, she refused and was promptly arrested for two days. Some delinquent workers received long sentences for a first offense. A woman deported to Irtysh fell ill and left her night shift guarding sheep, which resulted in two and one-half years imprisonment, forcing her to abandon her two children.[66] The law considered tardiness tantamount to absenteeism, punishable in the same manner, so that arriving at work twenty minutes late could land one in prison.[67] The penalty for *progul* in the camps was confinement for several nights in the *kartser:* the inmate received no food while locked in this cold, wet, punishment cell and had to work as usual during the day.[68]

Maria Jałoszyńska, deported from a village near Białystok to the Urals region, presents a typical experience. She was sent to work in a mine: "I was then 16, and forced to work like every adult worker. The work was very hard and dangerous. Every day two to three corpses were removed, and that's to say nothing of those who were disabled." Unable to fulfill the norm, she was forced to work two shifts, then threatened with separation from her family or a prison sentence. "The threats didn't help because I was too weak," she continues:

> Every day the work got harder and harder and the bread they gave less and less. After several months I was so exhausted and weak from hunger that I had to ask the doctor for an excuse from work, which was given only to those sick with a temperature of 40 degrees. He refused to give me the excuse and laughed derisively, "You're as healthy as a horse, you don't have a temperature, you're lazy, get to work." The tears ran down my face and I returned to the mine.[69]

For all of the exiles, whether arrested or deported, life became a daily struggle for survival, requiring great effort simply to procure some food for themselves and their families. Hard labor wore them down and threatened to deprive them of their humanity. A woman sent to a labor camp near Novosibirsk writes: "When I observed the livestock I came to the realization that the livestock had it better." One young woman, who had to cart dirt and stones for days, laments, "I turned into a draft animal." A compatriot echoes: "We were weak, hungry, desperate, and didn't know why or for what we must so live. We felt like the draft horses in the stables, from which they demanded work for a minimal amount of food."[70]

Labor through the Lenses of Gender and Class

Writing with bitterness, even disbelief, the exiled women unanimously decry the labor system under which they toiled. Besides denouncing the conditions of labor, they complain that *all* the exiles were forced to work, stressing indignantly that no regard was paid to such factors as sex, age, health, or previous experience. "They didn't take into account the old or the young, just drove everyone to work," writes Janina Niemczyk.[71] The exiles' response to the Soviet labor system reveals distinct gender and class configurations of the collective vision of the Polish nation. Above all, Poles protest that in treating the exiled population indiscriminately, Soviet officials ignored sexual difference, a foundation of the Polish economic and social organization, and thus restructured individuals' daily lives and threatened their identities. The lack of distinction between the sexes appeared to the Poles as a breakdown of order, a sign of barbarity.

Their reaction to labor in exile contains a second important component: Poles tended to regard themselves as a single unit, exploited in its labor by the Soviets. This unity, however temporary, overshadowed fissures within the Polish population. At the same time this vision set the entire Polish nation, as an ideal, against the Soviet (Russian) one, as a superior class, above the manual labor for which the latter seemed fit. These notions of gender and class were articulated as essential features of the Polish nation.

"Against All the Laws of Nature"

When discussing labor, Polish women object not simply to what they were subjected to as human beings, as formerly free individuals, or as unjustly exiled citizens of a previously sovereign country, but precisely as *females*. One of the most common refrains in the documents—by authors of both sexes—is that "women as well as men" were forced to work. Though initially only males were assigned jobs in her settlement, explains Stanisława Lisowska, "several days later even women were forced to work." Word of this situation reached Poles back in the occupied territories early in 1940. Fearful of the prospect of her own deportation, one woman wrote to her husband, who had fled Polish territory: "There have already been letters from those who were deported. They take them to Siberia to work in the woods. Women too."[72] The daughter of a policeman notes that in the brick factory to which she was assigned, women's tasks included carrying clay, shaping bricks, and loading the ovens: "In a word," she adds, "the very same as for men." One woman recounts laboring "just like all the men" in a mine. "Men and even women worked at felling trees, at building roads, at floating logs and clearing the forest," recalls another deportee.[73]

The juxtaposition of women and men working in the fields, the forests, the mines, and the rivers seems to have been both physically and cognitively jarring to most females, who considered themselves out of place. A teacher notes, "We were weak women, not accustomed to hard physical labor. We had to work alongside strong, capable men." Similarly, a woman sent to float logs down the river from forest clearings highlights the fact that "alongside men, women and children struggle just the same."[74] Men impart their distress at observing the plight of their women. "Grieving," begins one man, "we had to watch the Polish women who had to work their way through such high snow and in such extreme cold." Józef Bielawski laments that while working in the oil wells he "met 150 Polish women, most of them the wives of officers and government officials, doing hard labor."[75]

The simple phrases "women as well as men" and "even women" used so often in the documents carry great weight and express the outrageous treatment of female exiles. The strength of these remarks comes from the implicit assumption that women should be treated differently, for the Poles insisted on rigid distinctions between male and female labor, a distinction which Bolshevik ideology sought to erase. The Soviet commitment continued a long revolutionary tradition begun in the mid-nineteenth century by socialists who challenged the gender division of labor and refuted its naturalness, arguing instead that the notion stemmed from property relations and the mode of production. Following Marxist theory, the Bolsheviks located the source of women's oppression in the family and its role in keeping women out of wage labor, leaving them in a position of dependence. "If women were to be liberated economically and psychologically," historian Wendy Goldman explains, "they needed to become more like men, or more specifically, more like male workers."[76] Many early Bolshevik decrees strove to create opportunities for women's release from the shackles of the family into the public sphere. In the 1920s, economic chaos and continued sexual discrimination kept women from experiencing real changes in employment, but economic necessity coincided with Bolshevik ideology in the years of Stalin's industrialization drive and pushed women into the public realm at an unprecedented rate. Simply put, the campaign for modernization needed to exploit the productive capacity of women, and the 1930s saw a massive influx of females into the workforce, including traditionally male sectors. By the time the Poles arrived at the end of the decade, 42 percent of the workers in Soviet heavy industry were women, as were 21 percent of construction workers—a situation quite foreign to the Poles.[77]

In the countryside, the Soviet state attempted to transform peasant women into heroines of socialist labor, both to utilize their economic potential and to eradicate "backward" peasant attitudes, blamed for oppressing women. Efforts were made to turn rural women into tractor drivers, combine operators, and shock workers, who were glorified in the media well out of proportion to their numbers.[78] Millions of women joined the workforce in the 1930s, toiling at unskilled, low-paying manual jobs in agriculture and industry. Although these women hardly achieved equal opportunities of access, prestige, or pay, the Soviet government considered the "woman question" solved, by virtue of women's numbers in the labor force and their presence in fields previously considered the exclusive province of men. The New Soviet Woman was defined not by her role in the family, which the ruling ideology branded primitive, but by her role in production.[79] Soviet leaders lauded their state as the most progressive, having transcended social relations that they believed enslaved women and that characterized its Western rivals. What Soviet leaders denounced as petit bourgeois, the Poles embraced.

At the heart of the exiles' objection was the fact that women were treated no differently than men: Soviet leaders regarded their subjects as having generic bodies, equally capable of and liable for any physical tasks assigned to them. The Poles, however, stress that women, as a category, are essentially different from men. The violation of this principle appears not as a simple infraction of Polish cultural norms but as a disputation of nature itself. Polish females discuss the labor they had to perform predominantly "in terms of the 'natural' purposes and physical characteristics of women's bodies," rejecting what they perceive as the Soviet attempt to disregard nature.[80] "There was no allowance at all for the fact that woman is weaker than man. The work norms were the same for everyone," writes one woman. Revealing the same perception of what constitutes natural activity for women, another deportee complains that they "endure the same work—although in physical strength they are weaker." Describing life in a settlement, the daughter of a military colonist writes: "In hunger and cold we all had to go to work, though the work was very hard whether a woman or man we all had to work the same in the forest and the norms were so high that no one could do them." A village policeman's daughter, sent to work on railroad construction, scoffs, "They said that in their country women had to work like men, because they have the same rights as men."[81]

Polish men concur with the objections of their female compatriots. While describing their own labor in exile they repeatedly criticize the employment of women, using the same phrases. Some call it a tragedy.[82] Highlighting the importance of the reproductive function of the female body, men especially protest that neither motherhood nor pregnancy exempted women from work. "And that's not to even mention the periodic women's sickness," adds one man, referring to the menstrual cycle. Roman Flaczyński notes that initially women in his settlement received medical excuses from work for two days each month during their "illness"; the doctor, "our Pole," was soon reprimanded and forbidden to grant these exemptions. [83] According to these men, women naturally deserve special consideration in the time, amount, and type of work they perform. The situation in the USSR confounded them, for, as Bolesław Stankiewicz stresses, "There was no demarcation between work for women and for men."[84] Physical labor threatened to erase the distinction between the sexes.

Against the background of numerous campaigns promoting heroic labor efforts and the accompanying record mania, which attracted both male and female enthusiasts in the USSR throughout the 1930s, not a single adult Polish woman reports that she or any of her counterparts succeeded in achieving the work quota. There is only one instance of a Polish female writing that she could fulfill it, from a thirteen-year-old girl from a village near Wilno. In a matter-of-fact statement, devoid of commentary or judgment, she describes her life in a colony for Polish and Russian girls: "Sometimes I was a Stakhanovite, then I ate cutlets, drank milk, *kasha* and *piroshki* and I ate many other tasty things."[85] For her, the claim to being able to over-fulfill the work norm—thus earning the label and rewards of a Stakhanovite—seems to hold none of the negative connotations that older women associate with it. This sentence was crossed out with red pencil on her original statement by a member of the Bureau of Documents of the Polish Army in the East (AWBD) who prepared the testimonies for use by the Polish government, an action which reflects the social importance of this issue. Presumably such a deviant, successful at labor unnatural for her sex, had to be marginalized.

The notion of separate male and female space was both literal and metaphorical; identity stemmed primarily from the reciprocal definition of the sexes, whose presumed natures and complementary functions maintained the character and stability of the Polish nation. Women therefore resented doing jobs they considered belonging to the sphere of men's work. Alina Lukaszewiczówna notes that women and children had to separate metal from earth at a mine, "work that was difficult for men." Similarly, Helena Pieleszek angrily states, "At the collective farm there was not appropriate work for men, not to mention for women."[86] The categories of "men's work" and "women's work," in the eyes of the Poles, should remain distinct. Though Soviet women toiled similarly, some of the exiled females believed that they were given work most unsuited for them as women as an affront to their Polishness: they felt attacked because of their nationality, in terms of gender. Describing her work in a labor camp clearing forests, one woman notes: "The work in the penal camp was as if chosen for women, especially us from Poland."[87]

The blurred boundaries between male and female realms profoundly altered the social roles of individuals, disrupting the organization of the family and the identities attributed to its members. Females voice particular outrage that they had to work even when senior male family members lived with them in exile. In their vision of normal socioeconomic organization, the latter's labor should have been enough to satisfy both the demands of the Soviet state and the needs of the family. Men's wages in Poland were typically expected to support a family, a notion most women accepted. Women's wages were assumed to be supplementary to the family income, and men held the status of economic providers to family and nation. In exile, this ideal order could not even be attempted. "We all worked, women, men and children," states the wife of a military settler, noting that though her husband had supported her in Poland, his labor did not suffice to maintain the family in the USSR. One woman reflects on her shock at the strangeness of life in Kazakhstan: "I had in mind the image of our worker, whose wife is waiting for him with the children when he returns from work, and he feels the master of the house, he has some kind of property, works willingly." According to the author of a report to the Polish government on conditions of the exiles after the amnesty, Soviet men sometimes unofficially took their wives and children to the work site to help them fulfill, or even over-fulfill the norm; Poles, she stresses, are not fit for this system.[88]

The compositions of young Poles repeatedly depict the situation they encountered in the USSR as foreign and wrong. They write that back in Poland they had lived comfortably, in families in which the father alone worked to support six, eight, even ten children, as well as his wife. This natural state of affairs did not hold true across the border, a circumstance that sharply altered the social roles of all family members. Krystyna Sobierajska, who worked in the forest while in exile, compares this period with her previous life: "I had to work for the entire family which consisted of ten people and from it only three worked. My father worked in Poland alone for the entire family, and here three of us worked and couldn't earn enough and were hungry." Similarly, a schoolgirl from the Tarnopol province recalls that at home her father, a farmer, supported the family, which never knew hunger. In the USSR, she states indignantly, it was not enough that her father, mother, and two brothers worked: "I being 14 years old had to work in order to earn money for myself for a piece of bread." Another daughter of a farmer, fifteen years old when deported, writes bitterly:

> In Poland a worker's horse was treated better than a person in Russia, although they say that the working class in Russia is treated the best. In Poland the poorest worker, who has to support a wife and several children, lives better than a worker in Russia who works with his wife and children, as the child of a Polish worker does not lack milk or sweets, while in Russia a child doesn't even get enough black bread. The Bolshevik idea is beautiful but only in tales, in reality it's hell in place of life.[89]

In their nostalgia for home, these young Poles undoubtedly discount the contribution their mothers made to the family economy back in Poland. They may also have forgotten the important work that children performed on family farms. Nevertheless, their essays show the ideal vision of social organization espoused by the Poles, with a firm division of labor based on sexual difference.

Adult males, too, bemoan the breakdown of their accustomed socio-economic order. Referring to the common arrest of husbands and deportation of wives and children, men write of families falling into misery because of the lack of "the care of a father."[90] When deported along with their families, men endeavored to carry out their traditional roles, as Andrzej

Zinkiewicz conveys in this description of his life in exile: "I devoted myself completely to work, in order to keep my children from hunger and death." Such efforts often proved useless, and men agonize that while in Poland they alone had supported their families, in exile they worked hard, ruined their health, and yet watched relatives suffer. "I could earn enough only for myself," writes one Pole, "and my small children and wife were starving."[91] Men lament that their spouses, too, had to work, sometimes even their children, yet even their joint earnings did not suffice: "All members of the family do wage labor, which has a terrible effect on family life, and in spite of that they starve to death." Recalling his despair at his inability to support his family in Kazakhstan, one man writes, "their suffering was more painful than my own." A compatriot, remembering how his pregnant wife and teenage daughters had to work in the forest to earn their bread, likens the difference between his life in Poland and in Russia to that between heaven and hell.[92]

So anguished were some men at their helplessness before their families that they left them, rather than witness or contribute to their continued misery. One young man, deported after his father's arrest, felt he had no choice but to leave the settlement after the amnesty. "Going off to the army, I left my mother and younger brother in complete poverty," he writes, "instead of improving their situation I would have made it worse, for I wasn't in the condition to provide for myself." After his release from a labor camp, Feliks Kopacki happily located his family in Kazakhstan but found himself in a tragic position: "Since in my state of health as it was then I couldn't see any possibility of giving any kind of help to my wife and children, and could even become a burden for them, with ten rubles in the pocket of my ragged jacket, on 11 October 1941, after resting with my family for seven days, I bade farewell to my wife and my beloved sons."[93] Such testimonies express grief and humiliation at the suffering of loved ones and at the men's own degraded roles and suggest the injury done to their sense of purpose and worth.

Though men clearly opposed the system, their writings about their work experience differ from those of women. Men do not assert so categorically that they could not do the work required of them, and their explanations contain much more variation. At one end of the spectrum, men agree that their work in exile was "beyond the strength of a human being." According to Kazimierz Hryniewicz, "A strong man could not under any circumstances fulfill the norm."[94] Descriptions of the norm as a human impossibility contain a sweeping denunciation of the Soviet system of labor; the men's difficulties at work had little to do with themselves. At the other extreme stand those who did manage to do the required labor. Discussing the norm, Kazimierz Woropaj states that the most he did was 127 percent. "I belonged to the group of weak workers," writes another man, "not always reaching the norm." Others relate nonjudgmentally that their fellow countrymen fulfilled the quotas.[95] These claims, absent in women's documents, are not boastful. Most of them contain qualifications, such as this man's admission: "In Russia I was a Stakhanovite, but it was reflected in my health." Similarly, Mieczysław Pozewłucki writes, "The strong ones, with difficulty, could do the assigned work." Completion of the required labor did not necessarily stigmatize a male, though some men do refer to "fools" among the Poles who became Stakhanovites.[96]

Between the extremes of fulfilling the norm and never coming close to it are those men suggesting that the work quotas may have been achievable, though not for them. The reasons for their (sometimes individual, often collective) failure vary. First, many men claim that Poles were unfit for such work. Others focus less on inherent qualities of the Poles and more on the damage wrought on their bodies by their imprisonment. Jan Nowicki states that within two weeks in the camp, "fifty percent of our people became completely unfit for work." An army officer from Lwów explains that because of the conditions in the camp, the majority of Poles were not in shape to do more than 50 percent of the norm.[97] They may have been able to do the work, such comments suggest, were it not for the treatment they endured.

Some men attribute their failures on the job to their individual will. Simply put, they had no desire to do the work demanded of them, for the benefit of their enemies, and, therefore, never even tried to reach the norm. A farmer sent to work at railroad construction writes, "I was neither a Stakhanovite nor a shock worker and I did not try to be. My health and lack of desire did not allow me to do that." In a similar vein, a young man explains, "I was not an outstanding worker, and I didn't even try to be, as others did, who have long been gone from this world."[98] Such men emphasize their own choice and control, while women do not make such claims, falling back instead on biology and nature to explain their inevitable shortcomings at work.

Besides the choice to be poor laborers, men's documents contain another explanation, also absent in women's accounts. In the words of Jan Lipiński: "The norm was possible to fulfill and very easily so. You simply had to slip a few rubles into the hands of the foreman." Other men similarly discuss the real methods by which one fulfilled the norm, a system of connections and bribery amounting to favoritism and cheating. Some men contend that only other nationalities benefited from these machinations. "There were Russians working near us, and they earned a lot, they fulfilled 200–250 percent of the norm," writes a deported forester, "Nothing surprising about that—the foremen were Ukrainians, their friends, who knew how to prevaricate (they had twenty years of practice), so they cheated us, and gave to them."[99] Similarly, another man declares that in his camp Poles reached 50 percent of the norm, while Russians fulfilled it by bribing the foremen who were typically criminals. Some men explain that once they learned the system, they too took advantage of it. Kazimierz Biliński worked under Soviet brigade leaders of Polish origin, who could be induced to write down 125 percent when the workers actually fulfilled 25 percent: "In that way they made record-breakers, Stakhanovites, out of the Poles," he explains. "Wanting to keep themselves alive, the Poles had to adopt that wrongdoing." According to a judge from Gródek Jagielloński, those who shared packages from home with their supervisor got written down as having done more than the quota: "we said in the camp that the norm wasn't reached or exceeded by the one under whose name it was recorded, but by the pencil of the foreman."[100] Corruption provided the sole key to mastery on the job, not strength or skill.

These interpretations not only offer judgments on the system prevailing in the USSR but also explain the men's own changed status. Traditionally defined by their activity in the public realm, particularly their labor, Polish men experienced three changes in this regard while in exile, which compromised their own identity: they were deprived of choice in their jobs, many could not accomplish the required work, and they could no longer fulfill their roles as providers. While assertions that the work was simply too hard may have been accurate and sufficient for some men, others might have been drawn to more complicated explanations to counter their degraded gender status. Without systematic study of Polish men's relationship to work, which has not been attempted here, conclusions cannot be made about male identity. The issue of one's capacity to perform the required labor in exile does seem more troublesome for males, though. For females gender provides an unambiguous answer.

With male relatives gone, incapacitated, or ineffectual, many women suddenly acquired the role of economic provider for the family, one with which they did not customarily identify.[101] "At this collective farm I worked hard because I had obligations, I had to support a sick mother and three younger brothers," explains one young woman from a village near Białystok. "The work was terrible for me as I had never worked in Poland." Twenty-one-year-old Czesława Domiszewska, deported after her father's arrest, writes: "Having never worked at physical labor, I had to perform the hardest labor, the extraction of peat." Later she was sent to work in a sweater factory. "Here," she continues, "I worked until the end of my stay in exile as a common worker. I had to work even to the very last of my strength, as I had to support my sick mother and younger brother, waiting for that bit of black bread." She concludes: "With complete certainty I affirm that that country and government is the only institution in the world which in a refined and base and despicable way manages to abuse people in general and most of all the worker and his labor."[102]

Perhaps the ultimate affront, in the eyes of the exiles, was that mothers —including those of infants—did not receive exemptions from compulsory labor. This conflicted with their primary familial and social role, prompting surprise and resentment. "We all worked," writes one young woman, "even mothers with small children." "It was not taken into account at all that we have children," states a village woman. An officer's wife, singled out for punishment for refusing to work, remarks bitterly that the authorities decided to use her as an example to force others to work: "Who else to single out, if not a helpless woman who in addition has children, worries about them, for they are her only riches." A compatriot similarly persecuted for refusing a job, yet ultimately failing to withstand the pressures of the overseer, describes the trauma of the day she joined the work crew: "My fellow workers looked with compassion at the mother of three small children who was forced to go out to work while the other mothers trembled as they awaited their turn."[103]

The implications of this new economic role on women's functions as mothers will be explored in the next chapter. Here it is sufficient to note that regardless of what they actually were able to accomplish in exile, and of the existence of crèches and schools at which children could stay all day, women generally found their economic roles in the Soviet state incompatible with their identities and duties as mothers, particularly as Polish mothers. After the amnesty, a group of them sent a plea to the Polish Embassy begging for help for themselves and their children, whom they could neither feed nor clothe. Signed, "Polish Mothers of the Parabel' region in the Novosibirsk *oblast'*," the letter states: "They have taken away our husbands, they wear us down with work and hunger, harass us at every step. Some women with higher education (Polish schoolteachers) are forced to graze cattle. And so we ask you how to survive." In another collective letter six women deported from the Grodno district write that they, along with their children, are "in a critical situation," and beg for relief from the embassy. "They arrested our husbands before our deportation and we have no information on them at all," the plea states. "For the second year already we are trying with all our might to feed our children, in which we have great difficulty, as we no longer have the health or the strength."[104] The women felt incapable of fulfilling the functions they associated with men; at the same time, they were no longer able to perform their true duties, those of motherhood.

"Black Work"

To what extent were women's objections to Soviet labor demands a phenomenon of class? The previous socioeconomic positions of female exiles who hailed from the gentry or intelligentsia clearly fueled their denunciations of the labor they did in the USSR. When asked about her occupation in Poland, one woman from a noble family answered, "I have not worked. I ran my husband's house and I looked after my children." Schoolteachers and clerks likewise point out that they had never before worked at manual labor. "Of course none of us girls, who never before held an ax in her hands, could fulfill the norm," writes a woman employed at logging after her arrest for belonging to an underground organization. Anna Rudawcówna, a teacher from Grodno, states that a day's labor tending sheep or working on a construction site left her barely conscious in the evening: "We were weak women, not accustomed to hard physical labor." Another woman recalls: "We had manual jobs. No one could work according to his specialty."[105] For such women, former class status and the attendant experience of work made the burden of labor in exile only more onerous and contemptible.

While the violation of gender norms dominates the Polish government's criticism of the employment of its women at physical labor in the USSR, their social class often fuels the condemnation. A typical report on the condition of its citizens after the amnesty reads: "All deportees, regardless of their physical condition, age, sex or education were put on heavy manual labor." One document places particular emphasis on the socioeconomic status of the women—more accurately, of their husbands—to evoke the outrage of the situation: "That the wives of engineers, doctors, officers and similar people should have to live in temporary barracks suitable only for animals, and should have to work up to their knees in mud in the rice fields, for a piece of black bread, is by no means the worst."[106]

Some women felt they were singled out and assigned to the most difficult jobs precisely because of their former socioeconomic position in Poland, for which Soviet officials sought to punish them. According to a teacher from Białystok, "They sent women with education to the very worst, hardest physical labor, with that they mocked them." A former medical student of the prestigious Jagiellonian University in Kraków, employed at digging peat, notes bitterly that all the women in her group were used for unskilled jobs or "black work" (*czarna robota*), the least respected of all labor. Several women report being forced to perform useless labor meant merely to humiliate and exhaust them. Ada Halpern relates that when her transport arrived in Kazakhstan, the women were ordered to move piles of dung with broken pitchforks, in the rain. The commandant of the labor camp Vorkuta once ordered Barbara Szumska to dig to the bottom of the waste pile, insisting she remain there till finished. "One day we went to work," relates Feliksa Główkówna: "We were taken to a large stable where there was a huge layer of manure and were ordered to rake it, we then asked with surprise why there was so much and we heard the answer from the disgusting mouth of the Uzbek that they waited for twenty years for us to come and break it up."[107] These women understood their labor as punishment for their socioeconomic origins.

They did not misread Soviet intentions. Bolshevik ideology cast the Polish nation as reactionary, one led by members of the aristocracy and the bourgeoisie—exploiting classes destined, in the Marxist scheme of historical progress, for obliteration. The alternating labels applied to the Poles, aristocratic and bourgeois, defined them unequivocally as enemies of the Communist Soviet state, which claimed for itself the leadership of the working class. Denouncing Polish leaders for ruling "in their own class interests," one Soviet propagandist termed "lordly Poland" the "gendarme of capital." This rhetoric intensified in the 1930s as Stalin presented his industrialization drive as class warfare, pitting the proletariat against all of its class enemies: kulaks or wealthy peasants, private businessmen and traders, non-Communist specialists, independent-minded members of the intelligentsia, and other survivors of the old regime.[108] Subsumed under the label of "reactionary," such individuals were denounced as "exploiters and speculators," who must be broken or annihilated.

Terry Martin has found that though collectivization was theoretically a class-driven campaign, it quickly took on ethnic dimensions. Poles residing in the USSR suffered greatly from ethnic hostility at this time. Martin explains: "The popular identification of Pole and kulak was summed up in the rhyme '*raz Poliak—znachit kulak.*' Poles were bluntly told, 'You are being dekulakized not because you are a kulak, but because you are a Pole.'" In authorizing the deportation of kulaks from its western republics in 1930, the Politburo placed special emphasis on "kulak Polish counter-revolutionary elements" and thus embarked on what Martin refers to as the first case of Soviet ethnic cleansing.[109] Soviet leaders included the entire Polish population in the broader group of class enemies, and countless Poles recall the derisive use of the epithets "Polish lord" and "bourgeois lord" by *kolkhoz* chairmen, brigade leaders, prison guards, and neighbors, all who insisted that they would teach the Poles to work.[110] The previous occupation or wealth of an individual bore little relevance: Polish nationality alone sufficed to brand one a class enemy.

The typically emphatic nationalism of the Poles reinforced their enemy status. Marxists viewed the nation and the allegiance it inspired as a temporary phenomenon allied with the era they hoped to move beyond. Stalin called the nation "not merely a historical category but a historical category belonging to a definite epoch, the epoch of rising capitalism."[111] It would eventually give way to a world community with a single culture based on the proletariat, which, according to Marx, has no country. In the meanwhile, Soviet leaders strove to eradicate nationalist sentiment, considering it reactionary. Calling a Pole a bourgeois nationalist became another means of signaling his or her enemy status; in the perception of the Soviet leadership, nationality and class meant the same thing in the case of the Poles. And Poles certainly felt targeted because of their nationality. According to Maria Jurewicz, the work supervisor always recorded a lower output for Polish women than what they had actually accomplished. Others maintain that the norms were raised for Poles and that Soviet citizens received higher pay for the same work. A lawyer from Lwów explains that authorities and civilians alike believed that the Poles had now fallen into slavery because of the guilt of their government and, therefore, should be treated as slaves. In her own case, because of her weakened state of health, she proposed working as a medical assistant, but the doctor in charge insisted that her national origins rendered her fit only for hard labor.[112] All Poles became one enemy class in the eyes of the Soviet regime.

The reaction of Poles to their labor in exile demonstrates a similarly one-dimensional view of their nation, though with different adjectives and value judgments. Disapproval of women as physical laborers cuts across class divisions, suggesting a consensus on economic roles for women shared by Polish society at large. Condemnations of the Soviet use of female labor come not only from urban women or the so-called upper classes; rural women voice objections similar to (though less clear than) those of their more articulate compatriots. A conclusive analysis of attitudes toward labor according to class categories cannot be done, for many of these women do not identify themselves by previous socioeconomic position or occupation. Little can be said about the attitudes of women previously employed in factories, as the size of this group was small in the Soviet-annexed Polish territory, smaller still among the exiles as a whole, and virtually absent in the present sample. Yet peasants are highly represented. Unlike the women quoted above, they do not explicitly link their depiction of work in exile to their previous status or occupation, but they do take similar exception to their employment in the USSR.[113]

Since some of these females undoubtedly engaged daily in strenuous work back home, their categorical denunciation of having to perform physical labor in exile can perhaps be explained more through perception than objective reality—that is, by the attendant social and political framework and not actual unfamiliarity with manual labor. The commonplace nature of women's labor at home, seen as furthering the welfare of the family, meant that it was generally not perceived as work but merely a familial obligation. No matter what the extent of their labor or its economic contribution to the family, such women neither identified themselves as workers nor perceived the undervaluation of their labor. This contrasted sharply with their changed status in the USSR, where their labor, regardless of any likeness to what they had done before, was not only difficult but also involuntary and benefited a foreign and hostile entity. The women, therefore, denounce it outright, focusing not on questions of degree but describing it as incompatible with womanhood. Differences among women bear no relevance in this discussion. Even those women identifying themselves as "working people" (*ludzi pracy*), both willing and accustomed to labor, evince a traditional female work identity.[114] Moreover, they do not regard their labor as central to their identity; the maternal role remains superior to the economic one. Their statements indicate that they do not oppose working, as long as the job does not violate norms of proper female labor and does not diminish their strength, time, and proximity to the home, where they care for the family.

What emerges from the documents is a normative view of women, whose roles are governed by the sexual division of labor, assumed to originate in nature. The collective letter of a group of self-identified Polish mothers states: "We are exhausted by terrible work beyond our strength, for example, clearing trees on the taiga, pulling out stumps and roots, work about which our peasant women have no notion, not to mention women of the intelligentsia, women with higher education, accustomed to white-collar work." A woman from a village in the borderlands writes: "The old people did not remember women ever being employed at such work before the first women Poles (*kobiety Polki*) loaded rocks into the cart."[115] Though the exact prescriptions of women's work may vary among classes, there seems to be a perceived given about what women, as a whole, can and cannot, should and should not, do. One labor camp inmate refers to this essential nature of women while describing her work in the Siberian forest: "Did anyone pay attention to the fact they we couldn't do it . . . that as women we simply did not have the strength?" Similarly, a compatriot describes her job on a collective farm as "completely unsuitable for women, as not even every man could endure that work."[116] Women disapprove of the Soviet use of female labor not just on the basis of class but more fundamentally on gender norms.

The authors of Polish government reports also present the women of Poland, en masse, as weak and unaccustomed to manual labor. They voice outrage that "women as well as men" were made to perform physical labor, seemingly forgetting that many women previously worked long and hard on family farms, in factories, or at domestic labor. A report of the Social Welfare Section of the Polish Embassy discussing exiled peasants and farmers states that the work is extremely difficult "for our women, not used to that kind of heavy physical labor."[117] Underlying such statements may be an inclusive vision of women, taking as a given the need for restrictions on female labor. Alternatively, they may betray a myopic view of the Polish nation with a specific class configuration, according to which women, though not necessarily idle, are not made for manual labor at all. The word woman in this mind-set conjures up the image of a female engaged either in white-collar work or in purely familial and social duties, identified primarily through her husband. In this conception, women of lower classes prove invisible and inconsequential.

The category of social class can be more useful in understanding the experience of exile if approached in a less traditional way—not as a fixed identity, carried from one context to another and determinant of one's outlook, but rather as one piece of identity, in process, continually changing. As Joan Scott and Gareth Stedman Jones propose, class is better seen as "an identity historically and contextually created."[118] From this perspective, the most salient point for grasping the meaning of class in this experience is not a woman's previous socioeconomic position but the leveling of all Polish citizens that took place in the USSR. The altered context bore profound consequences for the social and material position of each exile. Those who had enjoyed high status in interwar Poland now became underdogs, in some cases even pariahs, in Soviet society; those occupying the lower socioeconomic rungs of Polish society did not receive special privileges under the Communist regime, for it considered them petty bourgeois or exploiters—read enemies—by virtue of their nationality, if not former class position.

Regardless of their status before the invasion, camp inmates and deportees were reduced to the position of having only their labor to sell. Divested of previous wealth and prevented from working according to their specialties, they enjoyed no choice in jobs; virtually all had to engage in some form of physical labor. The Poles sought to ameliorate their dismal economic position by searching for clandestine ways to earn money or set up trades. Former class status bore minimal relevance: while the wealthy owned more and higher quality goods in Poland, it did not guarantee that at the time of deportation they were in a position to bring many possessions with them, nor did it ensure the existence of relatives left behind who could send packages with items for trading. Thus even in terms of resources a real leveling occurred. One's material position in exile depended more on health, luck, ingenuity, and survival skills than on former socioeconomic position.[119]

Labor in Exile

One might argue that women of the upper classes would be disadvantaged, having never had to struggle for survival before, and thus not developing the resources and skills of which peasant and working-class women made regular use.

The circumstances in which dislocated Poles found themselves did not constitute normality—either compared with their previous lives or with their ideal notions; therefore, their work identities in exile probably bore only partial relation to what they had been before. Once taken across the border, virtually all Poles were reduced to the same socioeconomic position and acquired a seemingly similar class identity vis-à-vis the Soviets. As the statements cited demonstrate, this involved a consciousness of their disadvantaged position and outrage at their exploitation by the Soviet regime. If class consciousness is considered "political articulations that provide an analysis of, a coherent pattern to impose on, the events of daily life," it can be seen that the exiles largely shared the same daily experience.[120] In the face of this, class distinctions within the group tended to diminish, if only temporarily, and the Poles became a single disadvantaged class in the USSR.

The changed class position of the exiled women as a whole helps to account for the lack of variation across social classes in women's objection to labor on the basis of gender. Selective memory probably played a role: some women might have been engaged in physical labor back home and may even have been able to perform better at the jobs given them in the USSR than they were prepared to remember or admit (witness the crossing out by AWBD staff of one female's assertion that she could fulfill the norm). Although the productivity of the Poles' labor remains unknown, a tantalizing bit of evidence comes from an NKVD report from the Altai *krai*, stating that 75 percent of the Polish deportees there fulfilled the norm.[121] Finally, women may even have been willing to undertake similar types of labor, had the goal been of their own choosing, for the good of an independent Poland.

Despite isolated friendships, the exiles did not join with women of different nationalities along class lines. Instead, their statements reveal a general feeling of solidarity among the subset of deportees and labor camp inmates of Polish nationality. Many specifically state that their communities of Poles encompassed individuals from a broad spectrum of occupations and classes, who regularly gathered to celebrate Polish holidays and exchange news from home and who provided mutual assistance. The possibility cannot be excluded that women left unfavorable pictures out of their statements, that they disregarded incidents indicating tensions, particularly along class lines, within the communities of ethnic Poles. Yet even this case suggests important values and ideals shared by the Polish exiles as a whole, including solidarity, mutual aid, patriotism, and a sense of community, regardless of social class. When confronted with groups perceived as enemies and constituting a threat to their existence as a nation, this ideal served as a guiding force among ethnic Poles.

The statement of Franciszka Pączek provides a case in point. After the amnesty, Pączek, a peasant woman, worked as an orderly in a Polish hospital opened on Soviet territory. Though eventually evacuated with the Polish army to Teheran, she felt she initially received unfavorable treatment and ascribed it to her low socioeconomic status. Pączek writes that upon learning of the evacuations, she asked the officer in charge of supplies (Lieutenant Wolyński) to sell her provisions. This is how she describes the incident:

> Mr. Wolyński answered you don't qualify to buy because you're third category, that's only for officers and nurses, but not an orderly. My God some have to the point of overflowing but others nothing an orderly is not a person! thus our dear Poles though I am the mother of three sons whom I gave to the Polish Army and I myself work but I don't deserve, I thought that we all were undergoing hardship in this captivity and today such a distinction.[122]

Class tensions among Polish nationals surface here in a way that rarely occurs in the documents, suggesting cracks in the unity of the Polish nation, so often lauded by exiles and government officials. The importance of this image of national solidarity is indicated by the fact that the above-quoted passage was omitted in a version of Pączek's statement typed by a member of the AWBD. Though fissures in the facade of the unified Polish nation are undeniable, Pączek's statement actually underscores its wide appeal and possible attainment—albeit on a temporary basis—by implying that at least while under Soviet authorities, it was an ideal widely upheld in practice by ethnic Poles across class lines. Furthermore, by defining herself primarily as a mother, Pączek joins women of other socioeconomic groups who viewed their role in the nation and their own social significance in a similar light, thus pointing to a measure of consensus on the paramount role of women.

Given the trauma of forced exile, imposed by a national rival and based primarily on an individual's national identity and citizenship, gender and nationality take precedence over class identities, even in relation to the topic of labor. The structure of this population, once transported across the border, is vertical rather than horizontal: it becomes a fairly homogenous group, joined under the overarching category of nationality. With the leveling that occurs among the exiles as a whole, class identity converges with national identity so that being ethnically Polish, under the Soviet regime, is the same as being exploited.

Women frequently insist that *Poles* as a category could not perform the work demanded of them. "The norms at work were beyond our strength, so that none of the Poles were able to do it," writes a woman from a rural region of eastern Poland.[123] Men often concur. Conflating nation with class, they assert that the unskilled labor forced on them in the USSR fell beneath the Poles. "We worked there like the Russian *sovkhoz* members, but unaccustomed to hard labor, we couldn't match them in fulfilling the norm," writes one man. Individuals of other nationalities could do it, but not the Poles. In fact, one man brands the sole Pole in his camp who became a Stakhanovite a "100 percent Bolshevik," signaling his closer kinship to the Russians.[124] Similarly, women object to being made to do work they consider to fall in the domain of other nationalities—configured as having lower class status—constituting an outrage to their sex and nation. Aniela Kubicka writes scornfully, "Polish women were employed at the hardest labor on the same level as Soviet men." According to another deportee, "Polish women were doing work beyond their strength, for it was work done by the Kazakhs."[125]

Only one woman voices surprise that Poles could not perform at the same level as Soviet citizens: "The norm for Poles was exactly the same as that for the locals, but surprisingly not one Pole could fulfill it."[126] For most exiles, it seems a matter of pride, as if to say, "we Poles are not suited for heavy labor." The common association of Poles with nonphysical labor perpetuates the traditional disdain for manual labor that characterized prewar upper-class Polish society, and expands it to separate not Pole from Pole, but Pole from Soviet/Russian. The values associated with the nobility and intelligentsia, and projected on the nation, are widely reflected among the exiles. Since the Poles all represent a single class in the Soviet system, an exploited class of physical laborers, the ideal that the exiles articulate for the Polish nation directly opposes this status.

Conclusion

To the Poles, the equality that prevailed in Soviet economic life revealed a seemingly outrageous lack of recognition of the social consequences of sexually differentiated bodies. Soviet ideology and practice sought to make women more like male workers, and the job assignments, required output quotas, and working conditions seemed to have that effect. This is precisely what the Polish exiles abhorred. The dominant ideology of Polish society maintained the notion of separate male and female space, dictated by their roles in the family, which in turn seemed to stem inevitably from their different bodies and reproductive functions. The sexual division of labor posited that a woman's maternal instinct, understood as her natural or divinely ordained mission, prepared her above all for childbearing, nurturing, and fostering upright and devoted citizens of the nation. Though she could and often did work outside the home, these other tasks ranked as her highest obligations to society, rendering her economic role in the family or nation secondary. To use the words of Joan Scott, "Women inspired those behavioral characteristics on which depended, not so much a society's productive capacity or its wealth, as its stability and the bases of its social organization."[127] If the New Soviet Woman would be defined by her role in production, then in the eyes of the Poles, she would hardly be a woman, and they wanted no part of such disorder.

Although the reality of women's daily lives before the war was quite diverse, the ideal for women was not. In the trauma of the Soviet conquest and domination of the population of eastern Poland, women latched onto that ideal vision of womanhood and social order, which provided a measure of certainty in a sea of change, especially as the idea was seemingly backed by nature. Despite the changed situation in which the deportees and prisoners found themselves—probably precisely because of it—a new understanding of sexual difference did not develop. Rather, a more sweeping definition of womanhood prevailed, extending across class lines—one less differentiated than probably existed in interwar Poland, forged through shared daily experience of exploitation. The result appears to have been a collective identity, albeit temporary, sharing a common socioeconomic and political status and downplaying class differentiation within the group.

In coping with their lives in exile, Poles tended not to differentiate among themselves, but rather took pains to differentiate themselves, as a national group and a social class, from the Soviets—understood as the Russians. In deliberately blurring the boundaries between the sexes, the latter seemed to pervert both normal social relations and the laws of nature itself. The Poles set themselves against this aberrant nation as a single unit. In fact, one-dimensional thinking, in which class identity converged with national identity, prevailed on both sides. Soviet leaders considered Poles as a nation an enemy class; the Poles, in turn, saw themselves as a homogenous class, superior to those who currently exploited them. In the crucible of war and exile on the territory of the enemy, where a socioeconomic leveling occurred, class specificity faded, and one general normative view of women and Polishness emerged.

Many researchers have noted that the lines between the sexes are firmly drawn in wartime but that conditions are ripe for a renegotiation of gender roles.[128] The high number of women who typically move into jobs traditionally known as men's work, filling gaps caused by the mobilization of males to the front, represents the clearest example. In some Western societies, women have experienced material, social, and political gains from these changes and have fought to maintain them at war's close.[129] Gender roles underwent significant alteration by the labor demands imposed on the dislocated Poles. However, the women did not desire these changes: they had no choice in how they used their labor, the product of which benefited an entity they did not support, and their compensation barely kept them alive. Thus they did not embrace any of the corresponding changes in their social roles. Given the primacy of work in their daily lives and in their function in the Soviet state, the adoption of a new work identity based on their changed status would have rendered them labor animals and would have meant succumbing to the Soviet leaders and their system. Resistance and hope necessitated a rejection of that identity. Polish women, therefore, did not accept what they had to do as normal or even within their means, implying that their debased condition would not long continue, that their ultimate lot in life was not to labor and die in exile, as Soviet authorities sought to convince them. Fighting changes in their traditional functions in society, holding onto their identities as Polish women, the women maintained a connection to the home for which they longed.

4

"As Long as There Is Still a Polish Woman, There Will Also Be a Polish Question"

Family and Nation

The blurred boundaries between men and women in the realm of labor greatly distressed the exiled women. Sexual differentiation appeared to have little meaning in the USSR, and this left the exiles with a profound sense of disorder, a disturbing perception that females were unable to act as women should and that males could not function as proper men. Nowhere was this felt greater than in the family. In Polish society, the family bore especial significance for women, whose lives traditionally centered on the home. Women's domestic and maternal duties, attributed to female nature, seemed indisputable: they defined women's identity, structured their lives, and determined their role in the nation. The Soviet invasion and subsequent arrests and deportations completely disrupted these certainties. Many individuals were separated from their families. Once taken across the border and forced to spend most of their time at hard labor, women found the focus of their lives shift from the home and family. Restrictions on cultural expression, including religious practice and educating children in a national spirit, further impeded critical functions of Polish motherhood.[1]

Women often could not provide their children with the care necessary for survival. The loss of male providers seemed to put women's own survival in the balance. Unaccustomed to viewing themselves as independent, strong beings, women lived their days in ways that challenged, though did not revise, their conceptions of who they were or should be. They sought to retain that identity and stability through the family, in whatever incarnation possible. The traditional family was the model for their immediate families and for the organization of society as a whole; it also constituted the way many women imagined and related to the nation.

Partitioned Poland (1795–1918): "The Home-Fortress"

The home and family have traditionally carried great import in Polish society, particularly since the partitions of the late eighteenth century parceled the entire country among the Russian, Austrian, and Prussian empires. Deprived of political existence, Poles lost control of their public life. To varying degrees, over the next 123 years and across three differently administered partitions, Polish cultural life and national identity were also threatened, most vigorously under the Russians and Germans. Only the private realm remained beyond the control of the occupiers. With the loss of political independence, the Polish nation had to defend and preserve its private existence, its inner life, in order to continue. The home, therefore, acquired especial significance for the nation, representing "a last impregnable bastion of 'Polishness.'"[2] Gradually the home changed from a quiet nest to a home-fortress (*dom-reduta*). According to historian Barbara Jedynak, throughout the years of foreign domination, the home served as the "the Bethlehem of avengers" and "the stronghold of Polishness." The literature of the Polish Romantics portrayed homes as places that "sheltered tradition, memory and faith, the most essential forces for the revival and maintenance of national feelings."[3] The home was the source and training ground of individuals who not only would keep the memory and culture of the Polish nation alive but would also fight for its regeneration as a political entity.

Women, as child-bearers, nurturers, and caretakers of the home, thus gained particular attention in Polish society. According to Rudolf Jaworski and Bianka Pietrow-Ennker, the maternal role acquired "a special elevated status, as the family organization proved ultimately to be the only safe sphere in which Polish culture could be completely preserved and passed on to the next generation." The role of women in maintaining the nation was recognized as soon as the existence of the Polish state was threatened; in effect, women received citizenship in the Polish nation when the political state ceased to exist. The demise of independent Poland ignited a movement for social change that continued well into the nineteenth century. Reform debates emphasized educating females—not for their well-being but for the nation's. In the national discourse, Sławomira Walczewska explains, women were not emancipated but instrumentalized. Reformers concluded that women needed schooling in Polish language, history, and literature to disseminate that knowledge throughout society, particularly its younger generations.[4]

Women were widely attributed with a simplicity and spirituality that tied them to the past and imbued them with a pure form of Polishness. This notion was reinforced by reality—the near exclusion of women from public arenas. Jaworski explains that the home was considered a protected interior space, contrasting the hostile outside world:

> The internal-external model, which derived from traditional gender roles, was interpreted such, that on the basis of her special tasks at home and in the family, Polish women were thus far less exposed to damaging denationalizing influences than their husbands, who worked outside. Therefore Polish women could maintain their pure Polishness and as a result were particularly qualified and called upon to defend and transmit the special character of Polishness.[5]

The perceived needs of the nation strengthened the ideology of separate female and male spheres.

Patriarchal society merged with the Catholic worldview to produce an idealized symbol of women, *Matka Polka*, the holy mother of Poland. This model was built on the cult of Mary, the mother of Jesus. "Just as Mary . . . had been appointed to watch over the Polish nation," writes Pietrow-Ennker, "so too women—as Mary's successors on earth—were seen as being entrusted with the task of caring for the smallest unit of the nation, the family, and seeing that it had Christian values instilled in it." To this ideal, Polish Romanticism added the virtues of patriotism and sacrifice for the nation. The Polish mother became responsible for raising good Poles, preferably males, who loved and served the fatherland. As Bogna Lorence-Kot notes, a good woman was to raise her children well for the good of her nation and "for her own justification as a woman, mother, and Polish patriot." The traits associated with a proper Polish upbringing included discipline, respect for the authority of elders, Christian resignation, courage, altruism, patriotism, and absolute selflessness vis-à-vis the fatherland—even if that required the sacrifice of the family. The notion that Polish families would inevitably be called upon to make sacrifices to the "altar of the Fatherland" was prominent in Polish nationalism. As dying for the fatherland was the noblest of ends for males, conceiving and giving birth to future martyrs was correspondingly invested with a holy aura. Some women stepped out of traditional roles and served the nation like men—as armed insurgents—for which they suffered confinement in convents early in the nineteenth century and Siberian exile later.[6] Since the ideology of womanhood had no place for them, they were also marginalized and largely forgotten.

Guided by the positivists, in the 1860s, Poles began to turn from the fight for independence to focus on organic work at the roots of society. For women, this meant less emphasis on producing martyrs. Still charged with raising children in a patriotic spirit, women continued to sustain national traditions and history to keep the nation alive. They led patriotic meetings and history lessons in their homes. Praying, reciting poetry, and singing religious and patriotic songs became central features of family gatherings, especially on holidays. Women maintained connections to the past by preserving photographs, letters, family jewelry, and mementos from ancestral heroes. They also began a custom that outraged the Russian occupying authorities: wearing black clothing to signify national mourning for defeated Polish patriots of the armed rebellions. For these women, the Polish nation represented one large family, and they mourned its fallen members, even those unknown to them, as if they were related. Women also assisted compatriots by organizing covert study groups and underground schools, especially for poor children. In the 1880s, they helped create a system of secret university-level courses, called the Flying University, which rotated among private homes.[7]

Surveying the history of Polish women to the early twentieth century, Pietrow-Ennker concludes that women could be independent, active, and esteemed as long as they operated within the context of the family or the national struggle for freedom. Though a women's emancipation movement began in the Polish lands in the late nineteenth century, it differed from similar ones in Western Europe. Polish emancipation discourse continued to be tied with the national one, and women fought not for political rights or equality but for further education and more active participation in national life. Women's activism was still limited to defending the national culture and Catholicism; few women, even among the intelligentsia, departed from the traditional model of the woman-mother.[8] Social and religious ideology, demanding that they be free of personal ambitions and pleasures, linked the lives of women with others. A woman was expected to serve as divine protectress of the nation, demonstrating self-abnegation, religious purity, and patriotic fervor.

Independent Poland (1918–1939): "The Most Golden Chains"

Though the struggle to revive the Polish state succeeded at the close of World War I, the national discourse did not fundamentally change. On the eve and morrow of the triumph, the press spoke repeatedly of the unity of the nation and the duty of all Poles to merge themselves with the national unit, devoting themselves entirely to the life of the nation. A Catholic priest thus expressed the ideal to his female audience: "A Pole cannot live normally in isolation from his society; his own life interests—psychological and physiological—bind him to it. His personality unites him with other personalities in a certain whole, sometimes even merges with them, losing its individuality, the singular becomes plural and the feeling of 'I' changes then into the feeling of 'we.'" Discussions of the national unit presented the nation as an ideal family, characterized by a community of interests and the self-sacrificing cooperation of its members. Women's journals repeatedly proclaimed that "the family is the smallest unit of society," and constituted the building blocks of the nation. Familial happiness, insisted one writer, "represents the strength of society."[9]

Connecting the health of the family to the future of the nation, journals underscored the critical nature of the work of women: as tenders of the family and guardians of the hearth, they held the future of the nation in their hands. Despite the support women's journals gave to expanding women's activities outside the home, as discussed earlier, they espoused gender roles that retained the idea of a sexual division of labor and stressed the importance of women's traditional work in the home. This, many believed, not only accorded with the laws of nature, but also reflected and promoted the good of the nation. Through marriage and childbearing a woman must make sacrifices "for the good of the family, society, and country," advised a doctor: "Only in that way does a woman really become a useful member of society." The ultimate contribution a Polish female could make to the nation remained bearing Polish sons. This doctor explained: "We need youth capable of dying for the Fatherland, capable of heroic actions, and such youth should be born and raised by the brave Polish woman, it is she who in the present difficult time must give the country healthy boys and raise them into heroes, capable of giving their lives up for the Fatherland."[10]

The brave Polish woman retained other traditional duties to the nation: keeping alive the memory of the struggles and sacrifices of the forefathers, instilling love and respect for the Polish land, and guarding the ideals of Polishness. The model woman-Pole (*kobieta-Polka*) at the dawn of the new Polish state maintained "the traditions of our mothers," embodying "all that is whole-heartedly national, whole-heartedly Christian, and whole-heartedly democratic." Such women, considered spiritual life-givers to family members and the collective, were entrusted now with sustaining the unity of the fatherland. The woman-Pole therefore had to continue to be "a life-giving fountain-head, from which it is always possible to draw the faith, hope, and strength of the soul."[11]

The years of European peace and political independence for the Polish state entailed a move to a period of normality. Sovereign on its own territory, the Polish nation enjoyed a cultural dominance that contrasted the besieged condition of the century-plus of national struggle. Nevertheless, the focus on women's maternal duties did not cease, despite their achievement of political rights and their increased participation in education and the labor force. Women gained many rights after 1918, but patriarchal views impeded their ability to make use of them. Society did not wholly accept women's increased employment and continued to oppose their involvement in pure politics. According to historian Roman Wapiński, though more women, especially young ones, moved into public life, their public activity largely took place in the traditional realms of education, charity, and self-improvement. Even the women's movement, which remained an elite phenomenon, sought to widen women's horizons without diluting their ties to the family or, as Andrzej Chojnowski states, replacing the position of the "man of the household."[12] Messages about woman's paramount role as mother became more fervent as Poland entered the crises of economic depression and threat of war from Germany.

Throughout the interwar period, Catholic and women's journals discussed woman's vocation of childbearing, which demanded that she devote herself to raising children, nurturing her husband, and caring for the home, as her own primary needs and desires. "Woman, as they say, is born to love and to give herself to the one she loves," proclaimed a characteristic article. "That is why she finds complete satisfaction in marriage." Citing the pain a woman endures giving birth, this ideology regarded the mother as the living symbol of sacrifice. Catholic writing, in particular, focused on this notion:

> In the mother looms above all suffering. The suffering of delivering into the world, worry over health and life, the pain of illness and experience, the burden of the countless daily thorns, by which both the household and the outside world crown her heart. Moreover—in the mother we find something beyond the energy, the strength, and the authority of the father—something stronger than death—love. In love is included in one word all that we can say about a mother.[13]

The holy aspect of women's character and functions remained an important component of ideal womanhood.

The wife/mother symbolized the family, and the burden of maintaining its social status and reputation fell almost exclusively on her shoulders. A typical expression of this convention reads: "In her hands rest the harmony, order and health of the family, the spiritual atmosphere of the home; on the outside, the social position, and not rarely even the position of the husband in society, depends on how the wife carries his name, if she arouses respect and sympathy for him, or denigrates it with inappropriate behavior." Thus a woman had to take care not to tarnish the identity she assumed from her husband and also had to ensure that the family upheld it. Men were largely excused from this responsibility, as "the moral health of the family home" was considered entirely in the hands of women.[14]

The familial duties assigned to the female were transposed to the larger social unit to define her role in the nation. She bore responsibility for raising the nation's children by bringing her own offspring up as honorable citizens and patriots. Outside the family, she should fulfill the task "to which nature has called her": raising the moral and cultural life of the nation to a higher level. Describing the basic tasks of the female sex, one author declared, "We strive, as much as possible, to see to it that the Polish nation is spiritually reborn, that life operates on a firm moral basis."[15] Women, "for the good of the Fatherland," should engage in social work through charitable, cultural, educational, and sporting organizations; in the case of war, they must be prepared to uphold the faith and spirit of the nation's members and provide assistance wherever needed. These tasks required self-sacrifice, the hallmark of the mother. One writer urged women to struggle constantly against the claim that they were created to be happy; on the contrary, she asserted, women were made to build and maintain moral values. Helping in her own way to build a strong nation, a woman's endeavors "must be permeated with a deep sense of responsibility, must be pure service to the idea of the nation, free of ambition and personal viewpoints."[16] Just as a woman's identity in the family was intricately tied up with others, so it was in the nation.

Discussing the important role played by the mother figure in the history of the nation, one woman wrote, "I think that in no other nation is the figure of the mother as venerated as she is among the Poles."[17] Women's role in the nation, venerated, sometimes glorified, was nonetheless secondary. A woman was expected to act for the nation predominantly through others: by raising male heroes and loyal citizens, passing on cultural traditions, and taking care of the home—the brick of society, but clearly its smallest unit, the one most removed from public activity, power, and celebrity. To an extent that men were not, the Polish woman was urged to sublimate her own desires and interests to the family and in that way serve the higher good. The dominant ideology stipulated sacrifice and devotion to others as the way to her own self-fulfillment; any other contributions she might make to the nation were downplayed. Though this indirect service to the nation was glorified and women were depicted as the partners of men in the great work of the nation, men were given the leading, active, and powerful roles in that work. The deeds of men also gained the greatest respect and loudest accolades from society, which not only demonstrated the disproportionate value placed on male and female activity, but also obscured the diversity and significance of women's contributions.

"We were everywhere," proclaimed the female editors of *Bluszcz* of the struggle for national liberation, "in underground work, in secret schooling, in Siberia, in hard labor, in prisons and in exile, yesterday—and today, in the uprising and in the formation of the Legions." And yet, on the same pages, other women wrote in a way that undervalued their own contributions. Polish mothers were instructed to take their children to the graves of "our fathers," the heroes of the national struggle, and entreated to instill love and respect for the land of "our forefathers." Discussing the patriotic duties of

Polish women, a female writer praised the accomplishments only of "our fathers," and stated: "We are their sons."[18] The use of gender-specific language in such cases might be dismissed as rhetorical convention, as not expressing a literal meaning; common acceptance of this practice, however, does not erase underlying assumptions. The unquestioned use of masculine terms underscores the assumed naturalness of the notion that daughters and mothers did not occupy positions considered heroic and legendary; those were considered inherent to men. Such standards perpetuate the binary view of the activities attributed to the sexes, in which the female always takes second place.

Despite all the rhetoric aimed at women, in both literature and the press, glorifying their maternal duties as critical to the success of the nation, the Constitution of 1935 credits only the *sons* of the nation with the resurrection of the Polish state. Women were seen to be connected to the nation through the men they produced, nourished, and supported. The indirect relationship to the nation ascribed to females can be found in the law stipulating that a woman marrying a foreigner lost her Polish nationality. In such a case, she was automatically accorded the national identity of her husband, and she passed his identity to her children—a situation that did not apply to males who wed women of foreign nationality.[19] Apparently, nationality did not inhere in the female as it did in males; she could be deprived of it without her consent. Women's vaunted closeness to the nation bore no significance in this issue.

The idealized image of the Polish female as the self-sacrificing, pure wife/mother of the family and the nation persisted throughout the Second Polish Republic. Though media and legislation upheld traditional notions, we cannot assume that individual women did not challenge these precepts, either vocally or in the way they lived their daily lives. While this topic demands extensive research, some preliminary conclusions are offered, based on the writing and lifestyles of popular women writers of the period.

Polish literature of the 1920s and 1930s provides evidence of flux, disagreement, and increased choices for women. A wave of female writers gained extensive popularity in the interwar period, and many of them addressed the topic of womanhood. The issue of the female body, long a taboo subject in public discussion, even among advocates of women's emancipation, was first broached in interwar literature.[20] The works of acclaimed authors Maria Dąbrowska, Pola Gojawczyńska, Maria Kuncewiczowa, Zofia Nałkowska, Maria Pawlikowska-Jasnorzewska, and Gabriela Zapolska portrayed women with a wide range of personalities and social roles.

Refraining from placing women in idealized situations or emphasizing motherhood and the traditional virtues associated with them, they challenged stereotypical virtues and conventional roles accorded the female sex, showing instead the diversity and complexities of women. Their characters often flouted social conventions: they had affairs, left their husbands, and had abortions.

Some of these writers were explicitly feminist. According to one scholar, playwright Gabriela Zapolska "was the first to dare to give a woman's interpretation of the battle of the sexes and illustrate its social and moral background." Zapolska's *Moralność Pani Dulskiej* (*Mrs. Dulski's Morality*), one of the most popular plays of the period, attacks the hypocrisy of middle-class morality, particularly concerning sexuality and marriage, and ridicules the precept that "a woman should go through life quietly and calmly." The popular dramatist and poet Maria Pawlikowska-Jasnorzewska also offered radical social commentary. Her play *Egipska pszenica* (*Egyptian Wheat*) mocks conventional views of womanhood, which see its essence in motherhood and scorns traditional marriage for its double standard of sexual morality. In another drama, Pawlikowska-Jasnorzewska disparages the male view of women as instruments made to serve their husbands. Novelist Maria Kuncewiczowa created strong female protagonists lacking spousal or maternal affection.[21]

Conservative critics loudly denounced works they tagged "feminist," a term used as a pejorative. Zapolska's *Moralność Pani Dulskiej* was called a work "dictated by revenge." The inspiration for the drama, wrote the eminent critic Karol Irzykowski, was the hatred of a woman bent on adventure toward women with proper, regulated lives.[22] One male critic attacked *Egipska pszenica* as "a pack of biological, psychological and artistic nonsense." According to Irzykowski, Pawlikowska-Jasnorzewska's plays constituted "an attack on men." Likewise, the publication of Kuncewiczowa's stories in 1927 led to accusations of immorality, depravity, and "the undermining of the authority of motherhood." The Catholic press called the new literature scandalous and dangerous, "a terrible burden for the Polish soul," and denounced it for "containing an emphasis on the sexual side of life" and "all but propagating the negation of family virtues, divorce, marital infidelity, shamelessness, perversion."[23]

The lives of these authors also flouted social conventions; some left their husbands, went through numerous divorces, worked to support themselves, and even became single mothers. Certainly the lifestyles of the cultural elite cannot be taken as the norm for society, yet evidence exists that not all Polish women adhered to the ideal demanded of them. In a memoir written after the Second World War, one woman admits to paying little attention to her duties as a mother and found this to be characteristic of her milieu:

> Young, well-off mothers of that period did not, on the whole, appreciate the part they could personally play in the development of their children. If a child was well looked after, was clean, warm and well fed, by whoever was in charge, that was enough. A baby was only a baby, not a person in his own right. We, the grown-ups, had our lives and the children had theirs. I am sad and ashamed to admit it, but that seemed to be the general pattern.[24]

Other transgressions occurred throughout society. Though the numbers remained small, some married couples separated, while others lived together without marrying. Approximately 32,000 Polish Catholic women gave birth to illegitimate children each year, representing 5 percent of all live births by Catholics. Surveys of the period showed that the Catholic Church's stance against birth control was not always upheld in practice. The number of births per woman declined in the interwar period, demonstrating that family planning was a fact, especially among the intelligentsia. Although no statistics were compiled on the number of abortions in Poland, social critic Tadeusz Boy-Żeleński estimated it to be near one million per year.[25]

Society at large did not accept such choices. Church and popular periodicals denounced free love, divorce, prostitution, illegitimacy, birth control, abortion, and the dissolution of marriage and the family. According to historian Regina Renz, Catholic ideology was not doubted, and its main elements continued to dominate interwar Polish society. The authors discussed above paid a price for living according to their own wishes. After her first marriage, Zapolska had an affair that caused considerable scandal and for which she was ostracized from society; with no means of support, this celebrated author attempted suicide and eventually died poor and forgotten. The diary of Zofia Nałkowska contains an ever-present conviction that women's intellectual and artistic abilities were little valued.[26] This woman, the first to become a member of the Polish Academy of Literature, suffered through two unhappy marriages and, despite her talent and acclaim, ended up penniless, alone, and unhappy.

Certainly the ideal view of females did not capture the reality of the daily lives of all women. It constituted a normative vision, one which maintained considerable weight in Polish society; though many did not or could not live up to this standard, its importance cannot be dismissed. As British historian Mary Poovey explains, such an ideology might have accurately portrayed the lives of some individuals; "for others, it probably felt less like a description than a goal or even a judgment—a description, that is, of what the individual should and has failed to be."[27] For Polish women, the symbol of *Matka Polka*, virtuous, self-sacrificing, and patriotic, remained the model by which their roles in the family and nation were valued and judged.

In a speech in 1907, Zofia Nałkowska spoke of the hopes of Polish women, embodied in a new generation of women poets:

> These women tell us something new about the female spirit. Here for the first time—under the cover of pseudonyms, under the cover of the dullness of the printed word, we find not the apotheosis of motherhood, not the apotheosis of cleanliness and virtue—but the striving for individual freedom, dread of being placed anew on an ethical platform, rebellion against a new captivity—the striving for a free, conscious life, unhampered by even the most golden chains.[28]

The achievement of this goal for women as a group was not a legacy of the Second Polish Republic; many women did not find it desirable. In a characteristic article of the mid-1930s, one woman wrote that the feminist struggle belonged to the previous century; male and female fronts no longer existed. Instead, she concluded, both sexes must work together "for the general good of the nation, founded on two unchangeable elements—religion and families."[29] This was the legacy, more than any other, that Polish females took with them into exile.

Wives and Daughters

Both the exiled females and the authorities who drew up arrest orders and deportation lists attached great importance to women's familial relations. The NKVD gathered detailed information about the families of their charges. A widow deported from the city of Słonim reports that during the transport eastward she was suddenly taken for an interrogation: "In Słonim I was registered on my maiden name (Dubicka). But there it turned out that my last name, and also the fact that I am the widow of an officer of the Polish Army, was known." She was deported precisely because of that relationship. The occupying authorities largely viewed females as adjuncts to their husbands and fathers. Emilia Czternastek writes: "I was deported to Siberia for the 'guilt' of my husband Adam, who worked in army intelligence."[30] Of those women giving an explanation for their deportation, more than half attribute it to the occupation or social status of husbands, fathers, or brothers and more than one-third to the internment or arrest of such relatives. In the eyes of Soviet authorities, the identity of these women was almost wholly relational. Unless she committed some sort of transgression herself (in which case she was accorded her own identity and punished like a man), little mattered of a woman's own individuality—her background, her occupation, her actions, or her beliefs—once it was determined that her male relatives were enemies of the Soviet regime. The social status, suspect position, or crime of the men to whom they were attached, either through blood or marriage, branded females. Despite Soviet claims about the equality of the sexes, the most salient aspect of a female's identity appeared to be that of her husband or father.

Women generally mention this reason for their fate matter-of-factly. Jadwiga Komarska states: "On 13 April 1940 I was deported from Lwów on account of my husband, who was a lieutenant in the reserves and was taken in Russian captivity during the defense of Lwów." "Why I was arrested I don't know," writes Genowefa Maciorowska, who was deported from a village near Białystok, "probably because of my father and brother, who were arrested earlier than us."[31] The fact that women were exiled because of their men draws little commentary. That is not to say that the outcome caused no shock; certainly the women do not consider themselves guilty or deserving of retaliation for their relations. They do not seem at all surprised, however, that they were identified through their husbands and fathers. Their own fate appears an anticipated consequence of being Polish and female. On the whole, the women themselves tend to identify females relationally: their connections to others stand out as critical identifiers. They typically describe the populations in their deportation settlements as "children and mothers, wives of military men and the police."[32] Relationships with others constitute the basis of the identities of Polish women, who endeavor to uphold their connections, their roles, and their place in a larger whole—be it the family, the community, or the nation—throughout the ordeal of exile.

The importance of relationships to women's identity can be seen in their reactions to the division of their families. From the very first days of the invasion relatives were separated, sometimes by accident or as a by-product of other Soviet actions, often as a result of a deliberate decision by the occupiers. Many families were split simply because their members happened to be located at different ends of the Polish state when the war began. Since the invaders made it a crime to cross the new border dividing the Soviet-occupied territory from the German one, reunion became impossible. While men arrested for border infractions tended to be caught fleeing Polish territory to avoid arrest or to join the Polish army, many women went to the Gulag for trying to return home to parents, siblings, and spouses. One woman, stranded on the Soviet side of Poland, writes: "We were settled at the German and Russian border. We were separated by it from our families. Mothers from children, husbands from wives, but we didn't give up, we wanted to be together in this difficult time."[33] She was arrested trying to return home.

Arrest typically entailed immediate separation from family members, as in the case of Helena Dulko, who notes: "I left six children without any care in Poland under the Soviet Authorities I lost the whole farm, the oldest son 13 was abroad in Lithuania. Here I was with five children the youngest was just one-year-old still breast-fed." Sometimes women and children were arrested together, particularly when trying to cross the new borders. Though they briefly remained in the same prison cells, the children were eventually removed. Zofia Ćwiąkalska explains that "women who were arrested on the border with their children had their children taken away from them by force and they were given no opportunities to communicate with them, they were never told where their children were located."[34]

Even families deported intact did not always manage to remain together. Many deportees report losing family members through mere accident during the transports. Once the trains had passed out of Polish territory, passengers were allowed out of the cars at stops to try to obtain water or bread; foragers sometimes returned only to find that the train, with their relatives and belongings, had moved on without them. Stanisława Drozdowska's mother was left behind when she went for bread. Jadwiga Mateuszak was orphaned simply because, as she writes, "I left the train for water, the train left, and I was left behind."[35] This also occurred frequently in the chaos after the amnesty, as families traveled through the southern regions of the USSR seeking delegations of the Polish government. Often such separations proved irreversible. Antonina Proniewiczówna describes her experience:

> It was like this: Dad and Romek went to buy something and . . . were left. What despair! People consoled us that Dad would catch up to us. Unfortunately I thus lost the dear hearts of my father and brother. It was a real torment. From that time we starved, cried, and nothing more. Only the Lisowski family consoled us. After awhile several people got lost, but they caught up, but those who got lost with Dad and Romek disappeared without a trace.[36]

In other cases, individuals who fell seriously ill on the transports were removed from the train and taken to a hospital, while the rest of the family had to move on. Along the road, Helena Wołosiewicz's father was taken to a hospital. She went to get his address but fainted and ended up in a hospital herself, where she lay for days with a high fever; upon recovery, she learned that her father had died while her younger sisters continued somewhere on the train.[37] Such dissolution of families thus occurred through a combination of chance and the disregard of Soviet officials, who made no effort to help relatives stay together.

In one of the four massive deportations, the Soviet government deliberately pursued a policy of dividing families. The directive for the deportation operation of June 1941 contains precise instructions to this effect. The relevant section, entitled, "Manner of Separating Deportee from His Family," states: "In view of the fact that a large number of the deportees must be arrested and placed in special camps and their families settled at special points in distant regions, it is necessary to execute the operation of deporting both the members of his family as well as the deportee simultaneously, without informing them of the separation confronting them."[38] Demonstrating full awareness of the impact this separation would have on the individuals involved, the order instructs its executors to cloak their eventual intentions to avoid panic. Under false pretexts, agents must demand that the belongings of the male "head of the family" be packed separately from those of "the women and the children." The document further dictates: "The moving of the entire family, however, to the station should be done in one vehicle, and only at the station should the head of the family be placed separately from his family in a railway car specially intended for heads of families." Anticipating the trauma and possible resistance this action might provoke, the authorities hid their plans until the last possible moment. Helena Wiśniewska describes the instant she was suddenly wrenched apart from her male relatives: "A wail ran through the car. They are taking both my Daddy and brother, to this day we don't know about them. We say goodbye, Dad cries, brother cries, we all cry." For most of the females who endured the systematic separation of men from their families, those moments at the station were their final ones together. "At the station Nowo-Wilejka I was separated from my husband and I've never seen him since," writes a woman deported to Siberia.[39]

The dispersal of family members hit females exceedingly hard. The documents make clear that separation from loved ones was one of their greatest sources of pain and anxiety. In a cry of anguish Albertyna Korzeniowska recalls life before her arrest: "I had a child! A nine-year-old, wonderful girl, my whole world, a husband." Another woman, also arrested, describes leaving her daughter: "Our parting was brief. One can depict those experiences in a few words, but their tragedy can be understood only by one who has lived through similar moments. Three years have passed since those days, but I cannot recall them without bitterness and trembling." Władysława Walczak similarly tries to express her pain:

> On 21 May 1940 I was arrested by the order of the chief of the NKVD of Kustoev—they took me together with my daughter to prison in Ermak . . . that very same night they separated me from my child—and I heard only her cries and screams: "Mama! Mama!" I am in no condition to describe our separation and my experiences at that moment, one has to live through it to understand it. To hear the scream of one's child and be behind bars, not knowing what's happening, to be helpless, imprisoned, and for what? One could go insane.[40]

Men prove much less vocal about such separations, frequently remaining silent on the fate of their families. In many documents, the family situation of male authors remains entirely unclear. Even men who record spouses and children at the beginning of their testimonies often neglect to refer to them again in describing their ordeals. Sometimes such men were prisoners, without contact or information on their families, but in other cases they lived together with them in deportation settlements, yet discuss other topics. That is not to imply that men felt no concern for the welfare of family members; certainly some of them register their agony over the separation and uncertainty they endured.[41] The silences can possibly be attributed to long-held norms designating emotionality and preoccupation with family members as female traits, or to an aversion to airing private matters when such "larger" issues as the fate of the nation—the responsibility of males—were still at stake. Whatever the reason, relationships and family issues appear less critical in conveying the experiences and the identity of males than females.

Lamentations in official Polish documents of the division of families in exile typically stress that wives were separated from husbands and children from mothers. These statements focus on assumed dependencies. "Families were broken up," declares a report for the Polish government-in-exile, "children torn from their mothers, in accordance with instructions given from above, and husbands from wives."[42] In this formulation, hardship stems not merely from the loss of loved ones but from the separation of categories of individuals from those on whom they depend for care: children were thus left without their (natural) caretakers—mothers—and women were left without their protectors—husbands. The separation of brothers and sisters or even children from fathers does not receive the same emphasis. The effect of the division of a man and his children seems relevant only when he is cast as the head of the household, the breadwinner of the family. Men write only that families—not individual children—were without fathers, stressing the latter's material role.[43] In the tragedy of the Polish nation, women fall into the same category as children: helpless individuals cruelly left without their providers and protectors.

Women's own reactions to their separation from male relatives reveal a perception of gender roles closely following the traditional model of the prewar period. In self-depictions, females generally do not portray themselves as self-sufficient or strong but view themselves—by virtue of their sex—in need of men for material support and protection and eventual rescue. Many point out the absence of men in their deportation communities. One woman notes that there were twenty-eight families "without fathers" in her settlement. This situation filled many females with desperation, some from the very outset. Maria Grajanowski recalls the moment her brother was taken away at the train station: "With pain in my heart I watched his face moving into the distance and at that moment I was seized by complete resignation and lack of will to live, for after all our caretaker was leaving us, we were left alone." Similarly, a young woman relates that soon after arrival in the USSR her father died. "Our despair had no bounds," she writes, "we were left alone, helpless, without means to live, amidst the wild forest of Arkhangel'sk." One woman depicts the drama of the deportations as follows: "whole trains of helpless women with small children, left by the men who were in the army, and later all arrested and deported to Kozel'sk, Ostashkov and Starobel'sk."[44] These females could not imagine surviving without their men.

Certainly there was substance to these fears. Most females were accustomed to being supported by husbands and fathers and many had never worked outside the home. In reality, though, as the previous chapter demonstrated, no man was able to support a family on his own in Soviet exile. Not only did the regime require all adults to work but the meager wages and/or food rations usually did not suffice for even one person. Those families deported with fathers and husbands faced the same desperate material conditions and likewise had members perish from starvation and disease. Survival did not actually hinge on the presence or absence of male relatives because the head of the household was generally incapable of supporting or protecting his family.

The documents reveal a tendency on the part of the women to regard themselves as weak and defenseless, to designate the category of women as helpless. One young woman explains that by February 1940 most of the inhabitants of her native village had fled: "This step was impossible for my family to take because there was no one to decide that. We recently lost our dear father, who gave up his life for the Fatherland, fighting until the last moment for the freedom of its eastern border." Reading their words, one would think that the women lacked initiative and resourcefulness. They doubt their own agency. The testimonies of Polish women frequently contain as explanations the phrases, "we were weak women," or "we were only women." They refer again and again to "helpless mothers" and "defenseless women." Janina Kaziewiczówna describes the night the NKVD came to take her family away: "All this took place amidst great crying of the entire household, we and the kids of Mrs. Maliszewska cried the most, but we were defenseless as we were only women and children, so what could we do?" A teacher from Grodno offers a dramatic image of the civilian deportees: "The steppes of Kazakhstan . . . Sheep . . . And among them a crowd of helpless women and children, people without a home, without the Fatherland." Writing while still in the USSR, she ends her plea as follows: "Save us, don't forget about the thousands of helpless women and children left on the steppe of Kazakhstan. . . . Oh Brothers! SOS! SOS!"[45]

The ironic comments women make about the way that Soviet men treated them also imply weakness and passivity as defining characteristics of the female sex. Describing the moment she was taken from her home, Janina Kucharska scoffs, "Six of them, NKVD-men, came for us, two women." Bożena Ciszyńska makes more biting comments: "There is a lot one can say about the heroism of the Soviet army. I remember how that night, 13 April, four soldiers from the NKVD, with revolvers and bayonets pointed came to our apartment, and of whom were they afraid? Three women? Such things really are comical."[46] Other women write with similar derision about the behavior of Soviet prison guards, believing their numbers and their weapons ridiculously excessive for guarding female inmates. Commenting on the fact that a group of Polish females was escorted to prison under heavy guard, a woman arrested for her work in the underground snaps, "This Polish nation must be terribly dangerous, even in the convoy of women!" In a scornful assessment of Soviet actions in eastern Poland, Kazimiera Sawczak remarks: "Old people, women, and kids, young people under the age of eighteen—this was the element that was dangerous for 'our liberators.'"[47]

These statements reveal a widely accepted view of an essential nature of women as defenseless and nonthreatening. Poles repeatedly lump women —regardless of age or physical capability—together with minors and older persons, as beings needing male care. It seems ludicrous to these women (even the one actively involved in the underground) that officers could expect or fear resistance from females. Such mocking remarks are negative comments about Soviet males. To Polish women, they do not appear to act as real men, do not seem to understand basic truths about the differing natures of the sexes. Thus, the women deride both the masculinity of Soviet men and the normality of their society. "It's a disgrace for Soviet officers to go after a helpless woman with a revolver," remarks Zofia Dzieciejew.[48]

A contrasting picture of an essential male nature corresponds with these assumptions about the female sex. It adheres to this depiction from a Catholic journal in 1937: "In the father we see energy and strength, which defends, protects and obtains the means for support." Accustomed to viewing men as strong and protective, women voice alarm when they find another dimension to their character or deportment. Females are particularly disturbed by the incapacitation of their men by the soldiers and NKVD agents who came to deport them; they also report extreme unease at the sight of male relatives crying. Maria Wojtkiewiczówna writes, "I will never forget that pale face and those tears, which rolled from the eyes of my father."[49] Such breakdowns intensified an already chaotic and grievous situation, contributing to the upset of the natural order of things. Many females follow descriptions of their fathers crying with expressions of their own sense of despair and uncertainty: they seem to have lost all grounding and been overcome by a feeling that they "didn't know what was happening around [them]." A schoolgirl from Grodno describes a particularly troubling moment on the transport: "Crossing the border my Dad cried like a little child and said to me, child, we are crossing the border of our beloved Fatherland, we will not return to it again. From that grief and sadness, I didn't know what was going on, everything was lost for me."[50] The AWBD staff member who prepared a typed and edited version of this document crossed out the words "like a little child" on the original. Presumably the depiction of an adult male as childlike did not fit the desired image of a Polish man.

Though the tears reported in male statements usually belong to women, some men do admit to crying.[51] This occurs, above all, at patriotic moments, when initially crossing the Polish-Soviet border and later at the announcement of the amnesty and formation of the Anders army. In such cases, the unusual nature of male tears highlights the tragedy or intensity of the situation faced by the exiles, a national drama, rather than a personal one. Witold Rawicz-Olędzki writes that while subjected to vicious propaganda against Poland, "the most steadfast men cried, not to mention the women."[52] While women's tears could be expected, he implies, the fact that men cried reveals the extreme nature of Soviet treatment of the Poles.

The agony imprisoned women experienced at the sight or sound of Polish men crying is a common theme in their reports. Countless women recall being tortured by the cries of beaten men, seemingly sharing their pain; they state that they can never forget the terrifying sounds of their "fathers, sons and husbands being beaten." One woman relates being moved by the frequent cry of "Mama, mama," from men; "nothing more, no complaints, no requests." She continues, "they wanted only to go to their mothers, their own mothers, from whom they were used to seeking solace." That same cry evoked horror in another woman:

I had never heard the cry of adult men that they want to go home. For twelve hours from the basement *kartser* the cry—more accurately the howl—reached us of tortured men. I want to go home!!! Always the same tone and the same words. If that had been a child, even through the walls I would have shouted to him a lullaby about home—but an adult man, that complaint, that begging for home was more difficult than the cry of a child. What happened to him?[53]

Women anguished over their countrymen's transformation to something contrary to their ideal; reduced to fragility and powerlessness, these men became disturbingly similar to women and children.

Male prisoners also note the horrible effect beaten inmates' tortured cries had on them, but do not emphasize the screams of men. The walls trembled from the cries of those being beaten, one man notes, "My ears swelled from the screams, the cries, and fretful sobs." They seem particularly upset by the yelling and sobbing of women. "At night I often heard terrifying screams, even of women," writes Szczepan Zieliński.[54] Both sexes describe what seemed most out of place and torturous to them: women—the male cries of pain; men—the same from females. For women, the reduction of men to childlike crying twisted their notions of male deportment. And the screams of beaten women seemed incongruous to males: what were women doing in punishment cells? How could interrogators lay a hand on defenseless women? Both cases reflect what the authors perceived as the barbarity of Soviet actions, which reduced males to an inappropriate state and treated females improperly. Additional injury stemmed from the inability of either sex to provide its accustomed remedy: women wanted to comfort the wailing men, as they would a child, while men chafed at their inability to defend women.

Though not many express it themselves, men, often helpless to render assistance, were reportedly distraught at the change in their roles; witnessing this pained women. "The men, mostly from the intelligentsia, looked on their fellow sufferers with pain and grief, writhing in their powerlessness," writes a woman in the labor camp Iaia, when describing how Polish men reacted to their female compatriots there.[55] Some individuals experienced this within their own families. Jadwiga Cholon recalls: "My father, who suffered so much in German prison and never shed a tear from it, now looked at us hungry, awaiting help, and cried. Pain tore at our hearts seeing these dear tears." The bodies of Jadwiga Siwkówna's family members swelled from hunger: "Father could not look at this," she states, "but he couldn't help us in any way." Men's despair at their powerlessness may have been expressed mostly through silence. On the transports men were sullen and silent, explains Andrzej Żurek, "for how do you answer the cries and screams of children, 'Daddy, I'm cold, I want to go home'?"[56]

The Soviet economic and penal systems impeded men from fulfilling their traditional roles as providers and protectors of their families. Additionally, men had a clear responsibility to the nation—in the form of armed service—that ranked higher than their everyday duties to their families. This obligation appeared so natural that it was beyond question. Women relate as if inevitable the fact that men left them, often with numerous small children, at times of great distress. After Poland fell to its two invaders in 1939, many men fled the country, went into hiding, or joined the partisans; after the amnesty, they left wives and children behind on Soviet collective farms to join the newly established Anders army.

Though it was acceptable (and sometimes imperative) for males to flee their homes after the invasions, most women could not even if they so desired. Karolina Dominiakowa states that she wanted to leave her town after the invasion but could not escape because she had a small son to worry about.[57] Women describe the desperateness of their situation in exile and their wish to flee the horrible conditions and oppressive authorities in search of the Polish army; they felt constrained, however, by their responsibility for family members. In a collective letter written to the Polish relief organization, a group of women stranded in Kazakhstan depict their perilous existence and plead for assistance: "We are afraid, however, to leave on our own," the letter concludes, "for we have children, and we also lack the necessary material conditions." In an anonymous memoir, a woman writes that she met the amnesty with fear because she had three small children to look after and did not know how to leave with them.[58]

At the same time, young motherless girls describe being orphaned when their fathers left them to join the army. Genowefa Czyżyńska, deported with her family of seven, watched her mother and brother die at the settlement. After the amnesty, the rest traveled to Uzbekistan, where she recalls being sick and hungry and dealt yet another blow: "Daddy, having learned that a polish army was being formed decided to abandon us and go to the army to serve the Fatherland and then, if necessary go after the eternal enemy, to fight for independent Poland. And he left me very sick and the two little sisters with me. It was sad for us to live for we were four families. The other children had mothers, only we orphans were alone." Stanisława Drozdowska remembers the night the NKVD came for her family, giving them fifteen minutes to pack: "Mama is sick, Papa doesn't think about packing and my sisters ask where are we going." On the journey to Russia, her mother was lost, left behind when she exited the train to find bread; conditions later worsened for Stanisława's family. She explains: "Then they said that Papa himself couldn't earn for everyone and ordered him to give up three sisters to the orphanage and if not then they wouldn't give anything. Papa had to give up those three sisters. But if Mama had been there she wouldn't have given up the children."[59] Stanisława recalls her mother's eventual reunion with the family: "She learned that Dad gave those three little sisters to the Soviet orphanage and had a heart attack it was all Daddy's fault." Though men were regarded as the protectors of the nation, it was women who were charged with staying behind and caring for the daily needs of its children.

Men report setting out to join the army, leaving families in Central Asia with little or no hope of their survival. Some record it as a matter of course, stating simply that they left a wife and children with no means of support and have no further knowledge of them.[60] Duty removed the sense of choice. One man writes that in Uzbekistan, "I left my wife and children to their fate, and I myself hurried as a Pole to the Army, for the Fatherland called me."[61] Others express the conflict they felt between their obligations to the nation and to their families. Describing the wave of men leaving settlements for Polish outposts, one young man writes: "The families stay behind. Sorrow, sadness, but it's hard, you have to accept fate, maybe it's not for long." "With great pain we all left our families there on the steppe," writes another man. "The duty of immediate service to the Fatherland dominates everyone." Regardless of the rhetoric upholding the father as the "head of the household," responsibility for the family ultimately belonged to women.[62]

This is not to judge the men who left to fulfill what they believed was their duty to the nation, through which they ultimately sought to benefit their families. Rather, it highlights the accepted gender roles that determined and constrained the actions of both sexes vis-à-vis the family and the nation. Polish men were expected to serve the nation—seen as the highest cause—directly, primarily through military service. This did not conflict with their duties to their families, presumably the future beneficiaries of their actions. Women, on the other hand, faced different restrictions in their choices: if they had children or siblings who needed care, they were not free to leave them, even if to fight for the national cause. Women's greatest service to the nation, according to societal consensus, was indirect—through the daily care and maintenance of the nation's smallest unit—the family.

While taking care of the family, women demonstrated resourcefulness and often took bold action, further contradicting stereotypes of women's nature. Women, and often young girls, report extraordinary labor and risk taken to benefit others. The following account of life in exile comes from Wanda Wróblewska, who was fifteen when deported after her father's arrest:

> On the *kolkhoz* I worked at many different things. The work was very hard. You had to work or you'd go without bread. . . . My mother is sick and couldn't work, my sister and brother were too young to work for a piece of bread, so I, as the oldest, as the head of the household, couldn't watch as my mother and siblings were dying before my eyes. I worked as I could, sometimes completely hungry, but it made me happy that I brought 300 grams of bread to my family.

Others report spending any time free from their jobs searching under the snow for reeds to burn so the family would not freeze or stealing grain to prevent starvation. Krystyna Jurkiewicz recalls sneaking out to the fields to dig frozen potatoes, thinking only about her hungry and sick mother and not the fact that she could be sent to prison for her actions. Women routinely left their settlements illegally to go to towns to trade clothing for food for their families. "Above all it is forbidden to go to the *kolkhoz*—which women do anyway," explains a teenager. "There are also many cases of spending the night in the clink. The children are hungry and need milk. So mothers prefer to sit in jail so their children have milk."[63]

For the most part, women did not recognize their own strength and resourcefulness. They recount overcoming difficult struggles without self-praise or bragging; they simply did what they had to do to take care of others, with little hesitation, and typically attribute their survival to God, the Virgin Mary, or the Polish army. The steadfast actions taken by themselves or other women, actions that kept the deportees alive each day throughout the ordeal of exile, generally go unheralded. When women do recount their bold or heroic actions they typically do not own them. One young woman struggled to save her family after the amnesty by walking four times to the Polish delegation for aid; hungry and exhausted, she carried the food she obtained thirty kilometers back home. One of these trips left her bedridden for three days. "I don't know where I got the strength for that," she writes, using a phrase that follows many such tales, "the thought of keeping my closest ones from starving to death gave me strength and drove me on." The common use of that phrase by women—not found thus far in male testimonies—suggests that demonstrated agency and power contradict their basic image of who they, as females, are. During an interrogation, an officer put a gun to the head of one Pole, threatening to pull the trigger if she did not confess. "I don't know where so much strength in me came from," she writes. "I calmly answered, 'Shoot.'" Finding her mother to be capable of much more than she ever expected, one young woman writes: "I was surprised at the heroism of Mom, for everyone abandoned us, we were left alone."[64]

Reflecting on their travails in exile, women frequently state, "I don't know where I drew the strength to survive."[65] Men, however, seem able to take credit for their deeds, such as one who writes, "I endured it all, though it was hard." Władysław Kędzierski reports that a corporal in his cell asserted "that he was alive thanks to me, for there was a time when he fell into depression and was ready to end his life, and my persuading and convincing words saved him." Other men also claim to have taken it upon themselves to raise the spirits of others, and one describes storytelling sessions organized for that purpose "on my initiative."[66] They tell of attempts to organize acts of rebellion, such as strikes and escapes, not cloaking their agency or courage.[67] In contrast, women simply did not see themselves as "heroes" or "saviors." Furthermore, the threat of harm to family members significantly compromised their willingness to engage in outright acts of rebellion.

Soviet policies largely identified these women with the family and attacked that nexus as a way to demoralize them and impede resistance. Women's traditional functional and emotional attachment to the family became a weapon used against them, as Soviet authorities routinely threatened them with the welfare of loved ones. Manipulating females through their relationships, the authorities endeavored to obtain information on the whereabouts or activities of other Poles and to exploit the women's labor. Women's reactions to these attempts show the importance of their familial bonds but also demonstrate that females were not simply mothers, wives, and daughters; they were also, in a fundamental way, Poles. They sometimes identified with the nation in the same way that men did.

NKVD agents, in particular, exploited the importance of familial relations to their female subjects. Attempting to pry information from women prisoners, officers routinely stated that the women would never again see their families if they did not collaborate or foretold dire consequences that relatives would suffer in the case of continued resistance. "After all," comments one woman, "they understand the heart of a mother." Some women could not withstand the pressure, particularly if the consequence of acquiescing harmed no one but themselves. A peasant mother of five small children, arrested after her husband had joined the partisans, received an eight-year sentence to a labor camp. She recalls: "I ask them for what those eight years, they answered me, because I told them nothing and they said what kind of mother are you you don't feel sorry for your children, I didn't want to sign the sentence for them they said if I sign I will be able to write to the children and I signed the sentence for them with pain in my heart."[68] The interrogators apparently assumed that females were, above all else, mothers, wives, and daughters and that their bonds with others could be used to break them.

Local authorities used familial bonds as a tool to extract obedient labor from Poles in "free exile." Wanda Daszkiewiczówna writes: "Once when the commandant of the settlement sent me to work and I categorically refused, he, with great anger and hatred, locked me up in the club and kept me in captivity for two days. After two days he let me go saying that if I didn't give in, he would arrest my mother. With that kind of ultimatum—I had to go to work." All relationships fell prey. A woman deported with her husband explains that local authorities "had a strong weapon in their hands against us, for whenever they wanted us to do something they threatened to separate us. So we performed the most difficult work, fearing that they would go through with this threat." A fifteen-year-old deported from a village in the Nowogród *województwo* with her younger siblings experienced the same predicament. Since her mother was dead and her father in a Soviet prison, the responsibility for supporting the family fell entirely on her shoulders. She recalls hard work and constant hunger, yet adds, "I was afraid to miss even one day of work, so they wouldn't separate me from my little siblings."[69]

The dread of separation from children hung as a terrifying cloud over many mothers. In a protocol sent to Polish delegates from Kazakhstan, a group of women, all mothers, complains that the local authorities constantly threatened them with prison: "And after all, it is well known how easy it is to terrorize women by threatening them with tearing them away from their children." One woman, deported with her daughter after her husband's arrest, endured a long interrogation during which the investigator announced that if she failed to become an informant, they would shoot her husband and take away her child. After refusing to work because she had two small children to care for, Antonina Otto was arrested and initially resisted NKVD efforts to coerce a confession of counterrevolution: "They demand, then threaten my greatest fear, that they will take my children from me, that they will take them away and I will never see them. In that way they torment me. After all I am a mother, they know my weakness, but they stop at nothing."[70] Otto finally signed the statement and returned home after agreeing to report to work. The commandant won, she adds, and then used her as an example to force other mothers to work.

These tactics frequently brought women's attachments to family and nation into conflict. Soviet officials seem to have underestimated the sacredness of the Polish nation to its female members, who sometimes sacrificed their personal attachments and familial commitments for the good of the nation. Though family carried great importance for most women, struggle and even martyrdom for their country sometimes overshadowed it. One woman decided to leave her family and flee to Romania to join the Polish army. "I left Warsaw hungry, cold, dark, and went toward a new life," she writes. "Father, Mother, Brothers—I loved them all and it was not out of egoism that I thought about this new life. I was pushed by an energy, faith and desire for action so great, that everything was blocked out by its importance."[71] Like other Poles devoted to the national struggle, she ended up in a Soviet prison.

The documents contain abundant accounts of the cruel manipulation of familial relations, amounting to emotional torture, at the hands of Soviet security police. And they show the steadfastness of women who refused to succumb. After long imprisonment and many brutal interrogations, one woman was suddenly taken to a room where a feast was laid. Inviting her to eat, the NKVD officers expressed sorrow for her—she was young and had a father she dearly loved. Adding that they also had him in their custody, they promised freedom for both if she signed a confession, then threatened to shoot him in front of her unless she became an informant. Refusing, she realized, "at that moment I have no father . . . God and the Fatherland are dearer to me than my family." The NKVD tried to extract information from

Jadwiga Trautman, an underground member, and once drove her home to view her mother through a window, suggesting she could stay there if she agreed to collaborate. Trautman recalls: "I felt like rushing in and touching that precious being . . . and [I] heard behind me, 'so you will come tomorrow to the NKVD?' A moment of hesitation . . . (I am cursing you for that moment) . . . no! I rushed back to the car . . . no, no, no! We arrived at the prison and that same night I was taken for an interrogation." Her compatriot Eugenia Schmidt, arrested as a courier for the Polish resistance, faced interrogations during which "they threatened to take revenge on my daughter, who would die in prison." She yielded neither to such attempts at blackmail nor the threat of execution. Schmidt describes how, aware of the possibility of her own arrest, she had discussed it with her teenage daughter, stating her willingness to give up her dangerous activity at her child's request. The daughter, Schmidt reports with pride, told her to continue her work in the underground, saying, "I know what threatens us and I know that I don't imagine myself as anything else but a Pole, above all."[72] Loyalty to the nation cost such women great anguish, a price that many willingly paid.

These examples demonstrate that devotion to family members did not capture the entirety of women's identity as members of the nation and question stereotypical notions of their character and desires. Although the relational aspect of female identity was strong, some women also felt a direct relationship to the nation and willingly left parents and siblings—though not children—to fight for it, both in the aftermath of the Soviet invasion in 1939 and the amnesty in 1941. Others, like Schmidt, knowingly accepted the risk of separation from their families and engaged in clandestine work. Still others refused to yield to intimidation to sacrifice their principles for the sake of loved ones, for though they valued the family, they swore allegiance to a higher entity, the nation. The notion that Polish families would have to make sacrifices to the "altar of the Fatherland" persisted in the minds of many patriots, female as well as male. Alina Lukaszewiczówna took her dying mother and brother to a hospital in Kazakhstan, reflecting: "I accepted fate. If they depart I have to bear it quietly. I am a Polish woman and I can't cry. I only tell myself, 'They died in the struggle for the Fatherland.' It doesn't matter that they didn't fight with weapons in their hands." Dorota Majewska, who worked as a typist in the underground, reacted similarly when the NKVD arrested her. "I endured the arrest calmly," she writes. "Mama also didn't cry. It was as if she turned into stone. She said only, 'Yet another flame on the altar of the Fatherland.'"[73] When they wanted to pry information or labor from them, Soviet authorities, particularly the NKVD, did perceive women to be different from men. But in attributing to women a solely relational identity, these officials underestimated their identity as Poles.

Mothers of the Nation

The assault on the Polish family went beyond the physical separation of its members and the use of relationships as weapons. At its inception, the Soviet government advocated the Marxist notion of the "withering away of the family" as the key to women's emancipation. Transferring household labor to the public sphere, through such measures as communal dining and day care, would liberate women from the fetters of motherhood and allow them to freely participate in public life. As Wendy Goldman points out, the Bolsheviks attached little importance to the emotional bonds between parents and children and especially slighted the role of the mother.[74] The state, it was assumed, could easily take over the functions of childrearing. Early legislation took steps in this direction, but by the late 1920s, widespread social disorder plus the prohibitive cost of social welfare led the Party to deem these goals unreachable. It began to take a more conservative approach to family policy, leaving the burdens of housework and childrearing to women, while continuing to require their participation in the labor force and encouraging increased education. Since the regime had never sought to remake gender roles within the family, women essentially worked a double shift.

The Party remained ideologically committed to the idea of the equality of the sexes but in opportunistic fashion abandoned the notion of the withering away of the family because it proved economically unfeasible. The Stalinist regime moved instead to stabilize the family, neither for the good of the unit itself nor the well-being of its members but for its own ends: labor exploitation, social control, and increased fertility. Years of war, famine, poverty, the chaos of fast-paced modernization, Bolshevik legislation, and Stalinist repression had undermined family ties, a situation the regime had no desire to redress because it considered the family (and motherhood) a matter of social significance, not a private affair.[75] The Party wanted allegiance to the state to supersede all other loyalties among its population, and to that end, its organs continually undermined familial bonds and lines of authority. State-sponsored organizations and events monopolized the daily lives of individuals, young and old, taking them out of the home as much as possible; children were encouraged to inform on parents and spouses on each other. Above all, the Communists strove to have their agencies replace parents as the main socializers of youth.

The exiles became subjects of the same policies applied to Soviet citizens. Since the Poles came with a national allegiance troubling to the Soviet government, they found themselves especially targeted for "reeducation," which ran the gamut from persuasion to coercion, and even to destruction. Reeducation, applied also to native national groups considered unreliable by Stalin, was a means of "forcing them to forget their homeland and their culture."[76] In this way, the regime sought to "promote assimilation to a generalized Soviet culture."[77] For women from Poland, who saw their primary duty to the nation to be raising children into Polish patriots, Soviet policies compromised their identities as women and as members of their nation.

Women condemned to prisons and camps had no opportunity to care for their children or to make decisions about their futures. New mothers received no special consideration: those who gave birth while imprisoned were treated as wet nurses, allowed merely to feed their babies according to a schedule set by the authorities. Maria Karmińska, who endured these conditions, writes: "In prison I gave birth to a child, I wasn't alone, there were other mothers. We were not allowed to give our babies to our families, they treated us in a terrible way. They deported us to Russia with our children. There they took the children away and once a day for 15 minutes under a rifle we were allowed to see our children."[78] If the infants survived their first weeks, they were whisked off to Soviet orphanages, to be raised without knowledge of their backgrounds. Mothers typically received no word of the location of their children.

Although deported women typically remained with their youngsters, they anguished over their inability to fulfill their maternal duties. Certainly they tried. Despite state demands on their time, their own exhaustion, hunger, and illness, women endeavored to carry out their traditional duties in the home. Many of them refer to the double burden they endured, working all day, rising early, and staying up late to tend to domestic chores: "It was not taken into consideration at all that we have children, that we have to wash clothes, cook, chop wood, fetch water." A typical day for one deportee began this way: "I dragged myself up at five o'clock in order to fetch water, not only for myself but sometimes for our landlady, to cook a dish for the children, gather scraps for heat, wash clothes, etc., and only went to work at nine. I was constantly extremely exhausted." The women's testimonies reveal extraordinary devotion and self-sacrifice for their children. They spent days in jail for leaving their settlements illegally in search of food. They risked long imprisonment by stealing food and heating materials. They gave up their own rations, though famished from long days of laboring. "It is difficult for us mothers, aware of the goals and means of bringing up children, to bring them up well at present," writes a group of women in exile. "We try to give them the best of what we have. We ourselves don't eat, we don't sleep much, in order to give our children at least the minimum."[79]

Regardless of their efforts and sacrifices, women found that some of the obstacles erected by the authorities proved impenetrable; they simply could not fulfill the functions of motherhood that they deemed natural. Forced to labor all day, they had to deny their children their presence, their care, and their instruction. "It was not easy to part with the children and to give up the long hours I had spent with them, teaching my little girls and playing with my son," notes a woman ordered to work in the forest. When they left for work in the morning, mothers either had to leave their children alone or send them to Soviet institutions; both options tormented them. Aurelia Czech was deported with her newborn. "Upon arriving at the appointed place, I immediately had to go to work, otherwise I wouldn't have gotten bread and milk for the baby," she recalls. "When I went to work I had to leave the baby without care, only one who has suffered such things can understand what went on in my heart then." Paulina Rzehaków faced a similar predicament when, after the amnesty, her husband left to join the Anders army. "I was left alone with the children," she writes. "I continued to work digging canals—I locked the children in the hut during my absence. In the morning I made soup, left it on the burner, and Zytka, a five-year-old, fed her younger siblings. When I returned home, the children sat frightened and crying."[80]

Leaving children alone all day agonized mothers, who feared the ruin of their young. "Our children are deprived of normal conditions of growth," writes a group of mothers, desperate for assistance from Polish social welfare workers. The young not only lack nutrition, soap, and clothing, they explain, but since mothers cannot stay at home with them, "their lives are unregulated. The older kids lost years of learning, the younger ones, because of a lack of appropriate playthings and assistance, are late in developing." Another mother laments, "Our children are unhappy, neglected, persecuted by all. Often I wanted to sit down on the snow and cry, cry from despair." Just as women found that they could not act like true mothers in the USSR, they found that their offspring were different. Maria Żmigrodzka writes with distress that her youngsters, "no longer even resembled children."[81] "They get wild and will grow into regular savages and brigands," despairs another mother.[82]

Usually the sole alternative to leaving children alone all day was to take them to Soviet nurseries or, if they were older, to schools. In some locales, the authorities forced children to attend Russian schools, while in others they did little to enforce this regulation, leaving it to the parents' choice. Some mothers did take this option. Maria Szoska decided to leave her children at a Soviet nursery while she worked all day. The knowledge that they would be safe, warm, and fed did not alleviate her grief, however: "My heart often tore from pain, as I snatched my little ones from bed and still in darkness I carried one in my arms and the other I led by the hand, and I left them at the nursery and quickly exited, pursued by the cry and scream of the baby, 'Mommy, don't go!' "[83] Mothers dreaded sending children to day nurseries or schools because of the possibility that they would slowly cease to be *Polish* children. Indeed, Soviet schooling for the deportees aimed to destroy the children's sense of Polishness—to turn them, instead, into Communists, loyal to the Soviet state. It therefore sought to subvert Polish children's traditional learning of loyalty, hierarchy, and authority. Analyzing the overhaul of the school system in Soviet-occupied Poland, Jan Gross explains: "The new regime was concerned to capture for its own purposes the more general, the broadest learning that youngsters acquire in school, namely, the capacity for and habit of obedience, the recognition of authority beyond the family circle, and domestication, as it were, into membership in society." The attempt "to wrest children away from the old ways" involved encouraging criticizing and informing on parents, to undermine their authority and debunk the cultural heritage they passed on to their offspring.[84]

Women felt powerless to stem the erosion of their parental authority, a process that not only altered their children but also compromised their own identity as mothers. Anna Szwedko recalls several painful incidents seared into her memory, all demeaning to her as a parent. Her children began screaming when the NKVD came to deport the family, and, out of nervousness, Szwedko yelled at them to stop. The NKVD officer scolded her in front of them, stating that she would have to go to the USSR to learn to treat children properly.[85] One day in exile, Szwedko's youngest son watched a Russian family eating bread and asked his mother for some, but she had none. The little boy grew angry, told his mother she was no good and he would have the NKVD take her to jail. Women felt such humiliating and heartbreaking incidents evidenced the Soviet effort to wrest their children away from them.

Soviet schooling and propaganda contained radically new and challenging content for Polish children. They were forbidden to speak their native tongue and forced to learn Russian.[86] Classes in "militant atheism" mocked all religious belief and drilled into youth the idea that there was no God. "In school they taught us that Poland no longer exists, that there is no God," relates one child.[87] Soviet schoolteachers continually derided the Polish nation and forbade children to study Polish history or literature. Instead, they learned Russian history, the principles of Communism, and love of Stalin and the Soviet state. The results of this education began to manifest in young Poles. Women anguished over signs of atheism, loss of native tongue, and ignorance of Polish history. In their view, such developments bespoke their children's loss of Polishness. According to Irena Gajewska, the Soviet schools sought to "warp their characters and poison their souls with the poison of hatred toward everything Polish." Even sending children to day care to ensure that they were warm and fed during the workday seemed dangerous, as Bronisława Bartoszowa explains: "An agitator came to the daycare. She told the children how bad it was in Poland, that there was no God, etc. Evidence of the influence that she managed to exert on the children is the fact that four-year-old Krysia Walakiewicz told her mother that she would not return to Poland, because it was better in Russia." As a result of Soviet schooling, states Maria Stawowczykowa, in many families, the children's faith wavered, they no longer wanted to pray, they changed their behavior and the way they talked, and they acquired a hatred of the intelligentsia.[88]

Adults worried not merely about their own children but about the children of the nation. One woman expresses her distress about the fate of Polish children: "They took the children whose parents were in jail to the so-called *Det-Domy* [Children's Homes], gave them Soviet last names and brought them up in the spirit of Communism. The kids forgot how to speak and pray in Polish." Another woman bemoans that the Polish boys she encountered after evacuation to Iran, who had come from Russian orphanages, "had completely forgotten how to speak Polish, they were disobedient."[89]

The issue of maintaining the Polishness of the children was crucial to Polish women, and many willingly took risks to ensure it. Some of them lost part of their salary for keeping their children at home against orders; others went to jail rather than send their children to Russian schools. Maria Gołąbowa sat in jail for ten weeks because her son did not attend the local Russian school. Women faced persecution if their children defended their native country and beliefs in class, an action many mothers encouraged. Izabel Kaucka, for one, taught her son to say, "I am a Pole, I believe my own mother and not a Russian teacher."[90] Women's punishment for recalcitrant children included assignment to heavier work and the loss of the opportunity to purchase food and clothing.

Afraid that their children would lose their Polishness, women ran clandestine lessons, teaching Polish language, history, and literature, drawing directly from female ancestors who had taken on that task during the partitions. These activities, illegal in the Soviet system, were true acts of resistance. Many women instructed their children at home, even giving them lessons before setting off for work. Former teachers frequently continued their roles as educators in exile. Julia Argasimska, a teacher in a small town in eastern Poland, agonized over the demoralization of Polish children in Russian schools, where they heard "terrible lies" about Poland: "They were told, for example, that village women in Poland fed the little dogs of the Polish lords at their own breasts. The children I had taught in Poland very often came to me for clarification in such cases—I responded in such cases, not fearing what kind of consequences it would have. That for me was real moral torture." In a similar vein, Irena Sypniewska writes: "I was busy teaching children, two little boys came to me, and I taught them, and then was forced to stop as it came to the light of day. After the amnesty I continued this work in the open, I taught five boys and one girl."[91]

The importance women placed on providing children with a Polish education and keeping them from losing their nationality is perhaps best illustrated by the following case. Regina Ostaszkiewicz tells the story of a little boy she met on the transport from Poland who was deported with only his grandparents (the Stankiewiczes). When the local authorities decided to put him in an orphanage, everyone in the settlement reacted with despair. "My heart also broke," she writes, "for what will happen to a poor little Polish child, once the wild Bolsheviks snatch him away." Both grandparents tried to trade themselves so that the boy would not be taken, but their attempts met with refusal. Ostaszkiewicz explains what happened next:

> Then Mrs. Stankiewicz took Jerzyk and taught him who he is, that his name is Jerzy Oczepowski, that he is a Pole, a Catholic, repeated the prayer "Our Father" with him, that he comes from Polish Drohiczyn, that his father's name is Lucjan Oczepowski and his mother's is Wanda Oczepowska. She reminded him that if the Bolsheviks call him differently or tell him that he is a *Moskale*, don't agree, tell them he is a Pole and his name is Oczepowski. Grandmother taught Jerzy like this several times a day for four days, but she often stopped because she cried a lot. Mr. Stankiewicz also cried even though he is a man. No matter how many times one of the Poles came over, Jerzyk right away ran up and immediately said, "Please ask me my name," and then he repeated everything, for he learned well. And he told us that we should be calm, that he will always be a Pole, and will never become a *Moskale*, and he crossed himself and prayed.[92]

The situation presented an excruciating dilemma for mothers, who felt it their duty to bring up their children as Poles. A group of women seeking assistance from the Polish government-in-exile spoke for many: "We want our children to be raised in our spirit, not to forget their language and their nationality."[93] Should they leave their children alone at home all day, without care, often without food or heat, in order to prevent their Sovietization? Could they let their children suffer physically, for the sake of keeping them Polish?

This dilemma assumed gigantic proportions, with life and death stakes, for many women. Mothers frequently found that no matter what they tried, it did not suffice to keep their families alive. They watched their children steadily decline from hunger, exhaustion, and disease; the alternative was to send them to a Soviet orphanage. It is important to note that there was no unanimity on this issue. Isolated and exhausted, many women—even mere children, left with the responsibility for younger siblings after the loss of both parents—faced this dilemma on their own. Some, for reasons that do not lend themselves to analysis, kept their children with them. They were variously unable to part with their most precious beings, unable to give up on their own efforts to save them, unable to cease believing in the possibility of a miracle. Fearful of the consequences of sending a child to a Soviet orphanage, many women refused. Maria Podziadło lost both her parents and was left with four brothers, the youngest of whom was barely a year old: "In spite of difficult conditions I didn't give my brother to the orphanage and he died of pneumonia."[94]

For some, giving children up to certain Sovietization meant capitulating to the enemy, a price too great. Again, the notion of making sacrifices to the "altar of the Fatherland" surfaces. Some Poles felt that keeping children Polish was as important as keeping them alive. One woman explains this position:

> It is possible, I suppose, for persons who have never been put to the same tests to feel that we were to blame for such an attitude; to say that as mothers we were asking too much of our children; that no mother is justified in condemning her child to hunger and vagrancy for the sake of an ideal. To that, I can only reply that Polish mothers throughout the whole of Polish history have always asked much of their children and have persistently taught them to believe, as they had been taught themselves, that there are worse things than physical hunger, ill-treatment, solitude, or anything else that this world can do: and that it is first from these worse things, from perversion of the mind and abdication of the spirit, and not from the pains and fears of the body, that a Polish mother strives to safeguard her child. This, however misguided, is what we did feel, and what we continued to feel about the effect on our children of institutions utterly alien to us in character and officially atheist in program. And I think it cannot be true that we mothers loved our children any less than those mothers love theirs who think first of what they can do for them in this world.[95]

This defense maintains that no Polish woman was willing to give her children over to the Soviets: they would remain Poles or die. The truth of the matter is that this ideal of Polish nationalism conflicted with the love and humanity of many individuals. When watching their children slowly starve to death or succumb to disease, some women found that their own emotional attachment, and the Polish nation, lost priority. Some Polish women gave their children to Soviet institutions in the hope of ensuring their physical survival.

After laboring for seven months in exile, Eleonora Klidzia fell ill and could provide her children with neither food nor clothing for the winter. She writes:

I was seriously advised to let my children be admitted to the orphanage. And I had no choice. I couldn't count on anyone and the children were weak, suffered from bloody diarrhea, chicken pox, skin diseases from the incredible dirt. I realized I had to save them or let them starve. I knew that after my death they would be taken to the orphanage anyway. Death from hunger was the worst death I could imagine. At the end of November 1940 I took my children to the orphanage in a region neighboring Irtysh and they were admitted because of my disabilities.[96]

Another woman, forced to give her own sons to the orphanage because she could not feed them, explains: "I preferred parting with them forever, so as not to see their eyes, when they asked me for a piece of bread that I didn't have."[97] Similarly, a girl left in charge of her siblings after the arrest of her father and death of her mother finally decided, with the help of a brother, that she could not let her younger siblings perish. She recalls: "Once my brother got sick and was in bed for two months. I couldn't earn to support three people. At first we sold things, but that didn't last long. Hunger and misery took over us in our house. For weeks we went without a piece of bread. We were forced to give our sister and brother to the orphanage. It was 86 kilometers from the settlement. We parted from them with pain in our hearts."[98]

Soviet documents also register the desperation of Polish mothers unable to provide for their families, noting suicides and mental breakdowns, as well as the surrender of their children. The people's commissar of internal affairs in Kazakhstan reported: "In the Irtyshsk region the deported Pole Barbara Paniuk on 8.IX.40 came to the regional NKVD office with her small children. She left there three sons and two little daughters, stating, 'Take my children, they're starving, I can't feed them, if you don't take them, I'll soon sink.' Leaving the children, Paniuk walked out with an infant at her breast and disappeared (her corpse was never found)."[99] This report was written in October 1940, before the deportees had faced their first winter in exile.

The threat of death was real and overwhelming. Scores of women report witnessing the deaths of their offspring in exile. Children died in the arms of their mothers who were helpless to prevent the ravages of disease and starvation.[100] For many women, this helplessness and loss of their own issue deprived their lives of meaning and hope. Half of Czesława Greczyn's six-page report about her life in exile depicts with chilling detail the illness and death of her son. "Mothers each lost several children," she writes. "And the finger of God touched me as well and I lost my only child. I lived through a complete gehenna—I'm surprised that I'm alive." Greczyn describes living "like an animal," dirty and alone in a strange city, while her three-year-old son lay in a hospital bed: "Many times there were entire days when I had nothing in my mouth, there were moments when out of hunger I wanted to steal bread. . . . I lived this way three weeks, but would happily have suffered even longer, if my little one had lived, but things turned out differently." She learned that her son had died when she found his name crossed off the list of patients at the hospital. With considerable effort, Greczyn located his unrecognizable corpse. "Nothing was left for me—my heart broke," she writes. "I was alive, but I so desired death then." Her eventual evacuation from the USSR seemed pointless to her after losing her only child.[101]

Other women were apparently completely broken by the deaths of their children. Such cases are hard to document because these women would not have made it out of the USSR to tell their stories. Those who did get out, though, tell of the suicides of mothers who had lost their children.[102] A captain stationed at an outpost of the Polish army after the amnesty reports meeting over two hundred women who came to him with the same lament: "I can't go on anymore. I had two, three, four children, and now I am alone. I don't want to live anymore, do with me as you please, and do whatever you want with my things." The archives of the Anders army contain a letter written by a woman stranded in Central Asia, describing her desperate situation to her husband, a sergeant:

> Czesio—your son—died from hunger and exhaustion. I buried him. I am not able to describe the funeral because my eyes are filling with tears. . . . I had been working in exile for two and one-half years, including Saturdays and Sundays, only to save our children. But I can't anymore. I am too weak. I have decided to follow my children if Aniela dies. If not today, then in a few days, death from hunger will come.[103]

It is difficult, perhaps impossible, to analyze the implications for Polish women of the agonizing position in which they lived—fearing and often witnessing the death of their own children. Grief, anger, guilt, despair, and resignation are some of the complex feelings expressed by mothers who outlived their children. Adela Mrozowa, who lost her small son, speaks for many: "There are things that just do not lend themselves to telling, that one must suffer in one's own heart in order to understand, but I think that if there is hell on earth many of us went through the fire here."[104]

Yet even in the wake of these profoundly tragic losses, women remembered that they and their deceased children were Poles. With overwhelming frequency, females, young and old, reveal an intense preoccupation with the fact that their loved ones were buried in the USSR, that Poles had to be laid to rest in non-Polish soil. Czesława Greczyn writes bitterly about her son's death: "And I had to leave in that hated land that which was most dear to me, that which had been everything in the world for me." She notes a final irony: two months after her child's death she received 1,200 rubles by mail from her husband. Not only was it too late to save the boy, but she could not even erect a tombstone because of the lack of materials in "that damned country." Nevertheless, she erected a cross and a tablet, on which she inscribed, "Lesiu Greczyn, a little Pole."[105]

The exiles despaired over leaving the bodies of loved ones in "foreign Russian earth." This pain almost rivaled that caused by the deaths. Many individuals found their relief at being evacuated from the USSR tempered by sadness at leaving someone in that accursed soil. "Our departure didn't make me happy, leave for what? With whom? What is this, that I'll be in Persia and my dear Father lies in the wild steppe? I'll never see his grave," writes one woman. On the way to the evacuation point her mother also died: "Here in this wasteland my mama was left." One young woman cried when she finally managed to depart—not from sorrow at leaving but because she had to say good-bye to her "comrades left there in the cemetery," who, she asserts, died "on the road to the Fatherland."[106]

Women demonstrate an obsession with leaving markers at the graves of their deceased that would distinguish the nationality and religion of those left in the soil. They erected tablets and crosses and sometimes had them clandestinely blessed by priests.[107] Poles were unwilling to leave without planting a sign in the ground that contained their loved ones and compatriots, for the death of a Pole in exile was not seen merely as a personal calamity —it was a tragedy of the entire Polish nation. The number of deaths alone made it a national experience; in addition, survivors shared the deaths by investing them with a common meaning. Zofia Kruszelnicka writes about the loss of her daughter: "Even little Krysia died, she was buried in the field. Every one of us left someone dear in foreign land, the road was marked by graves and crosses, suffering and sadness, we traveled a real Golgotha." She endowed this tragedy with religious and historical meaning, which served to make it explainable and bearable. Another woman writes, "we are again bestowing all of Siberia with Polish graves . . . in order to rebuild Poland . . . in which God will help us." One of the clearest expressions of the mixed religious and historical understanding of the deaths, and the experience of exile itself, comes from a woman who lost her two-year-old son: "Soon my only son was lying lifeless on the upper berth, dressed in his best white suit, his yellow curls falling on his pale face while the red lips smiled. In his hands he held an image of the Virgin and a simple black cross, the cross of the Polish exiles. His head rested on a small bag containing a handful of earth— Polish earth."[108] This little boy joined the ranks of the martyrs for Poland. In the personal tragedy of losing their children, these women found a connection to the national tragedy, past and present. The national myth of the martyrdom of the Poles provided the women with a space and a language for expressing their personal suffering.

In the previous chapter, several collective letters, written by women still in exile who were seeking assistance from Polish delegations were discussed. These women point out the incompatibility of the economic role required of them by the Soviet regime with their own identities and duties as mothers. Typically, the letters bear such signatures as, "Polish Mothers of the Novosibirsk *oblast'*," suggesting that identifying themselves as Polish *mothers*, not simply as women or citizens, gave the petitioners more political and emotional clout because it stressed their singular importance to the nation. One collective letter begins with the authors identifying themselves as, "We Polish women." It too stresses not their own welfare but its importance for the welfare of others: "We ask for help, for we want to raise our children into brave and healthy citizens of our beloved Fatherland."[109] Their relationship to and responsibility for others is a key part of these women's self-definition as members of the nation.

In this regard, the case of Franciszka Pączek, the peasant woman who felt she was treated unfairly by Polish authorities after the amnesty, merits additional comment. Pączek bases her claim for equal treatment, despite her relatively low socioeconomic status, on fulfillment of her role in the nation:

the production of soldiers. "Thus our dear Poles though I am the mother of three sons whom I gave to the Polish Army," she writes angrily, "and I myself work but I don't deserve. . . ."[110] Like the women quoted above, white-collar workers, Pączek highlights her role in the nation as the mother of soldiers. She implies that having produced three sons for the Polish army, she has fulfilled her ultimate duty to the nation and is, therefore, a full and equal citizen.

Similarly, a young woman stranded in the Urals grounds her plea for assistance in surviving and ultimately leaving her settlement there in her usefulness to the fatherland. "I am not asking for anything for myself," Dalomea Nieznańska begins her letter, "but I want to give of myself all that could be useful for such a great matter as the rebuilding of our fatherland." She continues: "I love our fatherland and all the fellow countrymen so much, that I would like to help them. . . . I am certain that I could help much."[111] Although Nieznańska, age nineteen, does not emphasize her status as potential mother of Polish patriots, she nonetheless justifies her entreaty not on the grounds that she herself is a citizen of Poland or that she has suffered a great injustice at the hands of the Soviet regime, or even that she simply has no means to survive. Devotion to others and usefulness to the fatherland serve as the key legitimate claims, perhaps the greatest measure of worth, that she and these other women employ.

The Nation as Family

The family not only constituted the smallest unit of the nation, but also provided a framework for women's relations with conationals. Typically, the displaced women extended the values and roles dominating their family life to the wider community of exiles, expecting the same ideals to prevail: solidarity, cooperation, self-sacrifice, and devotion to the nation. These values often prompted women to actively resist Soviet actions and demands. What stands out in the documents is that women willingly put themselves at risk to assist others to whom they were often not related nor even acquainted. Reports abound of Polish doctors working in medical facilities who routinely gave their compatriots medical excuses from labor—the only legal means to miss a day of work—against official directives. Jadwiga Pawluś, an obstetrician, worked as a medical director and earned a relatively high salary. Her generosity in granting Poles exemptions from work led to her denunciation as dangerous and reassignment to heavy labor. Polish women who served as brigade leaders receive praise from compatriots for helping them by exaggerating production reports; they, too, soon lost their privileged positions.[112]

Women prisoners often took courageous action to alleviate the suffering of others, most frequently in response to the screams of men being tortured in prison basements. Horrified at the sounds, women sometimes protested the actions of the NKVD. A typical description follows: "The hollow strikes and the cries of beaten men reached us. Don't hit! One night at the end of May, from our cell there arose the cry of 62 voices: Don't hit! We had to scream at last—it was already beyond the tolerance of the most steeled nerves. This was a revolt against the injury of our close ones." Maria Pieszczek writes similarly of women's efforts to protect men during terrifying nights in prison: "They called people at night to interrogations which lasted till morning. We often heard the yells and screams of beaten men. After a scream from the women, 'don't beat the men,' the yells, the screams quieted down. After that we could hear whistles, keys. The chief of the prison packed several women into the *kartser* for revolting."[113] Women report that their entire cell registered its protest against the torture of Polish men, sometimes screaming or banging on cell doors, other times staging hunger strikes. In most cases, they had no idea exactly who these men were; nevertheless, they regarded them as their fathers, sons, and husbands.[114] Direct witness to the suffering of others also spurred acts of protest and disobedience, and women recount revolts against the abuse of cellmates. They raised a commotion when guards mistreated others or denied needy prisoners medical care. "If we saw that someone was threatened with the loss of life due to the lack of medical care," writes Bogusława Ptaszyńska, "then the whole cell staged a hunger strike and the sick one was only then taken to the hospital."[115]

These protests were collective actions, demonstrating both the solidarity of the women and the power of group initiative. Individual women also violated the rules and dehumanizing atmosphere of prison life, fighting back to protect or aid others in misery. Józefa Telemajer-Dorobkowa recalls a disturbing experience early on in her stay in prison:

> At night I was awakened by the terrible cries and screams of a woman giving birth, lying there next to me on the ground. . . . No one cared

what was happening next to them, everyone was vacuous and deaf to the screams and the pain of others. They were accustomed to it, or had lived through it themselves, or they awaited the same. I started to scream in an inhuman way and kick the door yelling for help, a voice from behind the door said, "shut up you stupid Pole, it's nothing, you'll get used to it."

Another woman records her impassioned reactions to the ill-treatment of cellmates. She recalls seeing a guard slam an iron door on the leg of a woman for walking too slowly: "I think it was then that, for the first time in my life, I got something like hysterics. I was unaware of what I was doing. My own shrill screaming brought me back to consciousness." On another occasion, a guard reached to strike her friend, a young woman she had taken under her wing: "Seized by a sudden passion of anger I too jumped up and faced him, my fists clenched. Never, never would he strike my beloved Marysia!" One young woman endured being locked in a cupboard, tied in a sack and beaten, and confined for five days in the *kartser* because she could not bear the sight of women fainting from lack of air in the cell and repeatedly knocked the grating off the window.[116]

Instances of women resisting on behalf of others far outnumber similar actions taken, or reported, for an individual's own benefit. Women typically took courageous action and risked punishment to alleviate the suffering of others, usually compatriots. Sometimes these others were new cellmates and oftentimes unseen and unnamed Polish males, nonetheless considered relatives, whose tortured cries came up from the prison basements. Nationality alone made these others family, drawing a feeling of connectedness and a readiness for self-sacrifice from these women.

Polish females also tended to form surrogate families in exile, usually composed of new acquaintances whose only links were a common nationality and the shared predicament of forced exile. Adolescents in prison, such as Janina Podlewska, report that older Poles took care of them. "There were cells in which there were many of our women from the intelligentsia," she relates, "who cared for me with all their heart and tried at each step to replace my mother."[117] Imprisoned women discuss deep attachments they formed to younger ones, whom they sought to aid and comfort. Young Poles alone in exile often felt they owed their lives to compatriots who took them in. One such girl writes, "God took pity on me and did not let me die." God's intervention took the form of a woman, a substitute mother, who, the girl explains, "took care of me like her own child and didn't let me die." Another girl lost her mother in Russia; an older couple cared for her and her siblings. "There would have been nothing to eat were it not for the kind Mr. and Mrs. Bartozaków, who cared for us like their own," she states.[118] This latter phrase occurs frequently in the documents, as children report being saved by fellow Poles who, though they had little themselves, did all they could to enable helpless children to survive.

Single or married, with or without children of their own, women willingly took on the responsibility for the children of others and tried as much as possible to minimize the consequences for youths of repressive actions against their parents. Kazimiera Brzezińska describes the hardship of a woman sent to jail for refusing to leave her infant and go to work: "The separation of a mother from her five-month-old child made a terrible impression on us, since I was feeding my own baby, for those two weeks that she was in prison I fed her baby." Similarly, Marta Midowa relates that though working hard on a *kolkhoz*, "at the same time I took care of an orphan, a twelve-year-old girl whose Mama died of exhaustion, leaving three orphans."[119] One can speculate that despite the extra burdens such responsibility added, these women gained comfort and satisfaction, both from assisting human beings worse off than they and from exercising the maternal and domestic functions they associated with females and linked with normality.

Surrogate families formed not only around orphaned children; women of all ages hooked up with others after deportation, living together in extended families, typically without men. These groupings enabled some of the deportees to avoid being parceled out to the homes of local Russians or Kazakhs, a situation that Poles dreaded. Together women sometimes built their own clay huts, salvaged abandoned ones, or pooled their resources to buy domiciles from the locals so they could stay with their own. Krystyna Schmidt recalls that when her transport arrived at its final destination, the passengers were indiscriminately divided among existing homes, so she clung to the women she befriended on the train: "Our group, which included six people, willingly joined together in one 'family,' afraid to be left alone among foreigners, and was settled at the end of the village." Similarly, Helena Lebracka explains that when the train arrived in Russia and passengers were being dispersed to different locations, they tried to band together in groups along ethnic lines: "Two other families went with us, the railroad inspector from Stanisławów with his wife and daughter, along with the wife of an official and her two children, together we made up one family."[120]

Often the deportees describe their entire community of exiles, numbering even into the hundreds, as "one big family."[121] Michalina Zajączkowska's transport ended up on a collective farm in Northern Kazakhstan, where, she writes, "We all lived like one great family, we willingly helped each other." Socioeconomic status made no difference within these groups, women frequently assert. Stating that the forty Poles in her settlement lived "like one family," Zofia Misiak explains: "Although the element among us varied, intellectuals and others, we understood each other and helped each other materially and morally." Similarly, a painter describes relations among her group of deportees: "The intellectual level varied but that was not a barrier in getting along."[122] These communities functioned similarly to the family back home—on whatever scale it was imposed, the family structure provided material assistance and emotional support to violently uprooted individuals.

These arrangements meant that time-consuming tasks, such as standing in line for bread, gathering manure for fuel, and picking berries and mushrooms for sustenance, could be shared. "The Poles, who totaled fifty people, lived in harmony," writes one woman. "They helped each other at their jobs, in taking care of the home, in material matters, and in general maintained very warm relations." Individuals reportedly shared packages from home with those who were starving: "If one had something," a woman notes, "everyone did." Caretaking and assistance, which required scarce resources, were not doled out according to bloodlines: common nationality meant that they were all related. "They even arrested women," explains Stanisława Jeżówna, "that means mothers, leaving children to their own fate, they were only saved because we took care of such orphans together we helped those kids."[123]

The women describe such examples of mutual assistance with appreciation and pride. The qualities demonstrated by the collective drawing praise are those traditionally expected of women: unity, devotion to others, and self-sacrifice. Two reports highlight the exceptional value placed on these traits. According to Irena Łopatniuk, "Relations between prisoners were good, there was great friendship and self-denial. We behaved one for all and all for one." In the same vein, a woman deported to a collective farm notes: "There was community between the Poles, one understood the other perfectly and helped each other. There was no selfishness or materialism."[124]

Similar praise for solidarity among Poles exists in men's documents. "All of Poland can be proud of these citizens, unyielding, and at every step emphasizing their Polishness," writes Czesław Bednarczyk. "Everyone lived harmoniously, helping each other."[125] Some men also employ the language of the family when describing communal life. In the internment camps, notes a farmer, "We all lived like brothers." A teacher from Słonim writes: "Poles in prisons and forced labor camps, with few exceptions, formed one great family, joined by a sincere patriotism, deep religiosity and mutual love." Tadeusz Jurczyk also characterizes the deportees on his *kolkhoz* as a united family.[126]

Men's documents, however, reveal a lack of unanimity on the issue. In striking contrast to those of women, they frequently report a lack of solidarity among the Poles. "We all lived by ourselves, like animals," writes Stanisław Lewicki.[127] Men complain that neither friendship nor cultural life existed among the Poles and characterize their mutual life instead with the words intrigue, suspicion, and malice. They recall fistfights and arguments in prison cells, on issues political and petty, and recount harassment and stealing by Polish criminals in the camps. "Personal relations were beneath criticism," writes Władysław Kryżanowski, explaining that everyone put their own interests first, never the good of the nation.[128] The majority of men spent their time in the Gulag, where a stricter regime prevailed than in the deportation settlements, and this situation may have caused greater fear of others and a tendency to withdraw into the self. But some men report the same of the settlements. "Relations among the deportees were not founded on complete respect of one family toward another, nor even of one person toward another," writes one man.[129] Men thus cast doubt on the cohesion of the Poles and suggest class-based antagonisms. Some men state that peasants and workers attacked members of the intelligentsia and denounced them to the NKVD. Others assert that small farmers were "Bolshevized."[130] Solidarity existed only within groups formed according to social class and occupation, such men claim, contradicting the picture of unity offered by most females.

When women report transgressions of Polish social norms, they appear to be perpetrated by non-Poles. Men, however, discuss individual Poles who acted disloyally to the nation and are seemingly unconstrained in revealing the existence of "bad" Poles in the community. They name Poles who joined the Red Army, became Communists, collaborated with the NKVD, criticized Poland, or took part in anti-Polish spectacles.[131] Józef Połcz recalls "meeting weak characters among the Poles" who "maybe from a desire to get a piece of bread" informed on others. In the internment camp, a POW relates, "a small group entered into the service of the NKVD, sullying the uniform of the Polish soldier, everything Polish." Similarly, Zygmunt Prędkiewicz maintains that NCOs did not stop believing in Poland: "I can't, however, say the same for officers of the Polish army, there were of course individuals who were outstandingly Polish, but unfortunately many so terribly lost heart that they tried to be complaisant to the Bolshevik authorities, so that it was embarrassing to watch."[132] Whereas women stress the selflessness and cohesion of the collective, men point out that the opposite often held true.

How to account for this significant gender difference in assessing relations among the Poles? Studies of survival in Nazi concentration camps have found a gender difference in the formation of networks of support, with females proving more active and males more isolated.[133] Though gender may have affected the tendency for individuals to form bonds with others, it is hard to imagine that the overall behavior of the Polish community could have been experienced so differently by males and females, particularly in the settlements where they lived together. It may be that just as women were more attached to the family, both in their daily existence and their identity, they were more bound to the idea of the nation as family. Because women viewed maintaining solidarity and morality as their responsibility, they may have needed to present their community as such, forgetting or marginalizing evidence to the contrary. Less invested in the notions of unity and selflessness, males apparently had an easier time seeing and reporting traitorous individuals, some of whom they may have seen as competitors. For men, the failures of others did not reflect on the individual recounting them; women may have felt differently. Strongly identified with the family and with others, women perhaps believed that the responsibility for upholding the reputation of these larger families rested on their shoulders, a perspective that would have influenced their efforts in that direction, as well as their perception and memory.

Just as the family was entrusted in the era of the partitions with the spiritual maintenance of the nation, so too did it embrace this mission in Soviet exile; as in the past, women led this work and reached out to compatriots to uphold their Polishness. Jerzy Świętochowski credits the "wives" on his *sovkhoz* with "protecting their Polishness from complete collapse."[134] Besides clandestinely educating children, they continued collective religious observance, shared Polish culture, and nurtured the hope of eventual liberation. Since the Soviet government persecuted individuals for engaging in these activities, maintaining Polish culture and faith also represented acts of resistance.

Poles made a point of observing religious holidays, especially Christmas and Easter, whether in settlements or camps. For these occasions the exiles endeavored to obtain special foods and gather to celebrate after work, usually with lookouts posted to warn of approaching authorities. They also held frequent group prayer sessions. Halina Blaszczakówna, deported to Northern Kazakhstan, writes: "We were forbidden to speak in our native language, but we didn't pay attention to that, we had gatherings of our own people, where we recited the rosary, prayers and liturgies together. . . . We did not want ever to accept that abnormal life." "We prayed together secretly, for we were forbidden to pray in groups," echoes Aurelia Karazinarczyk. "We didn't pay attention to that and prayed, because prayer was our entire comfort."[135] Continued practice of Catholicism was as critical to preserving the Polish spirit as maintaining Polish language and patriotism.

Against regulations, inmates staged cultural events in their cells and deportees gathered regularly to reaffirm their connections to Poland, sharing memories, information, and their cultural heritage. At nighttime, recalls Wanda Baczyńska, the Poles met "for political discussion, reading of newspapers, conversation, dreaming."[136] These meetings often took place in cemeteries and forests, away from the eyes and ears of local authorities who could throw such offenders into jail. A letter from home provided an occasion for gatherings to read and discuss its content. Deportees also read aloud any Polish books that they had managed to smuggle out with them, as one young woman recounts: "Each one of us managed to bring some kind of Polish book, which was read 100 times." If no such books were to be found, which was the rule in prison, Poles met to talk about books they had read, recite poetry from memory, or discuss films they had once seen. As one woman explains, "We gathered together after work in order to spend at least a couple of hours in our own company."[137]

Individuals sought solace, connection, and hope in these gatherings, much like they had in their immediate families back home. In the words of a woman from Przemyśl, "Our group of Poles (there were sixty of us) lived like one huge family—we helped each other and made each other feel better —we shared our worries and read letters from home together. Sometimes we all gathered together and then letters were read, prayers said, and we remembered those good times from long ago, for we lived solely on memories from the past." Many exiles credit these gatherings, this solidarity among compatriots, with their ability to withstand the ordeal. These extended families provided members with moral support and faith in the future, a religious and patriotic faith in the salvation of the Poles, and the rebirth of their state. "None of the Poles lost their spirit for even a moment," writes Zofia Chwialkowska, "All believed in one thing, that today or tomorrow this torture must stop, that the time would come when they would be freed from this captivity, that this 'special settlement' would end."[138] Countless women echo this sentiment, expressing a nearly unanimous attitude of religious faith and patriotic spirit.

Men frequently report something women rarely do: that some Poles were broken spiritually and morally. Reading men's documents one senses that the loss of hope, mental breakdown, and moral decline were not isolated exceptions, as women suggest. A "complete loss of morality occurred," states Adolf Sienkiewicz on the behavior of compatriots in the camp. "More than one would have given his soul for a piece of bread." They report high rates of depression, going mad, and suicide. Describing fellow countrymen as apathetic and completely broken, a village teacher asserts that "the Poles bore the camps much worse than Soviet prisoners."[139] Even more striking is the number of men admitting their own breakdowns. A small number of women report losing the will to live, typically following the death of their children, but they generally declare constant faith and hope. Many men, though, express the sentiment of Kazimierz Szpotowicz: "Each one of us understood that this is the grave of all hope." Male prisoners report being broken by interrogations and beatings. "The only dream I had in such moments was to obtain a needle, nail or pin and cut my veins," writes the former mayor of Nowo-Święciany. Reflecting on all that the Soviet regime had taken from him, Józef Bykowicz, an *osadnik,* writes: "They took all of my property—the earnings of a whole life. My wife and children were deported, to this day I don't know where they are, or if they remain alive. I'm afraid to think about it all, so that I don't lose my mind. I left that 'paradise' psychologically broken, in bad health, a cripple."[140]

Neither the accuracy of the seemingly greater spiritual and emotional strength of women nor the reason for the differences in reporting breakdowns can be ascertained. Women's reticence on such failures may again result from their traditional guardianship of the spiritual and moral health of the collective, be it the family or the nation. For them, Polishness embodied unity, selflessness, unwavering faith in God and nation; they bore the responsibility of upholding it and perhaps presented themselves and their communities as close to the ideal in order to hold on to their prescribed identity. Men may have felt freer to be candid on this issue because it was not integral to their identities or social roles. In that regard, the worst had already come to pass: their proven inability to defend home and fatherland, their complete subjugation to foreign enemies. Many reports of depression, suicide, and traitorous behavior come from the internment camps, from soldiers and officers dwelling on their defeat on the battlefield. Discussing widespread depression among the internees at Kozel'sk, one man writes: "The crowdedness, the military experience, thoughts about the Fatherland, and about one's relatives and the past, all caused nervous strain and impaired the health of virtually everyone in the camp." An internee in Starobel'sk describes a similar mood there: "Each of us still had before his eyes the family home and the tragic military defeat."[141]

Men generally concur with women that "great patriotism and Catholicism" form the basis of Polishness.[142] However, men are preoccupied with three attributes they consider critical to being a Pole, rarely articulated as such by females—refusing to be debased, fighting for the fatherland, and avenging the nation. One boy recounts stubbornly singing the Polish anthem on the transport so that surrounding people "would know that we are Poles and that we endured everything heroically." "Our Poles were mostly peasants," notes a man deported to the Arctic north, "fierce in their Polishness, and not allowing themselves to be disparaged or coerced in any way." Asserting that Poles prefer to die rather than submit to abasement, another deported man explains the belief that should their subjugation last long, they would have to "die in a Polish manner, in a soldierly manner."[143] These traits are not attributed only to soldiers or males but are presented as hallmarks of Polishness. In the words of Bazyli Bujalski, "All Poles, even the young, even eight-year-old children, displayed fortitude and resoluteness of the innate will." One man has this to say of female volunteers in the military: "These women were for the most part not skilled, very often barefoot, in rags. They lived 10–12 people in rooms of 4 x 3 meters. Despite everything, they worked extraordinarily, heroically." Describing the ambition of the Poles in his camp, a teacher pronounces the ultimate service to the fatherland: "To keep oneself alive at any cost, to endure everything, and after liberation, revenge!!!!"[144] In short, men highlight heroism and martyrdom for the nation, while females stress unity and sacrifice for others. Men and women accentuate different facets of being Polish that stem from their distinct social roles in the nation.

At the same time, women and men articulate some ungendered bonds to the nation. Women's reactions to the burial of relatives and compatriots in foreign soil reveal not only a spiritual but also a material connection to the Polish nation that they shared with men. The exiles longed not just for Poland as an abstraction but in very tangible terms. One woman recalls leaving a mandatory anti-Polish meeting in her settlement "thinking about Poland, the beloved Fatherland, of those Polish forests, hamlets, meadows, fields, mountains, and about our sea, that's all ours, Polish, it was and is the best, the most dear." In the minds of its adherents, Poland had a palpable existence, a plot of land marked off on the European continent, in which roots ran deep. In the words of Zofia Sicińska, "We were brutally taken from our homes, torn from the land, which is everything for a Pole, which he becomes rooted in, and which he can't live without." In her description of approaching the Polish-Soviet border, one woman expresses this deep attachment to the space conceived as Polish:

> I did not feel like speaking. The wheels rumbled mournfully. My mind was a blank, a dull vacancy. So it had happened. We were deported. Only then did I realize that it is far from being a matter of indifference where one dies and is buried. We gazed at the trees, the cottages and trees of Poland. It seemed that something was bound to happen, that to cross the frontier was a thing impossible, inhuman. Let them torture us to death, if only on our own soil.[145]

For these displaced persons, land itself had a nationality.

Individuals of both sexes expressed their connection to a common national history, which helped shape a sustaining identity as well as a collective hope for the future. Polish individuals often saw themselves as part of one family, sharing a drama that stretched back into history. As soldiers, often the grandsons and great-grandsons of Poles exiled to Siberia by Russian tsars throughout the nineteenth century, men easily fit themselves into the historical drama of the Polish nation. "Somewhere in the recesses of my brain arises the thought—just like our ancestors," one man recalls thinking as he was being deported. Women also claim a part of this legacy and repeatedly cast the journey eastward in a historical light, invoking the earlier banishment of Polish patriots. "We did not know where we were going," recollects one woman, "only when we were beyond the Urals did we understand that we were headed in the direction of Siberia, where many of our ancestors found death amid the taiga."[146]

For Poles, imprisonment or resettlement by the Soviet government represented much more than a personal calamity. All of the individual victims were linked by a shared destiny. One woman writes:

> The day 13 April was the day of my greatest tragedy, not because in one moment I lost everything, not because they didn't let me take a change of clothing with me, that had little meaning for me. Far worse was my despair, almost to the point of madness, as I got down on my knees and begged the chief of the NKVD to let me visit and bid farewell to my elderly and sick mother. The road to Siberia was difficult and it seemed that it might be without return, we were tracing the steps of our forefathers, who also were heroes exiled to Siberia for the cause of Poland.[147]

Her quick jump from her pain at being taken from her mother—an important symbol in the life of the nation—to the anguish she and others experienced at being torn from their fatherland, highlights that this was not just a personal, familial tragedy, but a national one. The victims cast the deportation of the Poles by the Soviet regime as a continuation of the historical drama of the Polish national family. This family included the descendants of those exiled by the tsars, even if they had never set foot on Polish soil. Mieczysław Krukowski describes such people: "In the very same place there were several families who, though having Soviet citizenship, nevertheless felt their polishness (sic) (they were the children, grandchildren and great-grandchildren of people exiled from Poland by the tsars)." The new exiles recount meeting Soviet Poles who treated them like long-lost relatives. One man encountered a Soviet Pole in prison who bemoaned "fate has sent even you to the Northern tundra, just like our fathers."[148]

Placing their own fate in this context, women largely accept the situation with quiet resignation. Though they did not actively seek this status, women too felt like martyrs for Poland. When the NKVD came for Renia Gręplowska, she recalls, "I understood that that is the fate of the Poles."[149] They believed that the upheaval resulted from God's will and that God would see them through the ordeal. Zofia Pająk demonstrates this conviction in her description of the calamity of the Soviet invasion and subsequent deportations:

Sorrow and despair gripped me, I knew that nothing would remedy this, it was necessary to accept fate. . . . We knew already in past historical times that our Fatherland was oppressed by enemies from the beginning; whenever it rose again some unexpected hurricane and some terrible wind again blew over our heads and again forced upon her the shackles of bondage, and our Poland endures suffering and torture and we do together with Her.[150]

The exiles not only saw themselves following the path of their Polish ancestors but that of Jesus Christ. Many Poles liken their ordeal to traveling the Golgotha road. "On the first day of the Resurrection of Christ," writes one woman of her evacuation from Russia, "we homeless Polish wanderers marched on to our own resurrection."[151] The traditional identification of Poland as the Christ of nations seemed to promise the resurrection, once again, of the Polish state.

For many individuals, this legacy, this group identity, provided meaning and even satisfaction, and enabled them to cope better. Janina Borak-Szyszko writes dramatically of her experience in prison:

My eyes were opened to a new, different, and unfamiliar world of baseness, cruelty, degradation—on the one hand, and nobility and heroism —on the other. The first type, who by the law of the fist imprisoned, tortured and murdered the very best and the youngest sons and daughters of martyred Poland; the others, who with dignity and heads held high, tread on the road along which for 150 years traveled each generation, a road which through sacrifice and blood leads to Siberia and hard labor. I was proud that I experienced, that I came into contact with, Polish reality, that I was a part of an unyielding whole.[152]

Sharing in the history of Poland was yet another way that women expressed a direct connection to the Polish nation, one unmediated by gender. It made them an integral part of the family of Poles.

Conclusion

When disaster struck the Poles in 1939, paralleling in its effect on the Polish state the previous calamity of the partitions, women had a ready-made legacy to guide them. They drew on traditional notions of womanhood and called upon history and religion to give meaning to their experience of exile and help them survive it. Women relied on the customs and mythology of the previous subjugation to face the new tragedy, to structure their daily lives in the USSR, to create a sense of order and identity in the midst of chaos, and to bolster their faith that just as the Polish nation emerged triumphant from the long years of foreign domination earlier, so would it again survive this painful episode. The nation thus offered women a means for survival.

For women, the most relevant and sustaining national myth proved to be that of the *Matka Polka*. The ideal of selfless and patriotic motherhood, a legacy of the years of partitioned Poland, during which Poles sought to keep the nation alive despite the loss of statehood, had remained the core of the ideology of womanhood, despite the broadening of women's activities in the interwar period. Motherhood was still the ultimate vocation for the Polish woman. Her greatest duty, attributed to biology, was to bear new Poles—the future of the nation. From this capacity presumably flowed her further duties: raising children and caring for the home. With the persistence of the ideal of woman as morally pure, in the image of the Holy Virgin, and close to the nation, she also remained the spiritual and patriotic educator of the nation. Seemingly backed by nature, religion, and history, this model gained new relevance for women in Soviet exile.

Despite the difficult conditions they faced, women devoted themselves to the welfare of family members, particularly the moral and patriotic health of children. While men's ultimate duty to the family and nation was to go off and fight for the fatherland, the daily welfare of the family was the primary concern of women. The ideals of patriotic motherhood applied to all females, setting standards for their relations with others in and beyond the home. Females viewed themselves (and were viewed by others) relationally: their connections and duties to others largely defined their own identities. Women sought to maintain their relationships and their roles in them, and in turn, such efforts enforced their sense of identity and belonging to the nation. For women, the good of the nation was typically served through others.

The qualities and duties assigned to the female in the family were transferred to ever-wider circles, to surrogate families, to the community, to the nation. Polish women related to the nation as to family, envisioning a large community whose members shared strong emotional bonds, a common history, language, religion, a joint destiny, and a tangible homeland. The sentiments of Maurycy Mochnacki, who wrote in the first decades of the nineteenth century, remained apt in the twentieth. Poland, he declared, "was more a people than a government, more a family than a country."[153] Women were expected to approach this family selflessly, fostering unity and morality —hallmarks of women's Polishness. Just as the immediate family was highly gendered, so too was the nation. Bound with running the public sphere, creating economic wealth, and, above all, sacrificing their lives to defend the fatherland, men received the highest authority and acclaim. While similarly based on patriotism and Catholicism, men's Polishness emphasized heroism, revenge, and a refusal to be debased.

The gendered nature of Polish national ideology is seen in the symbols invoked, both in the past and in the new calamity. The exiles longed for their homeland, always referred to as the fatherland. This image encompasses the material basis, the security and protection associated with males. Women seemed to need the fatherland just as they believed they needed their fathers and husbands, the army, and the government to support and protect them. The feminine counterpart to this masculine form of the nation, the *Matka Polka,* the mother of Poland, represents moral strength, devotion, and self-sacrifice. These gendered images of the nation parallel the gendered roles in the family.

Despite the force and comfort of the ideology governing women's indirect service to the nation, at times women manifested a direct relationship to it. Some females desired to serve the nation in the most traditionally masculine of ways—armed combat; they were prepared to sacrifice personal interests and even family to that end. Their bond to the nation was unmediated by their relationships with others. Women expressed their ties to the nation in other ways that had nothing to do with gender-specific roles or duties. Their deep connections to the land of Poland—the forests, fields, trees, even soil—and the history of its people represent further expressions of their membership in the Polish nation, a concept and a space that women shared with their male compatriots. The invocation of land and history in interpreting and surviving the experience of exile shows that both sexes did work within a common social framework and shared some notions about the physical and metaphorical meaning of the Polish nation, while at the same time they maintained bifurcated roles within it.

5

"Homeless in Her Own Body"

The Body and Sexuality

National identity provided a clear and poignant framework for women to understand and express their agony as unwilling laborers for the Soviet state and as mothers witnessing their children's loss of Polishness, or worse, of life. Connecting with the struggles of compatriots, past and present, with Catholic and Polish notions of sacrifice, women could take solace in suffering in the name of the fatherland. They used the nation as a neutral space where they could find meaning to articulate their hardships, which seemed to represent a fundamental aspect of being Polish. Shared tragedy rendered them Poles on par not only with their ancestors but also with men. Nationality thus provided a meaningful and comforting way to objectify some of the traumas the women endured in Soviet exile. Other violations affected women so specifically, however, that they could not talk about them in terms of the nation.[1]

The female body became a particular source of anguish, as women experienced both extreme physical abjection and the loss of boundaries[2] as a result of their conditions and treatment in exile. With painful clarity the women understood—and felt—that not only were the homeland and the home not inviolate but neither were their own bodies. This chapter examines women's responses to the physical hardships of exile, focusing on the socially defined image of the female body that served as a filter. The more gendered the indignities and assaults, the less relevant the category of the nation for discussing them. In other words, women found it relatively easy to discuss violations they could construe in national terms, particularly those that they shared with men. Transgressions of social norms regarding the female body, however, seemed impermissible in the traditional story of the martyred nation, and, therefore, were largely silenced.

Polish Victims

Much of the adversity the Poles faced stemmed from deplorable living conditions: overcrowding, hunger and thirst, frostbite or suffocation, exhaustion and disease. Women write freely about such problems that plagued the body in the most basic ways, affecting females and male alike. They vividly depict both the effects of these circumstances on their bodies and their efforts to cope with them. Discussing these hardships as crimes perpetrated by Soviet officials, the women appear unrestrained in speaking out and expressing their pain. It is the suffering of the Poles.

The exiles saw the Soviet regime as the source of their agony and felt its agents missed no opportunity to intensify it. The statements and memoirs frequently report the denial of medical attention to the Poles. Commandants and collective farm chairmen refused to grant even brief absences from work to visit a doctor or to care for a sick relative. Deportees report vainly begging local officials to transport them to the nearest hospital, which often lay hundreds of kilometers away. Zuzanna Nowosielska devotes her entire testimony to an accident that befell her son at work; the authorities would neither provide him transportation nor allow her to leave her job to help him.[3] Nowosielska tells the story of her son's accident "only to show how they treated us." Like many deportees, she asserts that Soviet officials deliberately treated the Poles worse than others. One woman writes that nearly a hundred Poles died within eight months in her settlement, among them three of her sisters; they were told the hospitals had no room for Poles. Reportedly, the pleas of Poles for assistance met with only contempt. When Irena Sroka tried to get help for her dying mother, the authorities laughed at her and said they had no need for Poles—there was more than enough land for their graves. Similarly, Jadwiga-Helena Szymkowska recalls that when accidents occurred among the deportees in her settlement, those in charge merely hissed, "*Poliak*—let her die."[4]

Many exiles perished well before the evacuations in 1942. The exact number may never be established because of inadequate documentation. Corpses of infants were simply thrown from the windows of the transports as they moved eastward from Poland. Relatives received no word about the fate of sick persons removed from the trains. In the settlements, deportees typically buried family members themselves, without the attention or assistance of local authorities. After the amnesty, when huge numbers of Polish citizens flocked to the southern part of the USSR, the death rate soared. The amassing of people in places unprepared to receive them took a great toll on individuals already weakened from months and years of hard labor in harsh environments, and epidemics claimed many lives, particularly among the young and the elderly. The original estimates of nearly one million deportees suggested double-digit mortality rates. The Polish government-in-exile calculated the mortality of its citizens as of 1942 at approximately 20 percent. Stressing the incompleteness of the data, researchers relying on Soviet documentation note that as of mid-1941, the NKVD estimated the mortality rate among the *osadnicy* (first deportation) at 7.4 percent and among the refugees (third deportation) at 2.3 percent. Many scholars consider 8 to 10 percent a reasonable estimate of the death rate among the deportees.[5] Research on the labor camps shows that the overall death rate in the Gulag was 6.7 percent in 1941, shooting up to 17.6 percent in 1942.[6]

Anecdotal evidence provides a startling picture. In Zofia Bukowica-Lipska's settlement of 450 families in Kazakhstan, 180 people died; she calculates a death rate of 50–60 percent among the children, a statistic that included her own son. Irena Czekałowska worked in a hospital at Poldnevitsa, where "tens of people died daily," making the settlement a "valley of death." "The children died like flies," writes Helena Pawłowska, using a phrase that repeatedly occurs in the documents: "Every few weeks someone among the Poles died. On 15 December 1941 I lost my son, he died as the result of complications from measles and diphtheria. The child died without any medical care, as there was no such thing."[7] The Ognowski family lost five children. In the Ropelewski family, the father, six sons, and two daughters perished from disease, exhaustion, and hunger. A widow deported with her five children was left with one daughter. Janina Sobelewska, deported at age fourteen, writes bluntly that her family died. While in the USSR she lost her mother, three sisters, and her grandfather; she was evacuated to Persia with her oldest sister, but, she concludes, "There my sister died and I was left alone."[8]

Some of the privations the Poles endured stemmed from the poverty and stark conditions of the locales in which they lived, exacerbated after June 1941 by the war being waged with Germany. Of course, it was Soviet authorities who chose to transport the Poles to some of the more inhospitable regions of the USSR. The harsh reactions to expressions of need intensified the suffering of the Poles and seemed to reveal a vindictive attitude toward them. Most important, though other national groups endured similar hardships under the Stalinist regime, the exiles understood that it was their connection to the Polish nation that caused them to be forcibly taken from their homes and subjected to such misery. Soviet citizens continually underscored this perception. "Polish lords" and "Polish dogs" became stock phrases in official and popular usage. Many exiles felt that they received harder work assignments and lower food rations precisely because of their nationality. As one woman declares in recounting her miserable existence on a collective farm, "the fact that I am a Pole was enough to sentence me and other deportees like me to living conditions comparable to slow starvation."[9]

The conduct of NKVD interrogators provided Poles the clearest evidence of the effort to inflict pain on their nation; it did not matter that the Stalinist regime treated those it considered its enemies, regardless of national origins, in the same manner. The NKVD largely viewed the Poles as foes because of their Polishness and all the qualities Soviet ideology ascribed to it: an aristocratic or bourgeois nature, national chauvinism, religious devotion, and opposition to Soviet Communism. Thus, allegiance to the Polish nation alone signaled to the Soviet government and its agents a real or potential enemy; in the paranoia of the Stalinist years, the distinction was irrelevant. "The NKVD saw a counterrevolutionary in each Polish man and Polish woman," explains a thirty-one-year-old teacher, arrested as a "dangerous element."[10] During interrogations, the officers fired streams of insults at them, including "Polish pig" and "Polish whore."[11] In the documents, women use the details of these interrogations, as those of the living conditions, to underline the current tragedy of the Polish nation.

Interrogations, as a rule, took place at night. "The NKVD most often operates under the cover of night," writes a Pole arrested for applying to return to the German partition of Poland, "They strike unexpectedly at the victims, surprising them. It's easier for them to act on and influence weary and sleepy people."[12] Frequently interrogations lasted ten to twelve hours at a time; in the pattern of the infamous "conveyer belt", these sessions would be repeated for days, even weeks, on end. Helena Ostrowska endured thirty-two nighttime interrogations, throughout which she was forced to stand. Wanda Rapiejko was insulted and beaten during sessions repeated daily for five weeks.[13] In a calculated manner, the drawn-out process wore the prisoners down. Some inmates were transported for questioning to distant locations in cargo trucks, in which they had to lie face down; prisoners awaiting interrogation could spend several hours in small rooms resembling closets. When finally summoned, they had to walk through long corridors to the appointed room. Once the session began, the interrogator might ask a few questions, send the prisoner back to her cell, then haul her in for more later. Bronisława Dziedziecka notes that this maltreatment served to keep the prisoner "in constant tension, nervousness, from the lack of sleep and exhaustion."[14]

The NKVD did not stop there but routinely employed violence, as well. The same techniques are reported again and again. NKVD agents apparently preferred to hit women in the face, using their hands, a rubber truncheon, or the butt of a revolver. They grabbed them by the hair and repeatedly slammed their heads against the walls, causing some of the women lasting damage, including the loss of teeth, vision, and hearing.[15] Interrogators frequently whacked their victims' fingers and hands; women report having their arms twisted and their legs repeatedly kicked. Often the women were ordered either to sit on the edge of a chair or to stand for the entire night; if they got up from the chair, or fell down, they were struck.[16] A few women report the use of electric shock.[17]

A common punishment was confinement in the so-called *kartser*, which might be translated as "cooler." This was a particularly severe basement cell, empty, very cold, frequently with its floor under water; in some cases rotting food or human excrement covered the floor. The prisoner was usually ordered to remove her clothing—although some women report being allowed to keep their shirts on. Janina Bohdzewicz, designated a dangerous element because she led a scout troop, writes: "We were . . . starved and held in cold, so-called *kartsers* or 'kartsers with water' (they say that these *kartsers* were more modern!). There usually you were undressed and either soaked or had your feet kept in cold water. . . ." Such confinement could last for several days, often without any provision of food or drink or opportunity to go to the toilet. Aniela Pawliszak, who was eighteen when arrested, was taken to such a cell and left there, the first time, for fourteen hours, without food or water; her second confinement lasted five days.[18] Women report falling gravely ill from this treatment. A teenager became so sick after confinement in the *kartser* that she was unable to stand for two months; Maria Hojak, pregnant at the time of her arrest, lost her fetus.[19]

Following interrogation or detention in the *kartser*, the victims were dumped back in their cells, often unconscious, febrile, or bleeding profusely. They received no medical care, so cellmates did their best to make the victims comfortable. Despite the shortage of space in the cells, inmates typically made room for those who had been beaten to lie down and tried to console them. Many women write of their horror at seeing damaged bodies brought back to the cells in the mornings, some of whom had been beaten in an inhuman way.[20] Janina Hobler recalls that "the blood froze in their veins" when they saw women return from being tortured and heard of their ordeals. In one cell, the inmates cried upon seeing a gray-haired woman return from her interrogation covered with blood. The beaten woman's response, recounted by Jadwiga Cwikowska, reveals an attitude commonly expressed by the Poles: "And that woman, seeing us crying, smiled, saying, 'It's nothing children, it's for the Fatherland,' her words sounded in my ears throughout the entire time of my investigation." Another exile notes: "Our Poland endures suffering and torture and we do along with Her."[21]

Like many others, these women downplay bodily pain. They boast of their ability to withstand physical pain and their refusal to cry in front of the perpetrators, expressing a view of suffering as ennobling and even necessary for a higher goal—here, an independent and sovereign Polish nation. In so doing, they appropriate the partition-era ideal of sacrificing oneself on the "altar of the Fatherland." Traditionally a male-gendered notion of sacrifice, it required men to give up their lives fighting for independence; women would bear and raise sons to continue the struggle. Claiming their own physical suffering to fall within the male tradition, the women effectively degender the masculine notion of sacrifice and patriotic devotion. Configuring their suffering this way renders it equal to men's. The women see themselves simply as Poles, martyrs for the fatherland.

This spirit holds true not just for those beaten by the NKVD. The nation provided women a framework for understanding and articulating physical pain and violence they shared with male compatriots—when they were starved, left to the mercy of the elements, refused medical care, or physically abused. Such privations and assaults can be called generic or ungendered—they affected women as physical beings but not explicitly female ones; the salient factor of their social identity explaining their plight was nationality. Being hungry or cold, or enduring a beating, did not elicit shame. Nor did it compromise a woman's sense of self as a Pole. Indeed, as the gray-haired woman quoted above suggests, for many exiles pain only strengthened national identity and the resolve to maintain it. Speaking of their misery, women could clearly externalize the responsibility for their injuries: the culprits were Soviets (regarded essentially as Russians), whether in the capacity of government official, prison warden, NKVD agent, collective farm chairman, or neighbor. The wretched living conditions and brutal treatment, as well as their agonizing consequences, reflected not on the victims but on the perpetrators. Themselves blameless victims, women openly discussed their mistreatment as Poles. In connecting them to the history and traditions of their martyred nation, such disclosures bolstered the individual's identity as a Pole. They also presented Soviet rule as criminal, executed by a people "disgusting and barbarous."[22]

Cleanliness

Not all problems connected with the body could be externalized, despite the context of national oppression. Some circumstances of exile left the body in a state that violated *social* requirements and expectations, thus injuring the individual's identity. The meaning associated with a particular situation could cause intense suffering, which sometimes equaled or even exceeded the physical discomfort involved. In some cases, the body was not even touched and yet was the source of great distress because the context compromised the individual's sense of self. Cultural notions about the proper deportment, condition, and treatment of the physical body, particularly the female one, create a social aspect to the body, the violation of which can be as dangerous to the individual as direct physical injury.

To introduce the complex problems associated with the female body as a social construct, the issue of cleanliness will be first examined. Though personal hygiene is another generic hardship in exile, it represents a transitional category, for it is at once a physical and social matter. Its effects have as much to do with health as with identity. With considerable detail and repetitiveness, the documents depict the horrible sanitary conditions in which the exiles were forced to live and the resulting anguish. While the filth that surrounded the women and the dirt and vermin that adhered to their bodies did not necessarily affect their sense of self as women, it did compromise their identity in other ways. Attitudes toward cleanliness reveal the cultural mediation of the relationship to one's body.

Sanitary conditions grew particularly bad in prison cells, dominated as they were by overcrowding and a lack of ventilation. In the best case, inmates were taken to the toilet one or two times per day, more typically only once every several days; some women report that they were not taken out for an entire month at a time.[23] In the meanwhile, they shared a *parashka*, a latrine pail, to relieve themselves. Bogusława Ptaszyńska relates that her crowded cell contained only one such bucket, which was not emptied daily, causing a constant stench. According to another woman, the cell became a virtual hell as the women developed diarrhea from the poor food.[24] The cells lacked running water, as did the crowded barracks in the Gulag. Though access to locations designated for satisfying physiological needs was better in the camps, these facilities were usually rudimentary latrines dug in the ground. The settlements also lacked toilets. "The conditions were worse then anything one imagines," writes a woman deported to Kazakhstan. "I simply could not have imagined, back in Poland, that it was possible to live in such conditions. It wasn't life, it was torture." Like many others, she reports living in a filthy mud hut "in which no kind of vermin was lacking."[25] Due to the rare opportunities to bathe or even to change clothing, as well as the dearth of soap, most exiles found lice and bedbugs unavoidable, often from the first days on the transports.

Vermin caused particular agony for prisoners. The inmates' clothing periodically underwent disinfection but reportedly came back with more lice than before. Some women describe the cell walls as red with blood from bedbugs. Prisoners spent hours each day picking off lice, sometimes in their boredom—for they were not permitted other activities—counting who could kill the most. Maria Idzikowska states that the lice and bedbugs made life hellish, but picking them off provided the only diversion in prison.[26] Women have trouble discussing their infestations. One prisoner notes that it was so disgusting that she cannot recall it without trembling. Summing up the environment in which they lived, Maria Pieszczek states, "The lack of air, overcrowding, the lack of water, soap, lice which attacked us in masses, all tortured us tremendously."[27]

Given these abysmal sanitary conditions, the issue of personal hygiene became an obsession for the exiled women, particularly those incarcerated. Many top their lists of the horrors of prison life with the infrequency of bathing and lack of soap and clean underclothing.[28] They state that prison officials, out of spite, made it extremely difficult for them to wash. Allowed to clean only their hands and faces, prisoners were punished if they attempted more; in some cases the entire cell faced reprisal if one was caught. "Once a day we were given a cup of hot water. You could drink it, but God forbid that you should wash yourself with that amount of water," relates one woman. "There were those who performed miracles: with one-quarter liter of water they washed themselves from head to toe."[29] The dilemma of the daily cup of water—to drink it or wash with it—comes up frequently in the testimonies of the women, who were accustomed to certain regimens and levels of cleanliness that they associated with home.

Accumulated dirt was a source of discomfort and potential disease. But the problem of washing also constituted an affront to personal identity, for it entailed an infringement of the private space in which cleansing, particularly intimate cleansing, takes place. The work of Georges Vigarello has demonstrated that a prime feature of modern cleanliness, beginning in the late nineteenth century, is its association with the private space.[30] Though he placed particular emphasis on the physical space in which it occurs, there is also a metaphorical aspect to this space: the autonomy expected in the relationship to one's own body. Polish women's obsession with cleanliness can be seen as a way to maintain their private sphere, the inviolable space understood to be connected with the body, which represented a key means of holding onto individuality in extremely dehumanizing conditions. Insistence on maintaining cleanliness represents a form of covert resistance in that it kept the enemy from invading and eroding private space; it preserved the individual's relationship with herself.

Washing was intricately linked with the women's identity in another critical way, for as "rituals of demarcation, [it] had a personal as well as a political significance."[31] Vigarello details the transition in Western societies from concern with purely visible dirt to the "pursuit of the microbe." Since this new notion of hygiene aimed at "invisible" cleanliness, it "bolstered a vigilance which was primarily social." Cleanliness, he writes, "did not only increase resistance, it assured order. It added to the virtues."[32] According to Alain Corbin, "The recognized influence of the physical on the moral bestowed value on cleanliness and neatness. . . . People shunned organic wastes, which reminded them of animality, sin and death."[33] In the modern world, cleanliness became moral, a sign of advancement with class, race, and national biases. Since washing was perceived to involve a civilizing process, continuing this practice—despite difficult conditions and the impediments posed by their captors—kept the women, in their minds, apart from mere animals. Eugenia Francuz notes that at the end of a two-month train journey, without access to soap and water, "all the people were like animals." "My friends and I often thought that it would have been better for us in Russia if we were not people," concludes another woman, "as the pigs were regularly fed, often given even bread and tea, and when we were given a little warm water we didn't know what to do with it, wash ourselves or drink it."[34]

Stressing the importance of cleanliness to the individuals of their group, some Polish women assert that this defined them as a collective. Jadwiga Świtalska, who served time in six different prisons, writes, "In each prison there was a lack of water and washing was made very difficult and they always called us 'Polish prigs' [czyściochy polskie]." Some women felt their cleanliness distinguished them from other nationalities. A woman deported to a state farm in Siberia notes that after one trip to the local bath she promised herself she would never go again: the locals were so dirty that they infested the newcomers with lice. She preferred using the nearby canal instead.[35] Women stress that they could not get used to conditions they found revolting, or that others felt at home in them. For many Poles, the dirt and bugs symbolized a perceived Soviet lack of culture. Cleanliness became a code for social status and was linked in the minds of Polish females with their Western, civilized, and superior identity. One Pole describes the Sunday ritual for the locals as picking lice from each other and killing them while sitting at the dinner table, using the same knife to then cut bread. She concludes dryly: "This is what appears to be hygiene, and even 'high culture' to the 'Soviet Union.'"[36]

Allied as it is in many Western cultures with moral and intellectual progress, cleanliness, or its lack, frequently becomes a way to characterize and denigrate entire groups. In contrast to the assignment of levels of cleanliness along national lines as these Poles do, a German woman imprisoned in the Gulag, who bore much sympathy for the Russians, offers a completely different distinction. "None of us had the strength to wash," she writes. "That means something for women, and particularly for Politicals, as most of us were."[37] This woman, a Communist, had little concern for national distinctions but did perceive a large gulf between herself, as a political prisoner, and the common criminals in the camp. Cleanliness served as a way to separate this woman's community along lines meaningful to her.

While some individuals maintain that the inability to wash proved especially onerous for women, the issue was not specific to female identity. Cleanliness constituted a generic problem; it affected individuals of both sexes, and men also object to the deplorable hygienic conditions.[38] Unlike the privations discussed earlier, such as hunger and cold, which were connected primarily with the physiological functioning of the body, this issue could not be entirely externalized. Certainly the exiled Poles blamed Soviet authorities for hindering their efforts to remain clean, but the consequences —the dirt, the stench, the vermin—literally and metaphorically tainted the body. The unwashed body is generally stigmatized because of the social meaning attached to cleanliness. The link in the modern Western mind of washing with privacy implies that the sanctity and autonomy of the individual impeded in maintaining his or her desired level of cleanliness are challenged. Furthermore, since cleaning is understood as an indicator of moral and cultural advancement, as a mark of civilization, the unclean body is suspect and inferior. Thus, not only did the inability to wash make the exiles' bodies uncomfortable and vulnerable to disease, it also compromised the identity of the individual as a civilized, Western, superior being. The exiles' efforts to maintain personal hygiene served to resist this degradation.

In reports by Polish men, the connection between cleanliness and personal autonomy receives particular emphasis. Though they prove similarly upset about the filth and the vermin, their descriptions contain subtle differences. Men are much less likely to elaborate on their feelings about the conditions or the meaning they held for them, focusing instead on factual information (the number of times they were taken to bathe, the amount of time allotted to it). Additionally, males noticeably refrain from making comparisons with individuals of other nationalities; they neither suggest that cleanliness was unimportant to others nor label it a Polish trait. In this way, the issue appears less tied up with the men's national identity than it does for women. Instead, men highlight the power relationship, expressing anger that they were *not allowed* to wash in their cells, that they were not given soap, that they were herded into bathrooms in huge numbers for only several minutes, rendering washing impossible. Through these complaints they impart a sense of being toyed with; the obstacles placed in front of maintaining personal hygiene were about diminution, the restriction of autonomy. Teodor Dobrowolski, for example, states that some prison functionaries "amused themselves" by sending large numbers of inmates to the toilet for a few brief moments, then "tore them away and pushed them into the corridor, not always allowing them to turn on the water and wash their hands."[39] The reader senses that rendering the men powerless in this intimate matter compromised male identity. It seems to have mattered to them more as male beings than as Polish or Western ones; the indignity stems less from the condition of their bodies than from their lack of control over them. For both sexes, the issue of cleanliness affected much more than the physical body; it touched the social body, as well.

Female Victims

Polish women encountered other situations that caused or intensified their distress because of the social meaning of the body. Their suffering diverged from men's as they endured gender-based indignities and assaults. Some of the gendered problems concerned the female body exclusively. More important for this analysis, they involved violations of the social norms attached to the female body. These norms take sexual difference as their starting point for prescribing and proscribing behavior along sexually differentiated lines, investing the body with social meaning and expectations that give the individual identity. The physical body need not be damaged nor even touched to cause agony; in many cases, severe injury is inflicted on female identity, which, though related to physical characteristics, is based on cultural interpretations of them.

The female body proved highly problematic for the exiled women, as their sexuality became a weapon in the hands of men with authority, a tool with which to humiliate and control them. This category of offenses, which victimized the women as females, encompasses a range of situations and conduct. In the ensuing discussion, the offenses are separated into three types, on an ascending scale of violence to the individual: mixing, invasion, and sexual exploitation. As the violence of the offense increased, so did the woman's level of internalization and tendency to take refuge in silence. Additionally, the nation increasingly lost its relevance as a way for women to understand and articulate their suffering. These injuries to the female body and identity robbed them of the words to name them and to express their full impact.

Mixing

The problem of the female body most frequently arises in women's testimonies in expressions of shock and disgust that women and men were not physically separated at times presumed proper and necessary—a phenomenon referred to herein as mixing. Simply put, in the USSR women and men were brought together in places, proximity, and at times that Polish women considered outrageous violations both of their human dignity and of nature itself.[40]

Mixing began with the very journey to the USSR, in the packed train cars, and often continued in prison cells and barracks. The regularity with which arrested women note, even in the briefest accounts, that they were initially confined in cells together with men, suggests the agony this circumstance caused them. "I was taken to prison and crammed into a cell with one hundred men," one woman indignantly states.[41] Another writes that in the first prison in which she was held, forty people were packed into a cell for ten, "women, men and children all together." She adds that her misery lessened in the next prison, where "the conditions were so much better, the cells were only for women and children." This separation seemed to restore a small measure of normality to a very chaotic and distressing situation. Leokadia Pelipczek echoes this assessment. "Conditions in prison were terrible," she writes. "For two months men and women sat together in one cell sixteen meters squared, altogether there were ninety people. . . . Only after two months was I transferred to another prison in Brześć where men were already separated from women." Polish men, too, found such mixing scandalous, as the following comment suggests: "It's enough that they threw into a women's cell a man in rags, who sat with the women for two weeks, and the prison officials didn't react to it at all."[42]

Some women include only the fact of this mixing in recollections of the cells. Many others include it in their list of distressing conditions, such as intense heat or cold, lack of air, lice and bedbugs, severe overcrowding, and a foul stench. This list merits pondering. The body experiences literal discomfort and pain from these plagues; it is completely unaffected by the mixing. Furthermore, the fact that the men included in the cells were fellow Poles, sometimes even acquaintances, did not make their presence any easier for the women to bear. In this close and intimate setting, the presence of men only violated the women's dignity and increased their shame; the documents convey no indication that the proximity of their men lent the women a degree of moral support or protection against the common oppressors.

Mixing was also a problem in free exile. The daughter of a forester notes, "The lack of space meant that women and girls had to sleep together with men." A farmer from the Wilno region thus describes her barracks: "men and women together in terrible crowdedness." Similarly, a postal clerk documents her cell-like barracks, which housed "six to eight families, men, women and children altogether."[43] Young women sent away on temporary work assignments, and their relatives, voice a common complaint about their quarters. Irena Król states that she was sent off to float timber and had to sleep in a tent with boys; because of that she did not undress at night, and quickly got lice.[44] The latter detail reinforces the unclean and improper nature of the mixed accommodations. Typically, they do not recall any specific incidents stemming from these living arrangements. The simple description of the situation expresses its indignity. The frequency of the complaint points to the violation the women felt and suggests a pronounced sense of modesty and even shame accompanying the female body, a body expected to be hidden from the public—particularly male—gaze.

Distress increased with the humiliation accompanying bodily needs and functions, especially on the transports. "All physiological matters had to be done in the open in the car in spite of a mixed company it couldn't be helped," writes Stefania Ulanowska. A hole in the floor functioned as the toilet. Some deportees report that when they were let out of the trains to relieve themselves, the situation proved little better: "When they let us get out for a moment for our needs, it wasn't possible to go a little further off, only close to the car and that's men and women together, and a soldier guarded."[45] The problem did not cease with the eastward journey. In some prisons, women were allowed to use the toilets only under the watchful eyes of male guards. Special settlers frequently found either no enclosed spaces for eliminating bodily waste or ones that were not separated by sex. The problem loomed large at the worksites. "Going to the toilet during work was disapproved of or even forbidden," writes a laboratory nurse forced to work in the fields. "We were not permitted to move even half a meter to some bushes, and had to take care of our needs in the eyes of the guard."[46]

In their testimonies, most women merely state these uncomfortable facts, without expressing their reactions.[47] A few, though, try to convey the anguish they felt. A teacher from Kraków writes: "At the stations or anywhere the train stopped we had to jump down from the high cars and, under the guard of the soldiers, crawl under the cars—everyone together, women, men and children. There was no shame. A person became an animal relieving the unavoidable bodily needs." What here elevates humans above animals? Mindfulness of the necessary separation of the sexes and a sense of shame in relation to the body. Jadwiga Jeleniewrza describes the same ordeal: "This occurred in the light of day, at the station, under your own car, in the eyes of the masses passing by and of the Soviet soldiers, everyone all together—women, men, the old, and the young. Many people fell seriously ill from this." A male deportee, similarly recounting how "women, children and men" had to relieve themselves alongside the train, comments: "In that way we began to appreciate what a 'great culture' exists in Russia."[48]

Part of the injury stemmed from the invasion of the private space and violation of personal autonomy connected with the body. But the women were not disturbed only by the lack of proper facilities or even the lack of privacy per se. None writes of feeling shame that unfamiliar women, foreign or not, observed them urinating, but they repeatedly underline that they had to take care of these needs in front of members of the *opposite sex*. This exposed their bodies and physiological functions in a way that they found highly uncomfortable and offensive to their notions of modesty. In Polish Catholic culture, as in many others, the burden of hiding the body weighed more on women than on men.[49]

Males also note the mixing of the sexes in exile, confirming that while the unaccustomed situation disturbed them, it was especially painful for females. "Each of us, and especially women and girls, were tormented," writes one man about the lack of privacy in the train cars.[50] When describing the mixed transports, men object more to the dismal conditions imposed on them and the domination they symbolized than to the exposure of their bodies to females present. Men are troubled by the fact that they were not allowed out of the cars, that they had to use a hole in the floor, throw their excrement out the window, or sit in filth. They do not report encountering guards of the opposite sex in the toilets. The documents analyzed contain only one male testimony complaining about having to relieve himself in front of open doors, in view of a guard. This prisoner emphasizes that the man watching him held a bayonet. Similarly, Polish men taken by ship to camps in the Far East complain that they could not go to the toilet because criminals attacked them.[51] Men's humiliation stems not so much from shame of the body but from the loss of power. The overflowing *parashka*, in which inmates were forced to relieve themselves all day, became emblematic of their situation. It testified, one man writes, to "the culture and freedom that the Red Army brought to the nation oppressed by 'lordly Poland.'"[52]

The language used in men's reports also suggests that shame played a lesser role in their reactions than in women's. Men seem less bothered by the details of their bodies and relatively unhampered in naming body parts, functions, and by-products. Their reports contain words and descriptions more graphic than anything in the women's writing. A doctor, age fifty-two, describes the "accumulation of excrement" which flowed down the walls of the prison toilet from the floor above: "The drains and floors of the toilet were covered with human feces and urine, we literally were up to our ankles in urine mixed with water." "We had to relieve ourselves right on the floor," writes Józef Sołczyński, "The strongest ones were on the sleeping boards, those sick with dysentery and the weak ones were dying on the floor in feces."[53] While women tend to convey the horrible conditions in their cells by noting the foul stench or frequency of fainting, men write more directly, describing latrine pails overflowing with feces and urine. They recall relieving themselves in their pants, boots, or food bowls, stressing that they were reduced to relieving themselves in inappropriate places.[54] As with the issue of washing, the loss of mastery presented the greatest problem.

Women found bathing facilities especially tormenting. They initially felt great joy at the prospect of a bath, particularly after spending several weeks locked in train cars. Irena Zmudzińska, a student from Lwów, relates: "At one station a pleasant surprise awaited us, as we were taken to the bath. With great relief I washed the huge amount of dirt from my body." Their initial joy, however, turned to horror and shame, for, as Zmudzińska states, there was something strange and unpleasant about the bath, something that the exiled women encountered throughout the USSR. "Whoever goes through such a bath for the first time suffers a great deal," explains

Eugenia Schmidt. "Inside the rooms, where you had to undress and bathe under a shower, was a male staff. The bath took place in their presence." "We had to strip and hand over our apparel to be steamed," recounts another woman. "We then had to approach the soldiers and receive from them a ridiculously small piece of soap, and after having washed, return to receive a towel and prison underlinen which was supposed to have been washed, and was handed to us one piece at a time." A librarian offers a vivid account of her first trip to a Soviet bath:

> Long ago, when I was a child, a little girl, I fantasized, I tried to imagine everything that I heard. I heard about heaven and hell. A strange thing, when I entered the "bania" [bath] I saw hell, just as I had imagined it in my girlhood. Hot, steaming streams of water, turned on briefly by the men attending the bathhouse—tens, maybe even hundreds of naked women—the water steaming, men screaming, "Faster, Faster!"[55]

According to many accounts, Russian men frequently walked in on bathing women, under the pretext of turning the faucets on or off, checking the stove, collecting clothes for disinfection, or preventing escapes. Some women consider these moments among their worst in the USSR.[56]

This experience aroused some of the greatest anger expressed by Polish women toward the Soviets. "What could we do in the face of this one more humiliation?" asks a teacher incarcerated at the labor camp Iaia. "Contempt was our sole defense. Passing naked down the long corridor we looked at the men with their horrid smiles as if they were many pieces of wood, until little by little they left off smiling." Anna Cieslikowska describes the self-control the ordeal required: "You had to overcome your embarrassment and humiliation, clench your teeth and control yourself in order to calmly bear the coarse jibes and not spit in those hideous faces, or not punch them between their eyes." She recalls having to wait, naked, while her clothes were disinfected:

> That waiting was the worst, as the whole band of dirty Russians [Moskale] attending the bath walked about the room, our escort guards also came in, under the pretext of watching so that none of us escaped. I don't know where I got so much strength to calmly bear all the humiliation. I was half conscious from the helpless rage. I felt that if one of those scoundrels approached me, I would douse him with boiling water or strangle him with my own hands.[57]

Though women often write that they bore the trials of exile with silence and fortitude, the situation in the baths unusually provoked them. Many of them screamed and protested. One woman states that the "disgusting treatment" by the men in the bath "was the last straw that breaks the camel's back." She continues: "We rebelled and made such an uproar that the men had to be withdrawn." An office worker from Warsaw recalls that after her first time in such a bath, she and the other women began a hunger strike to force the director to address their complaint. Typically, nothing came of the women's actions. "Protests did not help," writes one woman. "Protesting, I was pushed in my clothes under a stream of water."[58]

In contrast to the general tendency among the exiled women to strike out or resist in some way for the benefit of others, mixing in the baths represents one of the few circumstances impelling individual women to protest on their own behalf. Though physically unhurt, the exposure of their bodies to the eyes and jeers of Soviet men caused emotional pain, for mixing in the baths was understood as the ultimate humiliation. Having been taken from their homes and loved ones, deprived of their material possessions, the body represented the final frontier; it was all that the women still possessed, the last space of privacy and individuality. Leaving these women naked, Soviet actions reduced them to defenseless bodies, subject to the penetrating gaze of strange and hostile men.[59] Under male surveillance, the women became mere objects. Expressing outrage served to reject that status, to reclaim the right to privacy and to their bodies, to their identity as individuals and as a collective of females.

The strength of their reaction partly stemmed from the attempted deprivation of autonomy and individuality; in this sense the offense is a generic one. But gender plays a critical role. Private life, Gérard Vincent has suggested, can best be understood as "the range of the inarticulate"—the secret.[60] As for privacy regarding the body, it is precisely those parts of the anatomy that constitute physical sexual difference and serve as the basis of social distinctions of the same, that are considered private, and which individuals seek to protect from the intrusive gaze of strangers, above all, those of the *opposite sex*. That which most clearly announces one's sex, which reveals the individual as a sexual being, is considered above all else the person's own, and the most necessary to hide from others. The need to conceal these body parts and functions is deemed greatest for women, who are traditionally regarded as different from the male norm, their bodies viewed as the "other."

Before the war, Polish Catholic women continually received reminders of the necessity of covering their bodies. Throughout the interwar period, the Catholic monthly *Rycerz Niepokolanej* (*The Knight of the Virgin Mary*), by far the most popular journal in Poland, placed the burden of chaste deportment, seen as crucial to the health of the family and the nation, on females. Catholic writers denounced short skirts, thin fabric, low-cut or sleeveless blouses, skin-colored stockings, and short hair—anything, that is, that revealed or highlighted the contours or skin of the female body.[61] Immodest dressing, they cautioned, would cause females to lose respect and could harm the health of family and nation.[62] It was the duty of females to "defend virtue, faith and noble-minded influence on public and private decency."[63]

The exposure of the exiled women's most private parts to members of the opposite sex called attention not only to their nakedness and defenselessness but also to their femaleness, in a carnal sense, causing both shame and anger. The relative anonymity of the women in this setting enabled them to protest. Solidarity among the women made resistance possible because the group offered support and encouragement to find an outlet for anger and no doubt reduced the fear of painful consequences. Though it had little tangible result, protesting at least helped relieve some of the profound feelings of helplessness that women report experiencing. At the same time, the bond of nationality played an important role: in this situation the violation struck the women as a group of Polish females. Their protests served to oppose a further national conquest—the appropriation of their bodies. While they recognized themselves as victims of males, the latters' different and antagonistic nationality mattered, for it provided for an opening to speak.

Women's reactions to the mixed baths express much about their own feelings of modesty and their perception of Soviet culture. Their comments indicate that they viewed this perversion not merely as an act of cruelty against them but as an indication of the primitive nature of Soviet (Russian) society. The woman who used a hunger strike to protest notes that the director failed to remedy the situation and told them that they were no longer in Poland and had better get used to the mixed baths. Genowefa Wróblewska writes that when the "Bolsheviks" came into the room in which she and her compatriots were washing, "there arise among the girls screams and commotion, and a Russian woman, who was also present, showed great surprise, for, after all, in their country such an unclothed mixing of the sexes is a daily and most natural thing. Indeed, I later ascertained myself, being in the camps, that men staffed the women's baths." Yet again, Russians seemed to invert the expected social order that recognized sexual difference and preserved proper segregation. In this alien country, men ran the women's bath and women the men's. In the words of a forty-year-old office worker, "The male presence in the bathhouse during the women's bathing throws a suitable light on and adequately characterizes those who employ such methods."[64] The trauma reported by women who experienced mixing conveys the suffering Russians inflicted on the Polish nation and the perceived incompatibility and inequality of the two societies.

Invasion

As violations of private space and dignity became more individualized and invasive, beginning with body searches, the breaches were progressively internalized. Arrested women routinely endured searches by male NKVD officers. These women were forced to strip, whereupon their belongings and bodies were meticulously examined; usually several men presided. One of the aims was booty: the searches included the confiscation of personal possessions, from money and jewelry to items of clothing, religious medals, and photographs. "They took me to a room in which there were twenty men," one woman relates. "They went after my things like vultures." Wanda Baczyńska states that she was "searched and robbed" by the NKVD according to the "appetite and scruples of the searcher."[65]

These procedures also aimed to humiliate the women, for they were accompanied by jeers and insults from the NKVD agents and guards. Many women report bearing streams of profanities and being repeatedly called prostitutes—an aspersion on their chastity that deeply offended them. The epithets most frequently reported, and the ones wounding the women the most, insulted female sexual propriety, their own or their mothers'. Czesława Humaner was interrogated by a man she describes as "completely akin to Mephisto, a sadist respecting nothing," who screamed at her, "You sneaky woman, you bastard, fuck your mother, you bitch, you whore, you Polish officer's mistress." Such attacks struck the core of their identity. Eugenia Swojda, for one, states that her interrogator used such expressions that "as a woman I was driven to despair."[66] Though men bore similar profanities, they report being most disturbed by insults to God and nation, to "our government and General Sikorski."[67]

The NKVD subjected women to searches repeatedly, long after they had any possessions left to hide—further evidence of the desire to degrade them. The authorities made women stand on display. Kazimiera Zielecka describes her prison stay in Dniepropetrovsk: "We were strip-searched daily, and they kept us naked for several hours in the cold corridor." Helena Ryszkowska reports similar treatment at a labor camp near Sverdlovsk: "On days free from work they conducted detailed searches, sometimes with stripping us completely. The search sometimes lasted ten hours, even at times of great cold."[68] The female body became an object to be exposed and examined at the will of the officers.

Searches went beyond confiscating possessions and exposing bodies. Few women offer details about these additional procedures. Refraining from naming, they state merely that they suffered searches that were "brutal," "inhuman," "disgusting," and "humiliating." A fifty-seven-year-old woman from Lwów writes that the searches by the NKVD violated the dignity of a woman and a human being. "The searches were conducted in a vulgar manner," writes another woman, "offending female dignity." In a commonly vague way, Antonina Wawrzyńkowska notes briefly: "The night searches tormented us immensely, as we were ordered to strip—etc."[69]

Some women are a little more explicit, revealing to what the "etc." refers. "At night we were summoned to interrogations," writes Eugenia Pióro, "torturous searches were made, humiliating and offending female dignity (gynecological searches)."[70] Many women endured these invasive examinations but only those probed by female agents offer details. In these cases, male guards remained in the room. Cecylia Czajkowska recalls her experience:

> The nurse announced that I had to undergo a search. I didn't realize what that would be like, I thought it meant looking through my purse, pockets and overcoat, something of that sort. And then a horrible moment, the search was a medical body one. I suggested to the nurse, even begged, that she dismiss those soldiers during it, telling the nurse that I couldn't undress in front of them, I encountered loud, coarse laughter and profanities. . . . I will never forget the moment of that search.[71]

The woman whose belongings were taken by the twenty vultures, continues her description of that episode with the following staccato narration:

"But that's not the end. They see yet to the possibility that I surely could have hidden gold, or some kind of papers. Despite the fact that I am nearly naked. Another procedure. This time a woman searches. I am completely naked. She even looks in my hair, which she orders me to comb thoroughly with her comb. With dirty hands she examines me. I do gymnastics."[72]

Most of the gynecological searches, however, seem to have been performed by men. Women's increased humiliation is reflected in the style they use to report these searches: these descriptions are shorter and vaguer than those of examinations performed by women. A clerk from the city of Stanisławów states, "Searches were conducted among us every few days—conducted by men not constrained by the fact that we are women." "The first body search was performed by a Soviet officer," writes Zofia Zachwieja, an instructor for a Catholic youth organization. "The search crossed the boundaries of decency. There were no women to do the search."[73] Typically, the content is not discussed, no details offered, and no bodily parts or procedures named. The shame left by these ordeals precludes words. Comparison with documents of Polish men, who underwent similar searches, makes this readily apparent. They do not seem to have been searched by female investigators but point out that men stripped and searched Polish women.[74] Men too describe their searches as torturous but reveal more about the extent of the examinations. Some of them write simply that the investigators searched "in all possible places on the human body," or in "unspeakable places."[75] Others list these places, including the rectum. "They meticulously searched each naked prisoner," writes one man, "making them do knee bends, looking in the mouth and even the rectum."[76] This word does not appear in women's reports. Neither do females voice a desire for revenge, which males do in such cases.[77]

Unlike the numerous instances of protest to mixing in the baths, accounts of body searches do not recount resistance. A few women note that they begged, futilely, to have males leave the room during gynecological searches performed by females. Only one woman refers to attempts to protest: "Whoever among us resisted," writes Marta Baśkiewicz, "was taken into the corridor and beaten unconscious."[78] No other women report screaming, struggling, or appealing to higher authorities. Recalling the searches, the women are quieter about their reactions; shame and disgust come through, but anger does not. No doubt the individual's isolation during the examination intensified her fear of the outcome of any protest.

Body and Sexuality

Naked, vulnerable, subject to the probing of men with apparently unrestricted power, she had nothing to hold onto for support, from which she could speak out and resist. Moreover, the affront proved more devastating because this invasion was directed personally against her body. The touching, the attention to sexual organs, left a mark on the woman's body and psyche that she could not discard; the victim of body searches seems to have been branded, in her own mind, with shame and guilt.

In women's accounts of the baths, the greatest stigma fell on Soviet men for their base behavior. Not feeling any guilt, women could externalize the injury and find anger; in the group setting, they could even express it. The more personal and intrusive attack—the body search—entailed a shifting of responsibility for the shame. As isolated individuals, women did not construe this invasion as a collective injury done to the Polish nation. Their descriptions rarely contain references to the nationality of victim or perpetrator: only women and men are involved. Furthermore, the searches affected the physical body and especially damaged its social aspects. If women bear a responsibility to hide the female body and maintain its purity, then violations implicate their propriety. Though the offense stems solely from another (male) individual, the female whose body is invaded is traditionally considered dishonored. Unable to completely externalize this affront, she becomes much more reticent, both at the time of the offense and then in the retelling. One woman recalls her very typical reaction to such a search: "I kept silent, but felt as if I had been deprived of all human dignity." Another woman reacted similarly: "I didn't pay any attention at all, with lowered head, with eyes fixed onto space, I acted as if I saw nothing around me."[79] Few could find words to describe their experience; what they could express was their shame.

Sexual Exploitation

Encounters with the NKVD sometimes involved sexual coercion. Many women hint at such abuse of police power, but like the searches, this sensitive issue is rarely discussed with detail or openness. Dorota Majewska notes without explanation that in prison she realized that NKVD agents could do anything they wanted to a defenseless girl. One prisoner recalls that her interrogator said he had "special feelings" for her and wanted to help. Maria Norciszek relates that her investigator "in the most shameless manner undressed himself completely, took off his long underwear, and behaved himself like the most shameless pig." She does not elaborate. Another woman thus describes an interrogation: "Suddenly, for no apparent reason, my cross-examiner became extremely flirtatious. He got up from behind his desk and came and sat beside me on the sofa. I stood up and went to drink some water. He followed me and stood behind me. I neatly evaded him and returned to the sofa. Down he sat again beside me. And again I got up and went to drink water. Maneuvers like these lasted for a couple of hours." In a report rare for its bluntness, Eugenia Swojda declares that she had to defend herself from her interrogator's desire to rape her.[80]

Female prisoners were not free from the threat of sexual abuse once they passed beyond the closed rooms of the NKVD interrogators. After sentencing, which took place without a trial, the women were transferred to labor camps throughout the USSR. By all accounts, the camps were harsh and dangerous places, particularly for women. According to Elinor Lipper, a Dutch woman imprisoned in the Gulag, "The Soviet camp . . . is a university of crime; it has become a place of both physical and moral destruction." The criminals, she states, "raped all the women who took their fancy," and gang rape, called "falling under the trolley," was extremely common.[81] In his work on crime in Russia, Valery Chalidze notes that among the professional underworld, "the most highly valued expression of the sexual instinct seems to be rape, especially collective rape."[82]

According to the Polish accounts, in some places women were afraid to move a few steps from their barracks at night, "because men attacked them and raped them."[83] Male criminals, the infamous *urki* of the Gulag, made nighttime raids on barracks. These powerful criminals habitually played cards for other people's clothing and even lives. "When it came to women," Maria Olechnowicz states, "they played for the right to rape." She continues: "The winner is the first to commit rape, the others are bound to help him carry out the enterprise."[84] Camp authorities, many individuals assert, did little to prevent such behavior. Chalidze confirms this point, explaining that in the official view, "non-political criminals were still regarded as socially akin." Since political and class criteria designated the regime's main enemies, common criminals—thieves, rapists, murderers—generally enjoyed a better position than political ones. They also had relative freedom to exploit and terrorize the political prisoners, with, Chalidze adds, "the direct encouragement or connivance of the authorities." Personal narratives of camp experiences by non-Poles similarly insist that some sort of understanding existed between the criminals and the guards, to the detriment of the politicals—especially female ones.[85]

The Poles' accounts of their lives in the USSR depict a world in which sex was forcibly taken or used as a commodity with considerable frequency. Besides cases of attack and coercion, Poles write scornfully about encountering a form of sexual union involving only a degree of consensus. "The institution of 'camp husbands' is a rather curious phenomenon specific to the closed camps in the USSR," explains Janina Seudek-Malanowicz. "Men and women alike, after arriving, try to contract a concubinage for the period of stay in a given camp."[86] The term "camp husband" (*lagernyi muzh*) is common to the literature of the Soviet labor camps.[87] Also known as "protectors," these men served to improve the daily living conditions of their sexual partners by arranging lighter work, obtaining larger food rations, or providing them with foods (particularly sugar and tea) and material goods (like dresses, coats, and boots) impossible to obtain through normal channels. The positions of authority these men typically held in the camps made this possible. They also helped ensure that their lovers fulfilled their quota at work, at least on paper. According to one Pole, the only way a woman could fulfill the work norm was by "becoming the lover of one of the camp functionaries, which was easy to do, as they exchanged her every month or two, when they grew bored."[88]

As the name implies, these men also protected their women from the aggression of others. In some cases, this meant from the female criminals in the camps. A woman imprisoned at Sukhobezvodna in the Volga region explains that the criminal women customarily divided the possessions of a new arrival. If she did not acquiesce, her things were taken at knifepoint; she could only get them back with the help of "some strong man as her lover."[89] Camp husbands also protected women from other males. The response of one woman to what she feared would be a proposition or attack illustrates both the ever-present threat to women and the respect accorded other men's "property." Approached by a man whose "tiny eyes shone with animal desire," she responded resourcefully: "I do not know what inspired me to say that I was waiting for the superintendent. 'That's all right then,' he said, 'wait for your lover.' And off he went. I was truly lucky. No one acquainted with conditions in the camp would be surprised at my horror." Albertyna Korzeniowska learned of this prevailing order from a Russian man who approached her soon after her arrival. "He is grinning and laughing, witty," she recalls. "He tries to explain to me that the position of a woman in a labor camp without a man is very difficult, that he likes me very much, that he is looking for a lady friend."[90]

According to Barbara Szumska, a twenty-one-year-old accused of counterrevolutionary activities, the men in the camps particularly liked Polish women because they were "clean and 'ladylike' and not very accessible." Again, cleanliness and virtue become defining marks of the collective of Polish females. She relates her experience in the camp Vorkuta: "I remember it was in June 1941, just after the outbreak of the Russo-German war, some chief engineer-agronomist, a Georgian by origin. He liked my braids, he told me that with defiant frankness, and then proposed transferring me to a better position. They always start that way. I did not agree."[91]

The threat and reality of sexual exploitation was a fact of everyday life outside the Gulag, as well, for the testimonies of female deportees include incidents paralleling those recounted of the camps, be it abuses of police power, individual and gang attacks, or forced prostitution. They also express a fear suggesting the incidents were not rarities. Though the deportees did not face regular interrogations by the secret police, NKVD agents summoned individuals at will. In some cases, their intentions may have been sexual exploitation. Olga Słabowa, deported to Kazakhstan, describes being called to the central office at the factory where she worked. There, a well-dressed man suggested he could improve her position. "He was an official of the NKVD," she writes, "who offered me his companionship—with the goal of taking me to the barracks." Another woman describes being led by an NKVD officer to a dark office. After making sure the building was empty, he assured her that if she got on well with him she would have everything, and he would not submit a complaint against her to his chief.[92] Separated from male family members and little valued by the Soviet government, the women were generally defenseless, if not before the predatory intentions of such men of authority then before their capacity for revenge.[93]

Women in free exile write about pressure for sex from men who commanded their work brigades, directed their schools, issued ration cards, and ran the local administration. Jadwiga Jeleniewrza states that her brigade leader often recorded a lower level of work output (which determined food rations) than the laborers actually achieved: "Often the reason for this was the refusal of women-Poles to submit to the brigade leader." A homemaker deported to Kazakhstan writes that "from the side of the members of the administration there were disgusting propositions even rapes."[94] The deportees also feared drunken locals. One woman reports several visits her first night in exile from inebriated peasants who "wanted to make her acquaintance," which she learned meant simply, "I want to spend the night with you."[95] Relocation for temporary job assignments involved considerable anguish, as the young women shared sheds and tents with local males. Stating simply that these men behaved "very unpleasantly," one woman writes. "Every night that my sister did not return home tortured us with anxiety."[96]

Women sent to collective farms in Central Asia report abductions of young girls and the buying of wives, perversions of marriage that they describe in the same tone as their incarcerated counterparts discuss camp marriages. "Frequent cases occurred in the village of wives being bought for a certain amount of provisions," writes a woman who was told that she "could get a lot" for her friend. Most of the report of one young woman details the terror evoked by local men. She and her sister, otherwise alone in exile, joined two older women "for defense against the attacks of the Kirghiz and the Uzbeks, who in all sorts of ways, by rape and bribery, desired to take advantage of the misery of two hungry girls." The man who controlled bread rationing wanted to "marry" her fourteen-year-old sister, and his actions impelled them to flee the farm.[97]

While sexual harassment and the danger of rape seem ever-present aspects of their lives in exile, the way the women chose to discuss the issue renders it impossible to estimate the number of women raped. This holds true for the incidence of rape in the USSR in general, as the Soviet government ceased publishing criminal statistics in 1928.[98] Citing documents from Soviet archives, Stanisław Ciesielski concludes that local authorities continually took advantage of Polish women, pressuring them for sex in exchange for food."[99] Given the style in which the Poles broach the issue of sexual abuse, one cannot escape the suspicion that far fewer women were willing to vocalize the matter than experienced it. The women's writing reveals much about the sexual and moral norms they accepted and which formed an important part of their identity.

Most references to sexual violence are either general statements that such things occurred or tales of third parties. Irena Czekalowska notes vaguely that at the settlement Poldnevitsa, "there were even such cases where Polish girls were attacked with force." As a rule, names of victims do not appear.

Polish women working in the local sawmill, a woman relates, "were constantly exposed to verbal assaults and even rapes from the Soviet bandits—*urki*."[100] Those who relate this information keep themselves at a distance; it apparently happened only to others.

This phenomenon occurs frequently in relation to the subject of widespread rape. In a study of Southern women during Sherman's march to the sea in the American Civil War, Jane Schultz concludes: "Rape became for them an unspeakable crime—never named but referred to in oblique language as something that happened to other women."[101] More recently, investigators seeking to uncover the story of mass rape in Bosnia-Herzegovina initially found in personal encounters that though everyone knew of someone who had been raped, they met no one who identified herself as a victim. "If they do come forward they try to remain anonymous and avoid being labeled as rape victims," reports Vera Folnegovic-Smalc, a psychiatrist working with these women. She continues: "If they do come to a counseling session they usually begin by speaking about themselves in the third person (that is, they say that someone else has been raped)."[102] Polish women, too, speak of rape in the third person.

Though some women describe their own threatening encounters with Soviet (never Polish) men, not one rape victim appears among them. Or so it appears. Even the most detailed accounts of coercion and intimidation drop away in the middle of the story or note the woman's escape, so that not one of the authors, it seems, is actually raped. The most explicit and evocative account of a Soviet man's attempt to force a Polish woman to have sexual relations with him comes from Sabina Ziółkowska. After her arrest for trying to cross the Polish-Romanian border, she was searched by a male NKVD officer. "One after another he precisely orders me to remove pieces of my clothing," she writes. Ziółkowska continues:

> I tremble, he also trembles, I from fear and disgust, he? I still don't know. He starts to speak on '*ty*' [familiar terms]. See what I'll do for you? I'll write a nice protocol, at 4 in the morning there is a train to Białystok. You'll go on it, I'll take you to the station myself. Just stay with me till 4 AM, for this one night. In prison there are lice, you won't go there. You'll stay with me. He extends shaking hands for me, or rather at me. How disgusting. Should I scream or beg? Remain silent or persuade? I speak nervously. I think, after all I am alone with him. I tell him—you have your own friends, your own women, what do you want with me?

He puts on a record—some pretty, suggestive tango. Why does he put a record on, maybe he thinks that music will put me in the mood, or maybe he thinks that I will scream and he wants to cover my cry? Again he speaks, again he trembles. Don't be scared, you won't get pregnant. He takes a bottle of vodka out of the cupboard. I calmly try to persuade again. He understood me, but sent me to prison.[103]

The grammatical tense and pace of her account abruptly changes as she endeavors to get out of the situation. She is much less explicit in describing how the episode came to a close. What else did the agent do? Was something painful left out between her entreaty and her exit?

While Ziółkowska apparently succeeded in talking her way out of a dangerous situation, others report actually escaping. The woman taken to the deserted NKVD office managed to run from the building. A woman traveling on a train woke to find a man touching her body; she jumped away and hid all night.[104] Others fled their localities, illegally, to elude men who continually pressured them for sex. Another common strategy the women employ is to leave gaps in the narrative, so that it remains unclear how the situation turned out: it is not clear if the woman was raped. Without explaining what occurred after her interrogator removed his clothing, Norciszek immediately states that her interrogation concluded with a beating by another agent. Korzeniowska does not relate what happened with the man who insinuated that he wanted her as his camp wife, and neither does the woman who described her flirtatious examiner report how those humiliating sessions ended for her.[105] In general, either the women state that they refused or escaped, or they fall silent on the outcome of their threatening encounters, gliding past it to other topics.

The statement of Zofia Jernsiówna stands out for its focused and detailed expression of emotional trauma connected with sexual coercion. She depicts a painful incident in Siberia, in which a young deportee faces the choice of having sex with the son of the collective farm chairman in order to have her desperately ill brother transported to the hospital or of helplessly watching him die. The document also stands out for the distance between its author and the wrenching experience it describes, and thus serves as a clear example of how Polish women dealt with the issue of sexual abuse. Jernsiówna's entire document on her period of exile is devoted to the two days surrounding this decision. The episode is depicted vividly and emotionally but told in the third person, with no introduction or explanation of the characters, as if it is about other, unnamed people. It is hard not to assume though, that the experience is Jernsiówna's own.

Here is her retelling of the proposition made by the chairman's son: "He knows that she has to send her brother to the hospital, knows that she didn't get a horse, he can still save the boy, he can get a horse, but not for free—for a terrible price, the price of her." Given one night to consider, the protagonist sees the decision as one between sacrificing her brother or herself. "To sacrifice the life of the one who, after the death of Mother was the closest person to her, without whom she could not imagine her existence. To sacrifice her honor, and maybe her entire life and future for him." Willing to make that ultimate self-sacrifice, she delivers her brother to the young man so he can take him to the hospital and then reports to work. She returns home later in great distress, "knowing that disgrace and shame await her." There is no nobility or exoneration for her in this act of caring and sacrifice—only shame, which apparently adheres to the woman and not the man exacting such a high price. The episode ends similarly to those discussed above. When the man finally comes to her place at night to collect his payment, she continually evades his touch, then begs and pleads with him to leave her alone. By what she terms a miracle, he understands and leaves. She credits her savior as *Matka Boska*, the Holy Virgin.[106] Perhaps the story could not have ended another way and still be told.

Given the widespread nature of violence and sexual coercion, it is hard to believe that none of these women was actually overpowered and raped. Several interpretations are possible. These women may in fact be the lucky ones, who managed to escape being raped or taking part in sexual relations requiring them to sell their bodies. Those who were not so lucky either did not survive, did not make it out of the USSR to bear witness, or simply refused to recall their ordeals. Alternatively, these women may well have left the most painful facts out of their accounts. They might have changed the ending to create a memory with which they could comfortably live. "'Remembering' or 'not remembering,'" historian Klaus Theweleit points out, "simply means making decisions about the reality to be produced."[107] The latter possibility cannot be underestimated, for the stigma of rape and prostitution was strong in Polish society, causing silences.

Not only are the silences about rape telling but also the language used to describe the attempts. Rather than directly stating what went on, the women use euphemisms and ellipses to express the most objectionable behavior of the men, the most painful moments for themselves. The men "have special feelings" or offer "companionship." They simply behave "shamelessly" or "scandalously." A woman working as a janitor in Kazakhstan states that her superior "demanded impossible things from me."[108] The sexual content of the intentions and behavior remains veiled and references to the body minimized, if not altogether avoided. For this reason Ziółkowska's description, including the man's trembling and the acknowledgment of the possibility of pregnancy, is highly unusual. Even the verbs "abduct," "attack" and "rape" tend to be used only in abstract comments. This again resembles what Schultz found in the diaries of women in the American South. Calling rape "the unspeakable crime," Schultz explains, "women made a tacit agreement not to call rape by its name, referring to it obliquely instead."[109]

Polish women reveal a restricted range of emotions when recalling these dangerous moments. The more expressive statements use the words "shame," "humiliation," and "helplessness." They do not speak of such feelings as anger, hatred, grief, or a desire for revenge. Nor do they use the language of the nation, which would cast the abuse as an injury done to the Polish nation. Instead, in cases involving sexual coercion, the women isolate themselves and internalize the offense. Their Polishness means nothing when they are abused as women; neither does the nationality of the man seem relevant. The incident appears to reflect on the victim, not the perpetrator.

To understand what was at stake for these women, we can turn again to Jernsiówna's statement. Her narrative highlights the supreme importance to Polish women of their sexual honor, which precludes sexual relations for any purpose other than procreation within wedlock. She equates the physical death of the male (the brother) with the implicit moral death of the female. And the moral death results from socially illicit sex—even though coerced. The "price of her" is not literally her life, it is her chastity. The identity of the proper woman is thus distilled to her sexual honor, which provides a woman with self-esteem and standing in society. "Where rape is treated as a crime against honor, the honor of women is called into question," writes Rhonda Copelon. "Honor implies the loss of station and respect; it reinforces the social view, internalized by women, that the raped woman in dishonorable."[110]

Valuing a woman's honor, her sexual propriety, over her very life has occurred in various societies and across time. Anastasia Pavlova, a Bulgarian woman, related her ordeal at the hands of Greek soldiers during the Balkan

Wars of 1912–1913. Herself badly beaten and raped, she detailed her efforts to prevent her daughter's rape, stating, "My only consolation is that I saved her honor."[111] Studying the problem of mass rape of German women by Soviet soldiers in the aftermath of World War II, Norman Naimark found that "suicides were not uncommon when families faced the invading army and the threat of rape and humiliation." One document Naimark cites describes the actions of a professor who "killed his wife and daughters and then himself not to have to bear the anguish [of their rape]."[112] This attitude is not merely a relic of the past. Interviewers report that in the recent war in the former Yugoslavia (1992–1995), many Bosnian women stated, "I would prefer to be killed than raped."[113] Though this reaction may appear to individuals in some cultures to be so normal as to escape attention, it is a profoundly revealing description of the social identity frequently ascribed to —and internalized by—females. It tells her that her sexual honor (which in all too many cases she is powerless to control) determines her own and her family's social standing and ultimately the value of her life.

The importance of sexual honor to the identity of Polish women explains why they had to avoid the label of rape victim. The same holds true regarding forced prostitution. Most discussions of camp husbands include assertions that while such alliances commonly occurred, Polish women did not avail themselves of the men's costly assistance. "The type of job also very often depended on the so-called protection of 'superiors,' who for that demanded that they be paid highly, especially by women," writes Janina Bohdzewicz. "It was rare that Polish prisoners had better work; they were mostly assigned to the very worst labor." Despite the difficult life in the camp, writes Stanisława Widoła, "No one benefited from any kind of relief, which would have been the result of the favor of the commandant of the settlement and for which one would have had to give up the honor of a Pole or the reputation of a woman."[114] According to their testimonies, Polish women excluded themselves from such arrangements.

Polish men frequently echo this description of their compatriots, emphasizing the females' heroism and virtue. Piotr Cichocki describes the situation of women of various nationalities in his camp in Komi: "These women were used in many ways by the managers of different work divisions. One of the Polish women (I forgot her name), did not want to submit herself to the *prorabovi* [foreman] who divided work into brigades, so she was kept in the *kartser* for seven days, with only 300 grams of bread and ¾ liter of thin soup once a day." According to a male deportee, "None of the girls would have anything to do with the Soviets . . . our girls didn't talk to the collective farm men."[115]

One can only wonder about the accuracy of such characterizations. Polish females placed high value on their overlapping "honor of a Pole" and "reputation of a woman." The cultural and religious norms of modesty, chastity, and fidelity placed a great burden on them; lapses, for whatever reason, saddled the female with guilt. These norms barred women from seeking to improve their chances of survival through sexual relations. They may also have barred women who succumbed either to dire need or physical threats from admitting what happened to them, for internalized feelings of shame and dishonor almost inevitably result in silencing. An internal NKVD report on the condition of the deportees in Kazakhstan notes cases of mothers forced to sell their bodies for food or jobs.[116] And descriptions of Soviet penal institutions by some Polish men suggest that even Polish women might not have managed to maintain their virtue while confined there. Decrying the sexual debauchery prevalent in the camps, some of them note the high number of prostitutes, Russian and Polish.[117] Male prisoners recall overhearing the rapes—and they use that word—of Polish women through the walls during interrogations.[118] In a report written for Polish army intelligence, Stanisław Świaniewicz states: "Generally speaking, however, a woman in the camps for the most part very easily and quickly succumbs to forced prostitution. The question of food plays a large role here." Another man imprisoned in the Gulag, in a rare discussion of the depths faced by Polish females there, writes: "The lot of women in the work camps was horrible. I can say that it was worse than that of animals. They were treated like 'goods' to be used, traded for a piece of bread. If one didn't want to have a 'protector'—a so-called 'camp husband'—then she was ill-treated, her life made disgusting, so that we really must give the greatest credit to those not numerous Polish women who came through the hell clean."[119]

The picture this man gives challenges the self-representation of the Polish women. At the same time, it confirms the culturally accepted notion of dishonor previously discussed. Those women who succumbed, out of grim necessity, to the Soviet hell, became dirty; their bodies and social identities sullied. This man's characterization of the plight of women in the camps makes it clear why the women themselves would choose, even had to choose, to remain silent. Theweleit reminds us that one uses "'memory' to *construct a history he can live with now*." He explains: "The abstract 'memory' *rarely* talks about things that happened. It uses the names and events of the 'past' to construct the sort of present the constructor now wants to live in."[120] Apparently, to use the words of a woman who worked with Bosnian rape victims, "there was no discourse available to them in which the women could have revealed their experiences while preserving their dignity."[121] In such situations, even the discourse of the nation proved unavailable. The women not only felt that others would see them as defiled but also believed that of themselves.

Some parallels exist between the experiences of the exiled Polish women and German women under the Soviet occupation of their country that began in 1945. The latter experienced a period in which, according to Annemarie Tröger, "rape and prostitution became 'normal' sexual relations."[122] After multiple rapes, many German women decided to take on protectors among the Russian officers, essentially to prostitute themselves. They also ensured their survival by forming small supportive families, a space in which to discuss their experiences and support each other through them. This ability to deal with the reality of rape in a collective manner required "the conscious separation of the feminine body and the sense of self," which entailed the demystification of the notion of defilement and rejection of the burden of shame.[123] Atina Grossmann concludes that the German rape victims "felt victimized, violated, humiliated, but finally not guilty or responsible."[124] In contrast, Polish women's documents suggest that collectively and individually they were not able to make that detachment. The female body, wrapped in traditional Catholic taboos, remained at the core of their sense of self, their sexuality a source of guilt and shame, something to be denied or ignored. Unable to separate their sexual honor from their identity, Polish women of this period did not find a voice that would enable them to talk openly of what they suffered at the hands of Soviet men.[125] In such cases, even their national identity was overridden by their sexual one. Any victimization by Polish men was doubly silenced. If traumatized by rape or forced prostitution, women felt compelled to remain silent.[126] For them, the story of the nation in exile had no space for their suffering.

Sexuality

In these descriptions of sexual exploitation—told more as episodes involving female honor and shame than violence—sexuality is almost completely absent. As a manifestation of aggression, rape certainly has more to do with domination and humiliation than with sex, but it is carried out in a sexual way.[127] It is precisely their own sexual attributes that the women avoid mentioning, be it in the context of threatening encounters or their daily lives (which for some women still included their husbands). Almost everything connected with the physicality of the female body is cloaked or ignored in the women's discussions of their existence in exile. They demonstrate extreme reluctance to name body parts or processes associated with being female.

Though greatly concerned with hygiene and washing, women avoid the topic of menstruation. There are only two references to this bodily process in the women's statements—one of which is oblique and purely incidental —and two in reports by men.[128] In the first case, the woman notes that during her body search the NKVD officers confiscated all of her possessions: "They don't want to return even the belt indispensable at certain times for a woman." The second reference, more substantive, indicates a problem menstruation caused for imprisoned women:

> At the beginning of our imprisonment the greatest difficulty was the constant demand for cotton wool. This was given most unwillingly and in very small quantities. From time to time the nurse would exclaim, "Whenever will this end?" At first we did not understand what they meant. But after a couple of months of imprisonment their meaning dawned upon us. I am not sure whether something was put into our food which often had an unpleasant metallic taste. Whether owing to the addition of some special drug or not it is a fact that very soon most of us ceased to suffer from the usual female afflictions; there were few exceptions, who on the contrary, suffered severely and unceasingly. These were extremely miserable. The hygienic conditions were appalling and cotton wool was not to be had.[129]

Women in free exile, who no doubt found it nearly impossible to obtain cotton, refrain from mentioning this aspect of their difficulties. Nor do they express any anxiety connected with the cessation of menstruation, which likely accompanied their near-starvation.

Analyzing women's writings of the Holocaust, Marlene Heinemann found that fear of infertility due to amenorrhea was a common preoccupation.[130] Polish women express strong reactions to the loss of mothering functions, but they focus on the emotional aspects, avoiding references to the physical. They write at length of the pain of separation from husbands and children, and the inability to perform nurturing and educational functions associated with motherhood; they also focus on the difficulties befalling their offspring. Given that in many places the food situation in Soviet exile resembled that in Nazi concentration camps, even resulting in death by starvation, we can assume that many of the women ceased menstruating. However, they do not mention this fear or actuality in their writing. The physical aspects of being female, including their connections to motherhood, are avoided.

Pregnancy itself is discussed only in certain limited contexts. Ziółkowska's unusually frank account of harassment by her interrogator is the only one that touches upon the possibility of conception. Otherwise, only a few men register the occurrence of illegitimate pregnancies. Jerzy Świętochowski recalls "an unpleasant incident" in his settlement in Kazakhstan: "namely, one of the Polish women, the wife of a policeman (I don't remember her name), with two children, had a third child with a Russian, the head of the cafeteria. It happened undoubtedly in order to ensure her subsistence."[131] Despite the many allusions to rape and forced prostitution, women never mention fear of pregnancy, actual pregnancy, childbirth, or abortions that would accompany sexual encounters and attacks. If any of the exiled women struggled with the dilemma of an unwanted pregnancy, neither their agonies nor their solutions were passed on in written form after evacuation from the USSR.

Avoidance of the issue of unwanted pregnancies characterized Polish society before the war, as well. Although the Codification Commission worked on a draft of a new law on abortion throughout the 1920s,[132] the subject did not appear in the press until social critic Tadeusz Boy-Żeleński published pamphlets on the topic in 1929. He decried the silent character of Polish women in the debate: "Women—especially in our country, are shackled by a false shame in matters of sexuality, they are afraid. Just as before they allowed themselves to be dragged before the courts, to be condemned, without protesting against the murderous and senseless paragraph [of the criminal code], they maintain even now a surprising neutrality."[133] The reason? According to Boy-Żeleński: "[Women's] habit of dissimulation, silence about their own most essential matters, the lack of female solidarity." While debates on birth control and abortion go on around them, he remarked, women write letters about hairstyles and miss the whole matter. He considered this abstention characteristic of Polish women, noting that the Jewish women's journal, *Ewa*, broached the topic. As one historian points out, in the debate on abortion, the voice belonged to men.[134] When a few liberal women began writing in the 1930s on intimate matters previously taboo, including menstruation, contraception, and abortion, many women were offended.[135]

The issues of pregnancy and childbirth receive attention in the exiled women's documents neither as the outcome of rape nor as the result of consensual union with Soviet men. Rather, the topic is raised to illustrate that pregnant women did not receive proper treatment in the USSR. Expressing sympathy for such women and scorn for the authorities, Poles write of expectant mothers living in dirty and crowded prison cells and enduring beatings by the NKVD. They detail continued compulsory manual labor and lack of medical care, despite advanced pregnancy. And they describe the unsanitary conditions in which women gave birth—putting themselves and their babies at risk.[136] Though these problems, which portray the expectant mothers as victims of brutal foreign authorities, are openly discussed, the question of when these women were impregnated and by whom is rarely broached. The only point made clear is that pregnant women did not escape deportation; it appears that all the expectant mothers arrived in the USSR already in that condition—impregnated by their legitimate Polish husbands.

Pregnancy is linked with motherhood, not sex; the Virgin Mother seems to offer the guiding example to Polish women. The Catholic Church advocated this notion throughout the interwar period, promoting the cult of the Virgin Mary as the model for all Catholic females, including married women and mother heroes.[137] In this context, the realities of the female body seem admissible in public forums only when they concern the nation. Even when women write of the inability to breast-feed due to poor nutrition, the disclosure has more to do with nurturing others than anything physical about themselves. The women do not speak of their female bodies when they are simply uncomfortable or hurt, but only when their ability to mother Poles is jeopardized.

The topic of sex has two components in the women's testimonies. First, it always has a negative connotation. Second, it only surfaces in discussions of others. These two features are linked, as improper or deviant sexual behavior is used to characterize and condemn women of other nationalities. This aspect of sexuality will be discussed later. What merits attention here is that not only is deviant sexual behavior linked solely with women of non-

Polish nationality but any sort of sexuality at all. While the topic of sex comes up, sometimes graphically, in their discussions of *others*, Polish women simply do not present themselves as sexual.[138] The long-standing notion that proper women do not reveal their own sexual needs or desires persisted.[139]

Lesbians and prostitutes, concubines and promiscuous women seem largely absent from the Polish collective. The general image of women in Polish society seems to have supported, or even required this depiction. The following excerpt from a Polish government report highlights the assumption of the purity of its female citizens: "A very harsh aspect of Soviet imprisonment was that no distinction was made between political prisoners and criminals of the worst kind. Women suffered most from it, being kept together with prostitutes."[140] Note that the authors do not object to the proximity of murderers or thieves. Accounts of Poles under the other occupier, the Nazis, demonstrate a similar insistence on upholding the honor of Polish females. Several women voice shock and anger at a German attempt to recruit Poles for a brothel in the Ravensbrück camp. According to one of them, the proposition was so offensive that, "for the first time, we felt so enraged that we didn't give a damn about endangering our lives." Another insists that the sole Polish woman who volunteered was not like the rest of them; to "save the honor of Poland," they cut her hair to prevent her from joining the brothel.[141]

Not only are women of "improper" sexuality missing from the picture drawn of the collective of Polish women, so too are any women with sexual desire or experience even in the context of "legitimate" heterosexual unions. Feminization calls for the detachment from the body. In fact, any attention to the female body seems to offend their identity as proper women. As individuals and as a collective, these women, to use the words of Kathleen Canning, "efface the sexual or desiring body, the pregnant or nursing body, the body ravaged" be it by rape, unwanted pregnancy, or abortion, all of which we can well imagine, but not confirm in this experience of exile.[142]

Conclusion

From the moment they boarded the transports in eastern Poland, the exiled women were subjected to physical conditions and treatment ranging from uncomfortable to lethal. Some of the hardships and violence they experienced can be called generic, in that they did not concern the sex of the individual. Such afflictions as hunger and disease, or beatings, were shared by male and female Poles, who interpreted them according to a similar framework. Drawing on past experiences of their nation under Russian domination, Poles cast their agony in both historical and religious terms that rendered it explainable, bearable, and redemptive. The nation thus provided women with a space and a language for expressing some of their physical suffering—that is, when it did not call attention to their female bodies. In these cases, women could locate the reason for their targeting and their suffering in their Polishness—which further served to confirm their national identity—and could talk about it as the story of the victimized Polish nation. Shared tribulation conferred on the women equal status with Polish men.

Other forms of indignity and violence, however, contradicted women's identities as Poles. Gendered offenses, which targeted them precisely as women, did not seem to fit into the tragedy of the nation. Polish cultural norms of proper womanhood required detachment from the body and silence on its particular needs and agonies. Life in exile rendered this difficult: mixed living conditions and bathing facilities turned the spotlight on their femaleness. Women could recall such incidents because they occurred to them as part of a group, and left their individual bodies untouched. While women report feeling shame just remembering those moments, they were able to cast blame and scorn on the Soviet men who put them in such situations. Soviet authorities denied them personal privacy; in making the performance of physiological functions and hygienic processes public, they violated what to the Poles appeared a necessary and natural separation of the sexes. Such mixing offended modesty and entailed a promiscuity that upset social order, which required mindfulness of sexual difference. In such cases women could still cast the injury as one done to the Polish collectivity and that reflected on the base nature of their national enemy. The shame they expressed confirmed their identities as modest Polish females.

But the nation lost its relevance to women the more they suffered as females. Women who endured the transgressions of gynecological searches and sexual coercion progressively internalized the offenses. Cultural norms for coping with gendered transgressions intensified the injuries, so that what was done to a female by others tainted her body and compromised her identity as a woman. She became stigmatized, even in her own mind, by the acts of others upon her body. Feeling herself dishonored, she could no longer speak of the offense as a crime of the enemy. If she revealed herself to be a victim of rape (or a partner in a camp marriage), the transgression would be attached to her, more than to the perpetrator, damaging both her self-esteem and her social standing.

Describing their travails in the USSR, it was clearly easier for women to say "he beat me," or "he made me starve," than "he raped me." The former statements include a conviction that "he did this to me as a Pole," which gives a group allegiance that both upholds the individual and provides a space and discourse for voicing outrage, for expressing, "and I hate him/them." Sexual violation, however, contains a more secreted knowledge that "he did this to me as a woman," an identity that, on its own—deprived of the shoring up effect of national identity—apparently did not extend to the victims a sense of support and legitimate outrage. One can infer the inner response to such an offense as, "and I hate myself." While Soviet men could be presented as uncivilized brutes, who did not respect the norms regarding sexual difference, the fact that they raped women could be told only in the abstract. Only when the story was (seemingly) about other, unnamed victims could it be publicly presented as a crime of Soviet men.

If we consider how damaging rape typically appears to the victim or potential victim, so much so that she might choose death as her only recourse, then the silencing of the violation can be seen as the way out of that dilemma. At a time of extreme chaos, involving total dislocation, uprooting from all the mainstays of home, she needed those identities that were imbued with honor and esteem, that assured her place in a society that she knew and longed for and that gave her a sense of difference and superiority from the individuals and the nation that sought to degrade her.

The pain associated with the female body did not lead to the formation of a collective voice that could protest these more personal and violent transgressions, either before the Soviets themselves or a later audience of conationals. Since the wounding of the body came about as a result of the women's displacement at the hands of a national enemy, it helped—in the cases of generic bodily hardships and mixing—to mobilize their outrage and their resistance as a nation. But the more intimate and invasive the attack on female bodies, the less this seemed possible. Ultimately, the concept of the nation proved so masculinized that it had no room for talking about specifically female suffering. Women could appeal to the fatherland for understanding and expressing their pain only when it fell into masculine categories of suffering. Women's objections to mixing in the transports and the baths, to the searches and to sexual exploitation, contain no articulation of their position vis-à-vis men in general. They equate the pain that they are able to talk about solely with Soviet domination, marginalizing their experiences as females apart from the "Polish" qualifier. The women's statements suggest that all that is needed to alleviate their suffering is a return to home, to Poland. Any struggles that they faced there as women, at the hands of Polish men, were even less permissible in the story of the nation.

While waiting for that return, the women seem to have recreated home as a sense of certainty, security, and unity by upholding and asserting traditional Polish Catholic images of the proper female as a key aspect of their identity as individuals and as a collective. In doing so, they stressed female sexual honor, which involved excessive modesty, distance from the female body, and denial of their own sexuality. The best way they could find to deal with their female bodies was to cast them as part of the nation—as martyrs for the fatherland suffering like men, or above all, as mothers.

Polish deportees in Soviet Central Asia after the amnesty. *Source: Jan Karski Papers*

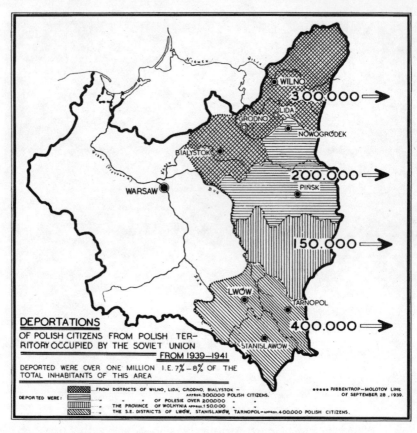

Map of the deportations from eastern Poland, prepared by the Polish Army in the East. It includes the original estimates of the numbers of persons taken, by region. *Source: Poland Ambasada (Soviet Union), Records*

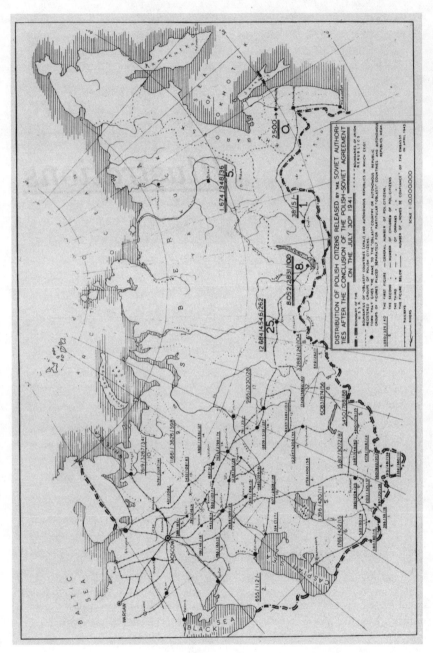

Map of settlements of deported Poles in the USSR, prepared by the Polish Army in the East. *Source: Poland Ambasada (Soviet Union), Records*

Polish family in Soviet Union. *Source: Władysław Anders Collection*

Passport photos issued to amnestied Poles: Zofia Kruszelnicka, Bronisława Rudzińska, Eugenia Woźniak. *Source: Poland Ambasada (Soviet Union), Records*

Cover of one woman's account of her time in the Gulag. Her document is one
example of the free-form memoirs written after the evacuations.
Source: Władysław Anders Collection

Polish women in the Soviet Union. *Source: Jan Karski Papers*

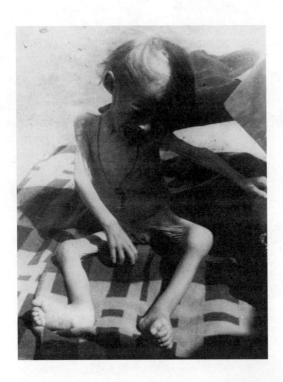

Polish refugee children in relocation centers in Uzbekistan, 1942.
By the time of the amnesty, many
of the exiles were in desperate
physical condition. *Sources: Jan
Karski Papers; Poland, Ministerstwo
Spraw Zagranicznych, Records*

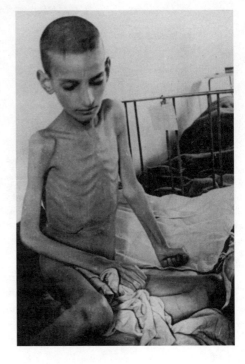

С. С. С. Р.

Народный Комиссариат

Внутренних Дел

УПРАВЛЕНИЕ
УНЖЕНСКОГО
ИСПРАВИТЕЛЬНО-
ТРУДОВОГО ЛАГЕРЯ

« » сентяб 194 г.

№ 015/6/49855

УДОСТОВЕРЕНИЕ

Фамилия, Имя, Отчество ЧАЙКОВСКАЯ

Цицилия-Христина Александровна

год рождения 1898 место рождения

г. Станиславов

На основании Указа Президиума Верховного Совета СССР—амнистирован как польский гражданин и имеет право свободного проживания на территории СССР за исключением: пограничных районов, запретных зон, местностей об'явленных на военном положении и режимных городов первой и второй категории.

При нем находятся Никого нет

Гр-н ЧАЙКОВСКАЯ Цицилия-Христина Александровна

направляется к избранному им месту жительства в к.г.т. Орджоникидзе, Ташкентской обл.

Удостоверение выдано на **три месяца** и подлежит обмену на паспорт.

Изложенное удостоверяется подписью и печатью.

Зам. Начальника Управления УНЖЛАГ'а НКВД
Ст. Лейтенат Госбезопасности   (ГОЛОВ).
Врид. Начальника 2-го Отдела   (ГАЛАТ)

МЦ 18613.

Soviet release certificate for Cecylia Krystyna Czajkowska, issued after the amnesty. Polish citizens were required to have such a document in order to leave their place of detention and travel to outposts of the Polish army.
Source: Poland, Ministerstwo Informacji i Dokumentacji, Records

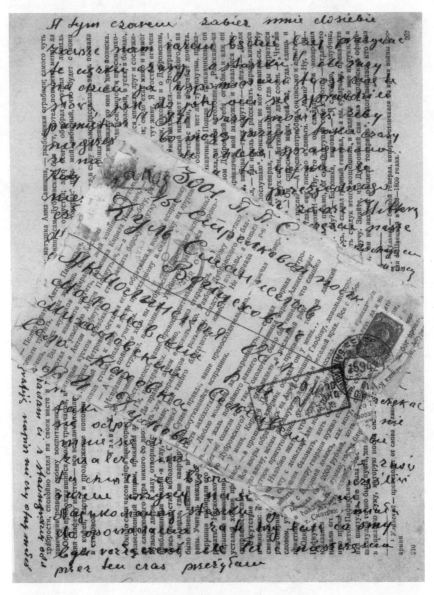

Letter from a Polish woman in Kazakhstan to her husband in the army, written on a page torn from a Russian book. The exiles wrote on whatever scraps of paper they could find. *Source: Władysław Anders Collection*

A Polish woman and her children still on Soviet territory receive rations from the Polish army after the amnesty. *Source: Poland, Ministerstwo Informacji i Dokumentacji, Records*

Poles in the USSR after the amnesty. *Source: Poland, Ministerstwo Informacji i Dokumentacji, Records*

Ob. Myszkowska Emilia
lat 28 zamiężn. ostatni
, Warszawie.

Dnia 5.I.1940r. zostałam aresztowaną na
Wileńszczyźnie za przekroczenie granicy jako kurier.
Umieszczono mnie w więzieniu w Berezyczu, po
3 miesiącach wywieziono mnie do Mińska a następnie
do Witebska. Przez cały czas pobytu w więzieniu
trzymano mnie w celach z natłoczonych aresztowa-
niami Polkami. Na badanie brano mnie nocą
do celi na ten cel przeznaczonej, przy badaniu
bito, w twarz kopano nogami, sadzano na krzesło
elektryczne celem wymuszenia zeznań. Śledztwo
prowadzone było przez 5 miesięcy, poczem wydano
wyrok zaoczny, oparty rzekomo na zeznaniach
świadków o przynależności mojej do organizacji
tajnej. Skazano mnie na 8 lat ciężkich prac
w obozach. Skończem zaś 1940r. znalazłam się
w Akmolińsku w obozie pracy.— Tutaj powości
śledztwo. Zarzucili mi kontrrewolucyjną agitację,
którą to miałam prowadzić w obozie pracy przez
podtrzymywanie na duchu koleżanek, którymi to
mówiłam, iż Polska będzie i my wrócimy do

Polish Women's Auxiliary in the Near East preparing dinner for soldiers.
Source: Jan Karski Papers

III

"We Polish Women Were a Model of Unity before Their Citizens"

Self-Definition through the Delineation of "Others"

Part III examines Polish women's relationship to individuals of other nationalities they encountered in exile, analyzing the ways they perceived—and defined themselves against—these others. Whether incarcerated or resettled, Polish women viewed their neighbors through a national lens that they seldom put down. Nearly all of their accounts separate the populations by nationality and generalize characteristics and behavior according to that criterion. Although a few hint at tension between Polish peasants and members of the intelligentsia, the distinctions and friction due to class do not compare, either in frequency or intensity, to the lines drawn between national groups. Such categorizations helped the women cope with the trauma of everyday life in exile, enabling them to create a refuge by consolidating their own national identity, a process that seemingly requires "the emphasizing of differences between one national community and another, and the effacing of differences within."[1] It is rare to read a report that does not deal with the issue of nationality.

One of the questionnaires prepared by the Polish army asks specifically for the ethnic composition of the communities of internees, prisoners, and deportees, thus illustrating the general importance of this information to Polish authorities. But women's accounts demonstrate that it is not a category imposed on them: they not only answer the question by recalling names and statistics regarding the different national groups, which stuck in their minds with noteworthy detail, but go on to describe the behavior and attitudes of individuals of the various groups. This attention to nationality occurs in discussions of other topics as well, from the invasion and occupation, to labor, cultural life, and living conditions. Some of the questionnaires do not ask about nationality at all, yet it creeps into the answers. And the unstructured prose accounts devote considerable attention to national differences and relations. Reading the statements, one gets the picture of sharply delineated ethnic groups, in day-to-day interaction and also in the minds of the women.

The New Demographics in Exile

The Poles faced a pronounced challenge once they found themselves in the USSR, where they encountered national groups both familiar and not. They were deported from their homeland together with other Polish citizens, including Jews, Ukrainians, and Belorussians. Individuals taken from the northern regions shared transports with Estonians and Lithuanians deported after the Baltic republics lost their independence to the Soviets. Incarcerated Poles found conationals in their cells while still on Polish territory, but once transported into the USSR, they were often surrounded by prisoners with whom they could not communicate. A woman sent to a labor camp near Krasnoiarsk reports living with people of the following nationalities: Russian, Tatar, Uzbek, Kazakh, Georgian, Armenian, Turkish, Chinese, Japanese, German, English, Finnish, Lithuanian, and Romanian.[2] Poles exiled to Central Asia often ended up living with Kazakh or Kirghiz families.[3]

The dispersion of Poles among other national groups on Soviet territory occurred commonly and deliberately. Polish women typically ended up in the minority, outnumbered in most cases by

Russians.[4] Women sent to the Gulag, in particular, report the dispersal of Poles among various camps in an apparent attempt to isolate them and sow distrust and demoralization. Maria Chrościechowska was separated from the Poles on her transport and put in a camp with nearly 2,000 Russians and only a dozen other Polish women. Aniela Pawliszak lived in a camp of 7,000 women, where over 70 percent were Russian and only 9 percent Polish. A teacher imprisoned in a camp at Karabas, which she called "hell on earth," was the only Pole in a large population of other nationalities.[5]

Statistics on the national composition of the Gulag population offer a sense of the place of ethnic Poles in the mass of humanity confined in the Soviet penal system. Recently published studies document 1.25 million individuals populating the camps in 1939. Poles made up 1.3 percent of the total Gulag inmates at the end of that year.[6] The percentage no doubt rose somewhat in the ensuing years as thousands more Poles were arrested in occupied Poland in 1940–1941. While Russians and Ukrainians constituted the majority of camp inmates (63% and 14%, respectively), disproportionately large numbers of other national groups were found in the camps, including Germans, Finns, Latvians, Lithuanians, Koreans, and Estonians.

Polish documents show that the ethnic composition of communities of deportees tended to vary less than in prisons and labor camps. Some groups of deportees were simply deposited in the wilderness of the Arctic north or Siberia, where they were the only residents for hundreds of miles. Poles in this situation had little contact with Soviet citizens.[7] Other groups ended up in settlements of exiled Soviet citizens, mostly kulaks, peasants punitively resettled as part of the collectivization campaign, or members of other suspicious groups displaced on Stalin's orders throughout the 1930s.[8] Transports of Poles were often added to these communities of exiles, where they lived closely with Russians, Ukrainians, Jews, Soviet Poles, and Volga Germans.[9] Finally, many Polish deportees were sent to collective and state farms (*kolkhozy* and *sovkhozy*), especially in Central Asia, where they lived among Soviet families of various nationalities, most frequently Russian, Ukrainian, Kazakh, Kirghiz, and Uzbek.

Polish women thus lived and worked in extremely close contact with individuals foreign to them. It bears remembering that the Poles came from a country in which their language, customs, and religion predominated, at least for the twenty years preceding the German and Soviet invasions. Exile robbed them of their cultural context. Gender segregation exacerbated the situation, for females spent most of their time in exile separated from the men of their own families and communities and, thus, lost another anchor of their identity. Men and women were segregated in prison cells and camp barracks and usually toiled in separate work brigades. The settlements contained more mixed groups, but the male population in free exile commonly consisted of the very young, the old, and the infirm, and after the Russo-German war began in 1941, local males left for the front in droves. Thus the able-bodied adult communities were largely and unnaturally female. The unfamiliar and unsettling demographics of exile undermined the coherence and authority of the uprooted Poles, who countered by reinforcing their own conceptions of national boundaries and gender certainties.

Gender plays a paramount role in their discussions of "others," for Polish women largely judge other nationalities through their female members. Traditions and expectations for their own behavior serve as universal measures for womanliness. Conflating individual women with the ethnic groups to which they belong, Polish women interpret differences from themselves as violations of proper norms, emblematic of the alienness and inferiority of the other groups as a whole. In this way Polish women can separate themselves from these others and their perceived improper behavior, thus defining themselves through contrast. In the words of Nira Yuval-Davies and Floya Anthias, women thus figure "as signifiers of ethnic/national differences—as a focus and symbol in ideological discourses used in the construction, reproduction and transformation of ethnic/national categories."[10] Given that they construed gender roles as natural, inherent to the female being, Poles' assessments of other women commented on the cultural and moral level of the entire nationality.

The quantity and character of the comments made about

women of non-Polish nationality vary significantly, depending on the degree of a group's alienness to the Poles and the extent to which it posed a threat to the cohesiveness and identity of the exiled women. On this basis, others are divided into three separate groups. The first consists of women criticized because of their perceived failures as members of the community of Polish citizens. This group, the focus of chapter 6, includes Jews, Belorussians, and Ukrainians likewise deported from Poland. Polish women felt especially threatened by the differences they perceived between themselves and women of Soviet Central Asia, the second group, and Russian women, the third. Not wanting to be like them, they used gender to attack these nations that they feared and abhorred. Chapters 7 and 8 examine the Poles' interpretations of Central Asians and Russians.

6

"They Abused Our Fatherland"

Coexisting with the National Minorities

In Polish women's accounts of their experience in the USSR, discussion of women of the ethnic minorities from Poland centers on their loyalty to the community and the nation. They did not perceive these women, compared with other peoples with them in exile, as alien. Because of their long history of coexistence, the Jews, Ukrainians, and Belorussians were familiar to Poles. The lives of the minority groups were "culturally intelligible,"[1] and thus did not directly challenge Polish women's own social roles. Consequently, the Poles do not focus their comments on intimate matters—the personal hygiene, sexuality, religious observance, or familial relations of these other women. In fact, most Polish women seem to have initially considered the national minorities as their own, as fellow members of a collective, citizens of one broad fatherland.

The challenge these others posed stemmed from national identity, for in manifesting difference or disunity, they threatened the authority and solidarity of the women as Poles. Though the question of loyalty to the nation was paramount, gender still mattered, for the Poles modeled the unity of the nation on traditional gender roles, with particular norms for the behavior of women. Accusing females of the national minorities of violating some of these expectations, ethnic Poles ultimately excluded them from the community of Poles, and indirectly rendered them lesser women. Nationality superseded gender in this relationship, but they were nonetheless intertwined.

National Groups in Interwar Poland

The Second Polish Republic was home not merely to the Polish nation but to large minority groups. According to official statistics, the largest group, Ukrainians, constituted 14 percent of the population, while Jews made up 9 percent and Belorussians 3 percent.[2] Still, ethnic Poles were the majority (69%). In compliance with the demands of U.S. President Woodrow Wilson and the Allies, the newly established Polish government pledged fair treatment of its non-Polish subjects and signed the Minorities Protection Treaty in 1919, guaranteeing civil and national rights to minorities. Additionally, Article 96 of the Constitution of 1921 asserted that "all citizens are equal according to the law. . . . The Republic of Poland does not recognize a privileged nationality."[3] In practice, however, the national minorities were at a decided disadvantage in interwar Poland. The issue of minorities' rights was a constant source of debate and acrimony among politicians, most prominently Roman Dmowski, the leader of the Polish right, and Józef Piłsudski, the leader of the left, who differed as to whether the resurrected Poland should be a nation-state or a multiethnic federation.[4] Throughout the interwar period, politicians and the press were preoccupied with the question of the place of these peoples in the Polish state.

The issue of minority peoples had not always been so contentious for Polish patriots. After the final partition of Poland in 1795, the Polish national movement—the concern of a small elite—focused not on who belonged to the nation but on regaining independence. After the loss of their state, Brian Porter explains, patriotic Poles "removed their nation from the material world in which tyrants could destroy and oppress, and they relocated it onto a transcendent spiritual plane."[5] Thus emerged the idea of Poland as a moral principle, a national essence. In the 1830s and 1840s, Polish romantics elaborated this notion, imbuing Poland with a mission to bring freedom to all oppressed nations. The poet Adam Mickiewicz cast Poland as the "Christ of nations," having the task of the earthly salvation of mankind and the regeneration of its spirit.[6] Such a notion of Polishness, based on the struggle for universal justice, required allegiance and participation, not ethnic homogeneity; it easily included Jews, who, after the partitions, came to be called "Poles of the Mosaic faith."[7] This idealism constituted the predominant expression of Polish nationalism at least until the 1860s.

The national idea began to change after the failed insurrection of 1863, which met with severe repression from Russian authorities. A new generation of liberals, the positivists, turned their energies from messianism and the fight for independence to "reawakening the vital powers of society" and began to conceive of the nation as an empirically identifiable society.[8] It was not, however, until the 1880s that a new wave of intellectuals, who rejected liberal tenets, began to define the nation according to rigid ethno-linguistic criteria. These thinkers, the originators of the National Democracy movement, embraced and mobilized the masses of peasants, heretofore indifferent to the nation and its politics. "In the process," Porter explains, "they constructed high walls of exclusion around the Polish nation, with solidarity and authority inside and hatred and violence outside."[9] By the beginning of the twentieth century, this exclusive form of nationalism regarded Belorussians, Ukrainians, and Lithuanians living on lands considered Polish as inferior peoples who would have to assimilate to the higher common culture of the Poles. It turned more virulently against Jews, casting them as an unassimilable other. According to Theodore Weeks, by 1912, anti-Semitism had become acceptable "at almost all levels of Polish society."[10]

Ethnic Poles regarded the reestablishment of a Polish state in 1918, after 123 years of foreign domination, as the triumph of their nation. For many, the long suffering of the Polish people justified organizing the state to fulfill the needs of ethnic Poles exclusively—to the detriment of minorities. Followers of Dmowski's National Democratic Party, in particular, believed that Poles would only prosper through "the most unsentimental national egoism."[11] Many Poles of all classes embraced the modern phenomenon of integral nationalism.

Despite its assurances to the Allies, the Polish government increasingly pursued chauvinistic policies. Much of its attention focused on the eastern borderlands, where ethnic Poles made up only one-third of the population. Ukrainians accounted for another third, while Belorussians, Jews, and peasants described as locals, each made up 10 percent of the total.[12] Some Poles considered it their duty to spread their enlightening influence in the region, the *kresy*. According to the National Democrats: "Where we can increase our strength and civilizing work, absorbing other elements, no right is forbidden us, we even have an obligation to do so." Piłsudski, who ruled from 1926 to 1935, sought to uphold older, nonexclusivist traditions of Poland and recognized the distinctness of the three nationalities. Nevertheless, he considered them ahistoric nations; it was, therefore, the duty of the Poles to lead them.[13] Increasing nationalism among some Ukrainians resulted in radicalization and even terrorist acts against the Polish government, which contributed to the spiraling tension among the various national groups. Tensions ran particularly high in the southeastern provinces, developing into violent clashes between Ukrainians, represented by the Ukrainian Nationalist Organization (O.U.N.), and Polish landowners and authorities. The government responded with a bloody "pacification" program in Ukrainian areas.

As the economy declined and the international situation grew more unstable and dangerous in the 1930s, the slogan, "Poland for the Poles," gained popularity. In 1934, the government repudiated the Minorities Protection Treaty. Resentment toward Jews, predominantly urban dwellers, resulted in economic boycotts, fistfights, and even pogroms. Anti-Semites increasingly characterized the Jews as ungrateful to their hosts, accused them of weakening the nation, and linked them to Communism, popularizing the myth of *żydokomuna* (Judeo-Communism). Piłsudski's cronies, who succeeded him to power after his death in 1935, gave in to popular anti-Semitism and instituted administrative measures to weaken the Jewish role in the economy and to drastically reduce their presence in academic institutions. The atmosphere prevailing in Europe at the time supported these developments; for Polish right-radicals, as for the Nazis, anti-Semitism "was intrinsic to social modernization and nation-building."[14] Hostility among the national groups within Poland mounted as the decade neared its end.

Increasing intolerance of national minorities constitutes a dominant trend in interwar Poland. The picture, however, is more complicated, especially for the eastern borderlands, the area the USSR invaded in 1939. Considerable evidence suggests that the national lines were not uniformly drawn so sharply. Jerzy Tomaszewski, a historian of national relations in Poland between the wars, asserts that even in 1939 many of the region's inhabitants either did not possess a strong feeling of nationality or were relatively indifferent to it.[15] In Polish political thought, the *kresy* signified the national margins.[16] This region represented a place of national blurring. Some elements of its heterogeneous population lacked a strong national consciousness. Many of these individuals, rural dwellers speaking Slavic dialects, possessed no clear-cut allegiance and found it difficult to answer the question on nationality posed by census takers. Some declared their nationality as *tutejszy*, meaning simply, "from here," revealing a regional sense of belonging. Peasants frequently identified themselves by the name of the region in which they lived—the "nation bore no meaning in their lives." One man explained of his fellow villagers: "As for national consciousness, the older peasants called themselves Masurians, and their speech Masurian. They lived their own life, forming a wholly separate group, and caring nothing for the nation."[17] According to historian Juliusz Bardach, this attachment to a locality persisted throughout the interwar period.[18]

The unconsolidated nature of national identity in the eastern portions of the country is confirmed by the government's efforts to Polonize these lands. In late 1920, the Sejm initiated a settlement program in which ethnic Polish officers and soldiers who fought in recent wars were given free plots of land (*osady*) in the east, with the expectation that they would serve as a polonizing element and policing force. Civilian colonists later received similar inducements to farm there. Education policies, though providing for some Ukrainian and Belorussian schools, consistently favored instruction in Polish. Additionally, the creation of the Frontier Defense Corps (K.O.P.) was undertaken not only to protect the eastern border but also to quell internal unrest and spread Polish propaganda. Not surprisingly, such endeavors served to increase hostility among the nationally minded elements of the other peoples there. Most importantly, they demonstrate the anxiety of the Polish government over an insufficiently Polonized population and its fear that ethnic Poles would fall under the influence of their Ukrainian and Belorussian neighbors—including those living across the Soviet border.[19]

The phenomenon of a regionally based identity also existed among some inhabitants of the historic Lithuanian lands in the northeast, though in a different form. It harkened to the days of the Polish-Lithuanian union (1569–1795), when many living there declared as their fatherland, in its narrowest sense, Lithuania, and in a broader sense, Poland. Consciousness as a Lithuanian stemmed from ties to the land, as a Pole, from connections to the larger political entity. This form of consciousness, with its attachment to a region or state, differs substantially from the modern conception of nationality based on ethno-linguistic ties and has been variously described as political nationalism, historical consciousness, and state patriotism.[20]

For some inhabitants of the historic Polish-Lithuanian lands, most notably Czesław Miłosz, this form of identity endured well into the twentieth century. Born in the city of Wilno (Vilna in Russian) in 1911, when it belonged to the Russian Empire, he grew up in the same physical place but in the new Polish state. A poet and writer in the Polish language, his roots in the territory of the old Grand Duchy of Lithuania, Miłosz refuses to tag himself with a conventional national identity. Rather, he claims allegiance to a native realm, a region defined predominantly by its mixture of languages, religions, and traditions. Such a mixture distinguishes not only the population as a whole, he emphasizes; the individuals inhabiting it are themselves a "mélange of Polish, Lithuanian and German blood."[21] While individuals claiming a pure nationality frequently disregarded this reality, there were also others, such as Mikołaj Michałkiewicz, the administrator of the diocese of Wilno, who declared himself, "a bit Pole, a bit Lithuanian, a bit Belorussian."[22] Such individuals could still regard Poland as their fatherland.

Similarly, some Jews claimed Polish as their nationality; many of those living in the cities were highly assimilated. Władysław Bartoszewski cautions against an unequivocal distinction between Catholics and Polish Jews, stating, "Jews had no reason to assume that Poland was not their country since they were loyal citizens of the state."[23] Though Zionists increasingly looked to Palestine as a home for Polish Jews, they did not represent the majority of the Jewish population. In the late 1930s, the assimilationist movement focused on educating the Jew "as a conscientious and true citizen of the Polish state." Though it criticized the state and demanded that it accord Jews equality, the movement "declared Poland to be the only Fatherland of its members."[24]

Historians of the eastern borderlands maintain that boundaries based on nationality were often less rigid and vital there. Divisions between peoples based on nationality were not as uniformly set as the statistics and rhetoric of the interwar years lead one to believe. As Tomaszewski writes, one of the problems with census data on nationalities is that they "pose unequivocal borders where such delimitations in the attitudes of people did not exist, as there were more or less numerous circles of intermediate character, mixing within themselves various cultural elements."[25] According to

Janusz Żarnowski, the eastern territories were distinguished by "the un-finished process of the formation of nations and crystallization of national boundaries . . . as well as the centuries long coexistence of mixed national groups."[26] Similarly, Roman Wapiński concludes that in the *kresy* closeness based on customs and language often prevailed over conflicts based on na-tionality.[27] Ezra Mendelsohn contends that relations between Jews and gen-tiles were better in the *kresy* than elsewhere in Poland.[28] Peaceful coexistence and indeterminacy must also be incorporated into the picture of relations among individuals of the various groups of eastern Poland. National con-flict alone, though certainly important, fails to capture the complexity of the region.

The bulk of women whose statements form the basis for this study lived in eastern Poland before their exile. They were not the politicians or intellectual elites who play a large role in the scholarly literature on national relations between the wars. Living largely in villages and small towns, such individuals have not been given direct attention in the literature, making it impossible to determine their prewar conceptions of nation and commu-nity. Undoubtedly, many of the women viewed these others according to prevailing stereotypes and had a negative opinion of them before 1939. For some individuals from the so-called national margins, borders between eth-nic groups may well have been blurred or less consequential. In daily life, most of these women probably had little need to draw impermeable lines around a small, homogeneous community. Likewise, a clear consensus on precisely what it meant to be a Pole was not necessary.

The situation changed drastically with the Red Army invasion of 1939. The Soviet regime, cloaking its actions under the announced intention of liberating the Ukrainians and Belorussians, brother Slavs, from the yoke of the Polish *pans*, tagged everyone according to their national origins, promot-ing rivalry and even violence between the national groups. In many instances, particularly in the weeks immediately following the invasion, differential treatment was meted out according to national identity. Finally, by striking out against everything that was Polish, including institutions, monuments, language, education, and religion, the occupiers fostered conditions in which ethnic Poles, confronted by a traditional enemy, asserted their Polishness. To maintain a distinct identity, to resist the pressures of Soviet authorities, and to respond to escalating interethnic tensions, many people erected bor-ders themselves, where perhaps none, or only weak ones, existed before. In the context of undeclared war, the lines separating national groups grew much more important and impervious. Ready-made stereotypes helped the Poles categorize the people around them.

Relations in Soviet-Occupied Poland

The Soviet regime sought to enact a social revolution in the territory its army occupied and initially seized upon politics of nationality as the means to that end. The invading Communists set out to destroy a state and social system largely ruled by and in the interests of ethnic Poles. Consequently, the occupiers used the grievances and aspirations of members of other national groups both to justify Soviet actions and to spur the minorities to turn against the Polish state and its upholders. The invaders encouraged chaos and violence: "Leaflets urged Belorussian and Ukrainian peasants to grab pitchforks, axes, saws and scythes and overwhelm the Polish landlords. . . . As the Red Army moved through the countryside and villages, political commissars and soldiers told the local peasants to take all they wanted from the landlords and rich farmers."[29] In the ensuing interethnic conflict, Polish nationality in many cases was enough to define one as an enemy and, therefore, a target for retribution. In the immediate postinvasion period, more violence stemmed from interethnic conflict than class struggle.[30]

Soviet propaganda appealed to some citizens of eastern Poland, who responded enthusiastically to the invasion and the calls to attack the old order. Though the extent of this cooperation with the invaders has not been quantified, evidence suggests its widespread nature. "For the record it must be stated unambiguously," asserts Jan Gross, that "throughout the Western Ukraine and Western Belorussia, in hamlets, villages and towns, the Red Army was welcomed by smaller or larger, but in any case, visible, friendly crowds. They were largely composed of young people from the so-called ethnic minorities—Belorussians, Jews, Ukrainians."[31] Similarly, Aleksander Smolar concludes: "The evidence is overwhelming: large numbers of Jews welcomed the Soviet invasion, implanting in Polish memory the image of Jewish crowds greeting the invading Red Army as their liberator."[32] Witnesses report that members of the minorities set up triumphal arches and waved red banners. They gave the soldiers flowers or presented them with bread and salt, a traditional ritual of greeting. They embraced and kissed the soldiers, sometimes even their tanks.

Jan Karski, a courier for the Polish government-in-exile, visited the Soviet-occupied territory late in 1939 and reported: "In most cities the Jews greeted the Bolsheviks with baskets of red roses, with submissive declarations and speeches, etc., etc."[33] Such cooperation reportedly extended beyond the initial invasion. Soon afterwards, some Jews joined militias and took posts in the new administration. According to a Jewish memorial book from the region, "The Russians trusted the Jewish population more than the Poles and the Ukrainians, and, therefore, the higher posts were allotted to the Jews." Karski also noted the influx of Jews into positions of authority or advantage, concluding, "in the vast majority of cases, their situation is better both economically and politically than it was before the war."[34]

Those Jews who displayed support for the new order did so for various reasons. Some acted out of ideological sympathy with Bolshevik goals. Jews played a large role in interwar Polish Communist organizations, in which they were overrepresented in membership and conspicuous in leadership positions.[35] For such persons, the Red Army's arrival brought hope for a more egalitarian society. But it was not only leftist activists who saw promise in the new situation. Karski elaborates: "The Jewish proletariat, small merchants, artisans, and all those whose position has at present been improved *structurally*, and who had formerly been exposed primarily to oppression, indignities, excesses, etc., from the Polish element—all of these responded positively, if not enthusiastically, to the new regime."[36] In other words, the new regime gave some Jews that which the Poles had denied them—leadership positions, material advantages, and elevated status. The new order seemed to promise an end to anti-Semitism. "The Communist ideal suited the Jews even more because it reduced the 'national question' to a perspective in which all ethnic programmes could be absorbed," explain Pawel Korzec and Jean-Charles Szurek. "The Soviet Union, perceived as stripped of national impediments, and as the 'homeland of the workers,' also constituted a homeland for the Jews."[37]

Some Jews welcomed the Communists as literal saviors. Several hundred thousand Jews fled the Nazi occupation of western Poland, where they faced grave danger, to find refuge in the east. For such individuals, the Soviet occupation appeared preferable. Likewise, practical concerns dictated acquiescence to the new policies. Refugees deprived of their homes and means of support had to comply with the new authorities to receive housing and jobs. Without relatives in the surrounding countryside to turn to, such individuals were particularly vulnerable. Even Jews native to the eastern provinces found themselves in a precarious position as time went on. "The destruction of trade, crafts, and the liberal professions—predominantly Jewish sectors—meant that the Jews had to look for a place in the new structure," write Korzec and Szurek. "They had no other choice, either because of economic uprooting or as a result of interracial conflicts."[38]

Other national groups acted from different motives. Some Ukrainians greeted the Red Army with joy, but typically for national rather than ideological reasons.[39] To Ukrainian nationalists, its arrival promised the fulfillment of national goals, which seemed to require the destruction of the Polish state—namely, the unification of Ukraine as a sovereign nation-state. Opposed to the status quo, such individuals eagerly cooperated with the occupiers, particularly by joining the new militias and replacing Polish schoolteachers and administrators, thereby usurping Polish authority.[40] Belorussians—largely landless peasants—hoped for the achievement of material goals, and often responded to the Soviet appeal to seize land from Polish landowners. Some individuals apparently indulged personal and emotional urges, using the invasion and accompanying chaos to settle old scores.[41] Individuals from all three minority groups engaged in activities largely to the detriment of ethnic Poles: denunciation and creation of lists for deportation, round-ups and arrests, participation in the new administration, formation of militias, land seizure and robbery, attacks and executions.[42] Of course, some Poles were guilty of the same.

Not all Jews, Ukrainians, or Belorussians viewed the arrival of Soviet troops positively. Like the Poles, the minority groups exhibited diversity in attitudes and behavior, and many individuals remained loyal to their state and their Polish neighbors. While discussing Jewish cooperation with the Bolsheviks, Karski also notes exceptions. "I have the impression that the intelligentsia, the wealthiest Jews and those of the highest level of culture," he writes, "rather think of Poland often with a certain fondness and would happily greet a change in the present situation [leading to] the independence of Poland."[43] Likewise, Ukrainians and Belorussians who owned land feared the arrival of the Soviets. Nor did initial acceptance or even collaboration prevent later mistreatment of non-Poles by the Soviet regime; once its authority was established, it set out to curtail the national, political, and economic aspirations of local supporters not in line with the Communist system. Thus Jews, Belorussians, and Ukrainians also ended up on cattle cars headed eastward.

Relations with the National Minorities in Exile

The documents suggest that interethnic conflicts and rivalries on Polish territory following the Red Army invasion set the tone for relations in exile. It is impossible to determine how the women regarded the national minorities before 1939, as they left no comparable writings from the pre-war period. Claims that Polish animosity stemmed solely from national minorities' cooperation with the Soviets or demonstrated hostility toward ethnic Poles cannot simply be accepted.[44] Whatever antagonistic acts did occur after the invasion stemmed from preexisting tensions and certainly reinforced negative stereotypes in the minds of the Poles. Without trying to apportion blame, it can be said that Polish attitudes toward Jews, Ukrainians, and Belorussians only hardened in exile. Polish women's documents display a negative overall assessment of all three minority groups. The critical nature of the Polish attitude toward the national minorities is highlighted in a memo written in 1943 by Lieutenant Telmany of the Bureau of Documents of the Polish Army in the East. Discussing whether the reports should be treated as historical documents and reproduced exactly as written or used as propaganda tools for the Polish government and, therefore, edited, he notes: "There is not a single statement in which one could not find at least one episode, paragraph or sentence, containing anti-Semitic or anti-Ukrainian sentiments, or describing how some segments of our population took the side of the Reds in October 1939."[45] The women's attitudes turn on the question of loyalty and betrayal.

It must be emphasized that the national minorities were fellow victims. Though the deportations primarily targeted ethnic Poles, Polish citizens of other nationalities, too, were arrested and deported from their homes, suffering similar maltreatment and deprivation. Traditional estimates break down the dislocated population as follows: Poles, 58 percent; Jews, 19.4 percent; Ukrainians, 14.9 percent; Belorussians, 6.3 percent; and others, 1.4 percent.[46] The majority of exiled Jews had fled Nazi oppression in the German partition of Poland and suffered deportation simply because they applied to return to the west—thus displaying, in the eyes of the occupiers, disloyalty toward the new regime.[47] While a few Poles note this ironic and tragic fate of the Jews, most offer no sympathy, condemning them as Communists or equating them with the criminals and worst elements of Polish society.[48] This also occurs in Polish discussions of Ukrainian and Belorussian women, who tended to be exiled for the same reasons as Poles—a fact Poles largely disregard. Describing fellow prisoners, many women declare that Poles were mainly arrested for political reasons, Jews for speculation and theft, and Ukrainians as common criminals. The level of intelligence of Poles, we are told, was high, while that of the others was uniformly low.[49] Polish women find it hard to concede similarity in the tragedy or moral character of their fellow victims.

Polish women generally did not conceive of these other women as belonging to other nations, as being a part of a whole other than the Polish state. The language used to describe them is possessive: they refer to "our minorities," "our Jews," or "Polish Ukrainians." This occurs when no differentiation, say, between Ukrainians from the USSR and Poland, is either needed or implied. This language suggests a separateness mitigated by long-term coexistence. For these women, common citizenship constituted an overarching category, at least in their initial expectations. Such comments as that of Amalia Jollesówna, reporting the joy of the Ukrainians at the arrival of the Red Army, highlight this implicit connection: "They broke from Polish citizens—Poles and Jews."[50]

Polish women's conception of the term "nationality"—its relationship to citizenship, blood, language, and religion—appears vague and shifting, rendering it impossible to state a consistent definition to which they adhered. On one level, Poles saw themselves as a distinct group joined by common language, religion, history, and customs. But the evidence provided in these documents suggests that the Polish collectivity did have room for the other groups, at least before the debacle of 1939. Though differences in language and religion rendered individuals less equal, there was still a sense in which these others could be Polish. Patriotism, devotion to the Polish state, and cooperation in promoting its welfare seemed to constitute the overriding criteria for being a Pole. Thus, one finds in the documents common usage of the terms, "Pole of the Mosaic faith," "Pole of Ukrainian nationality," or "Poles from Ukrainian families." These labels suggest the older, supranational conceptions of community and belonging, expressions of political nationalism or state patriotism. Some women use such labels as "real Poles" and "pseudo-Poles," further suggesting that ethnicity did not provide the sole definition of a Pole. The women's writings show that members of other ethnic groups could be considered Poles, as well. It may be that many ethnic Poles felt that those of different ethnic origin would always prove to be lesser Poles; but the reports and memoirs written after the amnesty reveal a need to prove this. In them, women use the criteria of patriotism, loyalty, and cooperation, rather than race, to exclude the national minorities from the Polish collectivity, narrowing its circle of membership.

In many cases, Poles present the minorities as excluding themselves, by declaration or by antagonistic behavior. Consider the following descriptions. A high school student deported to the Arkhangel'sk *oblast'* reports that in her settlement, "The Poles were all very close (I exclude the Ukrainians who constantly harmed us)." A typist sent to the prison camp Pot'ma states that "the Ukrainian women separated themselves and were hostile to the Polish women." Another woman writes: "The Ukrainians not only kept themselves at a distance but even outright declared themselves against the Poles, some even asserted that they didn't want to return to Poland."[51] In such typical cases Poles present the minorities as deciding themselves to scorn a collective to which they could have belonged.

The reverse proposition, that the minorities could be good Poles, remained a possibility. Janina Wawrzyńska offers the following description of her cellmates: "[The Ukrainians, Belorussians, and Jews] spied on us at every step and informed to the authorities things that happened and things that didn't. . . . Only in the camp, among shared hard labor, did they change their attitude toward us. With the passage of time, those who in prison informed and complained to the authorities, were good Poles in the camp." Another woman writes, "I must point out that the entire range of Jewish citizens of Poland were loyal in their opinions and never talked of Poland as anything but their own country, to which they wanted to return."[52] Although differences were never entirely erased, many Polish women recognized a bond that did, or should, link them with the others.

The women express a view of the broader nation as an extended family —though not an idyllic one. In the family of Polish citizens, the national minorities were the poor and distant relatives. Regardless of the bonds of common citizenship, community membership, gender, or familiarity, Polish females generally did not see women of the minority groups as equals and reveal an attitude of superiority toward them. Many use the vague term *Rusini* when referring to those women from Poland who spoke dialects of Ukrainian, signaling their perceived lack of a distinct national identity— especially one opposed to Polish identity. This conception echoes that of many politicians of the interwar period, who regarded the language and culture of Ukrainians, Belorussians, and Lithuanians merely as expressions of regionalism, the peoples themselves an "ethnic mass," whose allegiance was up for grabs by the strongest neighbor, either Poles or Russians. The notion that these others were of one family with the Poles was a constant in Polish political thought.[53] Most Polish women make it clear that they do not consider the Slavic minorities to be members of separate nations. If they grant them separate status, it is considered inferior or incidental to the larger entity of the Polish nation. For example, a woman from the town of Łuck writes that she was deported to Kazakhstan with Poles and Belorussians, adding, "I demarcate, since they gave such a nationality."[54] Polish women assume that the minorities were part of a larger whole, with attendant obligations.

Expecting these others to express a high level of patriotism and loyalty to the Polish state, the Poles became extremely resentful when this did not prove to be the case. Polish women did not suspect that their own foe might appear as liberator, friend, or a lesser evil to their neighbors. Beneath this lies a complete denial or lack of comprehension of the ways and reasons these others felt themselves to be different. Poles' demand for homogeneity comes through their scornful reports that some of their fellow deportees "now called themselves" Belorussian or were "representing themselves" as Ukrainians. They refer disdainfully to so-called Ukrainians or Belorussians.[55] In this way, Polish women attempt to erase the nationality of the minorities from Poland. Denying them their own identity, they turn the others from subjects into objects and obliterate their own suffering; if they do not have a separate nationality, they do not have a separate story to voice. The women thus privilege the Polish nation, and it alone becomes the subject of the narrative depicting the tragedy of the peoples of eastern Poland at the hands of the Soviet regime. The Poles are its victims and its heroes. The assertion by women of the minorities that they were not Polish posed not only a personal affront, but in the eyes of the Poles, one to the nation as well. They report such instances as treasonous.

Poles likewise took offense that these people "suddenly forgot how to speak Polish," "spoke only Russian now," or "refused to speak to us in Polish." Describing the "scheming" ways of "our *Rusini,*" one woman deplores the fact that "none of them even spoke in Polish," a complaint made against all three groups.[56] Simply put, many women of the national minorities spoke a language that was regarded as improper for them—both in the immediate sense of which Slavic language they used to communicate, and more broadly, in its unpatriotic content. In declaring their nationality to be something other than Polish, or in demonstrating their preferred tongue to be something other than Polish, individuals of the national minorities seemed to take an irrevocable step, for they asserted their difference from the Poles. Polish women understood manifestations of difference on these crucial grounds to mean that they were bad Poles and disloyal members of the community.

The reported hostility of Jewish, Belorussian, and Ukrainian women constitutes one of the most common themes in the documents. According to the Poles, they gloated over the fall of Poland, rejoicing that it no longer existed. They reportedly echoed the taunts of Soviet officials that the rule of the Poles was over and that Poland would never rise again. The phrase "your Poland" was even more bitter to Poles when coming from the mouths of former neighbors and fellow citizens. Living in crowded cells and barracks, Poles suffered from the slandering of Poland by the national minorities, who allegedly spread misinformation about how they had been treated there. Helena Antonewicz describes her transport to Russia as follows:

> My husband and I were the only Poles, the rest of the group were Jews. Some of them increasingly and more and more ruthlessly began to insult our national feelings with conversations in which they criticized everything that was Polish, and even expressed their satisfaction that Poland had lost its Independence. . . . It reached the point of a sharp exchange, which ended very painfully for my husband, as the upset caused him to cough up blood. From that moment the real torture began for us both.[57]

Bronisława Daszkiewicz, imprisoned for belonging to an underground organization, writes that the moral suffering she endured from insults to her patriotic feelings far outweighed the physical torture; the Ukrainian women in her cell, she adds, intensified it. Referring to one who bragged about her part in a terrorist act against the Polish state, Daszkiewicz deplores: "This one treated us unbelievably cruelly, saying untrue things about the Polish government and insulting the Polish nation."[58] Similarly, Irena Sypniewska writes: "Between the Poles and Ukrainians was an insane antagonism, at every step rang the epithets 'Polish pig' or 'Polish lord' [*pan*]. . . . We often heard loud praise for the Ukrainians for the number of Polish soldiers who had passed through their villages and were killed."[59] Women express shock and pain at hearing members of the minorities "tell macabre stories about their oppression by the Poles back at home." A great number of women might have written this statement: "It's hard to find the words to describe how they abused our Fatherland."[60]

Such incidents led to the identification of the groups, en masse, as treasonous. Typically Ukrainians are labeled nationalists, Jews as Communists, and Belorussians as "Communized" or "Bolshevized," signaling their misplaced allegiance to something other than the Polish state. Even without these labels, Ukrainians, Belorussians, and Jews are resented as ungrateful relatives, as Polish women voice outrage that "our national minorities," who, they felt, had it so good in Poland, could turn against their homeland, slandering and renouncing it.

Jews are especially singled out as turncoats, who switched their allegiance according to prevailing winds. In the Polish depiction, they are loyal to nothing—which the Poles consider incomprehensible and unforgivable. A woman from a village near Wilno writes:

> Only after announcement of the amnesty, several of them were ingratiatingly polite, and in contact with the authorities they all emphasized that they were Polish women. To the angry comment of an NKVD agent that several months ago during interrogation one of them said that she was a Jew and not a Pole, and now changed her nationality, she answered that one had to obey the authorities: the Soviets ordered us to put ourselves down as Jews and not Poles—so we said that—now you're allies with Poland—so we are Poles.[61]

Soviet authorities did, in fact, forbid many Polish citizens of different ethnicity to claim Polish nationality. After the amnesty, they refused to recognize them as Polish citizens, which was the criterion for release. The women, however, generally disregard the pressure exerted on the minorities to disavow Polish nationality; instead, they consider such cases proof of disloyalty. Furthermore, they do not register episodes of ethnic Poles renouncing their citizenship, rendering such behavior the exclusive trait of non-Polish ethnicity. Polish women present a similar picture of the Soviet passportization campaign conducted earlier in the occupied territories: "Among the Poles they met with a refusal, as everyone saw nonacceptance of the passport as his national obligation and preferred a difficult fate to the voluntary agreement to a citizenship that was degrading to him. The Jews acted differently. Many of them sought to accept the passport, in spite of the fact that two weeks ago they could be seen in the ranks of those registering for evacuation to the German occupation."[62] One detail left out here is that apartments and jobs were made available only to those who accepted Soviet passports: Jewish refugees from German-occupied Poland could less afford to resist the demands of the new administration. Poles apply a blanket obligation of noncompliance, regardless of differences in circumstances. The accuracy of the Polish depiction must also be questioned. For example, Ola Watowa, a Polish Jew deported to Kazakhstan, faced interrogations and went to prison for refusing a Soviet passport.[63]

Poles censure the others not only for verbal transgressions and explicitly unpatriotic actions but also for spoiling relations and making the daily life of their fellow exiles more miserable—which they also construe as unpatriotic. Some Polish women even assert that their own minorities treated them worse than Soviets did. Wincenta Paulo writes that initially relations in her cell were good. "Only when they started to make arrests among Ukrainian nationalists were relations spoiled," she continues. In prison cells and camp barracks, Ukrainian, Jewish, and Belorussian women reportedly served as provocateurs, often instigating fights with the Poles. Furthermore, one Pole asserts that "they managed to incite the Soviet women against us, telling them lies about conditions in Poland." Maria Arciszewska recalls such an incident: "Masha Kraska, a Jewish woman from Grodno—Trojecka Street—said in the prison in Petropavelsk that Jews in Poland didn't have any rights at all, that they were beaten and tortured, that there were pogroms, and when I pointed out to her that it was all slander, that the Jews had it very well in Poland, she turned the whole cell against me and the Communists almost killed me."[64] Polish women do not try to reconcile the claims of the national minorities with reality nor do they allow for legitimate grievances against ethnic Poles or the Polish government. Blind to the injustices that were perpetrated against the minorities in the interwar period, they operate from a strict code of loyalty and obedience. In this framework, those others are merely traitors, the Poles the victims. Polish women thus not only disregard unwanted truths but use the slanderers to construct a superior identity for themselves.

By far the most frequent complaint—and in the Polish context, most damning—against the minorities is that they served as informants, spying on ethnic Poles and reporting their activities and conversations to the NKVD. The majority of women who discuss the national minorities, whether they spent their time in prisons, camps, or settlements, make this charge.[65] The most odious aspect of their treasonous informing, it seems, was that it caused many good Poles to be arrested; some Poles even attribute the eventual death of imprisoned relatives to the initial act of denouncement by disloyal others. Antonina Siemińska was deported with her family to Novosibirsk; while there, a Jew denounced her husband as an officer, he was taken away and died—a sequence she links just so closely.[66] In nearly all of the women's stories of being set up or turned in, whether it happened to themselves, family members, or acquaintances, the culprit is a Belorussian, Ukrainian, or Jew.[67]

Significantly, the sin appears graver when it harmed Polish men. When the informant's victim is female, the narrator tends to mention a name or simply use the term "a woman"; if she adds more, it usually is that the victim was a mother who left behind a number of poor children. The tragedy of her loss lies in the fact that someone depended on her for care. Polish men punished because of the treason of the minorities receive a more pronounced emphasis, in terms depicting their patriotism and dearness to the Polish nation. Karolina Dominiakowa, disparaging the Belorussians, writes: "Thanks to them, five Polish patriots from the settlement were arrested." A high school student deported to the region of Novosibirsk reports that individuals of other nationalities went over to the Bolsheviks: "When there were gatherings for discussion in a certain apartment, their supporters crept in among the others and so delivered the best sons of the Fatherland into the hands of the Bolsheviks."[68] The gender-based differences in these depictions underscores the unequal relationship of males and females to the nation. Men—patriots, sons of the fatherland, defenders of the nation—have a direct relationship to it, while the family mediates that of women, whose own suffering is regarded as less critical to the nation.

Besides complaining about informing, women voice objections to a range of activities they attribute to the others and consider violations of the code of duty to the nation and community. The following assertions appear frequently. Only members of the minorities joined the Russians by accepting positions of authority in the camps. As brigade leaders, they were particularly cruel to Polish women, exhorting them to work harder and recording a lower output than they achieved. Non-Polish doctors refused to grant the necessary medical exemptions from labor to sick Poles, forcing them to face arrest if they missed work or further deterioration of their health if they went. Soviet authorities often arranged cultural events aimed at indoctrinating the exiles in Communist ideology: only Jews, Ukrainians, and Belorussians attended these films, plays, lectures, and parades.[69]

These claims are invariably juxtaposed to descriptions of Polish women, setting up a sharp contrast between Poles and non-Poles. The former reportedly refused to serve as brigade leaders to avoid pushing exhausted and emaciated women in their jobs. In rare cases when they accepted the position they soon lost it because of that very disposition. "It was characteristic that Polish women rarely lasted long in that function," explains a former clerk. "This came from the fact that they could not be ruthless in relation to their companions subordinated to them."[70] Women similarly report losing their positions as doctors or nurses for granting too many exemptions from labor, which they did to provide some relief to fellow exiles. Countless women assert that the Poles boycotted Soviet cultural events or whistled loudly as a group to drown out the offensive voices of the political instructors.[71]

Polish females valued both noncompliance with Soviet demands and a commitment to assist fellow exiles. They present the minority women as selfish people looking out only for themselves, serving the Soviet regime "for their own interests."[72] Jews, Belorussians, and Ukrainians, in the Polish depiction, routinely violated the cardinal values of mutual aid and solidarity. The women abhor the habit they ascribe to these others of placing their own interests above those of the collective, be it the nation or the small community in which they lived. This contrasts with the near monopoly on noble behavior the Poles confer on their own nationality.

Polish women blame individuals of the national minorities for difficult relations, maintaining for themselves an image of exemplary neighbors and innocent victims. They do not interpret the reticence or noncooperation of such persons merely as an anti-Polish stance. Instead, they see antagonistic behavior as evidence of the corrupted nature of the minorities, condemning them for not acting properly as members of their communities—whether the large collective of exiles from Poland or smaller ones based on ethnicity or residency. Poles report disapprovingly that Jews also informed on Russian women in the cells who openly discussed the terrible conditions in their country. The Belorussians and Ukrainians were "extremely susceptible and open to the influence of reshaping by the local authorities, for their own benefit," states Wanda Daszkiewiczówna. "Everyone lived for himself."[73] Women write that troubled relations prevailed not only between the Poles and the others but also within those groups. One woman notes that relations among women in her labor camp "were generally speaking, good." But she adds: "There were very bad relations among our Polish Jews, and in their relationship toward us."[74] Many Polish women seem unable or unwilling to notice community among the other nationalities. They concede to these others an ability to achieve solidarity mainly for hostile purposes, to harass the Poles.[75]

Without directly studying the experience of non-Poles in Soviet exile, it is impossible to make conclusions about their mutual relations. Certainly the unvaried portrayal by Polish women is suspect. A Latvian deportee, for example, offers an opposing view, asserting that in his settlement the Jews "supported each other far more than did other nations."[76] The writer Aleksander Wat, a Polish Jew, thus describes the Ukrainians with whom he shared a cell in Zamarstynów prison: "In comparison with Poles and Jews . . . theirs was a beautiful community, with excellent traits of loyalty and solidarity, with a natural sense of human hierarchy, not one that had been imposed on them."[77]

The perception of Polish women is crucial, not so much for the picture it gives of the others but for what it reveals about themselves. They see cohesion and mutual support as fundamental elements in their individual families and in the family of the nation. The relational nature of their identity is key: as mothers, wives, daughters, and Poles, they view themselves as existing in conjunction with others and having duties and obligations to them. Individualism and self-sufficiency are not qualities that draw praise from these women; solidarity and cooperation do. Hence, those whom they characterize as isolated and independent are lesser people. These insults fall not just on individuals but their entire nationality.

Having lost their homes and previous individual identities, Polish women found in the collective both an identity and a means for survival. They were profoundly disturbed by anyone who refused to cooperate or threatened this communal effort at survival. Such dangerous individuals had to become non-Poles. The projection onto others of what we most fear and reject in ourselves is a common mechanism in the cultural representation of others, enabling the corresponding definition of self.[78] In this context, the other women almost automatically became individuals who selfishly looked out for themselves, heedless of the good of any greater unit. "Some did not lose their spirit and kept others going," writes a woman deported to the Semipalatynsk *oblast'*, "others wanting to improve their daily lives, ingratiated themselves with the Soviet authorities (generally the Ukrainians)."[79] As a further illustration of such selfish tendencies, Polish women report that when they staged uprisings to protest the ill-treatment of fellow prisoners by the NKVD, members of the minorities often refrained from participating. Here is one such description: "Many times an uprising arose in the women's section, when the ear-piercing screams of tortured men reached us. The Jews did not take part. The Ukrainians, however, joined in solidarity with us. . . . The next day we did not eat breakfast. The Jews ate."[80] Such disloyal women, guilty of shirking communal obligations, stand in stark contrast to the Polish women, who present themselves as ever loyal and self-sacrificing.

The issue of faith in the future takes on great significance in the daily lives of Polish women and in their representations of non-Poles. While Polish women reportedly refused to surrender their faith in a just future and a return to home, the Soviet regime succeeded in breaking that hope in the others. Kazimiera Bola writes that the NKVD often summoned Poles for discussions, during which they tried to destroy their hope for the future: "They succeeded only with the Jews." According to Janina Seudek-Malanowicz, the Poles "were distinguished by a great faith in the future of independent Poland," while the Ukrainian women "were half convinced that the status quo could remain and they would be forced to stay in Russia till the end of their lives." This had serious implications for their conduct and loyalty. She continues that because of this lack of faith, "their behavior had a different character, more conciliatory and treasonous, full of fatalism." Even worse, Poles maintain, some minority women tried to destroy hope in others. A woman imprisoned with Belorussians and Jews writes: "They wanted to kill in me the hope, or rather belief, which intensified every day, that Poland would rise and that Poland had to rise."[81] Such accusations stand out boldly against the innumerable stories of how Polish women sought to comfort each other and keep hope alive.

The Poles clung tightly to the belief that they would obtain their freedom and see the resurrection of independent Poland. This was a difficult battle, as Soviet authorities and locals continually taunted them with the slogans, "Poland will never rise again," and "Your grave is here." Presented as a life and death struggle, maintaining hope is rendered a life-giving function. Furthermore, it is perceived as a particular capacity, even duty, of women. With their nation in danger, this rivaled their reproductive function in importance. In this sense, it became the duty of all women to become mothers, to offer hope and sustain faith in the future. The monopoly that Polish women seem to claim on this capacity renders women of other nationalities inferior women.

The taint of treason applies both to women and men of the minority groups but with different undertones. Women's descriptions of men of the national minorities focus on the period immediately following the Soviet invasion. They denounce Ukrainian, Belorussian, and Jewish men for robbing, beating, and murdering Poles; ambushing Polish soldiers; confiscating property; serving in the Bolshevik militia; replacing Polish administrators; denouncing their Polish neighbors; and assisting the NKVD in its nighttime missions to arrest and deport Poles.[82] Such men are presented mainly as thugs, lackeys, and opportunists. No accusations or suggestions of rape or sexual misbehavior are made. There is, however, a hint of impropriety in discussions about the women at this time. It is neither detailed nor explicit but implies that women of the minority groups did not uphold the standards of honor and chastity of Polish women. Jewish, Ukrainian, and Belorussian women wearing bright clothes, we are told, greeted the soldiers of the Red Army on the streets with flowers and cheers—acts of welcome and submission. In contrast, Polish females put on mourning clothes, in the tradition of their foremothers under the partitions. "Their officers expected smiles from our girls, but not one wanted even to look in their direction," recalls one young Pole. "We all dressed as modestly as possible, wearing black scarves on our heads." According to Maria Jurewicz, the Belorussians, "especially young girls," greeted the Russians with flowers, while Polish girls stayed in their homes. Hermina Halicka reports that "a great number of Jews and Ukrainians threw bouquets of flowers at their feet." Some reportedly kissed the soldiers.[83]

The suggestion of impropriety comes through some of the descriptions of relations in exile. A woman in a settlement in the Sverdlovsk *oblast'* writes:

> No one would accept any kind of relief which would have been the result of the favor of the Commandant of the settlement, and for which one would have to forsake the honor of a Pole or the reputation of a woman.

The Jews were lower in this respect, they often (not all, there were some courageous ones among them as well) searched for and found better living conditions, they exploited the situation and tried to live easier—not damaging their health—above the voice of conscience; as far as how often this happened, it was a daily occurrence.[84]

Another woman hints at similar behavior by Ukrainian women. Explaining that they acted differently, "more compliantly and traitorously," she immediately asserts: "In our labor camp not a single Polish woman tarnished herself with the conclusion of any kind of acquaintance with the Bolsheviks, all kept themselves distant from the Russians."[85]

The accusation of loose morals, sinful in the eyes of Catholic Poles, is not explicitly made against the women of the national minorities. Mainly Poles complain that their fellow citizens were not patriots. But since Polish women considered patriotism a highly moral matter, this failing reflected on the others' womanhood. These other women easily sell out their fatherland and their compatriots for material benefit—in a sense, prostituting themselves. In the eyes of some of their Polish counterparts, these other women fall to the level of common prostitutes—far short of ideal womanhood. In some cases, the affront to the Polish nation is considered so severe that the perpetrators are said to be worse than Polish prostitutes, who at least remain loyal to the nation. Some Polish women voice forgiveness and even praise for Polish prostitutes, who stole their bread and took the best spaces in the cells. The explanation lies in their patriotism. Despite their objectionable behavior, "at the same time they didn't let the Communists speak badly about Poland and came to our defense. They related kindly to pregnant women, children, and the sick. They did not like the Jews or the Ukrainians." In a similar vein, one woman writes that the Ukrainian and Jewish women "harassed us so much that even the prostitutes . . . turned out to be better Poles and came to our defense."[86] A similar view comes from a woman who spent the war years on Polish territory. Describing how several Polish women used their bodies to distract NKVD border guards to aid the escape of members of the resistance, she remarks with pride, "They may sell themselves, but not their country."[87] Patriotism raised even Polish prostitutes, considered the dregs of society, to a higher moral level than that of disloyal Ukrainian and Jewish women. The transgressions these women made against their fellow citizens appear worse than those of "fallen women."

In this way, national and sexual issues are conflated. In a memoir of his early life, Miłosz writes disparagingly of a chauvinistic legacy of the Polish gentry, which "liked to bring in the idea of treason at every step."[88] He suggests that Poles map the idea of treason onto issues, like marriage or selling off one's hereditary lands, which objectively have nothing to do with treason, but nevertheless are thus construed. In a similar way, these Polish women apply the notion of treason to such issues as language, identification, cooperation, and faith in the future. They also attach it to the matter of chaste behavior. The examples given above demonstrate a mapping of the notion of the good citizen onto the image of the good mother. In this overlapping of categories, immoral women, traitors, and non-Poles become one and the same. Concurrently, it constructs Polish women as both proper women and loyal citizens.

Significantly, the women do not cast aspersions on the sexual morality of Belorussian women, who draw the least harsh criticism from Polish women. Differences between Poles and Belorussians were less pronounced, and many of the women probably failed to see lines between the two groups. Before the war, the less-developed state of Belorussian nationalism resulted in less separatist and anti-Polish feeling. Simply put, the Poles felt less antagonized and less threatened by Belorussians: writing after their release, they have less to report about the Belorussians, fewer scores to settle, and probably less psychological and political need to excoriate them. While Belorussian females are often depicted as disloyal to the Polish nation and community, they are spared accusations that would take their condemnation a step further—that they are immoral. This charge is reserved for those peoples perceived as greater enemies of the Poles. Reading the Polish women's documents, one can chart a hierarchy of the others exiled with them. Polish prostitutes top the list as the least objectionable, beneath them fall Belorussians. Ukrainians and Jews compete for the lowest level, as the most offensive. By creating such a hierarchy, Polish women are reassured of their own superiority, of their own identity as proper women and patriotic Poles.

"Pseudo-Poles" and "Real Poles"

To maintain this hierarchy and the cohesiveness of their definition of a Polish woman, they must deal with exceptions: ethnic Poles who act improperly, and individuals of the national minorities who act ideally. Both seeming anomalies require explanation to fit into the framework by which Polish women ordered their world in exile. Not surprisingly, the explanation comes in the form of reference to their true nationality, a notion that enables the positive and negative traits to remain the property of Polish and non-Polish groups, respectively. This is a common practice in the construction of nationalisms. Geraldine Heng and Janadas Devan, who write on Singaporean nationalism, explain: "Differences within cultures and races . . . are converted to differences between cultures and races, into differences that strategically serve to distinguish valid, enabling, or potent cultural identities from those other identities reproduced as seductive and disabling, subverting the firmness of national purpose."[89] This mechanism underlies Polish women's discussion of exceptions within their communities. Even when describing individuals not fitting the stereotypes, the women continue to essentialize both gender and national identities.

Those ethnic Poles not fitting the definition of Polish women as exceedingly patriotic, civic-minded, chaste, self-sacrificing, and nurturing are marginalized through three mechanisms: general silence on the misbehavior of Poles, insistence that only isolated exceptions occurred, and the juxtaposition of descriptions of such outcasts with global condemnations of the national minorities, rendering the misfits more like the others than like us. While it is impossible to provide evidence of silence, common sense would question the seeming lack of uncooperative, selfish, promiscuous, or traitorous Polish women. Acts of collaboration and acquiescence during World War II—with either of Poland's enemies—have generally not found a place in Polish historical memory. In this regard, a cultural anthropologist has described the Polish nation as "obsessed with its innocence."[90] Władysław Bartoszewski noted the tendency to gloss over Polish participation in activities offensive to Polish national myths in the postwar period, when the blame for the evils of Polish Stalinism fell on others, especially Jews and Russians. "This insistence," he explains, "wholly without justification, of applying to another ethnic grouping standards of behavior which they were unwilling to apply to themselves, enabled the Poles to ignore their own participation in Stalinist crimes, and also, encouraged the idea that no 'real Pole' could ever have committed such crimes against his or her own nation."[91] One could say essentially the same of the wartime period. Though this strategy is difficult to document for the period of exile, the other mechanisms Polish women employ can be illustrated.

A teacher from Lwów recounts an anti-Polish meeting at which the deportees were ordered to take part in upcoming May Day celebrations: "Besides a few Jewish, Ukrainian and pseudo-Polish women, none of the Poles took part in the parade, in spite of expected repression from the Soviet authorities."[92] With the label of fake, those improper women are excluded from the collective of Polish women, despite their ethnic origins. Usually the exclusion occurs more subtly. Reporting that two women in her settlement served as informants, Róża Rederówna explains that one was a Ukrainian woman, the other a Pole, "who later married a Kazakh." A few paragraphs earlier she had scorned the local Kazakhs as dirty and verminous; treason and sexual transgression go hand in hand. Another woman describes informants in her camp, adding: "There was only one Polish woman, who had long ago left Poland and later ended up in prison, a great Communist." A deportee recalls that in her settlement several Belorussians, and "even" two Polish women, worked as informants.[93] In such instances, we are assured that the offenders cannot really be called Polish women. Having turned their backs on Poles and Poland, they are linked with others and rendered inferior. Or their numbers are marginalized, showing that they do not represent real Poles.

Confirming the improbability of Polish women's picture of uniformity, men report Poles breaking the codes of patriotic behavior with a relative casualness. Though they express their disappointment, men do not try to deny that the offender was actually a Pole. One man describes the informants in his settlement: "They were gamekeepers (Ukrainians and Belorussians) and unfortunately Poles, among them the military settler W.B." Polish men do not consider the national minorities to have a monopoly on traitorous behavior. Recounting his arrest, Władysław Kryżanowski discloses, "I was taken by a militia man, unfortunately a Pole." Many individuals—Jews, Belorussians, and Poles—reports one man, "had complete moral breakdowns, compromising us with slovenliness, begging, sycophancy, and often even denunciations." Mikołaj Zychała, explaining how some Poles sought better treatment, writes: "There were cases where purely Polish families, when giving out their personal information, put down on various lists the Ukrainian nationality, not Polish."[94] Men tend to present a more varied picture of Poles and their patriotism.

Male accounts of the national minorities, too, are less homogeneous than women's, their depictions less categorically drawn. They typically echo women's complaints, condemning the others for treason, betrayal, and persecution of the Poles.[95] While their stories generally concur with women's, Polish men do not present such a uniformly negative picture of these peoples. Some men blame the Soviets for causing divisions among Polish citizens. According to Jan Szczęsny, camp officials "tried to differentiate among the internees (incite hatred) . . . persuaded them to believe in differences in nationality and origins (Poles, Ukrainians, Belorussians)."[96] Men less unanimously dismiss the national minorities as common criminals, noting political prisoners among them. Positive assessments of the others appear frequently in men's testimonies, such as the following, from Antoni Drabowicz: "Former Polish citizens, Jews, Ukrainians and Belorussians, behaved themselves entirely properly with the Poles in the camp, they lived in harmony." Similarly, Piotr Ciesak recalls that in prison, Ukrainians, Jews, and Poles shared packages and cheered each other up.[97]

One also sees more cases of minorities proving to be good Poles in male accounts. According to a young journalist, the exiled Jews and Belorussians "accentuated their Polishness." "In spite of their unhappiness," writes another man of the Jews deported with him, "everyone always manifested their Polishness, didn't give up, and lived on the thought of returning to the Fatherland."[98] Aleksander Wat echoes the common portrayal of Poles and Ukrainians as enemies but presents a different view of the Ukrainian treatment of the Poles. "Even here, there were two groups of course, the Ukrainians and the Poles," he writes of prison. "That was the only place in years that a natural harmony existed between the two nations." Wat continues: "The Ukrainians related to the Poles with reserve but with incredible loyalty. We are enemies, but not here. Here we share common persecution. Relations were cold but incredibly polite."[99] Blanket generalizations about the national minorities are sometimes positive in male testimonies.

In Polish women's documents, such broad portrayals occur infrequently. Thus, the second exception to the national stereotypes is the good woman of the minorities, who acts like a true Pole. Other women qualify for this label by demonstrating loyalty to the Polish nation and solidarity with its citizens. Polish women tend to marginalize such individuals, suggesting that the behavior for which they are commended is atypical for their group. Unlike the condemnations, which are pronounced on groups, the praise usually refers to a few individuals. Wanda Dzierzanowska's group of deportees included a Jewish woman with her son, "who by her behavior, her civic attitude and ethical principles could serve as an example for many others." The fact that this good citizen was also a mother did not go unnoticed. Another woman, imprisoned in numerous labor camps, isolates several Jewish women as exemplary. She praises one of them for telling the Bolsheviks that they were liars and criminals and that she had lived better in Poland. In this case, patriotism went hand in hand with kindness to her compatriots, for the woman shared food she stole from the kitchen with the Polish women. Another Jewish woman reportedly refused to betray Poles to the NKVD, stating that her views "did not allow her to be an informant and secretly harm those who were weaker."[100]

In several instances, friendly relations resulted when a non-Pole recognized the real worth of Poland. "There were about 70–80 of us, 50 percent Jews, we lived together well," writes Julia Kwiatkowska of her community of deportees. "The Jews said that only now they knew how good it was in Poland." Similarly, Zofia Kruszelnicka reports approvingly of a Jewish girl, who, when asked by the Soviets where life was better, insisted on Poland. According to another woman, initially poor relations in her cell, attributed to the antagonism of the national minorities, ceased with time as they "turned out to be good Polish women."[101] Belorussian, Jewish, and Ukrainian individuals won the approval of Polish women when they joined in solidarity with the Poles and exhibited a similar patriotism. To be included in the collective, these others had to shed their differences with ethnic Poles, particularly regarding their views of Poland's past and hopes for its future.

Fellow Victims: Soviet Slavic Minorities

Many Polish exiles ended up living in close proximity to *Soviet* Ukrainians and Belorussians, who hailed from the eastern side of the Polish border. The exiles comment infrequently on these people but express a sympathy and respect for them that they seem unable to muster for their own Ukrainians and Belorussians. Since Soviet minorities do not play a part in the tragedy of the Polish nation, the Poles are able to recognize them as fellow, and blameless, victims, and can allow them their own story. As citizens of a different country, these Ukrainians and Belorussians can articulate their national identity without challenging that of the Poles, who carry no expectations of them as fellow citizens and do not perceive them as rivals. Nor do Poles see them as enemies, for they neither undermine the coherence of the Polish community nor represent the government responsible for the calamity of exile: Soviet equals Russian in Polish minds. Polish women therefore have little need to find fault with these other women and can instead see evidence of their goodness as women, mothers, and citizens.

Female deportees identified with these others because their daily lives had also been altered; in particular, they were also wrongfully deprived of their men. They also reportedly demonstrated sympathy and kindness, which enabled the Poles to see them as women in their customary terms. Anna Stahlowa describes a long evacuation march from prison in Kiev after the Nazi invasion of the USSR: "While passing through a Ukrainian village some women—because there were no men—handed us onions and garlic, sometimes even bread. Literally every woman in the villages was crying for her son or husband who had also been imprisoned. Those villagers welcomed us not as prisoners or enemies of the state but as their friends." Another trait rendering the Soviet Slavic minorities comprehensible and sympathetic was devotion to their own nations. According to one woman, the Soviet Ukrainians and Belorussians "were good people," for they "longed for their own country." They not only loved their own nation but also performed the customary function of mothers by transmitting its culture to their children. A Pole deported to a state farm in the Altai region praises Soviet Ukrainian mothers there for fulfilling their duty to their children and nation: "At each step the Ukrainians maintained their national distinctness, and their children, in spite of going to Russian schools, did not lose their national character."[102] Had these been Polish Ukrainians, these same traits would have been condemned as treasonous.

These others seem akin to Polish women because they express love for their nation, sympathy for the plight of the Poles, and sorrow at the break-up of their families. Polish women can only see these traits when they do not wear the blinders of nationalist tension and rivalry. Thus, they can comprehend the tragedy of the Soviet minorities and can allow its female members to be loyal citizens and proper women in a way that seems difficult for them in relation to Ukrainians and Belorussians from Poland.

Conclusion

The construction of national identity is a dynamic process, particularly vital during the trauma of war, as the Polish experience demonstrates. The Soviets did not create nationality conflict in the territory of Poland that they occupied. Tensions long existed among Poles, Jews, Ukrainians, and Belorussians living there. Yet individuals lived in relative harmony until society broke down at the instigation of the invaders. In villages and towns of the East, differences suddenly mattered more than they had in daily life before September 1939, when lines between ethnicities and cultures were not uniformly drawn, when different types and levels of nationalism coexisted. The testimonies of the exiled women reveal that this fluidity and indeterminacy ended in the course of the war. Their writing suggests that they had considered the Polish nation an extended family, which had room for the national minorities. They initially viewed these others as fellow citizens, perhaps not their equals, yet sharing the same fatherland. Polish women, therefore, expected loyalty and solidarity of them, denying legitimate cause for discord. Both in the aftermath of the Red Army invasion and then in exile, however, some of the minorities manifested differences in their attitudes toward the invaders as well as to the Polish state. The interwar years offered Polish women a ready-made way to view and condemn the minority peoples; their use of existing stereotypes makes it impossible to sort prejudice from reality in the women's reports.

The national minorities challenged (and were used by the Soviets to challenge) the women's solidarity and authority as Poles, including their understanding of the past and their vision for the future. When discussing Jews, Ukrainians, and Belorussians, Poles focus on the issues of loyalty and patriotism. Polish women establish these other women as traitors, reporting bitterly the welcome many of them gave to the Red Army. Regardless of the number of individuals involved in such acts or their motivations, perceptions of collaboration after the invasion activated the notion that the national minorities were quislings. Difficult relations in exile confirmed the idea that these others did not belong in the Polish nation, and the lines separating them grew more and more impervious. "Ethnicity arises in the interaction between groups," write Geoff Eley and Ronald Suny. "It exists in the boundaries constructed between them."[103] In the course of their exile, Polish women articulated well-defined boundaries between the various national groups that had resided in Poland, tagging each with a stereotypical identity: Poles as patriotic victims and heroes, the others as disloyal, due either to Communist proclivities, selfish national particularism, or moral failings.

In this process, Poles construe behavior that has nothing to do with conventional notions of treason, such as speaking one's native tongue, not providing assistance, or losing hope, as serious affronts to their nation. Polish women interpret differences that suggest distinct identities as evidence that the women of the national minorities are traitors; this forms a common theme in their reports about their experiences in Soviet exile. Indeed, at times it seems that presenting these others as disloyal citizens is one of the main aims of the Polish women. But through this process they suggest more than that. Nationality and gender are always intertwined, and the traits and activities that make these others failed Poles indirectly render them "bad" women. By mapping the notion of the good citizen onto the notion of the good mother, Poles make the minorities' failures as citizens of the nation and members of the community reflect on their status as women. If the women of the national minorities, in the eyes of the Poles, did not act similarly—did not express a deep patriotism, put the interests of the collective above their own or manifest caring and nurturing natures in their relations in exile—then clearly they were not acting like ideal women. In this way, the failures of the others to perform their proper functions in the nation and the community reflect negatively on their womanhood. Simply put, they do not appear as upright women. This denigration serves as the final act of exclusion from the collective.

Exclusion of these others enables Polish women, through contrast, to create a coherent definition of themselves and their community. They construct boundaries with an impermeability that may not have existed before. At the end of the odyssey, when the women are writing in Persia, they clearly espouse a modern conception of nationalism, based on ethno-cultural ties. This integral nationalism includes hatred and distrust of the alien and unfamiliar, accompanied by a feeling of superiority. It also embraces clear ideas about proper gender roles, defining for these females precisely what it means to be a Polish woman.

In the Polish accounts the tragedy of women—largely identified as mothers—plays a large role. It highlights the pathos and injustice of the nation's fate. This was a story largely denied to women of the national minorities. Though the deported Ukrainian, Belorussian, and Jewish women were also often mothers and endured similar agony, they are generally left out of this emotional picture. Instead, they play the role of villains, informers, and traitors who, unlike the Poles, are presented as blameworthy, or at least guilty in exacerbating the plight of the Poles. In this way they are deauthorized as subjects of the tragic story of eastern Poland.

7

"Barely Distinguishable from Animals"

Encountering Asia

The journey from life as a citizen of independent Poland to exile in the Soviet Union entailed the crossing of many boundaries, both physical and abstract. The one that caused the most anxiety was the border between Europe and Asia, West and East. Many Poles saw this as a very real, tangible border, located variously at the eastern frontier of Poland, the Ural Mountains, or the beginning of the steppe. Whether they staked out a physical marker or not, most Poles expected and sensed a profound difference once they had passed that border—in the people and their entire existence, a difference they feared and abhorred. The Poles attached their fear to the peoples as a whole and to the expanse they inhabited. The dread of Asia was palpable. Janina Borak-Szyszko writes that she trembled at the thought of Asia "and desired above all things to remain in Europe." Women and men similarly express the horror they experienced on the transports: "With a great cry we crossed the Polish border and went to a completely foreign and hostile land." They considered that "Europe remained a long way off, behind us." Janina Zbróg expresses this perception most vividly: "Each of us thinks with sadness that soon we will have to cross over the border of Europe. And unexpectedly, that moment arrived quickly. Among the trees appeared a white pillar with a white sign on which we could already from far away make out the black label, 'Europe.' And in a moment from the other side you could read, 'Asia.'"[1] Though certainly taking literary license here, she, like countless others, felt that she was not merely moving eastward but was passing into an entirely different state of existence. A hard line seemed to separate her former and future lives.

Crossing that boundary agonized the Poles because they felt they were leaving behind their entire civilization. "I sensed that they could send me in a direction in which I would meet no countrymen," writes Stanisław Bajkowski, "and I would be alone there among people of a race, culture and habits foreign to me."[2] Their apprehensions about the other side of this border echo long-held ideas about the East, as expressed by an exiled Pole in 1857: "For us, people of the West . . . the sky, the land and the people who live on [the steppe] are completely unknown."[3] Forced by Soviet authorities to live in Asia, in close proximity to its native inhabitants and in material conditions more destitute than they had previously known, the women from Poland refused to fit in, rejecting any blurring of the boundaries they perceived between themselves (Westerners) and the Central Asians (Easterners). One way to accomplish this was to pay these others little attention —especially females, whom they did not want to be like at all. Not allowing for any similarity between themselves and the locals—their neighbors, hosts, and coworkers—Polish women largely dismiss them as unquestionably unlike and inferior to the Poles. The boundary between Polish women and Central Asian women is a chasm that separated, in the Polish imagination, the civilized from the barbarous.

This general outlook toward the peoples of Soviet Central Asia shaped the way the Poles chose to discuss them, influencing both their comments and their silences. These discussions vary substantially, in quantity and content, from those analyzed in the previous chapter. Polish women focus extensive attention in their reports on women of the national minorities from Poland, largely describing and judging these collectives through their female members. In contrast, they have virtually nothing to say about the Kazakh, Kirghiz, and Uzbek women. Instead, they talk about these groups as a vague whole, reserving special comment for the males of these nationalities, who symbolize for Poles the threat and danger of Asia. Just as discussion of women of other nationalities expresses larger assessments of the groups as a whole, the silence on the Turkic women also reflects a profound judgment of the civilization to which they belong.

Encountering Asia

Attention to Polish women's treatment of the peoples of Soviet Central Asia can add to the understanding of their sense of their own identity and of order in the world. As George Fredrickson wrote when analyzing racial stereotypes, "If they tell us little that is reliable about the objects of such conceptions, they may reveal a great deal about those who hold them."[4] The attitude of the Poles toward Asia discloses much about their self-perception and their understanding of civilization, as well as what they feared might become of them in exile.

Contact with the "Asiatics"

Polish exiles had extensive contact with Kazakhs, Kirghiz, and Uzbeks, all Turkic peoples. Few of the women confined to prisons and labor camps report encountering individuals of these groups there; Turkic peoples were not incarcerated in high numbers. And Central Asia served less as a ground for labor camps than a place of punitive resettlement.[5] A great many women in so-called free exile refer in their reports to the Turkic peoples, in whose communities they were arbitrarily placed. The exact number of Polish deportees to Central Asia has not been established. Soviet documents suggest that 80–82,000 Polish citizens were deported to Kazakhstan, an estimate not universally accepted.[6] Most of the transports that left Poland in April 1940, filled primarily with the wives and children of men who had earlier been arrested, ended their journey in Northern Kazakhstan. Jędrzej Tucholski calculates that from this episode of deportation alone, 60,351 Poles ended up in the Kazakh Republic.[7] In a recent study, Piotr Żaroń estimates that as a result of the four deportations, approximately 150,000 Polish citizens—80 percent of them women and children—were scattered in at least 1,206 different localities in Kazakhstan.[8]

Other special settlers were directed further south to farms within the Kirghiz Republic. Additionally, waves of Poles released from prisons and camps in other parts of the USSR by the amnesty had to travel to the country's southern regions to reach newly formed Polish delegations. Soviet authorities routinely diverted their trains and forced them to work on collective farms in Kazakhstan, Kirghizia, and Uzbekistan. Finally, thousands of Poles were resettled from the Arctic regions to Central Asia after the amnesty at the request of the Polish government in London, in the hope that the better climate there would improve their chances of survival.[9] Masses of Poles thus straggled to the region from late 1941 through 1943; their mortality rate was high, compounding the difficulty of documenting the numbers. It is likely that several hundred thousand Polish exiles spent at least part of their time in the USSR in Central Asia.

These Poles were not isolated in all-Polish or even exclusively Slavic communities. The initial transports were divided upon arrival, their inhabitants scattered in many different localities. Poles were often added to existing collective or state farms, composed of the region's local inhabitants, with whom they frequently lived and worked in close contact. Many Polish women, simply deposited on the Central Asian steppe with their children, had to live in the corner of a one-room hut of a Kazakh or Kirghiz family.[10] Oftentimes they worked on the same brigades as native inhabitants of the region and, if sent off to do seasonal work, shared tents with them. Despite the fact that Poles had close, daily contact with Kazakhs, Uzbeks, and Kirghiz, they make remarkably little note of them in their descriptions of life in Soviet exile. The comments they do provide are uniformly brief, impressionistic, and lacking in detail.

This situation is highly reminiscent of past writings, memoirist and scholarly, on the subject of Poles in Kazakhstan that provide similarly scant and monolithic descriptions of the locals. Poles have a long history of association with the Central Asian steppe, particularly as a "prison without bars."[11] The Russian government began exiling Poles to Kazakhstan in the late eighteenth century and continued to do so throughout the period of partitions, particularly after the failed rebellions of 1830 and 1863. The meager literature on Poles in Central Asia before WWII offers little substance about the daily life of local inhabitants, their interactions with the Poles, or of the Polish understanding of their cultures.[12] The few scholarly works on the topic mainly discuss the general conditions for Poles in Kazakhstan, as well as their individual accomplishments, be they political exiles, geological and ethnographic researchers, or migrants looking for work. In some instances, the authors remark formulaically that good relations prevailed with the locals and that they engaged in mutual cooperation for survival. Yet these generalizations are rarely illustrated; when details are provided, particularly in cases of intermarriage, it becomes clear that the locals the authors have in mind are Russians.[13] Exiled Poles learned much from the locals, reports Michał Janik in 1928, including how to differentiate the government from the people and to see the Russian nation "as the victim of its evil government."[14] Such sympathy does not generally appear for the non-Russian locals. The true locals, the native populations, are absent in such assessments, seemingly irrelevant.

The Turkic peoples do sometimes appear in the texts but largely as objects, as the authors focus on the outstanding men, "representatives of Polish science and culture,"[15] and their contributions both to Western knowledge of the region and to the "enlightenment" of its inhabitants. "We Poles," exclaims one man exiled in the mid-nineteenth century, "were the first sowers of civilization and ethical ideas."[16] Similarly, scholars writing in the 1970s stress that the Poles exiled to Kazakhstan in the nineteenth century "rediscovered the Kazakh people for Western Europe and the entire world"; they "brought European civilization closer to the Kazakh nation" and "had a beneficial influence on the social life of Kazakhstan."[17] The following passage offers a typical description of the relations between Poles and the peoples of Central Asia:

> Polish-Kazakh contacts, characterized by humanism, were an element of the formation of the processes of consciousness of the peoples of the steppe, of the consolidation of regional and cultural identity. Poles were also active organizers of the democratic movements, which influenced the border population, sometimes gaining its active support. Coming often from the spheres of the nobility and the intelligentsia, they were the carriers of progressive ideas. They also often fulfilled an educational role.[18]

Thus, descriptions of the Turkic peoples of Central Asia are generally vague, condescending, and patronizing.[19] Little is said about what the Poles may have gained from peoples they considered beneath them, for they place them in a framework of the backward and primitive, receiving knowledge and assistance from the more enlightened Westerners—in this case, Poles.

While Poles exiled to Soviet Central Asia in the 1940s do not characterize themselves as active bestowers of enlightenment, they do see themselves as representatives of the West, vastly different from and superior to the local population. Stanisław Jałowski, deported to a state farm in Northern Kazakhstan, expresses this bluntly: "Whites from cultured Europe, we looked with repugnance at these ugly, slanted-eyed, flat-nosed people, so horribly dirty, breeding lice in their rags at the crotch. Their aversion toward the white race and the mistaken approach of the Soviets toward this half-wild nomadic people, brigands, arrested the development of progress on the Central Asian steppe." Polish men and women probably reached their places of exile with a racial stereotype of Central Asians as primitive and inferior and so paint them in broad, deprecatory strokes. Frequently describing their new neighbors merely as "a wild tribe of Kazakhs," they continually highlight their difference. "From every hut," one Pole recalls of her arrival, "Kazakhs came out to look at the white people from Europe." Another woman states that the majority of Kazakhs "hadn't the slightest notion of what kind of country Poland, as a European nation, was."[20] The Poles' idea of Asia seems to have been passed down in their culture and solidified during the years of exile. Whether as the result of individual experiences or merely as a means of preserving their trampled sense of order and hierarchy in the world, or both, Polish women largely maintain the old stereotypes.

The dismissive attitude toward the peoples of Central Asia as a primitive race remains a constant in Polish wartime writings; only in memoirs published decades later do more sympathetic and singular accounts occur.[21] The most numerous references in the documents to Kazakhs, Kirghiz, and Uzbeks alike are simple comments on their physical appearance and hygiene, blanket statements neither distinguishing between women and men nor singling out individuals. These references use the same few words and frequently exhaust the authors' attention to the local inhabitants of the steppe. One woman simply records this about life on a collective farm: "The local inhabitants—Kazakhs, dirty and lice-infested." In fact, this phrase is the most common description Poles provide of the locals in this region. "I never saw such dirty and ragged people," writes Danuta Dziewulska of the Kirghiz. Using the same adjectives to depict the Kazakhs, Ada Halpern states, "I rarely saw them clean and decently dressed, and they are an ugly type."[22] Another woman offers a more expansive description: "The Kazakhs are the rather degenerate descendants of the Mongols who overran and ruled Russia during the 13th to the 15th centuries. Their features betray their Mongolian origin and even now they retain many of their ancient customs, the most noticeable being a deep-rooted aversion to washing."[23] Such comments, from both males and females, surface not only in Poles' answers to questions about their place of exile and relations with the locals but also on such issues as their work and cultural life while there. "Work was difficult, among the Kazakh people," notes Halina Ziemba, "wild and unbelievably dirty." Others describe the despised hay-cutting season, when they had to work far away from the settlements. Then they lived "in tents, everybody altogether," one woman explains, "and it must be noted that the Kazakhs are terribly dirty."[24]

The focus on dirt in the descriptions of the peoples of Soviet Central Asia is overwhelming, and, therefore, suggests more than the authors' physical discomfort and concern for disease. Here the work of anthropologist Mary Douglas provides useful insight. Considering pollution beliefs and practices, she concludes that pathogenicity and hygiene are not the key issues; rather, dirt is a residual category, representing all the rejected elements of an ordered system. "Dirt offends against order," Douglas writes. "Eliminating it is not a negative movement, but a positive effort to organize the environment."[25] Seen in this light, the overpowering presence of dirt in the characterizations of the population of the steppe suggests two important perceptions held by the Poles. First, according to Polish terms, the locals lacked all order; they were without system, hierarchy, and culture. They are, thus, merely rendered as filth. Second, this portrayal sets up the local population, in its totality, as a rejected element of the Polish system. These others did not, and seemingly would never, fit into the Polish world with its well-defined notions of order and hierarchy.

The nearly exclusive focus on physicality—as if there were nothing more to note about these people—signals the scorn that Poles felt toward the Turkic peoples. Significantly, when describing their appearance or their homes, the Poles generally lump them together with animals. A young man records the following impression of his first entrance into a Kazakh hut: "I was stunned. . . . On [the lambskins] were seated people—I was considering whether such name might be given to them; they were stark naked, appallingly dirty and sprawling like animals under the influence of the warmth." "Those people really do not know anything about cultural life, primitive principles of hygiene," writes Halina Mijakowska of the Kazakhs. "They lived together with their lambs and sheep in dark smoky huts." According to another woman, newborn calves, cared for better than children, were sometimes taken into the family bed.[26] While Poles often remark on the animals that lived in Kazakh or Kirghiz huts, they tend to ignore the inhabitants.

Through their assertions and their silences, Polish women render the

Central Asians animal-like; they become physical beings lacking both cleanliness and culture. Krystyna Słowikowska records her place of exile as a Kazakh collective farm "inhabited by a completely primitive people, not possessing even a minimal culture, completely dirty." "As far as the culture of the Kazakhs goes," offers Leokadia Kapelańska, "it is so low that it's impossible to say much about it. I have in my mind now a picture of the Kazakhs, killing lice with their teeth, which is a terrible memory." Many women focus on this same image, calling it the sole Sunday ritual and using it to sum up the culture of Soviet Central Asia. This criticism also implies Godlessness, for the Poles often describe their own efforts to recreate Sunday mass or at least prayer sessions while in exile. The assumed cultural and moral bankruptcy of these peoples forms a common refrain. "The local people were Kazakhs, a wild people, descended from the Tatars," writes a 43-year-old woman from Lwów. "They raised cattle. Their moral level was terrible."[27] Poles demonstrate almost no knowledge of or sensitivity to feelings of allegiance, expressions of indigenous culture, or even adherence to Islam.[28] In their depictions, the Turkic peoples are simply devoid of culture and civilization. Using these two terms only in the singular, Poles equate difference on the part of these others with complete lack.

The Poles deny the Turkic peoples not only morality and culture but individual and differentiated group identities, as well. Their descriptions render the native populations of Central Asia a monolithic, essentialized "other." Rarely distinguished by ethnicity, these peoples are subsumed into one group of "Asiatics"; in this way, to the Polish mind, they stand simply as a foreign and primitive race. Most Polish women use several labels synonymously: Kazakh, Kirghiz, Uzbek, Mongol, Tatar. Teresa Czohańska believed that the only difference between Kirghiz and Kazakh was that the former word was illegal to use.[29] Few, it seems, note any more meaningful distinction. This is not a unique attitude; Europeans have commonly constructed different racial groups as a single entity, downplaying even known differences. The habit of white Americans of subsuming all the various tribes of Native Americans under the term "Indian" represents a parallel example.[30]

The scholar Benedict Anderson has written, "In the modern world, everyone can, should, will 'have' a nationality, as he or she 'has' a gender."[31] The erasure of nationality from the heterogeneity of the inhabitants of Soviet Central Asia stands out as especially important because of its significance in the Polish self-depiction and assessment of others. As their preoccupation with the properness of female character and behavior when describing the national minorities demonstrates, gender represents a critical aspect of the Polish women's understanding and evaluation of nations. More generally, it marks for Poles the level of civilization. Therefore, their perception of Central Asian females critiques the entire culture of the peoples of the steppe.

Women Erased from View

In startling contrast to their discussion of Ukrainian, Belorussian, and Jewish females, the Poles have little to say about Turkic women. Several factors precluded close communication and familiarity between the local and the resettled females, and seem to have preordained Polish women to devote the least amount of attention to the women of Central Asia. First, Turkic women came from cultures that traditionally sought to isolate females from public life. Second, they spoke Turkic languages, impenetrable to the Poles who could at least make sense of the Belorussian, Ukrainian, and Russian languages, all of which belong to the Slavic family. Though these points contribute to the Poles' lack of intimate knowledge of and interest in Turkic women, they do not sufficiently explain their relative silence on women of Central Asia.

To begin with, the cultures of the Turkic peoples of the USSR were not uniformly conservative with respect to women. Most Poles deported to Central Asia ended up in Kazakhstan or Kirghizia, where the women had never been secluded or veiled as they had in Uzbekistan.[32] And beginning in the 1920s, Soviet authorities, initially under the auspices of the *Zhenotdel'* (Women's Department) and later through women's clubs and other organizations, put considerable effort into disrupting the traditional social position of Muslim women and mobilizing them into more public roles.[33] While these attempts met with resistance and failed to transform gender relations among the Turkic peoples, the Soviet campaign for economic modernization did not slacken, and these women, just like their Russian counterparts, were forced to work for the state. They were largely employed at farming, sheepshearing, animal husbandry, and handicraft industry—precisely the tasks to which Polish women were assigned. After the outbreak of war between the USSR and Germany, local women made up the bulk of the labor force and largely managed the operation of the farms.[34] As for communication, by 1939 literacy rates for females in Central Asia had soared.[35] Soviet authorities placed great emphasis on getting girls to school, where they learned Russian; presumably they could communicate at least on a rudimentary level with some of the deportees.

Even if language differences made verbal communication with Turkic women impossible, one might reasonably expect descriptions and comparisons from the Poles, perhaps even recognition of the similarity of the plight of the Turkic and Polish peoples under Soviet rule. Living in close proximity to Central Asian women, in some cases for two or more years, Poles were in a position to observe and comment on various aspects of their lives—their health, the jobs they performed, their ability to fulfill work norms, the way they spent time outside work, the size and constitution of family units, the responsibility for child care. These issues draw note when women of non-Turkic nationalities are the topic of consideration. Significantly, Polish women's reports simply refrain from discussing and rarely even mention the Turkic women, be it as neighbors, hosts, coworkers or brigade leaders; they do not describe them as friends, adversaries, or even as mere curiosities. The Poles neither talk about them as individuals—they never name any of them—nor, on the whole, do they even distinguish between men and women. Most of the Poles' comments simply present them as a blur.

The silences are telling: Poles do not view the females of the Central Asian steppe as mothers or wives, nurturers or educators, or patriots—the roles through which Poles identify themselves and judge other women. The issues of nationality and patriotism, morality, family, sexuality, work, and religion, so important in depicting themselves and other nationalities, do not surface in relation to the Central Asian women. Nor do Polish women attribute to the latter other roles or identities. Jadwiga Wojciechowska, like many other Poles, reports that she lived with "terribly dirty Kazakh families." None of the family members draws her attention; beyond that statement, she notes only: "It was horrible for us to live together with the swine and sheep in indescribable filth."[36] Humans disappear into the dirt and animal kingdom. Interestingly, the Turkic women are not taken to task for the lack of order and cleanliness in the home, responsibilities that Polish women repeatedly assume for themselves in their own domiciles in exile. While Poles frequently denigrate women of other nationalities for their failures in this regard, they do not present Turkic women as having any special role that they either fulfill or fail to accomplish. Central Asian women merely fade into the scenery, along with the sheep and the filth.

Additionally, Polish women rarely mention children of the indigenous societies of the steppe.[37] In that world, as depicted by Poles, there can be no possibility of mothers or wives, either proper or improper ones. In the same way, since national or group identities are not acknowledged, there can be no talk of loyalty or patriotism. The Poles do not apply the terms by which they envision and present themselves to these other women. Simply put, while Polish women may register the existence of females, they do not present them as women with social roles and duties.

The absence of Kazakh, Kirghiz, and Uzbek women in the discussion and imagination of the Polish women signals their utter disdain for them. It is both the emblem and result of the great distance they perceived between these others and themselves. For these Poles, Central Asian women were completely unfamiliar; they shared neither past experiences nor common cultural roots. Furthermore, according to traditional stereotypes of Asia, the Poles did not conceive of the native populations as inhabiting the same world—their own being the civilized West, the others' the primitive East. Polish women seem to have imagined their worlds as parallel—their own clearly on a higher plane—with none of the thorny intersections that their own had with the more familiar and politically challenging worlds of the national minorities from Poland, or even more, the Russians. The Turkic peoples did not constitute a political threat. No history of enmity or rivalry existed between the groups; nor were the peoples of Central Asia the current oppressors of the Poles. Though the Turkic peoples were part of the USSR and oftentimes the executors of its authority, Poles did not equate them with the repressive, anti-Polish Soviet power, which they considered Russian. Nor did Central Asians represent the model of what that power sought to render the Poles; on the contrary, the Soviet government endeavored to remake the Kazakhs, Kirghiz, and Uzbeks, as well. As a result of these factors, Polish deportees considered the women of Central Asia largely irrelevant—an other to be despised, patronized, or mostly disregarded.

The deportees and the locals can both be regarded as victims of the same cruel authority, the Stalinist regime, which endeavored to mold both groups into loyal and productive subjects of the Soviet state. Possessed of a long-standing preconception and dread of Asia as the dark, primitive other, Polish women were unable or unwilling to see that similarity, to see the

Central Asians as fellow victims. They were unprepared to find, in what stood out in their minds as the dreaded uncivilized East, anything like what they knew at home. And so they did not find women like themselves. If they mention women at all, they deny any similarity; they erase their character, their voice, and their agency. The handful of comments specifically about women in Central Asia dismiss them as primitive or wild.

Maria Andrzejczuk recalls with disgust the common barracks in which she was forced to spend her nights: "In those lodgings we had to sleep in the company of Russian boys and wild Kazakh girls. . . . Who could fall asleep, when the shrieks and squeals of the girls and boys, whose moral level was beyond description, went on till late into the night? And what foolishness we heard, what profanity and blasphemy." One Pole relates how she and her compatriots continually encountered the senseless hostility of local Kazakh women. Though the Kazakhs did not use milk curd, they taunted the Poles who tried to obtain it, spilling their vessels and throwing stones at them.[38] Another woman claims that though the "Tatar" men in her vicinity spoke Russian, "the women know only their own simple language, which is made up of mostly short words." One of the longest descriptions of these other women comes from a Pole arrested for anti-Soviet activity. Her comments express the widely held disdain for the Central Asians, to whom she ascribes a vague identity of Mongol: "I was put in a cell with three Poles and three Soviets of Mongol origin, complete idiots, not knowing how to read, write, or even speak in Russian. They believed in the existence of the Tsar Nikolai, who was supposed to liberate them from the hated clutch of the NKVD." Adding that one of them was imprisoned for organizing a secret religious group, she continues: "That sounded ridiculous to me, as people with such a low intellectual level, barely distinguishable from animals, could in no way lead a secret organization."[39] When the Poles cannot simply ignore Central Asian women, they talk about them more as a species of animal than as other women.[40]

Given the fragility of their identity in exile and the uncertainty of their future, Polish women could not afford to view Central Asian women in any other light. They themselves feared becoming dirty, condemned forever to miserable mud huts, cut off from their religion and culture, robbed of the opportunity to fulfill the social duties they ascribed to women. All of these negative phenomena they considered primitive and attached to Asia. Would living on the steppe turn the Poles into Asiatics? Would the pressures of Soviet exile succeed in stripping them of their identities as Poles and women? Could they possibly become what they abhorred—mere animals, concerned only with the demands of biological existence?

Ambiguities and anomalies are threatening to one's long-held system of classification and order: if the Poles recognized these other females as women, accepting their differences in appearance, speech, roles, habits, and culture, then their own identity as women, their own certainty of who they were and would remain could be threatened. Half-identities are dangerous, for "the clarity of the scene in which they obtrude is impaired by their presence." But if those with ambiguous or half-identities are collected in one undifferentiated group, to use an analogy of Douglas, "a mass of rubbish," they gain their own place in the original ordering scheme—actually outside of it—and lose their threatening qualities. "So long as identity is absent, rubbish is not dangerous," writes Douglas. "It does not even create ambiguous perceptions since it clearly belongs in a defined place, a rubbish heap of one kind or another. When there is no differentiation there is no defilement."[41] With the erasure of the Turkic women from view, casting them into one undifferentiated mass, the concept of the civilized Polish female, an inhabitant of the West, remains intact, as does that of the wild and inhuman beings of the East. The Poles thus assure themselves that they do not belong in that other world.

"Jackals"

When Polish women talk about Central Asians, they envision a population seemingly without women, one that is threatening and destructive. Most of the actual encounters with locals that Poles recount are frightening. The Kazakhs, Kirghiz, and Uzbeks threaten some sort of damage or destruction, and the episodes highlight the perpetrator's aggression, criminality, and ability to inspire fear. Most of the actors in Polish women's stories of the steppe are men; their depiction of the men of Central Asia underscores the perception of a primitive population, one without the civilizing order of gender, and, therefore, more akin to animals than humans. Like their female counterparts, the men are not identified or judged on the basis of their social roles; they do not appear in the Polish documents as husbands or fathers, providers or defenders, workers or leaders. Males of Soviet Central

Asia attract the attention of Polish women mostly because they seem to embody the threat of violence and damage—the danger of dark, overwhelming Asia.

Helena Wiśniewska recalls that when she arrived in Uzbekistan, she was too scared of the locals even to move. "Those Uzbeks were terrifying, with knives at their sides," writes a student from Wilno. "There were seventeen of us Poles among those wild ones." "Terror seized us at the sight of these strange dark faces and people in rags," echoes another woman. "We had the impression that we were among wild people and that no one would ever know anything about what happened to us."[42] Poles' initial impressions generally did not change. Almost invariably, the non-Slavic inhabitants of Soviet Central Asia come across as a purely menacing people.

The natives of the steppe are the bogeymen of Polish children. Like adults, they make almost no note in their compositions of Central Asian women. The one exception found among the children's essays describes a girl's view of the Kirghiz: "The women looked like witches, and the men looked as if they would attack us."[43] More animal or monster than human, these people embodied the children's most terrible nightmares. Young Poles relate frightening episodes in which Central Asians reduce them to tears or assault their parents. One girl, age twelve when she wrote her composition, tried to dig a grave for her father who had died on the steppe. The Kirghiz reportedly tormented her by saying that dogs would eat him up; they also made her mother cry. Another girl of the same age lost both her parents after the amnesty and was stranded with her younger sister; the Uzbeks taunted her, saying that she would never reach the Polish orphanage but would remain in Uzbekistan forever.[44] A fourteen-year-old writes that life was terrible with the Uzbeks, who beat up her mother. Jadwiga Owsianik simply states that Uzbeks killed her father.[45]

As mothers, many Polish women saw the Central Asians in a similarly terrifying role, brutes who spoiled children and ruined families. Paulina Rzehaków had to leave her three small children alone while she worked all day. "When I returned home the children sat frightened and crying," she writes. "The Kazakhs frightened the children, banged on the door, and the little ones had convulsions from fear. There were no Poles nearby, in whose care I could leave the children." Another mother insists the Kazakhs corrupted Polish youth: those children who played with them grew wild and disobedient and lost their native tongue.[46]

Many Poles saw Kazakhs, Kirghiz, and Uzbeks and feared physical violence. Janina Dukjetowa reports that Kazakhs from her collective farm broke into her house at night and robbed her; no one responded to her screams. Another woman states that the local people in Kazakhstan beat both her and her daughter. And another complains, "The Kazakhs always beat us." "I stayed three nights with the Kazakhs without being robbed or murdered," reports a Polish countess, "but I saw no sense in tempting providence."[47] According to the documents, the already difficult labor became unbearable under Central Asian brigade leaders. One woman, employed at building barracks, remarks: "Our superiors were the Kazakhs, who beat and scolded us when the work was not done as ordered, sometimes it was too much to tolerate." A teacher, forced to cut and stack hay, writes that her ordeal was worsened by her coworkers, "the Mongols, especially that yellow Chink, [who] rages across the steppe like Satan." In a letter sent from her place of exile another woman expresses fear of her supervisor: "I've been assigned to some terrible Kazakh, I have to defend myself."[48]

In the documents, the dread of rape is continually linked with the Asiatics. Polish women seemed to carry this anxiety with them from the moment they crossed the border and arrived in the East. To many of them the mention of the word Asia or the sight of what was commonly imagined as an Asiatic—"strange sorts with dark faces and slanted eyes"—was enough to conjure the threat of rape.[49] A paralyzing fear gripped many women at the sight of an Uzbek, Kazakh, or Kirghiz man. This reaction to a group of others is not unique, for nations and races commonly project what they most fear and reject onto those who are different, particularly if visibly so. Rape and race are frequently intertwined in this way, as differences in appearance are invested with threatening meaning, and the resulting racial stereotypes can provoke irrational fears of sexual assault. In the United States, for example, the conception of the black man as a "beast-rapist" long held sway not only in the popular and literary imaginations, but scientific, as well.[50]

There are illuminating differences between the white American and the Polish vision of the racial other as rapist. First, the image of the Afro-American male had a dual nature, including a good, docile side, as well as a bad, ferocious one.[51] The Polish perception contains no good side, no childlike nature that would let the Turkic men retain their basic humanity. This possibly stemmed from the utter powerlessness that the women felt before them, for unlike the case of white males vis-à-vis blacks in the United States, these women had no authority or status over the Turkic population and had no need to rationalize paternalistic behavior. Significantly, the nineteenth-century Polish memoirs and reports of Central Asia revealing a condescending, sometimes paternalistic tone, lack the sense of fear and danger that pervades these accounts from the 1940s. The difference seems to be gender based. In the previous century, men composed nearly 90 percent of the Polish population in Kazakhstan; the women mostly followed banished husbands and fathers.[52] In sharp contrast, nearly 80 percent of the Polish deportees to Kazakhstan in the years 1939–1941 were women and children. They not only lacked authority in their new communities but also the protection and security of the men on whom they typically relied. Fear of physical and sexual violence lurks beneath the surface of their reports.

This discussion of the racial component of the women's fear of rape by local men should not be taken as discounting their anxieties or their stories. Certainly racial prejudices shaped both their initial attitudes toward these men and the content of their depictions of real or potential attackers. But the fears of many women seem to have persisted on the basis of experience, either direct or observed. The extent of sexual assault against Polish deportees in Central Asia cannot be documented any more than for the exiles in the USSR as a whole. Lacking a sympathetic government to turn to, the women had no recourse to police or court action. Soviet officials, interested in the deportees as manual laborers and potential political enemies, did not concern themselves with the issue. According to historian Shoshana Keller, local officials paid little attention to the rape or murder of local women either, focusing instead on the new crime of "preventing women from taking part in society."[53] Though Polish authorities subsequently wrote about the rape of Polish women, they did so either anecdotally or in the most general terms. Women's testimonies and memoirs frequently relate incidents that suggest sexual assault and recount threats and propositions. To one familiar with personal narratives from the USSR during this period, and the level of violence that they illustrate, the stories are plausible. Demonstrating the shortcomings of its campaign to liberate Central Asian females, the Soviet regime noted the persistence of crimes against them, including murder, rape, and the practice of "giving girls in marriage."[54] According to Gregory Massell, Muslim women continued to be abducted, like cattle,[55] and it seems that women deported to the steppe from Poland were not exempted from such treatment. Finally, in trying to understand what the peoples of Soviet Central Asia meant to the Polish women, common stereotypes and anxieties are more important than the reality and accuracy of the women's depictions; these are clearly accessible in the documents.

Before considering accounts of actual or threatened assaults, one more point of contrast between the traditional white image of African Americans and the Polish perception of Central Asians merits attention. Racist propaganda in the United States stressed the supposed excessive sexuality and even "sexual madness" of the black male.[56] Concomitantly, the white American stereotype portrayed the black woman as a symbol of sexual promiscuity.[57] In the Polish case, the sexuality of Turkic individuals is largely ignored. No picture of female sexuality comes through the Polish depictions of the Turkic groups, which is not surprising given the tendency to erase these women from view. Additionally, the descriptions of feared rapists focus on their animalism, so that the males appear not as men, but beasts. Thus, even rape, what we might label an extremely gendered behavior, does not mark these individuals as men but serves to underscore the belief that they belong to a primitive, uncivilized race.

Women frequently employ animal imagery to depict their encounters with men in Central Asia. In a dramatic narration, a Polish schoolteacher recounts her terror when approached by a man one night in a labor camp: "I looked and my heart stood still. The face of the speaker was terrible. His tiny eyes shone with animal desire. I have seen many curious types during my imprisonment and I have ceased long ago to be afraid of many things. But this squat figure, this Kalmyk face, seemed inhuman and filled me with horror."[58] Many women experienced a constant feeling of alarm while in the vicinity of the local men, a danger they liken to being among wild animals. One young woman was sent to work at a site where she had to live in an abandoned train car in the middle of the steppe. Nighttime terrified her: "I was afraid of the wolves, but I was even more afraid of the Kirghiz, who sometimes appeared there to assault and abduct young women." In a similar vein, a twenty-one-year-old describes her existence on a state farm in Uzbekistan: "We worked digging ditches, subjected daily to various propositions from our 'breadgivers.' We trembled at the very thought of the onset of night, the time of our rest. The drunken Uzbeks broke our windows and broke down the door, wanting to get into our barrack."[59] Women recalling their time in Soviet Central Asia even decades later evoke a similar atmosphere of fear. "Beyond town, at night," writes Krystyna Niemczyk, who was fifteen when sent to the Kara-Kalpak ASSR in Uzbekistan, "the people were more frightening than the jackals."[60] In an appeal to the Polish delegation for help, a woman stranded after the amnesty declares: "Fifty percent of the population here are Kirghizes, who are dangerous, attack defenseless women, rob and so forth."[61]

As explored earlier, Polish women demonstrate a profound reticence to broach issues revolving around sexuality. While their reports and memoirs express a sense of ever-present danger and relate threatening incidents, none of the authors actually identify themselves as victims of rape. Two firsthand reports of rape have been found in the archives, not in the statements and memoirs but in personal letters sent from Kazakhstan. Both letters were written by women to husbands. In the first, the wife of a Polish army officer writes: "I was the mistress of 30 herdsmen. I could no longer endure this, so I married the thirty-first herdsman. Now I carry the child of this herdsman in my womb. Life is terribly difficult. I beg you to forget about me forever."[62] The second letter states: "My life here is hell, but I have not had the courage to kill myself. . . . One day some herdsmen, more than a dozen, one after the other took advantage of me. As one of them showed a desire to keep me close to him I preferred that. I serve him as a wife. I carry a child in my womb. . . . I beg you, forget me forever, remake your life."[63]

These accounts cannot be confirmed, but their stories are plausible.[64] While noting the silence of women's memoirs regarding rape, Stanisław Ciesielski, in a study of the exiled Poles, concludes that "the attitude of Kazakhs toward Polish women was a special problem," especially because of "marriage" propositions and rape.[65] The reactions of the women quoted above do not differ from the reported reactions of Muslim women to such abductions. "Marriage by abduction" was a common practice in Central Asia, undertaken to avoid the high bride price (*kalym*). According to Massell, in such cases the woman became the wife of the man who raped her; fear and shame generally kept her from leaving or complaining.[66] Given the reticence shown by Polish women to discuss the issue of rape, it seems that only the desperateness of the situation and the intimacy of the relationship to the addressee makes such admissions possible. The assumed audience was a spouse, not the government or any wider public, as was the case for the authors of the testimonies. Neither in the correspondence nor in the vaguer reports do women try to gain anything—sympathy, assistance, revenge—

from the status of rape victim. On the contrary, they are so shamed by it that they see it as cause for the obliteration of the former self. In each of these letters, the woman considers herself defiled by her lot; instead of identifying herself as a blameless victim of a crime, deserving of aid and compassion, she accepts guilt and condemnation. Regarding herself contaminated, disgraced, unfit to return to her home and husband, she is prepared to give up her previous identity, her family, nation, and future because of the shame and stigma.

Two phenomena discussed earlier come together in this response. The first is Polish women's relation to the nation, which, to use the words of Anne McClintock, "was submerged as a *social* relation to a man through marriage."[67] In such cultural arrangements, family honor is defined in terms of the sexuality of women. Consequently, both males and females attribute disgrace to women who deviate from the norm. Second, the sexual act, illegitimate because outside of marriage, regardless of the violence or compulsion involved, tags the woman as guilty and unchaste. She bears the responsibility for the violation of her marriage vow. Failing in her social relation to the man, as his wife—which establishes her connection to the nation—she thus fails before the nation.

Without firsthand accounts of rape perpetrated by Russian or Polish men, it cannot be determined whether the stigma of rape alone or the idea of racial contamination rendered these women, in their own minds, unfit to remain Polish mothers. If the main role of a Polish woman was mother of the nation, then having been raped and impregnated by an Asiatic, a man not only of a different nation but a different race, she sees herself and expects to be seen by her fellow citizens as failing the nation, as wife, mother, and citizen. This leaves her unworthy of either her previous identity or projected future. Polish law would have encouraged this conclusion because it stripped a woman marrying a foreigner of her Polish nationality, shunning her from the collective.

The shame resulting from rape and the strength of the taboo against sexual activity outside of marriage are underscored by the way these women depict their situations. They neither state that they are continually raped nor forced or resigned to live with the man. Instead, they redraw the lines of the new situation, so that they serve as wife of the man, not his rape victim. Obliterating their past lives but drawing on them to make sense of their predicament, they cast their new status in terms with which they can live.

Wife and mother, even if out of compulsion, appear more acceptable roles than rape victim. Unable to avoid the reality of rape, these women essentially ask, in their very personal entreaties, that they be erased from the past and the consciousness of those with whom they shared it.

The women identifying themselves as rape victims write while trapped in the consequences of the act. They have not been released and have no hope of returning to Poland. Consequently, they seem to remake themselves to be able to live with the situation. On the contrary, women recording their experiences after evacuation from the USSR construct their memories in hopes of reintegration into their society. For them, the shame associated with rape can be left behind—at least publicly. Rather than recount actual incidents of rape or fill in the blanks of their vague descriptions, they can be silent and avoid that reality, which enables them to remain innocent Polish women, unstained by the stigma of rape, with their sexual honor intact.

While women are generally reticent about rape, and the few who identify themselves as victims do so because they have fallen out of Polish society, men break the silence. The cases discussed above and the issue of the rape of Polish women in Soviet Central Asia captured the attention of the highest Polish authorities. While female sexual honor and identity necessitated that women distance themselves from such offenses, men were not so bound. Males could broach and publicize the issue of rape and use it for their own national aims.

Studying the response to the rape of French women by German soldiers during World War I, Ruth Harris observed the same phenomenon. "If women's narratives of sexual violation were unadorned and often reticent," Harris writes, "propagandists preferred a strikingly gendered and emotive vision to illustrate the moral peril facing the nation." She demonstrates that at the hands of male soldiers, journalists, and propagandists, the "actual victimization of women was transformed into a representation of a violated, but innocent, female nation resisting the assaults of a brutal male assailant."[68] The issue of the male response to and use of the plight of Polish women in the USSR requires a more extensive analysis of Polish official and journalistic documents than can be undertaken here and rightly deserves its own study. The aim here is not to make conclusions about this topic but to highlight evidence suggesting a similarly gendered difference in the treatment of the rape of Polish women by an abhorred other.

At least in official capacities, Polish men were both more vocal and emotive about the issue of rape. A report written under the auspices of the Polish government-in-exile in 1943 discusses the fate of Polish women remaining on the Central Asian steppe. The author recounts the contents of a letter, similar to those discussed above, sent to another man, thereby moving the matter from an intimate, private sphere, where the woman sought to leave it, to a more public one: "One of the Polish officers in the Polish army in Scotland received a letter from his wife, sent by the Soviet government to the Mongolian steppe, in which she communicates to him that she will never be able to return to him, since in order to save their child from hunger, she had to accept protection in the yurt [tent] of a Mongol. She was infected with venereal disease and is pregnant."[69] The report's author emphasizes not the pain or the trauma the woman experienced but her family position and sacrifice. She seems heroic, since she accepted such a terrible fate to save the life of her child. The added information of venereal disease also stands out; no Polish women admit such infections in their own reports. Although women raise the issue of sexually transmitted diseases to signal the deviance and disgusting nature of others, it remains a taboo subject in their own society. In the male account, the assertion of infection serves to make the contamination of this blameless victim more complete, her martyrdom more evident.

Another official document uses an instance of forced prostitution, also reported in a personal letter, to convey the horrendous condition of Poles in Soviet Central Asia: "In the correspondence from Kazakhstan comes the dismal news of the fate of the deported Poles there. A mother with her two daughters is in the employ of a Kirghiz. At the same time, each one of the three women fulfills the function, in turn, of the wife of the Kirghiz—every ten days."[70] This author uses the story of the sexual subservience of a mother and daughters—not the widespread starvation, exhaustion, or illness—to convey the deplorable position, indeed, the violation, of the exiled nation.

Polish authorities recognized the propaganda value of these intimate stories. Minister of Defense Kazimierz Sosnkowski urged that they be made public, explaining that he felt it his duty "as a Pole and a citizen" to bring this information to light. More specifically, he suggested that they be used in dealing with American charity organizations.[71] The issue was perceived less as a matter of humanity or justice than as a national concern: government documents used the depiction of the plight of helpless women in a foreign and primitive land to epitomize the tragedy of Poland. Summarizing the consequences of Soviet aggression against Poland, one report states: "The fate of women who often fall into the hands of quite uncivilized natives is tragic."[72] The suffering of Polish women, particularly as mothers—saintly and stoic in their victimization—helped to portray the agony of the nation.[73] Poland, too, was weak but blameless, overcome and brutalized by its savage neighbor. The prime minister of the London-based Polish government in 1943–1944, Stanisław Mikołajczyk, used this metaphor to describe the Soviet takeover of Poland, calling it (as well as his wartime memoirs) "the Rape of Poland."[74]

Thus, while women tried to distance themselves from the reality and consequences of sexual abuse, the authorities effectively appropriated the act and the victimization as their own.[75] Commenting on the fate of Poles under the Soviets, Zdisław Łecki writes: "The Bolsheviks cast many Polish women, married and single, onto the Asiatic steppe, leaving them to the mercy of the nomads. These unhappy victims of Bolshevik culture, wandering across the steppe, were forced to sell their bodies to the owners of yurts—Mongols, who only under this condition agreed to give them shelter or a piece of dry bread."[76] Yet another high-level report, sent to three ministers of the government-in-exile concerning the condition of Poles in Soviet Central Asia, focuses on the same image: the Soviets are delivering our women to the wild Asiatics who rape. This document, also written by a man, states: "The women are given over to the prey of the collective farms, where they are compelled to submit to force."[77] This painful and humiliating situation also raised concerns about the future of the nation. As the biological reproducers of both the members and the boundaries of the nation, women ensure both its continuation and its purity. The Minister of Defense acknowledged this concern in his note, in which he urged that assistance be given to these "unfortunate ones," rape victims, "who, by the way, the reborn Poland will need in the future."[78]

In the stories of sexual abuse related by men, the offenders are not just males, not simply Soviet citizens, but Asiatics. For Polish men, defeated by both the Nazis and the Soviets, robbed of their entire country, this was a heavy blow, perhaps the ultimate humiliation. The mere fact of the rape of their women damaged their honor and pride; the information that the perpetrators, who were not even the conquerors of Poland, were of a race deemed inferior compounded the injury.[79] Polish men use the same condescending and essentializing terms as do women to denote the peoples of the Central Asian steppe: Mongols, Asiatics, and nomads. They stress the victimization of Polish women, and hence the Polish nation, at the hands of savages. The situation appears outrageous—the representative of culture and civilization at the complete mercy of the barbarians. Men thus appeal both to masculine pride and Western arrogance.

The female and male treatment of the issue of rape differ significantly: while women appear hesitant to discuss it, preferring to keep the details, the pain, and the shame in silence, men demonstrate a willingness to focus on the issue in a symbolic way. Both responses proceed from highly gendered national identities. They also underline constructions of women as the breeders of the nation, keepers of ethnic boundaries, guardians of the nation's health, and symbol of its honor. For individual women, rape becomes a personal responsibility, signaling their failure before husband and nation. Men's pronounced attention to the sexual violation of Polish women in Central Asia points to the symbolic nature of women's security, which "is often the last frontier men have to defend when all the other battles against colonialism and imperialism are lost."[80] They publicize tales of rape not to speak for the victims but to use the incidents as a clarion call for sympathy, outrage, and action on the part of Polish soldiers and of foreign opinion. Men view rape and forced prostitution not mainly as a crime against individual women but as an offense against the nation. The masculinized concept of the nation has space for women's violation when told in this way. The sexual violation of Polish women becomes an offense done to men, as "Poles and citizens," as well. Since it happened at the hands of men of a race considered primitive and savage, it was the ultimate humiliation, suggesting the contamination of the women and the nation, and the emasculation of the men.

Conclusion

In their accounts of exile to the USSR, Polish women describe and judge the Ukrainian, Belorussian, and Jewish nationalities through their females. While they devote much attention and emotion to the character and behavior of these other women, the Poles effectively erase the women of Soviet Central Asia from view. None of the issues by which they judge women of the national minorities from Poland, such as patriotism, solidarity, and motherhood, appear relevant in the Polish encounters with Turkic women. While it would seem that the Poles merely ignore the women of Central Asia, this act of erasure constitutes a characterization of the societies of the steppe, an insult. Obliterating the women renders the population without gender distinction: instead of women either upholding or transgressing roles and duties ascribed to them, we see only animal-like beings. Without mothers (and children), the population lacks all innocence.

The view of Central Asians as primitive is underscored by the Poles' picture of the males. Like the women, the Kazakh, Kirghiz, and Uzbek men have no names or social roles. They appear predominantly as attackers and rapists, more animal than man. In the vicinity of Turkic men, Polish women feared violence, contamination, and annihilation. Due to woman's biological and symbolic roles in the nation, the danger involved her identity and her future. For different reasons, the assault of Polish women appeared to Polish men as crimes against themselves. Polish men had lost much to the Soviet regime, and rape became an issue on which they could readily focus, one both intimately tied to their own identities and feelings as husbands, fathers, and protectors, and highly symbolic of the plight of Poland. Calling the men of Central Asia Mongols, Poles invoke the image of the invasion of their own territory in the thirteenth century, preserved in memory as an episode of rape and pillage, threatening the destruction of Western civilization.

The exiles feared the peoples of Soviet Central Asia because they and the space that they occupied represented the antithesis of Europe. The lack of discernible gender roles becomes one of the markers of the Asiatics' perceived lack of civilization, indicated also by the reported absence of cleanliness and intelligence, and of culture, religion, and nation. Without, in the Polish perception, meaningful distinctions and ordering categories, the Central Asians mainly appear as filthy beings who blend in and are at home with the animals and the dirt around them. Registering little else about their societies, the Poles effectively erase nationality and gender, aspects of identity crucial to their own sense of self and understanding of others, from the world of the Central Asians. Either blind to or not comprehending the locals' framework of social relations, the Poles conclude that they have none. They register nothing about family or communal life when discussing these others, apparently assuming that the issues so vital to themselves have no place in this other world. The inhabitants of the steppe, in this perception, are not individuals or nations, but merely a race, representing a world different from that known to and esteemed by Poles.

Depicting the Central Asian peoples as a vague mass lacking the elements understood as hallmarks of civilization, the Polish attitude resembles that of a colonial power to its subject peoples. "Western eyes," write Julia Watson and Sidonie Smith, "see the colonized as an amorphous, generalized collectivity of undifferentiated bodies."[81] Chandra Talpade Mohanty elaborates: "Colonization almost invariably implies a relation of structural domination, and a suppression—often violent—of the heterogeneity of the subject(s) in question."[82] This captures what the Soviet regime sought to do with its Polish subjects: to erase to the extent possible important aspects of their heterogeneity, including individual and group identities and cultural formations. Poles, in their imagination and their writing, treat in a similar manner those they considered beneath them. Though the Poles did not occupy a position of dominance over the inhabitants of Central Asia, such an attitude resulted from traditional stereotypes and the Poles' abject position within the USSR.

To the exiles, Soviet Central Asia symbolized the negation of Polish (Western) civilization. Women's trembling at traversing the border, their anxiety at crossing over into that alien state of existence, stemmed from a fear that they themselves could be reduced to the state that they described and abhorred. Not only would they lose their homes in the West, but also their identity as Poles and as women, their very humanity. Without the accustomed attributes of civilization, they would be degraded to the level of animals, Asiatics. "One had to stop being a 'human being'," writes a woman of her existence in Kazakhstan. "That life of primitive people was for us something atrocious. The overcoming of your 'I', the dependency on beings of such a significantly lower level of intelligence . . . it was a real gehenna."[83]

8

"You Can't Even Call Them Women"

Condemning the Russians

For many Poles, Asia represented all that was primitive, the antithesis of Western civilization of which they unequivocally considered themselves a part. In the writings of the exiles, the people of the steppe stand firmly outside the world of the Poles, universally abhorred, clearly a despised "other." This assessment serves as a reference for characterizing another important group of others: the Asiatics are used to signal and denigrate the essence of the most bitter foes of the Polish nation, the Russians.

Russians represent a more problematic group for the exiled Poles than do the peoples of Central Asia because they are at once highly threatening and uncomfortably familiar to Poles. As fellow Slavs, Russians generally look like Poles and speak a related language. Their country straddles the boundary between Europe and Asia. Poles approach the Russians with a historical legacy of enmity and despise them for what they have now done to Poland. Furthermore, they detest the way Russians live, fearing the Soviet regime's efforts to render the Poles similar. Situating Asia at the opposite extreme of the civilized West, the Poles use it to place Russians, both geographically and culturally. By continually juxtaposing the Russians to the "Asiatics" and often conflating the two categories, Poles signal an essential otherness of their historical enemies and recent conquerors. An intellectual arrested by the NKVD in Lwów in 1940 illustrates this perception as he recounts conversations in his prison cell with fellow Poles before their transfer to Russia:

> One of us would quote a striking analogy from Zatorski's book about Genghis Khan. Someone had read somewhere that Russians are a mixture of Mordvinians, Chuvash, Pechenegs, Khazars, Mongols and Tatars. The filthy square of our cell floor became the battlefield for the enormous thousand-year war between the barbarians and civilization, nomads and settlers. And bolstered by that far-ranging vision, we were ready to enter our Tatar captivity.[1]

Linking Russians with the peoples of Central Asia, the Poles locate their enemies in a different world; one Pole uses those very words—a different world—as the title of his memoir of wartime exile.[2] Another refers to Russians as the "Asiatic torturer."[3] Characterizing the true Russian nature as Asiatic also consolidates Polish identity as Western and civilized.

Poles represent the peoples of Soviet Central Asia as uncivilized, as animal-like, by ignoring or denying the existence of meaningful gender distinctions. Similarly, in their descriptions of life in the USSR, Polish women present the Russians as a collective that blurs the boundaries between men and women, thereby ignoring a hallmark of civilized society and subverting even nature itself. Poles voice particular scorn for Russians because this erasure of social distinctions between women and men was a conscious policy of their government. In the Polish mind, this lack of distinction marks Russian society as profoundly aberrant.

This depiction of Russians as other carries political implications. The message for Europe and the West, especially the wartime allies of the USSR, is that Russians are not like us but are part of the East. Poles do not belong in their orbit, nor should Western powers treat Russians as one of them, for Russians resemble the Mongols, the hordes of Asiatics who invaded the Central European plain centuries before, bringing only misery and destruction. Like the Mongols, Poles imply, the Russians constitute a threat to Western civilization and should not be trusted. This message was not just a matter of strategic or diplomatic importance conveyed by the Polish government-in-exile to the Allies. The view of Russians as alien and dangerous was not merely the notion of top political elites, but comes through the personal statements of countless women, expressing the way multitudes of individuals personally experienced Russians. For these Poles, the conduct (seen as the perversion) of the most intimate realms of daily life—the condition of the private sphere and of personal relations—represents the dangerous political meaning of Russians and their society. Gender is thus used to convey the political threat of the Soviets; more important, however, it is through gender that individuals who did not operate in the public sphere of high politics perceived and felt that threat.

In the Polish depiction of the Russians, females again bear the burden of differentiation. Their perceived improperness and even unnaturalness symbolizes the abnormal condition of Russian society as a whole. In contrast to their treatment of women of Central Asia, Poles focus much attention and emotion in their statements on Russian females; but they do so in different terms than those used for women of the national minorities from Poland. The issues of proper citizenship and solidarity find scant mention in discussions about Russians. Questions of whether they were loyal members of their own nation or contributing members of a community are seemingly irrelevant; these attributes are beyond their capacity. Instead, Polish women treat much more personal matters when considering this group, matters that comment on the most intimate aspects of the Russians as individuals. Thus, while women of the national minorities receive the labels of traitors and spies, Russian women are more frequently tagged as whores, child murderers, and shock workers. The national minorities are disloyal, while Russians are wild and degenerate. Among Central Asians Poles do not recognize women, while among Russians they see improper, perverted ones. These differences indicate both the intense scorn that Poles feel for Russians and the danger that the latter represent, for Russians threaten not just the borders of the Polish state, or the life of its soldiers, or the existence of its government, all of which are conventional perils of war. In reordering the lives of millions of Polish citizens, Russians endanger the most intimate sphere of existence and hence the very identity of each of those individuals. Ultimately, they threaten the character and existence of the Polish nation.

"Russia Is East, and Poland Is West"

The Soviet army that invaded Poland in 1939 confronted a nation bearing great antipathy toward Russia. It was a people whose psyche was saturated with historical memory, in which were fused the Mongol invasions of the thirteenth century, the partitions of the eighteenth, the suppressed rebellions of the nineteenth, and the bitter war of the early twentieth. Poles carried this legacy, compounded by the latest injustices, into exile in the USSR, where neither the stereotypes nor the injury were lessened.

In the documents, discussions about Russians take place within a traditional framework of West versus East. For centuries, West Europeans perceived Russia as an exotic other. Situating themselves firmly in the West, Poles emphasized their adherence to the Roman Catholic Church and their cultural ties to Latin civilization, which they contrasted with the Byzantine religious and cultural roots and the Asian features of the Russian land and society. In the Polish mind, Poland represented the outpost of Western civilization, bordered by the culturally inferior Russian empire of the East. In characterizing Russians, Poles have long operated out of fear and loathing, in a rivalry bearing high historical, emotional, and political stakes. As Norman Davies writes: "Poland's age-old contact with the Russians has brought nothing but bitterness and mutual mistrust. Russia is East, and Poland is West; and never, it seems, the twain shall meet. Poland's Westernism, therefore, is fundamental and compulsive."[4]

This long-held view did not adhere only to the Russian Empire, which had repeatedly contested and violated the borders of the Polish state. Well into the twentieth century, the metaphoric battle still found expression. A series of informational pamphlets put out by the Polish Information Center in New York during the Second World War illustrates the enduring Polish mind-set. Describing the *kresy*, the tract states: "Eastern Poland is the borderland of Western culture, civilization and humanitarian ideology. East of the Polish border stretch lands where Byzantine influence was predominant."[5] One pamphlet explains the nature of the Polish nation to the American people; the unannounced agenda is to distinguish it from the Russian one: "At the very outset of her national history, Poland elected to link her destiny with the West, rather than the East. Her national culture has always followed the pattern of Western civilization. . . . Poland prided herself on being an eastern outpost of Western Latin civilization."[6]

The changes in state structure and ideology brought by the 1917 revolution did little to alter the Polish view of Russia, for the enmity had not merely political roots—the conflicting claims and creeds of two neighboring powers—but represented cultural tensions as well. Polish scholar Jan Kucharzewski, who believed that the character of Russian society lived on after the fall of the old regime, captured this notion in the title of his seven-volume history of Russia, *From the White Tsardom to the Red*.[7] Poles did not separate Bolshevism from the nationality of its principal adherents. Even many of those sympathetic to the progressive ideals of the new regime viewed its representatives with condescension. Józef Piłsudski, longtime leader of the Polish Socialist Party, called Bolshevism "a purely Russian disease."[8] In his reminiscences, the writer Aleksandr Wat expresses an attitude common among Polish intellectuals toward the Communists before World War II: "To us those were people from 'over there.' Russia—a gigantic country, savage, neglected for hundreds of years, where a new life for humanity was to be built, and humanity would be organized on ideal foundations. A hundred some million people who were disadvantaged, unfortunate, but also half savage . . . every Pole had that impression."[9] Here, too, the geographical separateness of Poland and Russia, of Europe and Asia, reflected in the idea of Russians as people from over there, underscores the cultural separateness of the two sides.

Poles have represented the military conflicts between Soviet Russia and Poland in these absolute national and cultural terms. Neither lay people nor scholars have viewed the Polish-Soviet War of 1919–1920 merely as a conflict between two neighboring states, a contest over geographic borderlands. Historian Piotr Wandycz wrote that the Polish-Soviet War, like many conflicts before it, was a clash of civilizations, of Western and Eastern historical trends.[10] He echoes the traditional line of thinking, as expressed by the scholar of Polish-Russian relations, Wacław Lednicki, who stated that in any incarnation, Russia has always "utilized all the weapons of her own Eastern ideology; Eastern Europe became a battlefield on which two different, opposed, and even conflicting civilizations met."[11]

Many Poles viewed the Soviet invasion of September 1939 in a similar light, depicting it as an incursion of the Asiatics. Their descriptions repeatedly invoke the Mongol invasions of the thirteenth century. Women report uniform first impressions of the Red Army: Mongolian faces, drabness, dirt, disorder, danger. One woman offers this description: "On skinny, small horses, the dark Mongols, tawny faces, little slanted eyes, grey greatcoats, frayed at the bottom, with machine guns drawn. One is crouching, another cockily, insolently looking around. Asia! A hodgepodge. I watch, I'll never forget!" Writing from eastern Poland in 1940, another woman exclaims of the occupiers, "These are animals, it's the barbarians, they're Tatars."[12] Wat evokes the same image of the Soviet invasion: "Tanks, Russians, of course, mass meetings. . . . You know, those Mongol-like faces, those shoddy uniforms, those Mongolian caps with the raggedy peaks. It was Asia but in such mass amounts. Asia at its most Asian."[13] Like many others, Wat attributes the deterioration of Poland after the arrival of the Red Army to what the Soviets seemed to embody: "Asia, ragged, illiterate Asia." "The Russians seemed to bring decay to everything," echoes a woman from Wilno.[14]

This depiction did not originate in 1939. As Davies notes, "Ancestral memories of the Huns and the Mongols have been invoked on every occasion the Russian armies have marched on Poland from the East."[15] Even when the Russian army served a beneficial function, it provoked the same response. A woman who witnessed the flight of the hated Nazis from Poland before the advancing Soviet army in 1945 writes: "We furtively observe the Red Army, the soldiers who have 'liberated us.' With their long mustaches, slanting eyes, and yellow complexions, they seem more like the armies of Ghengis Khan than our own notion of liberators."[16]

This picture of the entry of the Russians renders it comprehensible to the Poles, who do not interpret the events of September 1939 as a defeat by a superior or even equal foe. The Red Army invasion is likened to the Mongol one, which swept across the Eurasian plains using sheer force to defeat governments and peoples, to the Western mind, of a superior civilization, lacking only in organization, force, and brutality. For Poles, September 1939 offered another illustration of the barbaric, Asiatic nature of the Russians and their state. Polish descriptions employ images not of an efficient, organized, and superior fighting force—that the Red Army proved to be—but of a ragged, disorganized, almost laughable band of ruffians, dangerous in their numbers and cruelty. The use of such words as "massive" and "hodgepodge" with an image of an undifferentiated mass, underscores the Polish perception of the group's primitiveness. Moreover, they are all alien; none of the writers acknowledge the Slavic elements of the Red Army, the features that made the invading soldiers similar to the Poles, presenting the Soviets instead as a totally Asian force.

The insights of anthropologist Mary Douglas again prove useful. Uncomfortable facts—the similarity of the Russians to the Poles and especially the superiority of their military—must be ignored or distorted so that they do not "confuse or contradict cherished classifications." Furthermore, as Douglas points out, half-identities or ambiguous identities are troubling, for they disrupt comforting notions of clarity.[17] If the invading Russian army is not sharply delineated from the victims, then its arrival and triumph endangers the Poles' sense of identity as superior and European. To bring some order to the chaos experienced in the fall of 1939, the Poles need to assign the invading soldiers an identity that fits into the Poles' established framework. The aggressors thus all become Asians, their victory attributable not to any cultural or moral superiority but to brute animal force, the same that had been exercised by the hordes who ravished East Central Europe centuries before. Like them, the Red Army is charged with bringing dirt and chaos, spoiling the order that the Poles had known: they have brought Asia into Europe.

The Poles maintain this boundary between themselves and the Russians in their contact with the nation as a whole, be it with soldiers, authorities, or civilians. Many women recall feeling great anxiety while viewing the "shabby landscape" and the "Mongolian faces" from the transports on their journey eastward. Often the men who perform the humiliating body searches or brutal interrogations are identified only by such a face.[18] A woman arrested for anti-Soviet agitation recalls being sentenced by a Russian "with a dreary face, resembling something between an orangutan and a chimpanzee." Drabness and brutality seem to sum up the people and the place. Maria Radzimińska describes an exception that she encountered, one that proves the rule. Surprised by the Europeanness (europejskość) of a Russian man she met in a labor camp, she writes that his was "the first human face" and he "the first civilized person" that she saw in Russia. Poles report that once they crossed the border into Russia, nothing made sense to them because they "all thought according to the categories of Western Europe." Summing up her experience in the USSR, one woman offers the following relatively generous view: "As a union of a European nation and Asiatic peoples, through mutual collaboration, the contemporary Russian is closer to the Asiatic than the European, has fallen lower in the hierarchy . . . this is seen in private, and especially, official life." Finally, Aniela Pawliszak, who survived Nazi captivity before her arrest and imprisonment in the USSR, speaks for many:

> The Bolsheviks made a strange impression on me: they are wretched people, who think only about how to fill their stomachs, for they are always hungry, and how to harm and abuse one who is weaker. They think and speak differently, for they live in constant fear of the govern-

ment and prison. They always lie, they never tell the truth. I have never seen the wild people of Africa, but I think that such barbarians as the Bolsheviks exist nowhere else on earth, although they pretend that they are like us, and always talk about culture.[19]

The Poles generally link the Soviet system, the Bolsheviks, with the Russian people, as a continuation of their past. Though aware of the abuses and deplorable living conditions prevailing in Soviet Russia, Poles usually do not conceive of the regime as a group of tyrants exploiting a helpless people. Rather, the system and all of its ramifications seem understandable to the Poles as a phenomenon from "over there," something indigenous to that foreign, incomprehensible Russian land. This national element, as an underlying explanation for the evils and ills of the Soviet system, is frequently absent from accounts of Soviet imprisonment written by non-Poles. Individuals from Western Europe who bear no historical grudge against the Russians, and whose own identity as Europeans was never contested, do not demonstrate the urgent need to highlight their difference from and superiority to the Russians. They tend to see a tragic nation plagued by an evil system and neither conflate the Soviet leaders and the Russian people, nor see a clash between civilizations. Elinor Lipper, a Dutch woman imprisoned in the Gulag, writes emphatically: "The Russian people, and the other peoples of the Soviet Union, cannot be equated with the Soviet government. Though they may have brought it into being, they are now the helpless victims of a ruling caste whose arbitrariness they must endure in silence. . . It is easy to condemn 'the Russians'—but to do so is to do the Russian people a great injustice."[20] Such statements rarely come from ethnic Poles, who see the people inhabiting Russian territory through a national lens clouded by historical enmity.

Some Poles do find good people among the Russians and write about them sympathetically. If they spent time in the labor camps, such men and women highlight the distinction between political prisoners and ordinary criminals, finding common ground with the former.[21] If deportees report kindness or friendship from local Russians, the latter tend to be older individuals, those who "remember the time of the Tsars."[22] In such cases, religious belief often serves as the link between the two peoples. Most of the favorable accounts apply to individuals or subgroups of the Russian population and not to the entire nation. Some authors register surprise when meeting with compassion from Russians. One deportee describes a close friendship with a young Russian woman, who was "the only pleasant or affectionate woman among the few native families in Korostelevka, where the bulk of the population was ready to exploit and spy upon the exiles." Similarly, another Pole records meeting "a Russian woman with a respectable soul."[23] Others attribute kindness from Russians to a "small drop of Polish blood" from ancestors exiled from Poland in the nineteenth century.[24] A few Poles can express compassion for the plight of the Russians without changing their negative attitude toward them. "And although Russians are our eternal enemies," comments one young woman. "I still feel sorry for them, that they live without freedom."[25] While some Poles display sympathy for Russians as victims of a ruinous government, most pay no heed to the distinction; the reigning system is considered endemic to the Russian nationality. In any incarnation, the Russians seem different to the Poles; inferiority is embodied in that difference.

"We Had Nothing in Common with Them"

Of all the nations that the Poles encountered in the USSR, the Russians were the most numerous. In the labor camps, Russians composed more than 63 percent of the total population.[26] Many deportees lived closely with Russians, even on collective farms in Kazakhstan and Kirghizia, to which large numbers of Russians had likewise been punitively exiled. Sharing cramped prison cells, common barracks, small huts, and daily labor gangs, Polish women had a close-up view of Russian women, with whom they compare themselves continually in their statements. These Poles did not see Russian women as resembling themselves and typically write with disgust about their character and behavior. Not only were these other women enemies, by virtue of their nationality alone, but they also constituted a model that the Poles rejected and, under the pressures of living conditions in exile, feared becoming.

Whether deported or arrested, Polish women generally characterize Russian women as primitive and disgusting, similar to Central Asians; dirt and disorder figure frequently in their descriptions. According to the Poles, Russians maintained no personal hygiene whatsoever. "We Poles, especially the women, even in the very worst conditions had to maintain some kind of order and cleanliness, at the very least passionately desire it, if conditions were so bad, like, for example, in prison," writes one woman. "They were different," she continues. "They slept on dirty floors, did not wash, and traded their soap for vodka; we were repelled by the women, with never-brushed hair that was infested with lice, which they covered with red scarves that were disintegrating from the dirt."[27] Many of the arrested Polish women, who prided themselves on their ability to clean themselves even when given only one cup of water per day, for both drinking and cleaning, assert this distinction between themselves and Russians.[28]

Like women of the national minorities from Poland, Russian women reportedly maintained no solidarity among themselves. Though this issue seldom comes up in relation to Russian women, it nonetheless serves both to differentiate the Russians and emphasize the definition of Polish women as a single cohesive unit. According to Olga Słabowa, the Russians were surprised by the closeness of the Poles. A woman deported to the Urals region writes: "The Poles were an example to the Russian people, they lived peacefully and together." "In spite of the danger from cold, hunger, and their bad treatment of us Polish women," writes Eudoksja Czerniewska, "I must firmly state, that the spirit of us Polish women was good and we were an example of unity in contrast to their citizens."[29]

The most lengthy, damning, and at times hair-raising descriptions of Russian women come from Poles incarcerated in the Gulag. Most of them brand the female Russian contingent there as "thieves, bandits and prostitutes." The overall impression one gets from reading Polish accounts is that while Poles were imprisoned largely as politicals, accused or guilty of activities and stances construed as unlawful according to the logic of the Soviet system, the bulk of Russian women were common criminals. "The camp is filled with a number of women," reads a typical account, "mostly criminals, bandits, thieves and prostitutes, the so-called *shalmanki*."[30] Stanisława Fornalewicz reports that her camp population included 300 women, half of whom were Polish, while the rest were "criminals, thieves and prostitutes." Similarly, Stanisława Krzemień writes that the women in her camp "were common Soviet criminals, mainly thieves, prostitutes and bandits. More than one of them had a human life on her conscience."[31]

Certainly criminals represented a powerful and oppressive force in the camps, one that affected the lives of nearly all inmates. In contrast to the picture presented in the Polish accounts, they did not, however, constitute the majority of the camp population. Documents from Soviet archives offer a rough estimate of the division between common and political criminals. An NKVD report records approximately 1.6 million arrests during the year 1937–1938, 87 percent of which were for political charges. The document also notes that of the total number of people sentenced "on cases of security police" from 1921 to 1938, 30 percent were common criminals.[32] Outside estimates place the percentage of common criminals during the period in which the Poles were incarcerated between 10 and 15 percent of the total labor camp population. Camp narratives—other than these brief ones by Polish women—also suggest the preponderance of politicals in labor camps at this time.[33]

On the whole, Polish men likewise refer to the Russian population in the prisons and camps as common criminals. "The Poles were political prisoners," writes a fifty-year-old machinist, "the Russians—criminals."[34] They similarly describe them as "people without faith or conscience." One man presents two cases as emblematic: a boy incarcerated for raping a seventy-year-old grandmother, another for impregnating his sister.[35] Polish men also report that Russian criminals terrorized them by raiding their barracks, stealing their last rags, and committing murder.[36]

A noteworthy difference between male and female accounts is that the former do not render criminality and immorality exclusively Russian traits. While women write as if the reprehensible individuals, particularly in the camps, were all Russian, men acknowledge that Poles also belonged to this group. "There was no lack, however, of even common criminals among the Poles," notes Mikołaj Tutorski, "smugglers, thieves, bandits." Others recall sharing transports with Soviets and Poles "of the worst criminal element."[37] Though they also bear no love for the Russians, Polish men seem less absolute in attributing negative behaviors based solely on nationality. They also compare themselves with these others less frequently and less emphatically than do Polish women. More independently based, men's identity does not seem to need this strategy in the way that women's does.

Some Polish women do note the presence of politicals among female Russian prisoners, showing their awareness of differentiation among the Russian group. This knowledge, however, does not often result in identification with or compassion for them. Janina Królikowska states that among the Russian women in her camp were politicals, criminals, and prostitutes: "The moral level, without exception, very low. Their attitude toward the Polish women, full of hate." Another woman writes: "There were also some better-educated Russian women—mostly spies, as I discovered later on, several nondescript creatures of no special character."[38] Similarly, in a 1946 exposé of the tragedy of the Poles under Soviet rule, another woman states that there were many politicals in the camps, but "the mass of them are every bit as primitive, as illiterate, and as inarticulate as the mass of common criminals"; she adds, "many are Asiatics."[39] A young woman from Stołci reports sharing a cell with Russian women murderers, speculators and politicals. She remarks, "The Russian women were prominently distinguished by their lack of morality."[40]

Even the "wives" in the camps, Soviet women imprisoned solely because of their marriage to men arrested in the purge of 1937, were typically perceived as distant and alien. Some Poles attributed a lack of intelligence, morality, or compassion to these female spouses of arrested officials, professors, and artists, who were probably quite like the Polish wives. Such stereotyping may well have taken place in Russian perceptions of Poles, as well. "We naively thought that we would find among them companions in our misery," writes one Pole.[41] This lack of commiseration is significant, for many of the Polish women were similarly taken from their homes because of their relationship to men considered dangerous by the regime. National distinctness precluded identification and community based on gender or class. On the whole, Poles did not identify with Russian politicals and rarely crossed national lines to form friendships with them. Only a few Polish women reached the same conclusion as Lipper, the Dutch woman, who relates that in the Gulag she gradually realized that all the others were as innocent as she was.[42]

Instead, most Poles take pains to demonstrate that Russian females are nothing like them. Just as the Turkic females seem to lack the attributes of women, so too are Russian females rendered incomprehensible. While the Poles accomplish this portrayal of the Central Asians through silence, they explicitly denounce the Russians, frequently describing them as a species unknown to the rest of the world, thereby taking them out of Europe and putting them in Asia. Stanisława Kowalska, recalling the female inmates in the camp Karaganda, writes: "The boldest human imagination could not create the model of the Soviet criminal. Comparison with animals would be the greatest compliment for this case of humanity." The most common terms used in discussions of Russian women prisoners are "inhuman" and "beyond description." Another Pole expresses similar shock about the female criminals in her camp, whom she considers simply inconceivable to the outside world: "I never imagined that a person could fall so low morally—completely depraved." The younger ones particularly horrified the Poles. Antonina Brzozowska regards the *besprizorniki* (homeless youths) she encountered, children sometimes aged twelve or thirteen, "something resembling a person only in the construction of the body, even the language they use is not similar to a human one."[43]

Describing Russian women, Poles repeatedly assert: "We were terribly afraid of them, and rightly so, we had nothing in common with them and their 'mother' language."[44] Two women arrested for border infractions explain why the language used by Russian women disturbed them: "Their vocabulary has no equal in the world, there is so much blasphemy, pornographic obscenity, and abuse of everything human." "Here, for the first time in my life, I heard words that probably don't exist in any dictionary in the world." Among the Russian women in the labor camp Pot'ma, one woman asserts, "reign indescribable clamor and vulgar invectives, about which Western Europe has no notion."[45] Countless statements record the same reaction, as does a report written for the Polish army after the evacuation. "In conversations about sexual intercourse the women are as cynical as the men, and as immodest in their language," the male author writes. "They use, without the slightest embarrassment, the same expletives and obscenities."[46] According to one woman: "The bad language which the women criminals use is so obscene that it is quite unbearable and they seem to be able to speak to each other only in the lowest and coarsest terms." A Pole from Lida was also repelled by Russians in the camp, who, she remarks, "in no way could be called women."[47]

When discussing the speech of Russian females, Poles continually interchange three condemnations: it is not properly feminine, not humanly decent, and alien to Europe. Accepting men's swearing, they conflate norms of gender, morality, and Western culture. In this construction, European becomes synonymous with exhibiting distinct gender norms, with the weight of distinction on the female. Those who violate them "in no way [can] be called women." Such females are not only not European, but they are closer to animals, just like the nondescript women of Central Asia. Significantly, while female Jews, Ukrainians, and Belorussians are accused of using language unbefitting Polish citizens, Russians are condemned for using language unnatural for women. Rendering Russian females nonwomen and animal-like, this denunciation goes far beyond that made of the national minorities from Poland, who remain both human and European in the eyes of the Poles.

Russian women violate other norms of female behavior, we are told. They seem such a horrifying breed that even male guards fear them. A Pole arrested for belonging to an underground organization emphasizes the vicious behavior of the Russians in her camp, stating: "These women were so terrible that even the guards yielded to them."[48] No respect or awe resides in this statement; the behavior of these women does not count as resistance to the authorities. Rather, such comments point to the abnormal state of both sexes in Russia. One Pole thus describes the activities of her fellow female inmates at Kolyma: "The retching, the wild cries, the dancing and stamping of feet, the brawling, fornicating and wild-cat fighting went on night and day. Even the men were afraid of these women. The commandant was afraid of them too."[49] Poles recount attacks on the women's barracks by other women, often the result of a card game with acts of robbery or murder at stake. This type of entertainment required the loser to perform these acts or be killed. Shocked at such female aggression, Poles found it horrifying that male authorities, from whom they expected protection by virtue of their gender, were too afraid to interfere.[50] At least one such incident was resolved in a way that set things right for the Poles, despite the authorities' refusal to help: "The uproar was terrific—the women yelled, screamed the skies down, until the men came to our rescue. These were Poles—they lived in barracks not far away."[51] The Russian guards may simply have been callously indifferent, but in the minds of the Polish women, their reticence, interpreted as fear of the monstrous females, signaled the inverted order of the world in which they now lived, where females were not even women and males did not act like men. Only Polish men acted properly here, fulfilling the role of brave protectors of victimized women; among the Polish nation at least, order still prevailed.

The behavior of Russian men in this and similar instances contradicts the anticipated norms for male behavior. This apparent reversal of expected gender roles, seen as upsetting nature, becomes emblematic of the distorted order of the Russian nation. Feminist scholars have found that gender frequently serves to represent and condemn situations of chaos and danger. If "gender relationships are seen as timeless, unchanging, outside social and political systems," writes Joan Scott, "then that which changes them is not simply wrong but counter to the natural order."[52] In the political struggle between Poles and Russians, a struggle taking place on the most intimate and the most public levels, Poles use gender to construct Russian nationality as primitive and perverse.

Poles accept the national minorities deported with them from Poland as fellow Europeans and contest only the definition of the Polish nation; therefore the grounds for comparison and complaint stem predominantly from issues of patriotism and solidarity. They pay scant attention to these matters in their discussions of Russian women, focusing instead on issues they perceive to lie at the core of individual identity and social order. Russians represent a much greater danger to Poles and contest their identity on several levels. In response, Polish women condemn their Russian counterparts on the most intimate grounds, that which most differentiates women from men as social beings, focusing on three topics: labor, family, and sexuality. Polish women use the standards by which they define themselves to show that Russian women do not resemble them in the least.

"Criminals, Prostitutes, Child Murderers and Shock Workers"

As depicted by Poles, Russian females did not observe the norms for women: they ignored personal hygiene and swore like men. They further blurred the lines between the sexes in performing physical labor. Whereas Polish females defined themselves primarily as mothers and nurturers of the nation, the women they encountered in the USSR seemed to have little connection to these roles. The most obvious and lauded role fulfilled by Russian women was that of worker—typically physical laborer. From its earliest days, the ruling Communist Party sought to grant females equality, understood as liberating them from domesticity and providing them full access to public realms. This became a real possibility after Stalin launched his drive for rapid industrialization in 1928. Tying the goal of female independence with that of reconstructing the economy along socialist lines, Stalin's regime stressed the participation of women in economic life, both in agriculture and industry. "Gender differences between men and women were being leveled as women were now considered in theory to be the same as men," writes Anne Gorsuch, "and women and men worked and played together in new ways and new places."[53] Historians generally concur that the need to rectify the acute labor shortage that developed in the late 1920s far outweighed concern for women's welfare. The combination of declining real wages and the failure to restructure gender roles meant "the promise of female independence was never fulfilled."[54]

Nevertheless, the rapid and spectacular rise in the numbers of women engaged in wage labor, particularly the traditionally male-dominated sectors, suggests that a measure of leveling did occur. Upon observing a group of women engaged in heavy labor, one Soviet intellectual remarked, "They were indeed sexless."[55] From 1928 to 1937, 6.6 million women joined the workforce. Unprecedented numbers of females entered the industrial sector: in the year 1930–1931 alone the percentage of women in heavy industry rose from 22 percent to 42 percent.[56] Whether individual motivation stemmed from coercion, economic necessity, or support for the Party's goals, "the gendered dimensions of industrialization were figured in the reimaging of the Soviet woman as a liberated, reconstructed persona who symbolized and simultaneously served as a yardstick for Soviet progress."[57] Women's labor in the agricultural sector likewise intensified, and Stalin lavished praise on the women of the countryside who broke production records, commenting, "I have never met women like these. These are entirely new people."[58]

Poles echo Stalin's assessment but with opposite implications. They frequently comment on the pride the widespread participation of women in the labor force inspired in Communist authorities, as well as in many Russian females. Helena Antonewicz recounts the scolding she and other Poles endured when they criticized the work of a brigade of Russian women on a construction site: "Shut up! Don't ever say that the women of the Soviet Union work poorly—they are Stakhanovites and you are not shock workers at all, you're a shifty people."[59] The high numbers of working women and the type of labor they performed, as well as the expressions of pride accompanying these details, struck the Poles as a strange phenomenon. In fact, the issue of women and work in the USSR also interested officials of the Polish army and government-in-exile, to whom it revealed the extreme otherness and danger of Poland's rival. One of the aims of the massive documentation project undertaken among the evacuated Poles was to expose the "true" nature of the Soviet system to the Western world. This task could be aided, it was apparently assumed, by providing information on women's labor, a signal of the "uncivilized" nature of the USSR.[60] One of the forms the army circulated among the newly released exiles bears the title, "Women's Questionnaire," and contains a section specifically concerned with the employment of Soviet women.[61]

Discussing this issue, Poles of both sexes report a pervasive abnormality. "It was often said that 'a woman has two hands and feet like a man, so she is obliged to work the same as men,'" notes a man from Lwów. "In labor no difference is made between women and men," explains Maria Szoska. "The conviction prevails that a woman is as equally suitable as a man to every kind of work, and that there is no labor she cannot perform, the weaker physical construction of the woman is not taken into account, it is thought of as a bourgeois fallacy."[62] Convinced of a basic nature inherent to all females, some Polish women place the blame for the transformation of women in the USSR to an unrecognizable form on Soviet leaders. Maria Sicińska recalls making bricks with two Russian women: "They were used to physical work, because they had never done anything else in their lives, but cursed their fate, their country, their leaders for turning them into labor animals." Wisłowa Krzyańska voices similar compassion for individuals compelled to live in a way that violated their essence as women: "In Russia there is equality for women, but they are burdened with hard labor, which in the entire world is performed only by men. The work surpasses the strength of women and separates them from that which is the most dear that they possess, their children."[63]

Other Polish females consider not only Soviet leaders deviant but the women as well, because they could manage the difficult labor and often executed it eagerly. According to Janina Wawrzyńska, Russian women easily fulfilled the high work quotas. Assertions of Russian women's ability to perform difficult labor and even exceed the norm are nearly always accompanied by illustrations of the inability of Polish women even to approach it. "The Soviet women outstripped us," states Zdisława Peszek. "They earned much more, and we got nothing." Another woman, forced to work on the construction of a hydration system, asserts, "Several Russian brigades fulfilled the norm, but we Polish women fulfilled 20–40 percent." Similarly, a 31-year-old woman who worked digging canals and building roads could not reach 50 percent of the norm. Near her worked a brigade of Russian women, of whom she reports: "The Soviet women fulfilled 90 to 100 and even higher percentages of the norm, once on the notice-board it said 112 percent."[64] Though most Polish women saw Russian ones as uniquely capable of the work, the situation was not so clear cut. As a few Poles note, Russian women sometimes managed to fulfill the norm only because of the help of "boyfriends."[65] And according to statistics of 1936, women were underrepresented among those who exceeded their work quotas: 23–24 percent of Stakhanovites were female.[66]

Russian women did not earn respect for their hard labor from Polish females, who considered them backward and ignorant—in a word, "Asiatic." Anna Szwaglisówna writes of her female coworkers:

> As a rule such women, accustomed as they are to work from their early childhood, don't complain. Some are even proud of their equal rights. But all this tells on their health. They are hoodwinked by the praise they constantly hear and this prevents them from realizing that they are being exploited and even if they did realize it they would have to bear it without protest, though the work they have to do is against all the laws of nature.

Another deportee echoes these comments. Noting that Russian women can perform physical labor which is "beyond the strength of our Polish and Ukrainian peasants," she finds it a sign of the primitiveness of their society: "In the more backward parts of Russia the women are still treated as beasts of burden in the Asiatic way and, in sober truth, I believe that when it comes to lifting and carrying weights, they beat the men."[67]

For Poles, equality in the workforce implied sameness; as far as women and men were concerned, the notion struck them as abominable. Many Polish women scorn the loudly proclaimed equality of the sexes in the USSR, regarding it a sham, the very goal an impossibility. Young Poles express especial sensitivity to this issue. In a composition about her observations of Soviet life, written in a school in Teheran after the evacuations, Halina Borowik states: "The Constitution speaks of the equal rights of the woman. She works hard and often takes the place of the man. She enjoys no respect whatsoever." Another essay writer declares: "The position of women in Soviet society is a curious one. The constitution gives them absolute equality of rights. In practice, this equality means solely that she has to work as much as a man." One young Pole worked on a collective farm with other girls, pushing wheelbarrows of dirt and stones up an embankment. She scoffs that according to the Soviets, "this means the emancipation of women, the equality of the sexes."[68] Another Pole, forced to cut and haul beams from the forests near Sverdlovsk, found the quota required of her impossibly high. Though she often felt like giving up, she did not leave her work, knowing that she would immediately land in prison: "and I had absolutely no desire to sit in prison with the female, fully equal, citizens of the Soviet Republic, who attained the honor of having the same equal rights to work as men."[69]

Poles felt the situation deserved only derision, perhaps pity, and wanted no part of such equality. Above all, they objected to a startling and unnatural lack of difference between women and men. One man labored in the forests alongside women, who, he explains disapprovingly "dressed just the same [as men], in pants, so from far away you couldn't tell the women from the men, and in that way, according to the laws of the USSR, women became equal to men and worked together with men."[70] This lack of difference threatened the Poles' conception of normality, in which the separation of the sexes in labor tasks and social roles seemed an absolute. For them, the Soviet order was not only painful, but also incomprehensible, for it disturbed the natural social and economic order. While Russian women were able to adapt and become labor animals, the Poles would not, and presumably could not. Polish women resisted this degradation, refusing to relinquish that which made them women: their physical weakness and duties in the home. They adamantly maintained a traditional distinction between the sexes, for it represented a firm dividing line between what was Polish and Russian, between the civilized and the primitive.

Abnormally fit as physical laborers, Russian females are correspondingly unfit as wives and mothers in Polish depictions. Russian girls marry early, remarks one Pole, adding that "family life is, however, very loose." Divorce, Poles stress, is extremely easy to obtain, requiring merely a signature or payment of a fee. An officer worker from Brześć-nad-Bugiem scornfully reports meeting a Russian woman who had married four times. A midwife recalls with distaste asking a Russian how she could willingly give up her own child: "She smiled nervously and answered that it's already the fifth child from the fifth husband, and two of her husbands did not accept their children." Such occurrences provoked shock and revulsion. Polish women considered the loose and temporary union that epitomized for them the Russian family to be a mere mockery of the word. One woman deported to the Urals writes: "In Russia there is officially no prostitution, so a Russian woman told me, they call him husband even when it's only one night, financial considerations, however, play the greatest part."[71]

The Poles were not the only ones to notice the plight of the family in the

USSR. Faced with extreme social turmoil, including impoverished women abandoned by husbands and masses of homeless waifs indulging in crime, the Soviet government enacted measures to strengthen the family in 1936, reversing nearly two decades of legislation intended to render it obsolete. Following Marxist theory, the Bolsheviks considered the abolition of the family central to women's emancipation. "A bastion of inequality," the family merely enslaved women, argued Bolshevik leaders, who prophesied the withering away of the family in the new socialist order. Marriage would become superfluous, replaced by free unions of equal individuals. Household labor, which Lenin described as "barbarously unproductive, petty, nerve-wracking and stultifying drudgery," would no longer tie females to the home.[72] Such tasks would be transferred to the public sphere, executed in communal centers; childrearing, too, would become the responsibility of the state.

Throughout the 1920s and early 1930s, individuals availed themselves of the revolutionary measures the Bolsheviks enacted soon after achieving power. Huge numbers of women flocked to hospitals for legal abortions: in 1926 there were 1.3 abortions per 1,000 people; by 1935 the number had jumped to more than 13. The birthrate fell. The USSR had the highest marriage and divorce rates in all of Europe by the mid-1920s; four out of every five marriages in Moscow ended in divorce.[73] Far from bringing liberation, the looseness of the marriage bond had tragic consequences for women, for despite the full employment of the period of the Five Year Plans, real wages steadily decreased. Abandoned by husbands, women fell into poverty, and many children were left to the streets, adding to the population of *besprizorniki*.[74] Along with the world war, revolution and civil war, famine, collectivization and dekulakization, mass arrests and deportation, the socialist family legislation of the early Soviet period contributed to the disintegration of the family with no effective institutions to assume its functions. In the words of Wendy Goldman, "The family had not withered away gradually, it had been smashed."[75]

In 1936, the Stalinist regime turned to repressive and pronatalist measures in an effort to promote family responsibility, turning its back on earlier Bolshevik ideas and rendering the family "an indispensable unit in the state's control of its citizenry."[76] The new laws sought to strengthen the family in the interests of the state, which was concerned about falling birthrates and the possibility of war. New decrees prohibited abortion, made divorce more difficult to obtain, and increased parental responsibility. Propaganda touted the new socialist family as "exhibiting a higher form of comradeship and cooperation" than its capitalist equivalent. A new cult of motherhood dominated women's journals, reminding females that in addition to joining the labor force, they had an obligation to the state to procreate.[77] Following the dictates of socialist realism, Soviet propaganda presented happy and hardworking families with numerous children, ignoring the conditions that rendered such a family the stuff of dreams. Polish women, however, noticed only these conditions and the accumulated damage to Soviet families and not the hopeful rhetoric.

The women unanimously conclude that Russian females are not real wives and mothers. They agree less on the cause. Some Poles locate the problem of the family in the character of Russian women themselves, finding them cruel and incomprehensible beings, who bear no love for their offspring. "Mothers generally don't give their children much love," writes a deportee from Wilno. "They see in them their entire anguish, the reason for their hard work." There are reports of Russian mothers abandoning their babies, hitting, kicking, and burning them. Halina Wojtowicz relates: "For two months I was in the company of only Russian women, mostly degenerate thieves and street bandits. One of them had a four-month old baby. She was sadistic and made him suffer by beating him and dipping him into hot water, so the baby barely survived each time. Many of the women suffered from venereal disease, many openly had intercourse with male prisoners, being ashamed of nothing." Here we find the worst imaginable degeneration of the female: criminal, immoral, immodest, contaminated, and capable of infanticide. Russian females, so incapable of fulfilling their proper roles as women, reportedly commit the greatest outrages: they kill their own husbands and children. They, thus, turn into the opposite of what is expected: life-givers and nurturers. One woman from Tarnopol, the only Pole in a camp among hundreds of Russian women, remarks, "They were mostly criminals, murderers of their husbands and children." Another Pole describes the women in her barracks: "The Russian group was made up of different elements, prostitutes, child murderers, criminals, bandits, and politicals."[78]

Russian men do not escape all blame for the diseased families. They do not draw the same degree of condemnation as women; they are not called wife killers or child murders. Nor are they chided for their promiscuity per se. But some Poles criticize them for their habit of casting off wives and rejecting their children, leaving them to fend for themselves. Just as Russian women fail as wives and mothers, these men fall short in their roles, as well. One Pole thus sums up her observations: "In their country a husband is not the guardian of the family and the father of the children."[79]

While nonetheless considering the conduct of Russians entering into casual sexual unions immoral, some Poles demonstrate an understanding of the dire economic circumstances of Russian women in freedom, an awareness that rarely surfaces in depictions of women in the camps. In these more sympathetic accounts, Polish women focus instead on the impossibility of creating a real family—of functioning properly as a woman in the USSR—a particularly terrifying circumstance for the exiles. "In general," remarks Wiktoria Krasowska, "a woman has the same rights as a man, she even holds high posts, but she cannot occupy herself with the home and children. . . . In Russia children are raised by the street." Fulfilling their labor obligation to the state, Russian women are unable to meet family obligations: "The Soviet woman is not happy, and thus a happy family and children are not created by her. She has neither the time nor the possibility to make a warm home, from which happiness radiates the environment. She has not the strength to separate herself from the gloom and the cursed work of fulfilling the plan."[80] Such accounts suggest some level of identification with the plight of the Russians.

In this place where they were forced to live, Polish women reportedly witnessed the destruction of what they considered the most important sphere of personal and social life—the family. They describe the Soviet family as one monstrously deformed, in which all the essential ties between its members are violated, all of its functions abrogated. Polish men concur. Witold Czerny, for one, declares that "contemporary Russia has no concept of the family."[81] Children are raised by the government and its institutions or by the streets. Separated from their families at an early age, youths go to school or work; they learn from teachers and political instructors, their mothers losing all influence over them. Russian children are taught to spy and inform on their parents; they learn in school that there is no God and consequently laugh at parents who still believe.[82] Taught to respect Lenin and Stalin, children neither obey their parents nor respect older persons. "Old people still believe, but they must hide this from their children," explains Liliana Bankierówna. "Youths are brought up in the spirit of nonbelief, demoralized, as nothing is sacred for them, they don't understand them [believers] and don't have a feeling of love for their near ones, love or respect for their parents." The home, too, is radically altered: rather than a private, safe place, it has become a public one, permeated with fear and mistrust. "People cannot trust each other, even in their closest family," writes a Pole who devotes especial attention to the degradation of intimate relations. "In his closest family a person feels like a hunted dog, the wife spies on the husband, and the husband the wife," she continues. "Is it possible in such an atmosphere of mistrust to raise children, can they develop from them worthy and noble people? Is it possible to think about family happiness?"[83]

For most Polish women, the question of the ultimate cause of the deplorable state of the family in Russia is moot. They assert that the Soviet family is alien and depict with no uncertainty the results of the inverted order they witnessed in exile. Crime and prostitution are rampant; there are reports of alcoholism and incest.[84] The women write about stunted and depraved children, the offspring of these pseudo-families. "The children are mentally retarded and physically incapable of working," notes a deportee. Such children, we are told, look like animals and show no trace of intelligence. One woman, commenting on the absence of real mothers, writes: "Kids, left without care, they develop in an improper way. They develop unhealthy fantasies and perversions." And those numerous children in orphanages, she states, "instead of growing up to be engineers and pilots will be criminals and hoodlums." Irena Szołkowska expresses the pathos and the irony of the situation. She writes that she felt sorry for all the youths brought up in Soviet orphanages, for they seemed like the lowest prisoners: "But the Soviets see them as the future of the nation!"[85] This observation offered more evidence of the inversion of the normal social order. "What else can be expected," asks a Pole, "in a country where a woman gets three years for burning her child alive and ten for having been the wife of a political prisoner?"[86]

The Poles distance themselves from the dismal unit of the family in the USSR. "In general," writes one woman, "their raising of the young is fundamentally different from ours."[87] They regard the workings of the Russian family and its role in society as a phenomenon from "over there"—a corruption of the natural social order, in which the family is a smoothly functioning unit of the nation, not at odds with it. They object to the fact that duty to the Soviet state has overridden duty to the family. This alien situation contrasts sharply with the Polish conception of society, in which the proper family is a crucial part of the nation and hence its state, and in which individual roles in the family have parallel roles in the state, resulting in a harmonious social structure, binding individual, family, and nation.

At the same time, such visible proof of the disrespect for the traditional role of women and the ability to erode it could only be threatening to them. The same economic imperatives that precluded Russian women from being true wives and mothers posed a severe threat to the exiled Poles, who wanted desperately to maintain their own families and their functions in them. But their daily lives in exile seemed to preclude serving as wives and mothers, as nurturers of the nation. As a measure of security, the Poles maintain their distance from the Russians. Russian women belong to a primitive world, one foreign to Poles: "You can see in their faces the effects of a primitive struggle for daily life, which we see only among wild animals. . . . In general relations between women and men have been deprived of any kind of spiritual basis. Their life together resembles that of two animals." The fear, however, that this could happen to themselves often lurks below the surface. A woman deported with her husband writes: "They did not yet manage to destroy in us the bonds of family, as they had already managed to do among their own citizens."[88] Polish women's continued maintenance of these bonds, of their social role in the family, was a way to retain the identity with which they were comfortable, their place in the civilized world.

In both critical aspects of daily life and social organization—labor and family—Polish women depict Russian women as their direct opposites. They do this even more emphatically with the issue of sexuality. The depiction of virtuous versus deviant sexual behavior commonly serves as an emotionally charged way to separate "us" from "them." Condemning the most intimate aspects of the lives and identity of a group of individuals renders them abhorrent others, prompting a visceral reaction that political and ideological differences can rarely produce. This maneuver has the corresponding effect of presenting the original collective as proper and superior, thereby deserving of victory in conflict with the others. The Polish portrayal of Russians represents a clear instance of the use of women's sexuality for national purposes, in which "the distinction between one ethnic group and another is constituted centrally by the sexual behavior of women."[89] The widespread characterization of Russian women as openly and aggressively sexual alone signals their otherness to Polish women. For these Poles, in accordance with Catholic doctrine and tradition, female sexuality is legitimate only within the bounds of marriage, and it constitutes an exceedingly private and taboo subject. They react strongly to the excessive and public nature of sexuality that they witness among Russian women.

The Poles' discussion of the sexual behavior of Russian females paints them, almost as a rule, as immoral and degenerate. For many, this was an automatic assumption, predicated on the well-known Communist principle of free love. Among the leading Bolsheviks its most vocal champion was Alexandra Kollontai, who encouraged the abandonment of bourgeois sexual morality. "The sexual act should be recognized as neither shameful nor sinful," she wrote, "but natural and legal, as much a manifestation of a healthy organism as the quenching of hunger or thirst."[90] Promoting the concept of free union based on love and respect was a component of the campaign to emancipate women. To these ends, early Bolshevik legislation had granted legal equality to women, replaced religious with civil marriage, and made divorce easily obtainable. Illegitimacy had been abolished, and abortion made legal and free.[91]

The consequences of the new laws, in combination with the tremendous upheavals of the early Soviet period, quickly began to manifest themselves. According to Goldman, "Women joined with soldiers, strangers, and temporary providers in casual, short-term unions. And for many the new communist morality encouraged and justified looser forms of behavior."[92] By 1920, newspaper articles criticized the results. "There is unimaginable bacchanalia," wrote one commentator. "Freedom of love is understood by the best people as freedom of depravity."[93] The decrees of 1936 reversed the original Bolshevik ideas and sought to reinstitute social conservatism, but the effects of earlier policies and social traumas still plagued Soviet society in the early 1940s.

Though small in numbers, the female common criminals, the *bytovichki*, also dramatically shaped the Poles' opinion of Russian females. In the literature on Soviet camp life, by Russians and non-Russians alike, female criminals are notorious for brutal and disgusting behavior.[94] Many of them grew up on the streets, part of the *besprizornye*, the orphaned and abandoned children who traveled in gangs and lived by petty crime. Local investigations in the 1920s found that the majority of homeless girls lived from prostitution, often commencing their work after first being raped. According to historian Alan Ball, "By their middle teens, many ranked as veterans, and

reports of prostitutes no more than eight to ten years of age appear in numerous sources."[95] Gonorrhea and syphilis were common among these females, who typically lived in close contact with the criminal underworld.
By many accounts, youths sent to prison typically emerged "as more formidable practitioners of the crime for which they were sentenced." Taking
a tougher stance against juvenile delinquents, in 1935, the regime decreed
that children as young as twelve accused of theft, rape, assault, and murder
would be tried as adults, so young offenders, too, ended up in the Gulag.[96]
"Contact with this new type of animal caused indescribable torture,"
writes one Polish woman who encountered them there.[97]

Descriptions of Russian women often set them off immediately from
the Poles by characterizing them en masse as prostitutes and whores. Many
Poles recount sitting in prison cells and dirty barracks "filled with Russian
prostitutes."[98] Janina Podlewska remarks, "I was the only political among
women of loose morals." "In Kiev," reports another woman, "they distributed us among the cells amidst Russian prostitutes and thieves."[99] In Polish
narratives, prostitutes are described in the same breath as the vilest criminals. One woman calls the "bandits and prostitutes" imprisoned with her
an assortment of "half-humans, half-animals." "There were about seven or
eight Polish women, a dozen or so Ukrainians and Jews, and the rest were
Russian women bandits, criminals, child murderers and prostitutes," explains Franciszka Howorka of her cellmates. "The Russian prostitutes and
bandits made everything hard for us. . . . They always threatened to kill us."[100]

Clearly, Polish women hold prostitutes in extremely low regard. But
once again nationality steps in and lends the category a kind of permeability,
for while detesting prostitutes in general, and using the label to signify the
perceived inferiority of Russian women as a whole, Poles manifest a special
leniency toward prostitutes of their own nationality. Poles who admit that
women were arrested and exiled from Poland for prostitution do not entirely disown them but compare them favorably with Russian prostitutes.
It is not, however, a matter of their patriotism, which excused Polish prostitutes' immorality in comparisons with women of the national minorities.
In this case, they are simply considered better. A teacher imprisoned in
Siberia discusses fellow inmates: "It's not even worth talking about their
moral standards; it's hard to imagine that they could be so low. In Lwów I
encountered our—Polish—'dregs of society,' but in comparison with that
same sort of people—citizens of the USSR—ours—those women on the

absolute lowest level—have a very high moral level." Wanda Lisowska writes: "Luckily, the Polish women lived alone. In those conditions we felt good even in the company of prostitutes (from Poland) who so mercilessly embittered our lives in prison. Even in comparison to these women, the behavior of Soviet citizens was wrong."[101] Significantly, the women of whom she speaks were not common criminals but mainly wives of dignitaries and artists who had earlier been arrested. After disparaging prostitutes, many women imply that even "our" prostitutes are better than the Russian women they encountered. Polish prostitutes appear in only a handful of testimonies, and few women seem to have dwelt on the dilemma they posed to the idealized picture of Polish women. Having marginalized their own profligates, they focus instead on the immorality of Russians.

According to the Poles, one of the defining characteristics of Russian women is an unbridled sexuality. Poles commonly describe Russian women as vulgar and immodest. In an impassioned account Janina Seudek-Malanowicz states: "The moral level of Soviet girls is terrifying, there is no such thing with them as ethics, religion, good upbringing, daily etiquette. I had the impression that these were wild women, primitive to the highest degree, degenerate." One of the deported women notes: "The morality of Soviet women is beneath any criticism. There is freedom in relating to men from the youngest years." Another Polish woman voices shock that Russian females "were deprived of any kind of modesty."[102] Poles judge the keen interest Russian women seemed to manifest in erotic matters entirely unnatural and immoral. Seudek-Malanowicz writes with disgust, "the question of pleasure, in every form, was the foremost idea of each of them. Incredible sexual debauchery, everything was loudly called by name in public discussions, not restrained by anything."

Polish women were repelled by Russian females who publicly engaged in sexual intercourse in the camps, a practice Aleksander Solzhenitsyn also discusses.[103] "Many of the women suffered from venereal disease," states one Pole, "many openly had intercourse with male prisoners, being ashamed of nothing." Women report witnessing orgies in their barracks. Izabela Jasel describes an incident at the camp Karabas: "And then a terrible night, a visit by some fourteen bandits, the boyfriends of our companions. An all-night orgy!" "Morality in general—on the level of animals," remarks Janina Gąsowska. She illustrates: "It happened many times, that at various times during the day and night men appeared in the women's rooms, infiltrating from their own quarters, enclosed by barbed wire, and before the eyes of everyone present had sexual orgies." The Russian women described by Poles act out of a wild, animal passion, unrestrained by civilities. "Pairs of Lesbian lovers, as well as mixed pairs making love, could be met everywhere day and night, mostly near the fencing or in the privies, but also in the canteen—a daily sight. It would put one off any idea of love once and for all. Animals are certainly less gross."[104]

This leads to another vice attributed to Russian women: perversity. Not only did they participate in orgies with men but also with other women. The few Poles who broach the topic claim they had never before heard of such depravity. One of them notes that among the Russian women in the camp she first encountered "lesbian love, a universal practice in these camps." She continues: "It is a most revolting practice. Everybody knows pairs of such women, and they make no attempt to conceal their habits. Those who play the part of the man are generally dressed in men's clothes, their hair is short and they hold their hands in their pockets."[105] The pronouncedly masculine appearance and violent behavior Poles report witnessing from Russian lesbians further underscores their "unnaturalness." A Polish teacher recalls an encounter with a Russian woman in prison: "When one of the prostitutes tried to induce me to lesbian love, and when I reacted appropriately, she beat me with her fists, threatening that she would kill me if I didn't agree, but luck would have it that that same day she had severely beaten another, and that one in all likelihood died in the hospital, and she was transferred to solitary confinement as punishment. So I was left alone." Completing the picture of debauchery, Poles report rampant venereal disease among the Russians. One woman offers a vivid picture of life with these women: "Venereal diseases are very rife. You had to eat the slop that they gave us with disgust, seeing that the bowls aren't washed, that next to you a half-rotted face was bent over your only food for the entire day. And drinking water from one jar at work, when you know from your neighbor that she has syphilis in an advanced stage." Stefania Działkiecowicz remarks that "in the cell was filth, lice, and infected women, mostly Russians."[106]

Polish women are remarkably open about sexual and bodily matters when describing Russian women. They use words and evoke images that never surface when discussing their own bodies, presumably believing the things they recount bear no relation to themselves. Maria Norciszek, a Polish Catholic from Sosnowiec, was in her late twenties when arrested by the NKVD. She gives the most detailed and painful account of the behavior of Russian women in a camp near Novosibirsk, recalling "shamelessly degenerate women," masturbators who delighted in spreading their pubic lice to the Polish women. "Those women," she writes, "were infected with various venereal diseases and during baths smeared us with their infected secretions." Furthermore, they "started to have shameless orgies only to spoil the young girls . . . and in the most shameless way made our lives disgusting and hopeless." Others also maintain that Russian women deliberately tried to corrupt young Polish ones. Not only were these women revolting, but they also tried to render the Poles similar. Norciszek reports that only one Polish woman "followed the conduct of these women." But just like the individuals who informed and were revealed to have Ukrainian blood or non-Polish husbands, this woman, too, is rendered a "pseudo-Pole." Norciszek adds that this woman "loudly declared that in Poland she never had bread to eat, and out of spite, abused everything that is Polish. . . . She informed about everything that went on in the cell to the NKVD."[107] The world of sexual deviance is left to non-Poles.

The phenomena of camp husbands and protectors similarly evoke the shock and disgust of Polish women, who focus not on the practicality or possible necessity of it but on the morality. When a Russian woman tells Zofia Pamfiłowska that many women have prison husbands and children, she feels stunned: "I look with eyes opened wide, not feeling like believing, to me it's something incomprehensible." Józefa Wojciechowska writes: "The moral aspect of the camp was the worst. People live in pairs like animals, always in shifts. Women who swore worse than the men sell themselves for bread, a little flour or butter or some kind of stolen rag."[108] Other Poles write about it more calmly, though not without distaste. "The idea of a camp husband, or a camp wife, is a very common one," explains one woman. "It is most curious that intelligent Russian women from among the political prisoners mostly choose for lovers men from among the lowest criminals. The authorities have nothing against the universal and public lovemaking. On the contrary, they rather encourage it as an entirely natural and normal thing." Both this woman and the author of the following remarks stress the behavior of the females involved, deeming it more strange than that of the males: "Thus like a man, so too a woman, after arriving, tries to strike up a concubinage for the period of time in the given camp, they are even themselves certain, that the moment that one of them is transported to another camp, contact automatically ceases, and they go for another."[109]

Polish women write about camp marriage as an alien practice observed from a distance, peculiar to Russians. "A Russian man told us that if their women were in our position, they would already be in the keeping of a man," writes Aleksandra Wodzicka, "rather than bear everything with such steadfastness, and work like we did." She continues, "Marriage proposals were frequently made to us. Only they never understood that if she had a husband in Poland, it could be an obstacle to another marriage."[110] What it seems they could not understand, she might add, is that Poles are just not like Russians.

Knowledge of conditions in the camps makes such coupling appear necessary, even inevitable.[111] To begin with, the combination of extremely low food rations, the lack of adequate clothing, and the extraordinarily demanding physical labor made it hard for a woman to survive without assistance. Lighter jobs, an extra jacket, or a supplement to meals came only from the *urki*, the hardened criminals, who lacked scruples but frequently had the access and power to get what they wanted. They then passed on benefits for the sexual and domestic services of a "wife." Second, no woman was safe from rape. Criminals often bought and sold women or lost them at cards; nighttime raids on women's barracks and gang rapes were common occurrences. After such abuse, a woman frequently chose one of the attackers as her protector, who at least temporarily became the only one to have access to her. As the letters from Kazakhstan discussed earlier show, it was a lesser evil.

According to Solzhenitsyn, "It was precisely in the camp that the women would either be broken or else, by bending and degenerating, adapt themselves."[112] It must be remembered that most Soviet inmates received long sentences and, therefore, had less recent memory of or expectations for a different kind of life, as the Poles did. Unlike Poles, Russians had no one to count on for liberation. One must also recognize that the couplings, however temporary or practically inspired, could provide some bit of warmth and comfort in an inhuman setting; some were probably motivated by love. They can also be regarded as a reworking and adaptation of traditional gender roles in extraordinarily harsh conditions. Through camp marriages Russian women may have attempted to hold onto their own social roles and maintain some semblance of their previous identities.

Most Polish women witnessing these liaisons do not express such considerations. Aghast at the conditions and adaptations, they focus their disgust not on the government, the system, nor even the men involved, but largely on Russian women, whom they regard as uniquely disposed to such behavior. The Poles consider Russian women, particularly the criminals, a breed unknown elsewhere, a deviant group with no counterpart in the rest of the world. It is useful to compare this stance with the opinions of women of other nationalities. Margarete Buber-Neumann, a German who spent a total of seven years in Stalinist and then Nazi concentration camps, offers a different view. Of the "Asocials," specifically the prostitutes, she writes, "the type is fundamentally the same anywhere . . . for me these women were victims of society in one way or the other."[113] Similarly, the Dutch-born Elinor Lipper, imprisoned at Kolyma, expresses great sympathy for what she calls the "relatively innocent character" of the Russians. Like Buber-Neumann, she draws the line between criminals and politicals. Lipper admits an ambivalent attitude toward the former, whom she considers "products of social injustice combined with hereditary degeneration and feeble-mindedness—people whose fault lay not in themselves but in their stars."[114] At the same time, she detests them for making her life miserable. For both of these foreigners, who came to the USSR willingly, nationality plays no role in their assessment and condemnation of others. It is difficult to imagine such treatment of Russian women coming from the pen of a Polish exile, whose sense of national identity faced constant attack.[115]

Polish men also describe Russian females as immoral, though they mention them less frequently. "Girls aged eight to fifteen are debauched like old, experienced prostitutes," writes Stanisław Bajkowski, "soliciting any man, using vulgar expressions, three-quarters of them have venereal diseases." Polish men also note the casual nature of sexual relations in the camps. They do not, however, declare it a completely Russian phenomenon. Józef Andruszkiewicz describes life in a labor camp: "As far as the moral condition of these prisoners, it was terrible: stealing, perverse sexuality—this was promoted by the presence there in the camp of women of loose morals, both Russian and Polish." In this account, such behavior does not reflect solely on the women. Andruszkiewicz continues, "Each Ivan had his Marusia, and before the eyes of everyone in the barracks took care of his lewd needs."[116] The topic of homosexuality does not come up in men's documents, though a memoir published in 1998 by a Polish Jew sent to Kolyma contains reports of men raping other men.[117] The topic of male homosexuality, in any form, appears even more taboo than either lesbian relations or heterosexual rape.

On the whole, Polish women render the Russian contingent and the criminal/degenerate element in the camps synonymous. None of their accounts about women of other nationalities, not even the minorities from Poland, report such objectionable behavior. Regardless of what may have really happened, these women link excessive and deviant sexuality with Russian females; Polish women thus remain modest, chaste, and innocent. Even more than the issues of labor and family, sexuality serves to differentiate Polish and Russian women.

Conclusion

The spectrum of people Polish women encountered in exile, and felt the need to talk about, included minority groups from Poland, Soviet Central Asians, and Russians. The national minorities were closest to Poles, geographically and culturally. At the opposite end were the peoples of the steppe, distant and utterly foreign. The Russians occupied a middle ground between the two. Geographically, they straddled the border of Europe and Asia; ethnically, they were a mixture of European and Asian stock. The Poles considered them alien—culturally, emotionally, and ideologically. Yet there was an undeniable familiarity: many Russians looked like Poles, they spoke a related language, and shared a long history of mutual contact. This very familiarity, this hateful closeness, made the foreign aspects of the Russian women weightier for Polish women. To pose a threat to one's identity, an other must be at least a little familiar, must present an alternative to that which one takes as given or natural. The complete outsider may cause fear but is usually interpreted as a threat to one's physical existence and rarely impinges on one's conception of the self. In the context of forced exile, Polish women found Russian women dangerous to their individual and collective identities. These Poles needed to place the perceived differences of Russian women in the forefront of the discussion about them and to explain them in a way that relieved the challenge they posed.

At the same time, the alienness of Turkic women could be dismissed. The peoples of Central Asia represented brute force and darkness to the Poles; they seemed *too* different and primitive to be considered rivals, particularly the females. But the remaining groups of others—the national minorities from Poland and the Russians—were in fact rivals of the Poles, contesting space, power, and identity. While Jews, Ukrainians, and Belorussians challenged the women's notion of what it meant to be a Pole, Russians more fundamentally contested their idea of what it meant to be a woman. This challenge confronted them daily and multifariously: in the loss of home, the demands made upon them by Soviet authorities, the ever-present propaganda, and the example of Russian women around them. Polish women roundly rejected that example, believing that Russian females were a species of their own, something that they themselves could never become. In fact, to some Poles, they did not even appear to be women at all.

Polish women saw Russian women as primitive beings in an uncivilized society, one distinguished above all by the lack of proper separation, between men and women, between public and private. Russian women, they found, acted like men, in the realms of labor, family, and sexuality. Not fulfilling any of the functions Poles deemed proper to their sex, Russian women seemed like animals. Polish women express great fear of the gender blurring they experienced in the USSR, for it seemed to deprive the world of order. The family not only provided the foundation of Polish women's identity but also supported the social hierarchy and enabled the maintenance of the nation. In their view, the family ranked of least importance in the lives of Russian women, whose fundamental identification was as workers, often physical laborers. Poles found gender roles in the USSR beyond their comprehension and therefore saw no meaningful distinctions between women and men. They interpreted the situation not as cultural difference but as evidence of a lack of civilization. Russian women are thus used in Polish women's testimonies for both a personal and a national aim: by showing that they do not exhibit the proper behavior of their gender, they are thus rendered inferior. They and their entire society, which knows not of the natural separation between women and men, become barbaric, "Asiatic." This enables the Poles to hold their conquerors and oppressors in complete contempt. All that Poles took for granted about the world seemed absent in this alien place. Describing her period of exile, one woman writes: "In this unique time I experienced the reality of all rules and doctrines being trampled, all that I have been taught since childhood. The bonds with everything that is good and sacred were being torn—I entered a new life—a life of Russia."[118]

In the accounts of their exile in the USSR, Poles demonstrate a strong consciousness of their existence on a geographical, ideological, and cultural border between Europe and Asia. The Soviet transgression of Poland's eastern boundary was only the latest of many incursions from the East. The Westernness of Poland, as a state and a culture, held great symbolic importance for the Poles, particularly after the momentous upheavals of the autumn of 1939. The incorporation of the *kresy* into the USSR erased the eastern boundary, while the Germans annexed or occupied the western Polish territories. The Nazis contested Poland's conception of itself as an entity in the West. Situating Poland on the other side of the border, Nazi ideology lumped Poles together with their eastern neighbors, casting them all as one group of inferior Slavs. The Poles thus found themselves in a highly precarious position, suffering assaults from both directions to their geographical and political positions and to their cultural identity. As a result, Poles writing about the Russians are highly sensitive about their relationship to Europe and Asia and adamant about situating themselves to the west of the border between these two geographical and cultural entities.

Conclusion

The Nazi invasion of Poland on 1 September 1939 dealt a violent blow to the Polish state that the Soviet invasion from the east, sixteen days later, rendered lethal. These two border transgressions represented the first of a series of violations that the Poles were to experience in the Second World War. Both the Nazis and the Soviets ascribed a homogeneous identity to the Polish population that justified, in their respective ideologies, domination and violence. In the Nazi mind, Poles constituted an inferior race, suitable only for slave labor and eventual destruction; the Soviets painted the Poles as exploitative lords, vassals of the capitalist West. Reorganizing their society and reeducating its members, the Soviet regime forced Poles to toil for the goals it dictated. Neither occupier intended to allow the expression of any identity among its subjugated population other than the one it bestowed.

Poles in the Soviet-occupied territory endured the overturning of their established order, including the obliteration of previous lines of hierarchy and authority. They also suffered erasures of personal boundaries, for Soviet authorities exercised their considerable power over both public and private life. Since the Soviet leadership wanted much more than a military defeat of Poland, it struck out against women and children, as well as men who served in the army and government. The home also became a place of battle, as even the most personal aspects of daily existence were subject to interference by the occupier. NKVD officers barged into homes in the middle of the night, terrorizing the inhabitants and confiscating whatever they wanted, sometimes even the domiciles themselves. Property, privacy, and autonomy were under siege.

The new regime shattered communal and family life, arresting Poles at will, and forcing hundreds of thousands of them to move across the Polish-Soviet border. The Poles equated this border crossing with a complete loss of order and felt they were leaving behind not merely their homes and communities but civilization itself. Women exiled to prisons, labor camps, collective farms, and deportation settlements in the interior of the USSR experienced constant trauma. Nothing seemed familiar or normal. And no aspect of their existence remained free from violation—not their families or homes, their possessions, their religious beliefs or national consciousness, not even their bodies.

In this hostile environment, in which climate, poverty, disease, the bitterness of the local population, and the policies of the Soviet government conspired to make their lives a living hell, women felt their identity, as individuals and as a collective, under constant attack. The Soviet government strove to suppress all manifestations of Polish national feeling, turning its bearers into obedient laborers and subjects of the Communist Soviet state. The exiled women were forbidden to gather for prayer, wear religious medals, celebrate their holidays, sing patriotic songs, read Polish books, or teach their children the Polish language or history. They bore frequent and vicious insults, along with assertions that Poland was dead and God did not exist.

These individuals suffered indirect attacks on their identity as well. The conditions in which they lived and the regimen imposed on them compromised their identity as women in various ways. Their feelings of modesty and propriety bore affronts in the form of indiscriminate mixing of the sexes in places they expected to be segregated, invasive body searches, and sexual propositions and abuse. Forced to work at hard physical labor, women considered their jobs improper for their sex. As mothers, they faced obstacles in fulfilling their duties at every step. Unable to devote their time and energy to their families and without necessary material resources, they saw their children deprived of care, education, and religion; they saw them waste away from disease and hunger; they saw them die. Not only could women not fulfill their role as guardians of the moral health of the nation; in many cases they could not even ensure the physical well-being of their offspring.

These violated components of their identity—nationality and gender—were by no means distinct. The exiled females construed the definitions of womanhood to which they aspired—and which they found constantly assaulted in the USSR—as fundamental aspects of their nationality. Drawing on past prescriptions for proper womanhood, sanctioned by Polish historical experience and the Catholic Church, these women invoked traditional notions of sexual difference as one of the key ordering elements of their own existence, of the Polish nation, and of civilization at large. According to this traditional view—not specific yet fundamental to Polish culture—the sexual difference of the female body inevitably led to a differing female nature, which contrasted and complemented the correspondingly essentialized male one. As a consequence of her biological reproductive role, a woman had distinct duties in the home, centering on the care and raising of children, nurturing the spouse, and guarding of the moral health of the family. These functions also determined women's role outside the family. Their central importance in the home rendered their participation in the national economy auxiliary. They were to contribute to the nation through others by producing and raising young patriotic Poles; supporting men who would fulfill the more publicized and powerful roles in the national economy, military, and administration; and providing a positive moral influence in society. This required extreme devotion and self-sacrifice from women; additionally, they were expected to protect the secrets of their sexually differentiated bodies through excessive modesty, chaste deportment, and avoiding illegitimate sexual relations. Such requirements served the nation, as female sexual honor was invested with important social meaning that reflected not only on a woman's own social standing but also on the men to whom she was linked, and the nation as a whole.

In the chaos and trauma of exile, where lines between women and men were continually transgressed and even deliberately blurred, Polish females drew on these traditional conceptions of gender roles to provide a sense of order to their uprooted lives and social relations. At the same time, a leveling of identity occurred among the community of Polish women. Differences within the group faded and objectionable behaviors were projected outward. Class divisions, in particular, lost significance, as the whole collective took on the same class identity and aspirations under the exploitative Soviet regime. Even formerly shunned prostitutes were accepted if they maintained solidarity and exhibited patriotism in exile. Caught in a sea of change and violence, women strove for unity, kinship, and certainty and adopted a homogenized view of what it meant to be a Polish woman. They used the recognition and maintenance of proper gender differentiation to signal their difference as a collective from others, defined on the basis of nationality. Adherence to these norms, understood as respect for the laws of nature, served to rank other nations on a scale of normal to perverse, civilized to primitive. Others were tagged with such labels depending on their degree of alienness to the Poles, the historical legacy they shared, and the intensity of the threat they posed to the dislocated Poles.

Polish women erected boundaries between themselves and the others with whom they were forced to live, particularly Russians and Central Asians, whom they cast as uncivilized. Establishing such boundaries helped counter the fluidity and the physical and psychological violence that engulfed the women in exile. These borders set them apart from others and also served to define the content of their own collective, one characterized by propriety, solidarity, and patriotism. Thus assured of their difference, Polish women held onto an idealized memory of the past and a vision of a better future, a return to home.

This strategy appears particular to the females exiled and to stem from their distinctive position in the nation. In the documents, men compare themselves less with individuals of other nationalities and denounce them less categorically. They also tend to present their own collective as more varied than do women, allowing for bad elements among the Poles: in male accounts, acts of treason and immorality are not the sole province of other nationalities. These gender-based variations in representing the collective and the other seem rooted in the differing sources of male and female identity. Because a woman's identity tended to be relationally based and heavily linked to notions of honor, the properness of the collective to which she belonged played an important role in both her self-perception and her social standing. Men, typically defined more by their individual achievements and positions, could be more secure in the independence of their identities from the collective. The presence of unsavory elements in their midst did not seem to compromise each of the group's members. Similarly, men's assessments of others were less enmeshed in their own sense of self. Women, accustomed to being judged on the basis of those to whom they were joined and charged with maintaining the unity and the honor of the nation, invariably compared themselves with those around them. Males, more invested in their independent activities in the public realm, had less need to do so. The exiled men focused their hopes on regaining control. They sought to recapture their damaged identities in the outlets open to them: military service and revenge.

Besides revealing crucial mechanisms by which national groups cope with the loss of autonomy and sustained attack on their identity, this book offers a view of the development of modern Polish nationalism in a period of collective tragedy. The women of this study came from all walks of life. The group included peasants and teachers, homemakers and doctors, clerks and countesses. These women hailed from the eastern borderlands of Poland, a society of flux and diversity, where the level of national consciousness varied widely, as did its content and articulation. Certainly tensions existed among the varied citizens of Poland in the east and sometimes erupted into violence. But Poles lived there together with Jews, Belorussians, and Ukrainians in relative harmony until the Red Army invasion of 1939. At Soviet instigation, nationality quickly came to define individuals and stamp one's enemies in the occupied territory. The new rulers encouraged hostilities and clashes among the nationalities, played upon existing stereotypes, and helped create new ones. In the hothouse of exile in the USSR, inflamed tensions among the peoples from Poland only intensified. The Poles faced several traumas connected with their national identity. They suffered the loss of statehood and sovereignty. Their nationality, no longer privileged, faced deliberate attack from the Soviet regime and its enforcers, as well as hostile locals. And Poles felt challenged by fellow citizens who did not manifest the unanimity that Poles expected regarding their state. Over the years of exile, the lines between the national groups from Poland hardened, gaining an impermeability that did not exist before. By the time this experience came to a close, these Poles largely believed that the Ukrainians, Jews, and Belorussians no longer had any place among their nation. Coexistence seemed neither realistic nor desirable.

The experience of foreign domination and oppression completed the move of members of the Polish collective from vague or undeveloped national feeling, regional identification, or political nationalism to the modern type based on ethno-linguistic ties. Could one imagine a person from the *kresy* still identifying him- or herself as simply "from here" after 1945?

Conclusion

War, occupation, and the realities of the postwar Polish state cemented the exclusive sense of nationhood. The combined result of the Holocaust, the redrawing of state borders, and population transfers was a homogenized state, almost exclusively Polish and Catholic. Poland lost its Jews, Germans, Ukrainians, Belorussians, and Lithuanians, as well as the people who earlier claimed allegiance simply to a region. Many Poles felt that they needed and deserved the fulfillment of the dream of the interwar nationalists, a "Poland for the Poles." In 1945, the Allies sanctioned the incorporation into the USSR of the eastern Polish territories occupied by the Red Army in 1939. Between 1944 and 1948, nearly 1.3 million Poles chose to be repatriated from that land into the new Poland.[1] This massive westward migration revealed both the Poles' inability to live with the nationalities now dominant in that territory—Ukrainians, Belorussians, and Lithuanians—and their desire to leave the USSR.

While most of the Poles evacuated from the USSR in 1942 relocated to foreign lands, other exiles did return to Poland from the Soviet interior.[2] In the early postwar years, Polish-Soviet agreements led to the repatriation of approximately 300,000 Poles from the USSR. Although the transfer of Poles ceased in 1948, new repatriations occurred in the late 1950s, returning an additional 245,000 Poles to their nation's state.[3] A study of the development of nationalism among Poles under German occupation is needed to complete the picture of the wartime legacy for Polish nationalism. It is clear, though, that the experiences of Poles under Soviet occupation and in Soviet exile had an enormous effect on the national imagination and lore. The injuries of World War II magnified the historical rivalry and enmity between Poles and Russians. Soviet involvement in the establishment and administration of the Communist regime in the Polish People's Republic and the silence it imposed on wrongs done to the Poles, including the crimes of Katyń and the mass deportations, further intensified the animosity. The returned Poles' previous experience with communist rule and the Gulag contributed to anti-Russian sentiment and the marked resistance the nation exhibited toward the imposition of Soviet-style Communism. For example, Poles rejected Soviet notions of the emancipation of women, to the extent that the Polish Communist regime began removing women from so-called men's jobs after the death of Stalin.[4] The effect of the war on women's roles and identities in the early years of the reborn Polish state demands extensive investigation. The research for this book suggests another legacy of Soviet domination: a re-embracing of traditional notions of female (and male) identity.

This analysis of women's experience of wartime exile demonstrates that Polish nationality is not an overarching category of identity, shared alike by all members of the nation. The Polish nation examined here was built on gender-based roles. Men and women owed different things to the nation. Considered the providers and protectors of the nation, men enjoyed a direct relationship to it. Women were accorded an indirect relationship to the nation, which dictated that they serve it and fulfill themselves through the family. Men and women, operating in separate but complementary roles, replicated the immediate family in the guise of the nation. Thus, it was a woman's maintenance of the roles ascribed to her in the inner circles of her life that assured her access to and benefit from the nation. For their public roles, men received the greatest acclaim and privilege.

Polish men and women did enjoy common ties to the fatherland. Individuals of both sexes shared connections to the land considered to be Polish, to the history of its people, and to a religiously imbued vision of their destiny. Notions of the tangible and metaphorical existence of the nation served to unite across gender lines. Religion and patriotism formed the basis for both women's and men's Polishness. But it was also highly gendered. Women's Polishness called for purity, selflessness, and fostering unity among the collective, while men's placed more emphasis on the individual, highlighting heroism and a refusal to accept humiliation. Women who did not fit the prescription for Polish females, or who desired to serve the nation in more masculine ways, were marginalized or unrecognized, often even by themselves.

Ultimately, the Polish nation, articulated as heroic and righteous, had a very masculinized character, even in its victimization. Women could use their national identity as a way to cope with hardships and indignities when they suffered like men or in ways that fit into the idealized identity accorded them. The nation, however, seemed to have no room for their suffering as females when they were raped or forced to sell their bodies to survive. Women felt compelled to remain silent about these injuries, which seemed to diminish them as women and as Poles. Men could cast this abuse as part of the drama of the nation, but it became their story, not the women's. In the men's telling, stories of sexual abuse were less about women's pain than the violation of the nation and the barbarity of the perpetrators, the national enemy.

Conclusion

Finally, these women demonstrate that both nationality and gender are categories of identity and belief that reach down to the most personal and vital levels of human activity and existence. Though both socially constructed, neither is a mere abstraction. Furthermore, both nationality and gender represent much more than tools for manipulation by politicians and propagandists. They are embraced by individuals and used to provide order to their daily lives and social relations. Certainly these categories have negative uses and effects. Gender norms are used to denigrate and exclude women who fail to conform to traditional prescriptions for sexual behavior, familial devotion, and public ambition; they can severely limit the activities and aspirations of both females and males. National identity often results in the judgment, dehumanization, and maltreatment of individuals belonging to different nations, who often become the inferior and despised other. And yet, these categories of meaning and identity do offer individuals and groups something of positive and necessary value, particularly in times of crisis and chaos. The norms of gender and nationality provide both constraints and comforts. In the trauma of wartime exile, they can offer desperate individuals strategies for survival.

For Polish women exiled to the USSR, embracing the tenets of traditional patriotic womanhood and strengthening bonds with other members of the Polish nation provided support, order, and meaning. Torn from their homes, separated from family members, and subjected to many forms of abuse, these women needed identities that would give them honor and esteem, an assured place in society, a sense of difference and superiority from those seeking to degrade them. Essentialized constructions of gender and nationality provided these supports. In their daily existence in exile, women often proved themselves stronger and more capable of taking on the roles of providers and protectors of their families than they expected. Unwilling to alter their notions of their own identity or of the ideal social order, the women did not incorporate heroism or physical strength into their identity. Instead, they embraced traditional definitions of womanhood, casting them as crucial parts of their nationality. In the face of continuous abasement in the USSR, these forms of identification upheld their connection to home and their faith in the future, enabling them to survive an experience they called "hell on earth."

Notes

Introduction

1. One woman, Janina Muśnicka Lewandowska, a second lieutenant in the Polish Air Force, was slain at Katyń. I am indebted to the late Jan Karski for sharing this information with me in conversation. See *Lista Katyńska. Jeńcy obozów Kozielsk, Ostaszków, Starobielsk zaginieni w Rosji Sowieckiej* (Warsaw: Agencja Omnipress-Spółdzielnia Pracy Dziennikarzy i Polskie Towarzystwo Historyczne, 1989), 111.

2. The Soviet government did not admit its guilt for the crime at Katyń until 1990. See *Izvestiia* 14 April 1990. On the taboo subjects in Polish historiography, the so-called blank spots, see Takayuki Ito, "Blank Spots in Polish-Soviet History: Pandora's Box or Catharsis?" in *Facing Up to the Past: Soviet Historiography under Perestroika,* ed. Takayuki Ito (Sapporo, Japan: Hokkaido University, 1989), 259–89; Piotr Wandycz, "Introduction to the Blank Pages in Polish Historical Issues," *Polish Review* 33, no. 3 (1988): 267–70.

3. See Bronisław Kuśnierz, *Stalin and the Poles. An Indictment of the Soviet Leaders* (London: Hollis & Carter, 1949); Władysław Wielhorski, *Los Polaków w niewoli sowieckiej* (London: Rada Ziem Wschodnich R.P., 1956).

4. See Joseph Czapski, *The Inhuman Land* (New York: Sheed & Ward, 1952); Janusz Zawodny, *Death in the Forest: The Story of the Katyn Forest Massacre* (Notre Dame, Ind.: Notre Dame University Press, 1962); Stanisław Świaniewicz, *W cieniu Katynia* (Paris: Instytut Literacki, 1976); Louis Fitzgibbon, *Katyń* (New York: Charles Scribner's Sons, 1977).

5. See Hoover Institution Archives (hereafter HIA), United States Department of State, Office of International Information, *Inside Soviet Slave Labor Camps, 1939–1942;* Sylvestre Mora and Pierre Zwierniak, *La Justice Soviétique* (Rome: Magi-Spinetti, 1945); David Dallin and Boris Nicolaevsky, *Forced Labor in Soviet Russia* (New Haven, Conn.: Yale University Press, 1947). Gulag stands for Glavnoe Upravlenie Lagerei, the Main Camp Administration.

6. See Melchior Wańkowicz, *Dzieje rodziny Korzeniewskich* (Rome: Oddział kultury i prasy, 2 korpusu, 1945); Ada Halpern, *Liberation, Russian Style* (London: Maxlove Publishing Co., 1945); Danuta Tęczarowska, *Deportacja w nieznane. Wspomnienia 1939–1945* (London: Veritas, 1981). One early book contains first-hand accounts of Soviet exile: *Dark Side of the Moon* (London: Faber & Faber, 1946), republished as Zoe Zajdlerowa, *The Dark Side of the Moon. A New Edition,* ed. John Coutouvidis and Thomas Lane (New York: Harvester Wheatsheaf, 1989).

7. Irena Grudzińska-Gross and Jan T. Gross, eds., *War through Children's Eyes*

(Stanford, Calif.: Hoover Institution Press, 1981); Jan T. Gross and Irena Grudzińska-Gross, eds., *"W czterdziestym nas matko na Sybir zesłali . . ."* (London: Aneks, 1983).

8. Jan T. Gross, *Revolution from Abroad: The Soviet Conquest of Poland's Western Ukraine and Western Belorussia* (Princeton, N.J.: Princeton University Press, 1988).

9. See Józef Jasnowski and Edward Szczepanik, eds., *Napaść sowiecka i okupacja polskich ziem wschodnich. Wrzesień 1939* (London: Polska Fundacja Kulturalna, 1985); Keith Sword, ed., *The Soviet Takeover of the Polish Eastern Provinces, 1939–41* (London: Macmillan, 1991); Julian Siedlecki, *Losy Polaków w ZSRR w latach 1939–1986* (London: Gryf Publications, 1987).

10. See, for example, Julia Hubert-Budzyńska, *Syberyjska dziatwa. Wojenne losy Kresowiaków* (Lublin, Poland: Norbertinum, 1993); Zofia Sierpińska, *Anatema* (Łódź, Poland: Klio, 1994).

11. The NKVD executed 3,900 Polish prisoners in Khar'kov and another 6,300 in Kalinin. See *Katyń. Relacje, wspomnienia, publicystyka* (Warsaw: Wydawnictwo Alfa, 1989); *Katyń. Dokumenty ludobójstwa. Dokumenty i materiały archiwalne przekazane Polsce 14 października 1992 r.* (Warsaw: Instytut Studiów Politycznych Polskiej Akademii Nauk, 1992); *Katyń. Dokumenty zbrodni*, 2 vols. (Warsaw: Trio, 1995).

12. See Aleksander Gurjanow, "Cztery deportacje 1940–41," *Karta* no. 12 (1994): 114–36; "Sprawozdanie z dyskusji dotyczącej liczby obywateli polskich wywiezionych do Związki Sowieckiego w latach 1939–1941," *Studia z dziejów Rosji i Europy Srodkowo-Wschodniej* 31 (1996): 117–48.

13. See Keith Sword, *Deportation and Exile: Poles in the Soviet Union, 1939–1948* (New York: St. Martin's Press, 1994); Albin Głowacki, "O deportacji osadników wojskowych w ZSRR (w NKWD)," *Mars. Problematyka i Historia* 2 (1994): 111–44; Stanisław Ciesielski, *Polacy w Kazachstanie w latach 1940–1946. Zesłańcy lat wojny* (Wrocław, Poland: Wydawnictwo Uniwersytetu Wrocławskiego, 1996).

14. Quoted by Sword, *Deportation and Exile*, 31.

15. The first evacuation included 43,858 individuals and the second, 69,247. Approximately 64 percent were army troops and the rest civilians. Siedlecki, *Losy Polaków*, 134.

16. Stanisław Kot, *Listy z Rosji do Generała Sikorskiego* (London: Jutro Polski, 1955), 58.

17. HIA, Władysław Anders Collection, 1939–1946 (hereafter AC), box 76, Akta Wewnętrze Biura Dokumentów (hereafter AWBD), no. 061243, Por. Telmany, Notatka, 6 December 1943.

18. In 1944 the work was transferred to the Ministry of Information and Documentation in London. Kazimierz Zamorski, *Dwa tajne biura 2 Korpusu* (London: Poets and Painters Press, 1990), 10–15, 203–7.

19. AC, box 76, AWBD, Notatka w sprawie zbierania i opracowania materiałów informacyjnych o Rosji Sowieckiej, 20 November 1943. English translation from Gross, *Revolution*, xiv.

20. These documents are in the Władysław Anders Collection. On the acquisition of the collection, see Maciej Siekierski, "Hoover Institution's Polish Collections: An Overview and a Survey of Selected Materials on Polish-Soviet Relations," *Polish Review* 33, no. 3 (1988): 325–41.

21. Quoted by Gross, *Revolution*, xvi.

22. Zamorski, *Dwa tajne biura*, 24.

23. Gross, *Revolution*, xix–xx. I have used the original protocols, comparing them with the typed versions when possible.

24. Kazmierz Zamorski suspects that the Anders army did not want the intended recipients to learn the horrible truths contained in the letters. Zamorski, *Dwa tajne biura*, 157.

25. Stanisław Mikołajczyk, Papers, 1938–1966 (hereafter MIK); Poland, Ambasada (Soviet Union), Records, 1941–1944 (hereafter AMB); Poland, Ministerstwo Informacji i Dokumentacji, Records, 1939–1945 (hereafter MID).

26. HIA; Rosarkhiv/Hoover Archives Project (hereafter RHP).

27. In a note delivered to the Polish ambassador just hours before the Red Army crossed the border, V. M. Molotov, people's commissar of foreign affairs, explained that the invasion did not constitute an act of war. In the view of the Soviet government, the Polish state no longer existed, having disintegrated after the German invasion on 1 September; the entry of the Red Army was necessary to save "defenseless" fellow Slavs—Ukrainians and Belorussians. *Polska w polityce między-narodowej (1939–1945). Zbiór dokumentów*, vol. 1, *Rok 1939* (Warsaw: PIW, 1989), 564–65.

28. See Miriam Cooke, "Wo-Man, Retelling the War Myth," in *Gendering War Talk*, ed. Miriam Cooke and Angela Woollacott (Princeton, N.J.: Princeton University Press, 1993), 183.

29. Biddy Martin and Chandra Talpade Mohanty, "Feminist Politics: What's Home Got to Do with It?" in *Feminist Studies/Critical Studies*, ed. Teresa deLauretis (Bloomington: Indiana University Press, 1986), 209.

30. Rhonda Cobham, "Misgendering the Nation: African Nationalist Fictions and Nuruddin Farah's *Maps*," in *Nationalisms & Sexualities*, ed. Andrew Parker, et al. (New York: Routledge, 1992), 46.

31. Geoff Eley and Ronald Suny, "Introduction: From the Moment of Social History to the Work of Cultural Representation," in *Becoming National: A Reader*, ed. Geoff Eley and Ronald Suny (New York: Oxford University Press, 1996), 7.

32. See Adam Mickiewicz, *Księgi narodu polskiego i pielgrzymstwa polskiego* (Kraków, 1922); Maurycy Mochnacki, *Dzieła Maurycego Mochnackiego* (Poznań: Nakład ksieg. Jana Konstantego Zupańskiego, 1863).

33. Jerzy Jedlicki, "Holy Ideals and Prosaic Life, or the Devil's Alternatives," in *Polish Paradoxes*, ed. Stanisław Gomułka and Antony Polonsky (London: Routledge, 1990), 41.

34. Brian Porter, *When Nationalism Began to Hate: Imagining Modern Politics in Nineteenth-Century Poland* (New York: Oxford University Press, 2000). See also Miroslav Hroch, "From National Movement to the Fully-Formed Nation: The Nation-Building Process in Europe," in Eley, *Becoming National*, 60–77.

35. See Benedict Anderson, *Imagined Communities: Reflections on the Origin and Spread of Nationalism* (London: Verso, 1991); E. J. Hobsbawm, *Nations and Nationalisms Since 1780: Programme, Myth, Reality* (Cambridge: Cambridge University Press, 1990).

36. See Jerzy Jedlicki, *A Suburb of Europe: Nineteenth-Century Polish Approaches to Western Civilization* (Budapest: Central European University Press, 1999); Andrzej Walicki, *Philosophy and Romantic Nationalism: The Case of Poland*

(Oxford: Clarendon Press, 1982); Andrzej Walicki, *The Enlightenment and the Birth of Modern Nationhood. Polish Political Thought from Noble Republicanism to Tadeusz Kościuszko* (Notre Dame, Ind.: University of Notre Dame Press, 1989).

37. Quoted by Peter Brock, "Polish Nationalism," in *Nationalism in Eastern Europe,* ed. Peter Sugar and Ivo Lederer (Seattle: University of Washington Press, 1969), 317.

38. For example, see Joachim Lelewel, *Polska, dzieje i rzeczy jej,* vol. 20 (Poznań: Nakład ksieg. Jana Konstantego Zupańskiego, 1864), 223, 225; Wacław Lednicki, *Life and Culture of Poland as Reflected in Polish Literature* (New York: Roy Publishers, 1944), 315.

39. Cyprian Norwid, *Pisma wszystkie,* vol. 9, *Listy 1862–1872* (Warsaw: Państwowy Instytut Wydawniczy, 1971), 62–64.

40. Mary Louise Roberts, *Civilization Without Sexes: Reconstructing Gender in Postwar France, 1917–1927* (Chicago: University of Chicago Press, 1994), 14.

Chapter 1

1. AC, box 45, vol. 15, no. 14468.

2. An estimated 80,000 Polish troops fled to Romania and Hungary in September 1939. Ryszard Szawłowski, "The Polish-Soviet War of September 1939," in Sword, *Soviet Takeover,* 32.

3. This order was given by the commander-in-chief of the Polish army. K. Skrzyman, "Wkroczenie Armii Czerwonej do Polski, 17.9.39," in Jasnowski, *Napaść sowiecka,* 68.

4. A resolution of the Congress of People's Deputies of the USSR signed by Mikhail Gorbachev in 1989 admitted the "probable" existence of the protocol. See *Izvestiia,* 27 December 1989. Only in 1992 did the Communist Party announce that the original protocols had been found. See *Izvestiia,* 30 October 1992.

5. *Documents on Polish-Soviet Relations, 1939–1945* vol. 1 (London: Heinemann, 1961), 40.

6. On the night of 17–18 September, the Polish government, diplomatic corps, and high command crossed the border into Romania. On 30 September power was transferred to a new Polish government assembled in France. It moved to England after the collapse of France in June 1940 and operated out of London until 1945.

7. AC, box 43, vol. 10, no. 11942.

8. *Polska w polityce międzynarodowej,* 564–65.

9. An article in the Soviet journal *Krasnaia Zvezda* on 17 September 1940, a year after the invasion, stated that there were 230,670 internees. Cited in Wielhorski, *Los Polaków,* 12. Wielhorski notes that since some of them were released soon after their capture, the Polish government estimated the number of POWs interned in the USSR during 1941 at 180,000. In a new study of Communist repression, Nicolas Werth uses the figure of 230,000 POWs. Nicolas Werth, "The Empire of the Camps," in *The Black Book of Communism: Crimes, Terror, Repression,* ed. Stéphane Courtois, et al., trans. Jonathon Murphy and Mark Kramer (Cambridge: Harvard University Press, 1999), 209. An alternative estimate of the number of prisoners of war, based on new research, is 125,000. Albin Głowacki, *Sowieci wobec Polaków na ziemi-*

ach wschodnich w II Rzeczypospolitej (Łódź: Wydawnictwo Uniwersytet Łódźkiego, 1997), 258.

10. Gross, *Revolution,* 188–89.

11. AC, box 41, vol. 9, no. 10744.

12. Jan Malanowski, "Sociological Aspects of the Annexation of Poland's Eastern Provinces to the USSR in 1939–41," in Sword, *Soviet Takeover,* 80.

13. AC, box 43, vol. 10, no. 11735; box 45, vol. 14, no. 14317.

14. AC, box 41, vol. 8, no. 10685; box 48, vol. 21, no. R2153; box 54, vol. 36, no. R7835.

15. AC, box 43, vol. 10, no. 11945.

16. AC, box 45, vol. 14, no. 14238; box 45, vol. 15, no. 14455.

17. AC, box 38, vol. 5, no. 6083; box 53, vol. 34, no. R7126.

18. AC, box 45, vol. 13, no. 14229.

19. Shortages quickly arose of foodstuffs and material goods due to the frantic purchases by Soviet soldiers, suddenly confronting an abundance of goods that had either been in short supply or nonexistent in the USSR. Later, underproduction, compounded with the rising demand from the influx of refugees, Soviet officers and their families, intensified the shortages.

20. AC, box 45, vol. 15, no. 14456.

21. AC, box 43, vol. 10, no. 11931. See also AC, box 41, vol. 9, no. 10744; box 45, vol. 14, no. 14233.

22. AC, box 44, vol. 12, no. 12676; box 45, vol. 14, no. 14238.

23. One of the first attempts to count the number of Polish citizens forcibly transported to the USSR took place in 1940, even before the deportations had ceased. Two members of the Związek Walki Zbrojnej (Union for Armed Struggle), Aleksandr Klotz and Wanda Ptaszkówna, traveled illegally to the USSR to investigate the living conditions of the exiles. Their report estimates a total of 950,000 deportees, 200,000 internees, and 250,000 arestees, concluding that 1,400,000 individuals were taken from Poland. "Obliczenia Klotza," *Karta* no. 12 (1994): 107–10.

24. The lowest approximation I have seen is one million. AMB, box 44, "Sprawozdanie Działalności Opieki Społecznej." The slightly higher figure of 1,150,000 is in an undated report of the Polish Embassy in Kuibyshev. AMB, box 7, "Położenie obywateli polskich i organizacja pomocy." A 1944 report of the Polish Ministry of Foreign Affairs, "Obliczenie ludności polskiej deportowanej do ZSRR w latach od 1939 do 1941," estimates the total number of exiled Poles at 1.25 million. Cited in Gross, *Revolution,* 146, 193, 287. One report in the papers of Stanisław Mikołajczyk, prime minister of the Polish government in London, calculates 1.7 million exiled Poles. MIK, box 18, folder "November 1941," untitled; box 18, folder "November-December 1941," untitled.

25. Two additional groups of Polish citizens relocated to the USSR during this period, one forcibly and the other not. Many Polish citizens were evacuated eastward from Polish territory in June 1941 when the German army invaded the USSR. The other group consists of the so-called free people who went voluntarily to work there. Many of these volunteers joined industrial labor brigades, having been promised high wages and excellent living conditions; medical personnel and entertainers also accepted work in the USSR. According to a note from Beria to Stalin dated 15 January 1943, a total of 21,860 individuals from eastern Poland voluntaily accepted

jobs in the USSR; 32 percent of them were ethnic Poles. *Konflikty Polsko-Sowieckie 1942–1944,* ed. Wojciech Roszkowski (Warsaw: PAN, 1993), 34. My research turned up one woman whose family, Jewish refugees from the German partition, went to the USSR after her father accepted a job there. Finding the conditions deplorable, they escaped back into Poland but were later deported. AC, box 46, vol. 15, no. 15550. Another woman traveled to Russia with her musician husband, who got a job in a touring orchestra. AC, box 36, vol. 3, no. 2164.

26. Władysław Wielhorski considered the best approximation to be 1,585,000 Polish citizens. Wielhorski, *Los Polaków,* 14–16. Jan Gross estimated the total at 1.5 million. Gross, *Revolution,* 194. Julian Siedlecki calculated 1.7 million. Siedlecki, *Losy Polaków w ZSRR w latach 1939–1986* (London: Gryf Publications, 1987), 45. Zbigniew Siemaszko concluded 1,646,000. Zbigniew Siemaszko, "The Mass Deportations of the Polish Population to the USSR, 1940–1941," in Sword, *Soviet Takeover,* 217–18.

27. Gurjanow, "Cztery deportacje," 125. While confident in his conclusions, Gurjanow makes it clear that they involved a significant amount of guesswork. He found no "passenger lists" for the 204 documented transports. No figure for the June 1940 deportations appeared in any of the documents of the convoy troops. The records did not differentiate transports of prisoners from those of deportees, leaving him to rely on other clues to distinguish them. Additionally, the records of one regiment contained lists for two transports not included in the summary reports of the convoy troops. Such considerations lead me to view Gurjanow's figures as preliminary.

28. "Sprawozdanie z dyskusji," 123. See also Głowacki, *Sowieci wobec Polaków,* 320–403.

29. Wojciech Materski, "Martyrologia obywateli polskich na Wschodzie po 17 września 1939 r.," in *Zbrodnicza ewakuacja więzień i aresztów NKWD na kresach wschodnich II Rzeczypospolitej w czerwcu-lipcu 1941 roku. Materiały z sesji naukowej w 55. rocznicę więźniów NKWD w głąb ZSRR. Łódź, 10 czerwca 1996 r.* (Warsaw: Główna Komisja Badania Zbrodni Przeciwko Narodowi Polskiemu, 1997), 8–9; Daniel Boćkowski in "Sprawozdanie z dyskusji," 130–35. Vyshinsky claimed there were 291,137 deportees. Stanisław Kot, *Rozmowy z Kremlem* (London: Jutro Polski, 1959), 84.

30. Andrzej Korzon, in "Sprawozdanie z dyskusji," 124. Krzysztof Popiński, "Ewakuacja więzień kresowych w czerwcu 1941 r. na podstawie dokumentacji 'Memoriału' i Archiwum Wschodniego," in *Zbrodnicza ewakuacja,* 73–74.

31. One researcher found, for example, that in the Wołyń province those charged with carrying out the roundup and transport of a specified number of families actually "overfulfilled" the plan. W. S. Parsadonova, List do Andrzeja Korzona, in "Sprawozdanie z dyskusji," 128.

32. Some deportees report that family members not on the lists for deportation joined the transports voluntarily, even illegally, so as not to remain alone. Other individuals ended up on the trains simply because they happened to be in the home of a family that was taken. Deportees recount losing family members who got left behind at train stations while searching for food, fell ill and were removed from the transports, or died along the way. Such cases seem not to have been documented by the convoy troops.

33. Grzegorz Hryciuk, "Deportacje ludności Polskiej," in *Masowe deportacje radzieckie w okresie II wojny światowej,* ed. S. Ciesielski, G. Hryciuk, and A. Srebrakowski, 2nd ed. (Wrocław: Instytut Historyczny Uniwersytetu Wrocławskiego, 1994), 43. See also Małgorzata Giżejewska, "Deportacje obywateli polskich z ziem północno-wschodnich II Rzeczypospolitej w latach 1939–1941," in *Studia z dziejów okupacji Sowieckiej (1939–1941). Obywatele polscy na kresach północno-wschodnich II Rzeczypospolitej pod okupacją sowiecką w latach 1939–1941,* ed. Tomasz Strzembosz (Warsaw: Biblioteka Ziem Wschodnich, 1997), 88.

34. Ciesielski, *Polacy w Kazachstanie,* 43. Additionally, it is not clear if the convoy troops were the sole division used for the deportations; perhaps regional and republic-level forces also took part. Ewa Kowalska, in "Sprawozdanie z dyskusji," 138–39. Grzegorz Hryciuk raises the issue of small-scale deportations, not captured in data on the major episodes. Hryciuk, "Deportacje," in Ciesielski, *Masowe deportacje,* 41. One scholar reports that small-scale deportations began in November 1939. Andrzej Paczkowski, "Poland, the 'Enemy Nation'," in Courtois, *Black Book,* 370.

35. Valentina Parsadonova asserts that Głowacki's statistics come from a period when the Soviet government only counted ethnic Poles as Polish citizens. Based on her own research of Soviet archives, she concludes that 321,800 *families* were deported, amounting to nearly 1.2 million individuals. V. S. Parsadonova, "Deportatsiia naseleniia iz Zapadnoi Ukrainy i Zapadnoi Belorussii v 1939–1941 gg.," *Novaia i noveishaia istoriia* 2 (1989): 36, 44.

36. This holds true both for the central and Russian archives and for those of the other relevant republics. See Giżejewska, "Deportacje obywateli polskich," in Strzembosz, *Studia z dziejów okupacji Sowieckiej,* 87–88.

37. Korzon, in "Sprawozdanie z dyskusji," 127; Marek Tuszynski, "Soviet War Crimes against Poland during the Second World War and Its Aftermath: A Review of the Factual Record and Outstanding Questions," *Polish Review* 44, no. 2 (1999): 200; Paczkowski, "Poland," in Courtois, *Black Book,* 370–71.

38. One researcher recently affirmed the long-accepted number of Polish citizens forced into the Red Army of approximately 210,000. Leon Antoni Sulek, "Wojenne losy Polaków żołnierzy Armii Czerwonej (1940–1945)," *Zeszyty Historyczne* 99 (1992): 30.

39. MID, box 98, folder 6, S. Świaniewicz, "Więziennictwo Sowieckie," for Sztab Naczelnego Wodza, Oddział Wywiadowczy, 1942. This report appears under the name of Ernst Tallgren in Dallin and Nicolaevsky, *Forced Labor,* 3–17.

40. Analyzing this group according to nationality, he found that among ethnic Poles arrested in the years 1939–41, 8 percent were women. Krzysztof Jasiewicz, "Obywatele Polscy aresztowani na terytorium tzw. Zachodniej Białorusi w latach 1939–1941 w świetle dokumentacji NKWD/KGB," *Kwartalnik Historyczny* 101, no. 1 (1994): 125–30. Jasiewicz estimates that for the entire region 90,000 individuals were incarcerated. He used card files of the NKVD for the Belorussian part of the former Polish territory; such records have not been found for the Ukrainian part. Another researcher similarly suggests a total of 90,000 –100,000 arrested persons. Albin Głowacki, "Organizacja i funkcjonowanie NKWD na kresach wschodnich II Rzeczypospolitej w latach 1939–1941," in *Zbrodnicza ewakuacja,* 39.

41. Paczkowski, "Poland," in Courtois, *Black Book,* 370.

42. Estimates of the percentage of women and children among the exiles range

from 30 percent to 60 percent. One undated report by Polish authorities in the USSR estimated that of the total number of Poles exiled there, 25 percent were women and 30 percent children. AMB, box 7, "Położenie obywateli polskich i organizacja pomocy." Zdzisław Łęcki offers a combined estimate for women and children of 30 percent. MID, box 2, folder 6, Z. Łęcki, "Działalność Związku Sowieckiego na terenie okupowanych ziem Polski od dnia agresji 17.9.39 do lipca 1941," 10 March 1942, 16. A third report claims 50 percent were women and children. MIK, box 18, folder "November–December 1941." On the basis of a study of 260,399 Poles in forty-seven different provinces in the USSR, one Polish official calculated that 37 percent were adult women; this computation was made nearly three years after the first deportations and does not capture those who had already perished. MID, box 96, folder 6, "Zestawienie statystyczne mężów zaufania i obywateli polskich w ZSRR. Stan w dniu 1.XII.42."

43. Kuśnierz, *Stalin and the Poles,* 86; Wielhorski, *Los Polaków,* 15–16; Siedlecki, *Losy Polaków,* 46.

44. Gross, *Revolution,* 193–207; Siedlecki, *Losy Polaków,* 45–47.

45. Siemaszko, "Mass Deportations," in Sword, *Soviet Takeover,* 225.

46. See Hryciuk, "Deportacje," in Ciesielski, *Masowe deportacje,* 33–35.

47. From *Czerwony Sztandar,* quoted in Hryciuk, "Deportacje," in Ciesielski, *Masowe deportacje,* 35.

48. RHP, fond 89, opis 69, del. 3, reel 22. *Osadniki* used in original.

49. RHP, fond 89, opis 69, del. 4–7, reel 22.

50. Forest workers, like railway workers, apparently were deported because of their knowledge of the terrain and its navigation that would aid the operation of an underground resistance.

51. Document from Nikolai Bugai, "'Specjalna Teczka Stalina': Deportacje i Reemigracja Polaków," *Zeszyty Historyczne* 107 (1994): 89–90. On the terminology used for each group in Soviet documents, see Gurjanow, "Cztery deportacje," 122.

52. Hryciuk, "Deportacje," in Ciesielski, *Masowe deportacje,* 62.

53. RHP, fond 89, opis 14, del. 9, reel 5. A total of 21,857 were shot.

54. Hryciuk, "Deportacje," in Ciesielski, *Masowe deportacje,* 63.

55. RHP, fond 89, opis, 69, del. 8, reel 22.

56. A total of 1,600 Jews were repatriated to the General-Gouvernement. Hryciuk, "Deportacje," in Ciesielski, *Masowe deportacje,* 53.

57. Hryciuk, "Deportacje," in Ciesielski, *Masowe deportacje,* 65.

58. The latter two territories were annexed from Romania, partly into the new Soviet Socialist Republic of Moldavia and partly into the Ukrainian republic. Gurjanow estimates that 17,000 people were deported from Moldavia. Gurjanow, "Cztery deportacje," 121. According to Werth, 31,699 people were deported from Moldavia and another 12,191 from the Romanian territory incorporated into the Ukrainian SSR. Werth, "Empire of the Camps," in Courtois, *Black Book,* 213.

59. According to Gurjanow, 10–13 percent of the deportees on five transports that left Western Belorussia died as a result of German bombings on 24 June and 12–15 percent were injured. Gurjanow, "Cztery deportacje," 66.

60. RHP, fond 89, opis 18, del. 5, reel 6.

61. Hryciuk, "Deportacje," in Ciesielski, *Masowe deportacje,* 67.

62. AC, box 43, vol. 10, no. 11945; box 45, vol. 14, no. 14441.

63. AC, box 45, vol. 13, no. 14205.

64. AC, box 41, vol. 8, no. 10451; box 45, vol. 14, no. 14386; box 48, vol. 20, no. R1882.

65. AC, box 42, vol. 10, no. 11318.

66. RHP, fond 89, opis 69, del. 3, reel 22.

67. AC, box 42, vol. 10, no. 11325.

68. AC, box 41, vol. 9, no. 10744; box 48, vol. 21, no. R1941; box 45, vol. 13, no. 14204; box 36, vol. 2, no. 1613; box 45, vol. 14, no. 14248; box 41, vol. 9, no. 10721.

69. AC, box 45, vol. 14, no. 14285. See also AC, box 41, vol. 8, no. 10393; box 40, vol. 7, no. 8994.

70. AC, box 38, vol. 5, no. 6811.

71. Hryciuk, "Deportacje," in Ciesielski, *Masowe deportacje,* 39.

72. AC, box 36, vol. 2, no. 1907; box 36, vol. 2, no. 1896.

73. AC, box 41, vol. 9, no. 10741; box 48, vol. 20, no. R1568; box 53, vol. 34, no. R7141.

74. AC, box 45, vol. 15, no. 14454. See also AC, box 44, vol. 12, no. 12621.

75. AC, box 36, vol. 3, no. 2228; box 42, vol. 9, no. 10745.

76. AC, box 41, vol. 8, no. 9968.

77. AC, box 44, vol. 12, no. 12627; box 44, vol. 13, no. 14007; box 45, vol. 13, no. 14193.

78. AC, box 39, vol. 5, no. 7271; AMB, box 33, teczka A, tom 3, Janina Dukjetowa; AC, box 42, vol. 9, no. 10754.

79. See AC, box 39, vol. 5, no. 7179; box 40, vol. 6, no. 8418; AMB, box 33, teczka A, tom 3, Janina Duczyńska.

80. AC, box 43, vol. 10, no. 11908. See also AC, box 36, vol. 3, no. 2263; box 43, vol. 10, no. 11940.

81. AC, box 36, vol. 3, no. 2230; box 41, vol. 8, no. 10214; box 36, vol. 2, no. 1613.

82. AC, box 38, vol. 5, no. 6811.

Chapter 2

1. AC, box 42, vol. 10, no. 11639.

2. A few women either went to the USSR of their own accord—following a husband who accepted a job there or fleeing the advancing German army—or were simply stranded there on a trip when the war broke out. The remaining women do not provide enough information to determine whether they were arrested or deported.

3. The remaining 15 percent do not provide the date of their deportation. For comparison, using the traditional estimate of 990,000 deportees, the breakdown for the entire group is: February, 22 percent; April, 32 percent; June 1940, 24 percent; June 1941, 21 percent. The revised figures break down as 44 percent, 19 percent, 24 percent, and 13 percent, respectively.

4. The NKVD reports that 82 percent of the February deportees were ethnic Poles; it offers no such data on the April deportees. Hryciuk, "Deportacje," in Ciesielski, *Masowe deportacje,* 45.

5. Jews composed approximately 59 percent of the June 1940 deportees.

Siemaszko, "Mass Deportations," in Sword, *Soviet Takeover,* 224. Paczkowski offers a much higher estimate of 84 percent. Paczkowski, "Poland," in Courtois, *Black Book,* 372. Many deportees in the fourth deportation came from the Wilno area, which was populated by Poles and Lithuanians. No nationality statistics on the final deportation have yet been found in the NKVD archives.

6. An early estimate from the Polish Embassy placed the proportion of ethnic Poles at 52 percent. According to Siemaszko, it reached 58 percent. Siemaszko, "Mass Deportations," in Sword, *Soviet Takeover,* 230. Recent research suggests a higher proportion of ethnic Poles among the deportees, 63 percent. Hryciuk, "Deportacje," in Ciesielski, *Masowe deportacje,* 68. Only Parsadonova suggests a significantly lower percentage of 33. Parsadonova, List do Andrzeja Korzona, in "Sprawozdanie z dyskusji," 128. No comprehensive statistics have been found for those arrested. Jasiewicz found that among individuals arrested in what became Western Belorussia, 59 percent were ethnic Poles. Jasiewicz, "Obywatele Polscy," 125.

7. See Parsadonova, "Deportatsiia naseleniia," 37; Sword, *Deportation and Exile,* 50–51, 58–59.

8. Only 6 percent of the women explicitly state their religion.

9. A nearly equal proportion (47%) does not provide the information or professes ignorance of the reason for deportation. A few women understand their fate as mere chance, reporting inclusion in mass roundups of Poles. Six deportees attribute deportation to their relationship to another woman, an arrested mother or sister.

10. They worked in the postal service or military bureaucracy.

11. AC, box 54, vol. 35, no. R7178.

12. See AC, box 45, vol. 13, no. 14178; MID, box 98, folder 6, Świaniewicz, 16; Robert Conquest, *The Great Terror: A Reassessment* (New York: Oxford University Press, 1990), 127, 204, 235.

13. Twenty-one percent give no reason for their arrest.

14. See AC, box 36, vol. 3, no. 2232; box 44, vol. 12, no. 12629; box 48, vol. 21, no. R1936. Studying arrests in the region annexed to the Belorussian SSR, Jasiewicz found that border transgressions accounted for the highest number of incarcerated women. Jasiewicz, "Obywatele Polscy," 130–33.

15. AC, box 43, vol. 10, no. 11942.

16. AC, box 39, vol. 5, no. 7355.

17. AC, box 54, vol. 36, no. R7839.

18. AMB, box 33, teczka A, tom 3, Zofia Stojak; AC, box 54, vol. 35, no. R7157.

19. Only 53 percent of the females record their age. Their average age is twenty-six.

20. AC, box 40, vol. 7, no. 9067; box 41, vol. 8, no. 10431.

21. AC, box 43, vol. 10, no. 11893.

22. Janusz Żarnowski, *Społeczeństwo Drugiej Rzeczypospolitej 1918–1939* (Warsaw: Państwowe Wydawnictwo Naukowe, 1973), 342.

23. AC, box 38, vol. 5, no. 6079.

24. Additionally, 9 percent lived in the Białystok province of the central region, part of which the USSR also annexed. These women are not included in the data for the central provinces.

25. The term is not clearly definable. See Roman Wapiński, "Kresy: alternatywa czy zależność?" in Wojciech Wrzesiński, ed., *Między Polską etniczną a historyczną*

(Wrocław: PAN, 1988), 10–11; Marek Wierzbicki, "Stosunki polsko-białoruskie w okresie okupacji sowieckiej ziem północno-wschodnich II Rzeczypospolitej (1939–1941)," in Strzembosz, *Studia z dziejów okupacji Sowieckiej*, 5. In designating the borderlands, for many people *kresy* referred to the parts of Poland that had been directly administered by the Russian Empire after the partitions, that is, the region east of the Congress Kingdom. Others simply used the term to designate the eastern portions of the interwar republic. I use it in the latter sense, including those territories of the former definition, plus the provinces of eastern Galicia and the Białystok province of the central region; all of them belonged to "Poland B." Using the administrative divisions of interwar Poland, I include the following *województwa* in the *kresy:* Wilno, Nowogród, Polesie, Wołyń, Lwów, Tarnopol, Stanisławów, and Białystok. Annexed to the USSR in 1939 (and 1945), these provinces (though only part of the Białystok *woj.*) became Western Belorussia and Western Ukraine.

26. Żarnowski, *Społeczeństwo*, 340–43.

27. Żarnowski, *Społeczeństwo*, 156–57. For Polish villages as a whole, the rate of illiteracy for women reached one-third.

28. Only 57 percent of the individuals record this information.

29. Among the women who do not indicate their occupation, 26 percent lived in rural areas and another 26 percent in urban areas; 48 percent do not provide their place of residence, either.

30. Jasiewicz, "Obywatele Polscy," 127.

31. Data from, *Drugi Powszechny Spis Ludności z dn. 9.XII.31 r. Mieszkania i Gospodarstwa Domowe. Ludność. Stosunki Zawodowe. Polska* Główny Urząd Statystyczny Rzeczypospolitej Polskiej, Statystyka Polski, Seria C, Zeszyt 62 (Warsaw: Nakładem Głównego Urzędu Statystycznego, 1937).

32. AC, box 45, vol. 13, no. 14199; box 45, vol. 14, no. 14258.

33. See AC, box 38, vol. 5, no. 5637; box 45, vol. 13, no. 14214; box 52, vol. 31, no. R6081.

34. The average time between arrest and sentencing was nine months. Jasiewicz, "Obywatele Polscy," 118.

35. The women report being held in the following places on Polish territory: Augustów, Baranowicze, Białystok, Brześć, Grodno, Kołomyja, Lida, Łuck, Lwów, Mińsk, Oleszyc, Pińsk, Przemyśl, Rawa Ruska, Skole, Słonim, Stanisławów, Tarnopol, Wilejka, and Włodzimierz. In the USSR, the women were most commonly imprisoned in: Borisov, Dnepropetrovsk, Kiev, Gomel, Khar'kov, Moscow, Odessa, Orsha, Smolensk, Starobel'sk, Sverdlovsk, and Vitebsk. Polish women were largely incarcerated in the following labor camp complexes. (1) Kar-lag (Kazakh SSR), including Akmolinsk, Karabas, and Karaganda, 30 percent; (2) Temnikov cluster (Mordovsk ASSR), especially Pot'ma, 23 percent; (3) Various camps in the region of Novosibirsk, particularly Barnaul, Iaia, and Tomsk, 19 percent; (4) Various camps in the Sverdlovsk *oblast'*, 6 percent; (5) Smaller numbers of women were confined in: Kras-lag (Krasnoiarsk *krai*); Vorkuta, Pechora, and Ukhtizhma (Komi ASSR); Kotlas (Arkhangel'sk *oblast'*); Starodub (Orel region); Vetluga Camps (European Russia); Petropavlovsk (Northern Kazakhstan); and camps in the Mariisk ASSR.

36. The remaining individuals (14%) do not record their location in the USSR.

37. These people include the so-called kulaks, Volga Germans, and ethnic Poles from the area east of the Polish-Soviet border as established in 1921.

38. Some women (1%) record their place of residence simply as a farm. The remainder, one-quarter of the deported females, does not indicate where they lived in exile.

39. AC, box 45, vol. 14, no. 14233.

Part II

1. AC, box 45, vol. 15, no. 14473. See also AC, box 36, vol. 2, no. 1570; box 36, vol. 2, no. 1610; box 36, vol. 2, no. 1587.

2. AC, box 53, vol. 33, no. R6589. See also AC, box 36, vol. 2, no. 1884; box 42, vol. 10, no. 11667.

3. RHP, fond 89, op. 69, del. 5, reel 22.

4. AC, box 38, vol. 5, no. 6106. See also AC, box 46, vol. 15, no. 15527; box 46, vol. 16, no. R165.

5. AC, box 48, vol. 21, no. R2001; box 45, vol. 14, no. 14289.

6. AC, box 36, vol. 2, no. 1598; AMB, box 33, teczka A, tom 3, Paulina Rzehaków; AC, box 42, vol. 10, no. 11223.

7. Hryciuk, "Deportacje," in Ciesielski, *Masowe deportacje*, 50, 59.

8. AC, box 36, vol. 2, no. 1884; box 43, vol. 10, no. 11930; box 36, vol. 2, no. 1871.

9. AC, box 45, vol. 15, no. 14479. Krystyna Słowik, deported to Kazakhstan, tells the story of a mother caught stealing coal to prevent her children from freezing to death: she received a one-year prison sentence and her children were taken to Soviet orphanages. AC, box 43, vol. 10, no. 11742.

10. MID, box 198, folder 8, Ada Halpern, "Liberation—Russian Style," March 1944.

11. AC, box 36, vol. 2, no. 1884; box 42, vol. 10, no. 11377; box 39, vol. 5, no. 7127.

12. AC, box 45, vol. 15, no. 14456; MID, box 198, folder 8, Halpern; AC, box 45, vol. 13, no. 14229. See also AC, box 42, vol. 9, no. 10745.

13. AC, box 45, vol. 15, no. 14479; box 79, folder 16, letter, Irina Beskownik to Andrzej Beskownik, 8 September 1942; box 45, vol. 14, no. 14273.

14. See AC, box 36, vol. 2, no. 1596; box 42, vol. 10, no. 11638; box 44, vol. 12, no. 12627.

15. AC, box 42, vol. 10, no. 11223; box 42, vol. 10, no. 11377; box 36, vol. 2, no. 1950; box 54, vol. 35, no. R7162.

16. MIK, box 18, folder "September-November 1941," "Relacja z Kazachstanu."

17. AC, box 36, vol. 2, no. 1955. See also AC, box 36, vol. 2, no. 1598; box 41, vol. 8, no. 10074.

18. AC, box 41, vol. 8, no. 10059; box 42, vol. 10, no. 11668. See also AC, box 43, vol. 11, no. 12149; box 48, vol. 20, no. R1882.

Chapter 3

1. AC, box 48, vol. 21, no. R2239; box 42, vol. 10, no. 11673; box 46, vol. 15, no. 15544.

2. AC, box 52, vol. 31, no. R6090.

3. AC, box 42, vol. 9, no. 10753; box 42, vol. 10, no. 11668.

4. Joan Wallach Scott, *Gender and the Politics of History* (New York: Columbia University Press, 1988), 64. The essays in this book inspired many of the ideas in my analysis. Polish perspectives on women and labor were not unique but continued the nineteenth-century discourse prevailing in Western Europe, which understood gender as a "natural" sexual division of labor. See Joan Wallach Scott, "The Woman Worker," in *A History of Women in the West*, vol. 4, *Emerging Feminism from Revolution to World War*, ed. Genevieve Fraisse and Michelle Perrot (Cambridge, Mass.: Harvard University Press, 1993).

5. Maria Nietyksza, "The Vocational Activities of Women in Warsaw at the Turn of the Nineteenth Century," in *Women in Polish Society*, ed. Rudolf Jaworski and Bianka Pietrow-Ennker (Boulder, Colo.: East European Monographs, 1992), 145.

6. Nietyksza, "Vocational Activities," in Jaworski, *Women in Polish Society*, 153, 155, 158–59.

7. Zofia Daszyńska-Golińska, *Przyczynki do kwestji robotniczej w Polsce* (Warsaw: Nakład Ministerstwa Pracy i Opieki Społecznej, 1920), 11.

8. Nietyksza, "Vocational Activities," in Jaworski, *Women in Polish Society*, 154. See also Danuta Rzepniewska, "Kobieta w rodzinie ziemiańskiej w XIX wieku. Królestwo Polskie," in *Kobieta i społeczeństwo na ziemiach polskich w XIX w.*, ed. Anna Żarnowska and Andrzej Szwarc (Warsaw: Instytut Historyczny Uniwersytetu Warszawskiego, 1990), 36–68; Anna Żarnowska, "Aspiracje oświatowe kobiet w rodzinach robotniczych w Królestwie Polskim na przełomie XIX i XX wieku," in *Kobieta i edukacja na ziemiach polskich w XIX i XX w.* Part I, ed. Anna Żarnowska and Andrzej Szwarc (Warsaw: Instytut Historyczny Uniwersytetu Warszawskiego, 1992), 123–54.

9. Renata Siemieńska, *Płeć, zawód, polityka. Kobiety w życiu publicznym w Polsce* (Warsaw: Uniwersytet Warszawski, Instytut Socjologii, 1990), 80. Women both had a higher rate of illiteracy than men and attended places of vocational and higher education in lower numbers.

10. "O prawa wyborcze kobiet," *Bluszcz* 53, no. 29 (20 July 1918): 213–14; "Kobieta w pracy zdała egzamin na 'piątkę'," *Moja Przyjaciółka* 3, no. 13 (10 July 1936): 250.

11. Katarzyna Sierokowska, "Przegląd piśmiennictwa poświęconego dziejom kobiet w Polsce międzywojennej," in *Równe prawa i nierówne szanse. Kobiety w Polsce międzywojennej*, ed. Anna Żarnowska and Andrzej Szwarc (Warsaw: Instytut Historyczny Uniwersytetu Warszawskiego, 2000), 10.

12. As agricultural laborers, men earned 50–60 percent more than women. Żarnowski, *Społeczeństwo*, 122, 86. In white-collar work, however, the difference was not as great. Siemieńska, *Płeć*, 80–81.

13. Scott, "Woman Worker," 424.

14. These calculations are based on information from the Second General Census of 1931. The last taken in the interwar republic, this census gives an incomplete picture of women's participation in the labor force and does not allow for calculation of the number of women actively engaged in labor outside the home. The statistics divide the population into two groups: those employed in agriculture and those employed in all other fields. The tables also demarcate the population as active or passive, the latter encompassing those persons supported by someone working actively in a listed field. In attempting to calculate the percentage of women

gainfully employed, the figures for the active population are used. Data from *Drugi Powszechny Spis*, 61–64, 73.

15. The working age is defined as 15–59, thus the total number of women in this group is calculated as 9,827,572. Data from *Drugi Powszechny Spis*, 32–41; Hanna Jędruszczak, "Employment in Poland in 1930–1960. Dynamics and Structure," *Acta Poloniae Historica* 18 (1968): 255.

16. Siemieńska, *Płeć*, 80; Żarnowski, *Społeczeństwo*, 217. Only 13 percent of women working outside agriculture were white-collar workers. Anna Żarnowska, "Kierunki aktywności zawodowej kobiet w Polsce XX wieku (do 1939 r.)," in Żarnowska, *Kobieta i edukacja* part II, 166; Siemieńska, *Płeć*, 54–55; "Po Sowietach - najwięcej kobiet studuje w Polsce," *Moja Przyjaciółka* 3, no. 17 (10 September 1936): 344; Żarnowski, *Społeczeństwo*, 192; "Polki na międzynarodowym kongresie prawniczek," *Moja Przyjaciółka* 3, no. 18 (25 September 1936): 368; Siemieńska, *Płeć*, 81.

17. Data from *Drugi Powszechny Spis*, 73–78; Żarnowski, *Społeczeństwo*, 164, 165, 170. See also Włodzimierz Mędrzecki, "Kobieta wiejska w Królestwie Polskim. Przełom XIX i XX wieku," in Żarnowska, *Kobieta i społeczeństwo*, 130–38. Women in the village were exhorted to maintain this division of labor throughout the interwar period. See for example, Abuz, "Rola kobiety w gospodarstwie rolnym," *Moja Przyjaciółka* 3, no. 23 (10 December 1936): 497.

18. See Stanisława Kielczyńska, "Kobieta dzisiejsza," *Moja Przyjaciółka* 3, no. 3 (10 February 1936): 35–36; F. Pisarzewska, "Stanowisko kobiety dawniej, a dzisiaj oraz następstwa," *Moja Przyjaciółka* 3, no. 14 (25 July 1936): 274; Helena Ellerówna, "Czy kobieta powinna pracować zawodowo?" *Moja Przyjaciółka* 3, no. 4 (25 February 1936): 52; "Na 100 mężczyzn wypada 123 kobiet w Polsce," *Moja Przyjaciółka* 3, no. 3 (10 February 1936): 34; "Kobieta w pracy zdała egzamin na 'piątkę'," *Moja Przyjaciółka* 3, no. 13 (10 July 1936): 250. Begun in 1933, by the end of the decade this bimonthly journal boasted a circulation of 100,000. Andrzej Paczkowski, *Prasa Polska*, vol. 3, *1918–1939* (Warsaw: Państwowe Wydawnictwo Naukowe, 1980), 250–51. Among its dominant features is its celebration of the accomplishments of women, both in Poland and abroad, in economic, political, academic, and social realms; it thus offers new role models—women active and accomplished outside the home.

19. "O prawa wyborcze kobiet," *Bluszcz* 53, no. 29 (20 July 1918): 213–14. See also Dr. Budzińska-Tylicka, "O prawa kobiet," *Bluszcz*, no. 43 (26 October 1918): 317; Scott, *Gender*, 106; this magazine, a social-literary weekly with practical supplements, had a circulation of 10,000. Paczkowski, *Prasa*, 281–82.

20. Dr. Gabryela Majewska, "Wiec kobiet polskich," *Bluszcz* 53, no. 47 (23 November 1918): 351; Dr. E. R., "Cel pracy kobiecej," *Bluszcz* 54, no. 1 (15 October 1921): 2; Sławomira Walczewska, *Damy, rycerze i feministki. Kobiecy dyskurs emancypacyjny w Polsce* (Kraków: Wydawnictwo eFKa, 1999), 111.

21. Dr. Władysław Chodecki, "Małżeństwo i wojna," *Bluszcz* 53, nos. 33–34 (17/24 August 1918): 242; "O prawa wyborcze kobiet," *Bluszcz* 53, no. 29 (20 July 1918): 214.

This is the underlying message of *Moja Przyjaciółka* as well. Despite praise of women's accomplishments and the exhortation to extend their work in society, its authors continually depict women's real work, both in terms of their own nature and the good of the nation, as raising families and ensuring the moral order of society.

22. Maria Warychówna, "Zadanie obecnej kobiety," *Moja Przyjaciółka* 3, no. 6 (25 March 1936): 92; Konstancja Hojnacka, "Kobieta w roli żony towarzyszki życia," *Moja Przyjaciółka* 6, no. 12 (26 June 1939): 337–39. See also Janina Habernówna, "'Na ślubnym kobiercu,'" *Moja Przyjaciółka* 6, no. 1 (10 January 1939): 5.

23. Its circulation reached 800,000 in 1939. In the words of one historian, it thus had the most brilliant career not only of all the interwar journals in Poland, but also of Europe. Paczkowski, *Prasa*, 242, 245.

24. Rycerz Niepokalanej, "Naprawa musi iść z góry," *Rycerz Niepokalanej* 15, no. 5 (May 1936): 130; S. B., "O mojej matce," *Rycerz Niepokalanej* 16, no. 1 (January 1937): 4.

25. Anna Żarnowska, "Kobieta w rodzinie robotniczej. Królestwo Polskie u schyłku XIX i na początku XX wieku," in Żarnowska, *Kobieta i społeczeństwo*, 174, 181.

26. Wanda Krahelska-Mackiewiczowa, "Czy jest praca 'lepsza i gorsza'?" *Moja Przyjaciółka* no. 12 (26 June 1939): 348; Wanda Krahelska-Mackiewiczowa, "Pracy należy się szacunek," *Moja Przyjaciółka* 6, no. 14 (25 July 1939): 412; M. Rulikowski, "Nowe pole pracy dla kobiet," *Bluszcz* 53, no. 10 (9 March 1918): 74.

27. This definition of class is from Gareth Stedman Jones, *Languages of Class: Studies in English Working Class History, 1832–1982* (Cambridge: Cambridge University Press, 1983), 101–2. See Anna Żarnowska and Andrzej Swarc, eds., *Kobieta i praca. Wiek XIX i XX* (Warsaw: Wydawnictwo DiG, 2000), 42. Kathleen Canning, "Gender and the Politics of Class Formation," *American Historical Review* 97, no. 3 (June 1992): 754; Janeen Baxter, "Is Husband's Class Enough? Class Location and Class Identity in the United States, Sweden, Norway, and Australia," *American Sociological Review* 59 (April 1994): 233.

28. Żarnowski, *Społeczeństwo*, 340–44, 349.

29. Żarnowski, *Społeczeństwo*, 286–87, 266–67, 272–73, 196, 216.

30. Żarnowski, *Społeczeństwo*, 186–7.

31. Aleksandra Jasinska-Kania, "National Identity and Personality Patterns in Poland between the Wars," in *Poland between the Wars: 1918–1939*, ed. Timothy Wiles (Bloomington: Indiana University Polish Studies Center, 1985), 118; Żarnowski, *Społeczeństwo*, 289, 349–51.

32. Cited in Żarnowski, *Społeczeństwo*, 352–53.

33. *Concise Statistical Yearbook of Poland September 1939–June 1941* (Glasgow: Polish Ministry of Information, 1941), 8, 11.

34. Quoted in Canning, "Gender and Politics," 737.

35. Hiroaki Kuromiya, *Stalin's Industrial Revolution: Politics and Workers, 1928–1932* (Cambridge: Cambridge University Press, 1989), xi–xiii.

36. On decrees, see Moshe Lewin, "Society and the Stalinist State in the Period of the Five Year Plans," *Social History* 2 (May 1976): 155; on militarization, Lewis Siegelbaum, *Stakhanovism and the Politics of Productivity in the USSR, 1935–1941* (Cambridge: Cambridge University Press, 1988), 285; on starving workers, Lewin, "Society and the Stalinist State," 160; deportee, AC, box 51, vol. 27, no. R4565.

37. RHP, fond 89, opis 69, del. 5, reel 22. See also Hryciuk, "Deportacje," in Ciesielski, *Masowe deportacje*, 48–50.

38. AC, box 46, vol. 15, no. 15544; box 45, vol. 14, no. 14255; box 45, vol. 14, no. 14322; box 36, vol. 3, no. 2248.

39. AC, box 53, vol. 34, no. R7139. See also AC, box 36, vol. 3, no. 2281; box 43, vol. 10, no. 11690.

40. Hryciuk, "Deportacje," in Ciesielski, *Masowe deportacje*, 64, 67.

41. AC, box 45, vol. 14, no. 14280; box 45, vol. 14, no. 14309; box 44, vol. 13, no. 14007.

42. AC, box 41, vol. 9, no. 10719; box 38, vol. 5, no. 6080; box 36, vol. 3, no. 2284; box 36, vol. 2, no. 1576.

43. AC, box 45, vol. 13, no. 14212; box 56, vol. 42, no. R9734; box 48, vol. 20, no. R1873; box 45, vol. 14, no. 14399; box 38, vol. 5, no. 5637.

44. See AC, box 39, vol. 6, no. 7902; box 43, vol. 10, no. 11909.

45. AC, box 43, vol. 11, no. 12222.

46. See AC, box 36, vol. 3, no. 2269; box 45, vol. 13, no. 14226; box 55, vol. 39, no. R8778.

47. AC, box 39, vol. 5, no. 7271; box 45, vol. 13, no. 14194. See also Eugenia Huntingdon, *The Unsettled Account: An Autobiography* (London: Severn House, 1986), 128–31.

48. AC, box 41, vol. 8, no. 10059. See also AC, box 46, vol. 15, no. 15530; box 39, vol. 6, no. 7829.

49. AC, box 42, vol. 10, no. 11330. See also AC, box 45, vol. 14, no. 14395; box 43, vol. 10, no. 11690.

50. Lewin, "Society and the Stalinist State," 153.

51. Six women report working in offices, fifteen in hospitals and clinics, six in kitchens, and two in nurseries. Wiktoria Oleksiak was fired from her job in a canteen when the war broke out and sent to work in a factory because she was the wife of a Polish officer. AC, box 36, vol. 3, no. 2248.

52. AC, box 52, vol. 30, no. R5639; box 44, vol. 12, no. 12611; box 53, vol. 33, no. R6668.

53. AC, box 36, vol. 3, no. 2217; box 43, vol. 11, no. 12154; box 44, vol. 12, no. 12598.

54. AC, box 38, vol. 5, no. 6106; box 43, vol. 11, no. 12149.

55. AC, box 38, vol. 5, no. 6112; box 52, vol. 30, no. R5627.

56. AC, box 45, vol. 13, no. 14229.

57. AC, box 36, vol. 2, no. 1568; box 42, vol. 10, no. 11377.

58. AC, box 36, vol. 3, no. 2217; box 50, vol. 25, no. R3589; box 39, vol. 5, no. 7365.

59. AC, box 40, vol. 7, no. 9590; box 36, vol. 3, no. 2248.

60. AC, box 43, vol. 10, no. 11685; box 48, vol. 21, no. R1937; box 44, vol. 13, no. 14008.

61. AC, box 36, vol. 2, no. 1884; box 42, vol. 10, nos. 11377 and 11638; box 44, vol. 13, no. 13970.

62. AC, box 43, vol. 10, no. 11687; box 36, vol. 2, no. 1950; box 36, vol. 3, no. 2253.

63. AC, box 39, vol. 6, no. 7902; box 48, vol. 21, no. R2273; box 45, vol. 13, no. 14197. Deportees who reported a salary typically received one-two rubles per day;

64. AMB, box 33, teczka A, tom 3, Małgorzata Utnik. See also AC, box 52, vol. 30, no. R5643; box 54, vol. 35, no. R7177.

65. AC, box 39, vol. 6, no. 7846; box 41, vol. 9, no. 10741; box 38, vol. 5, no. 6102.

66. AC, box 42, vol. 10, no. 11673; box 42, vol. 10, no. 11325. See also AC, box 48, vol. 21, no. R1951; box 50, vol. 25, no. R3583.

67. AC, box 48, vol. 21, no. R1984; box 44, vol. 12, no. 12624. The 1932 law on absenteeism was revised in 1938 to include tardiness. Vladimir Andrle, *Workers in Stalin's Russia: Industrialization and Social Change in a Planned Economy* (New York: St. Martin's Press, 1988), 160.

68. AC, box 40, vol. 7, no. 9590; box 42, vol. 10, no. 11639.

69. AC, box 39, vol. 5, no. 7196.

70. AC, box 41, vol. 8, no. 10059; box 36, vol. 2, no. 1576; AMB, box 33, teczka A, tom 3, Małgorzata Utnik.

71. AC, box 45, vol. 14, no. 14337. See also AC, box 43, vol. 11, no. 12507; box 52, vol. 30, no. R5636.

72. AC, box 50, vol. 25, no. R3583; MIK, box 15, letter, Lola to Staszek, 12 April 1940. See also AC, box 48, vol. 22, no. R2417; MID, box 99, folder 9, "Poles in the Soviet Union: Recollections of an Ex-prisoner"; MIK, box 18, folder "November–December 1941," Confidential Report.

73. AC, box 54, vol. 35, no. R7356; box 54, vol. 35, no. R7164; box 36, vol. 3, no. 2211.

74. AC, box 43, vol. 11, no. 12507; box 45, vol. 15, no. 14460. See also AC, box 45, vol. 13, no. 14189; box 48, vol. 20, no. R1873.

75. AC, box 49, vol. 23, no. R2912; box 35, vol. 1, no. 1253.

76. Wendy Goldman, *Women, the State and Revolution: Soviet Family Policy and Social Life, 1917–1936* (Cambridge, Mass.: Cambridge University Press, 1993), 11.

77. Natalia Pushkareva, *Women in Russian History: From the Tenth to the Twentieth Century*, trans. and ed. Ewe Levin (Armonk, N.Y.: M.E. Sharpe, 1997), 259; Goldman, *Women*, 312.

78. In February 1939, women constituted 30 percent of the medal winners in the agricultural sector of the Ukrainian SSR. Though most of them did not hold the most prestigious positions, those who did became public heroes. Matt Oja, "From Krestianka to Udarnitsa: Rural Women and the Vydvizhenie Campaign, 1933–1941," *Carl Beck Papers* no. 1203 (July 1996): 19–20.

79. Oja, "Krestianka," 7.

80. Scott, *Gender*, 154.

81. AC, box 42, vol. 9, no. 10754; box 42, vol. 10, no. 11525; box 43, vol. 10, no. 11690. See also AC, box 48, vol. 21, no. R2275; box 75, AWBD, D1267; box 45, vol. 15, no. 14460.

82. AC, box 37, vol. 3, no. 3494; box 56, vol. 40, no. R9089.

83. AC, box 39, vol. 5, no. 6710; box 41, vol. 8, no. 10689. See also AC, box 44, vol. 12, no. 12697; box 47, vol. 19, no. R1231.

84. AC, box 35, vol. 1, no. 492.

85. AC, box 45, vol. 13, no. 14227. The term arose from the exploits of Aleksei Stakhanov, who in 1935 set a record for hewing coal and was held up as a model worker to be emulated in all fields. Stakhanovism became both a method of mobilization that granted material rewards for "heroic" labor and a weapon against

undisciplined managerial and technical personnel. See Andrle, *Workers in Stalin's Russia*, 182–99; Siegelbaum, *Stakhanovism*.

86. AC, box 45, vol. 13, no. 14175; box 48, vol. 21, no. R2170.

87. AC, box 42, vol. 10, no. 11639.

88. AC, box 48, vol. 21, no. R2249; box 43, vol. 10, no. 11685; MIK, box 18, folder "September–November 1941," Ola Jaszkar, "Sprawozdanie o stosunkach panujączch na osiedlu p. n. 'Czwarty Skład'/Maryjska ASSR posiołek nr. 13."

89. AC, box 43, vol. 10, no. 11907; box 43, vol. 10, no. 11897; box 42, vol. 10, no. 11527. Boys write similarly. See AC, box 58, vol. 46, no. R11468; box 58, vol. 47, no. R11589; box 59, vol. 49, no. R12345.

90. AC, box 41, vol. 7, no. 9678. See also AC, box 35, vol. 1, no. 1037; box 46, vol. 16, no. R00305.

91. AC, box 59, vol. 48, no. R11955; box 36, vol. 2, no. 1397.

92. AC, box 42, vol. 9, no. 10748; box 41, vol. 9, no. 10719; box 43, vol. 11, no. 12062. See also AC, box 42, vol. 9, no. 11159.

93. AC, box 35, vol. 1, no. 1037; box 37, vol. 4, no. 3661.

94. AC, box 36, vol. 2, no. 1722; box 41, vol. 8, no. 10694. See also AC, box 61, vol. 53, no. R14614; box 66, vol. 71, no. 15975. It is worth noting that in October 1939 there were more than two million Stakhanovites in the USSR; by July 1940 the number increased to three million. Siegelbaum, *Stakhanovism*, 147, 280.

95. AC, box 35, vol. 1, no. 358; box 44, vol. 12, no. 12696; box 35, vol. 1, no. 78. See also AC, box 39, vol. 5, no. 7473; box 52, vol. 30, no. R5588.

96. AC, box 58, vol. 45, no. R11166. See also AC, box 47, vol. 18, no. R1047; box 39, vol. 5, no. 6900.

97. AC, box 50, vol. 25, no. R3862; box 54, vol. 36, no. R7677. See also AC, box 41, vol. 8, no. 10172; box 40, vol. 7, no. 8828.

98. AC, box 43, vol. 10, no. 11962; box 43, vol. 11, no. 12018.

99. AC, box 36, vol. 2, no. 2126; box 41, vol. 9, no. 10719. See also AC, box 35, vol. 1, no. 607; box 37, vol. 4, no. 4502. Interviews with Russian emigrés conducted under the Harvard Project attest to the power wielded by foremen, who reportedly responded above all to offers of vodka and sex. Siegelbaum, *Stakhanovism*, 166.

100. AC, box 39, vol. 5, no. 6586; box 40, vol. 7, no. 9602; box 45, vol. 15, no. 15052.

101. AC, box 42, vol. 10, no. 11673; box 43, vol. 10, no. 11903; box 48, vol. 21, no. R1947.

102. AC, box 48, vol. 21, no. R1986; box 55, vol. 39, no. R8618.

103. AC, box 48, vol. 20, no. R1575; box 42, vol. 9, no. 10753; box 42, vol. 10, no. 11676; MID, box 198, folder 2, Countess Czarkowska-Golejewska, "A Journey to Soviet Siberia," London, 1944. See also AC, box 44, vol. 12, no. 12627; box 44, vol. 13, no. 14023.

104. MIK, box 18, folder "September–November 1941," letter, Matki Polki rejonu Parabiel obl. Nowosybirskiej to Poselstwa Polskiego w Moskwie; box 18, folder "November–December 1941," Zajawlenie, "Do Opieki Społecznej przy Ambasadzie w Kujbyszewie."

105. MID, box 198, folder 2, Czarkowska-Golejewska; AC, box 43, vol. 10, no. 11942; box 43, vol. 11, no. 12507; box 48, vol. 21, no. R2271.

106. MID, box 99, folder 9, "Poles in the Soviet Union: Recollections of an Ex-Prisoner;" box 2, folder 4, "The Situation in Soviet-Occupied Poland." See also MID, box 91, folder 9, Confidential report, "Deportations from Soviet-Occupied Polish Territories," July 1944.

107. AC, box 36, vol. 3, no. 2215; box 42, vol. 9, no. 11207; MID, box 198, folder 8, Ada Halpern, "Liberation—Russian Style," March 1944; AC, box 43, vol. 10, no. 11698; box 45, vol. 14, no. 14284. According to Żarnowski, individuals employed at *czarna robota* were at the bottom of the social hierarchy in interwar Poland. Żarnowski, *Społeczeństwo*, 93, 104, 322.

108. Feliks Kon, *Pol'sha na sluzhbe imperializma* (Moscow: Gosudarstvennoe Izd., 1927), 4, 7, 14; Kuromiya, *Stalin's Industrial Revolution*, xiv–xv.

109. Terry Martin, "The Origins of Soviet Ethnic Cleansing," *Journal of Modern History* 70, no. 4 (December 1998): 837–40. The phrase translates as, "If you're a Pole, then you're a kulak." See also M. Iwanów, *Pierwszy naród ukarany. Polacy w Związku Radzieckim 1921–1939* (Warsaw: Państwowe Wydawnictwo Naukowe, 1991).

110. AC, box 45, vol. 13, no. 14212.

111. Quoted in Robert Conquest, *Soviet Nationalities Policy in Practice* (New York: Frederick A. Praeger, 1967), 61.

112. AC, box 36, vol. 2, no. 1950; box 47, vol. 19, no. R1271; box 48, vol. 20, no. R1568. See also AC, box 42, vol. 10, no. 11652; box 45, vol. 13, no. 14229.

113. See AC, box 44, vol. 13, no. 14010; box 48, vol. 20, no. R1571; box 53, vol. 34, no. R7068.

114. See for example, AC, box 42, vol. 9, no. 10753.

115. MIK, box 18, folder "September–November 1941," letter, Matki Polki rejonu Parabiel obl. Nowosybirskiej to Poselstwa Polskiego w Moskwie; AC, box 53, vol. 34, no. R7139. This woman does not provide her age or occupation; she lived in a village in the Wołyń województwo.

116. AC, box 42, vol. 10, no. 11639; box 41, vol. 9, no. 10744.

117. MIK, box 18, Polish Embassy in Kuibyshev, Social Welfare Section, folder "November–December 1941," untitled report. See also MIK, box 18, Polish Embassy in Kuibyshev, Social Welfare Section, folder "November–December 1941," letter from Kazakhstan, 10 November 1941; MID, box 142, folder 1, no. 4810; AC, box 48, vol. 20, no. 4566.

118. Scott, *Gender*, p. 59.

119. Both in the archival and published material on women's wartime experience, though, cases abound in which women from extremely privileged families demonstrate great strength and resourcefulness. See for example, Christian von Krockow, *Hour of the Women*, trans. Krishna Winston (London: Faber & Faber, 1992); Krystyna Sosabowska, *The Bridges I Have Crossed. A Polish Woman's Reminiscences* (Edinburgh: Albyn Press, 1985).

120. Paraphrased by Scott, *Gender*, 56.

121. Cited in Parsadonova, "Deportatsiia naseleniia," 36. Productivity is not delineated according to the sex of the workers.

122. AC, box 43, vol. 11, no. 12394.

123. AC, box 48, vol. 21, no. R2210. See also AC, box 53, vol. 34, no. R7141; box 36, vol. 2, no. 1908.

124. AC, box 48, vol. 22, no. R2363; box 52, vol. 30, no. R5588. See also AC, box 38, vol. 4, no. 5120; box 39, vol. 6, no. 8043.

125. AC, box 41, vol. 8, no. 9968; box 52, vol. 30, no. R5640. See also AC, box 35, vol. 1, no. 115.

126. AC, box 54, vol. 35, no. R7394.

127. Scott, *Gender*, 157.

128. Margaret Higonnet et al., eds., *Behind the Lines: Gender and the Two World Wars* (New Haven: Yale University Press, 1987), 5.

129. See Arthur Marwick, *Women at War 1914–1918* (London: Fontana Paperbacks, 1977); William Chafe, *The American Woman: Her Changing Social, Economic and Political Role, 1920–1970* (Oxford: Oxford University Press, 1972).

Chapter 4

1. The quotation which I use as the title for this chapter is attributed to Otto von Bismarck, cited in Rudolf Jaworski, "Polish Women in the Nationality Conflict in the Province of Posen at the Turn of the Century," in Jaworski, *Women in Polish Society*, 63–64.

2. Jaworski, "Polish Women," in Jaworski, *Women in Polish Society*, 55.

3. Barbara Jedynak, "Dom i kobieta w kulturze niewoli," in *Kobieta w kulturze i społeczeństwie*, ed. Barbara Jedynak (Lublin: Wydawnictwo Uniwersytetu Marii Curie-Skłodowskiej, 1990), 72, 83.

4. Rudolf Jaworski and Bianka Pietrow-Ennker, "Preface," in Jaworski, *Women in Polish Society*, v–vi; Walczewska, *Damy*, 44, 46; Bogna Lorence-Kot, "Klementyna Tanska Hoffmanowa, Cultural Nationalism and a New Formula for Polish Womanhood," *History of European Ideas* 8, no. 4/5 (1987): 437.

5. Jaworski, "Polish Women," in Jaworski, *Women in Polish Society*, 56.

6. Magda Monczka-Ciechomska, "Mit kobiety w polskiej kulturze," in *Głos mają kobiety. Teksty feministyczne*, ed. Sławomira Walczewska (Kraków: Convivium, 1992), 96; Bianka Pietrow-Ennker, "Women in Polish Society. A Historical Introduction," in Jaworski, *Women in Polish Society*, 1; Bogna Lorence-Kot, *Child-Rearing and Reform: A Study of the Nobility in Eighteenth-Century Poland* (Westport, Conn.: Greenwood Press, 1983), 7; on motherhood, Jedynak, "Dom i kobieta," in Jedynak, *Kobieta w kulturze*, 86–87; on armed insurgents, Irena Homola-Skąpska, "Galicia: Initiatives for Emancipation of Polish Women," in Jaworski, *Women in Polish Society*, 72; and Bogna Lorence-Kot, "Konspiracja: Probing the Topography of Women's Underground Activities. The Kingdom of Poland in the Second Half of the Nineteenth Century," in Jaworski, *Women in Polish Society*, 38.

7. Siemieńska, *Płeć*, 161; Jedynak, "Dom i kobieta," in Jedynak, *Kobieta w kulturze*, 79, 81–82, 88–90, 100; Lorence-Kot, "Konspiracja," in Jaworski, *Women in Polish Society*, 31–38; Adam Winiarz, "Girls' Education in the Kingdom of Poland (1815–1915)," in Jaworski, *Women in Polish Society*, 105–7.

8. Pietrow-Ennker, "Women in Polish Society," in Jaworski, *Women in Polish Society*, 24.

Walczewska, *Damy*, 57–58; Natali Stegmann, "Wielkopolskie wzorce kobiecej aktywności społecznej w życiu codziennym kobiet na przełomie XIX i XX wieku," in *Kobieta i kultura życia codziennego wiek XIX i XX,* ed. Anna Żarnowska and Andrzej Szwarc (Warsaw: DiG, 1997), 367–68.

9. Ks. Czesław Oraczewski, "Samowiedza Narodu," *Bluszcz* 53, no. 48 (30 November 1918): 358; Aleksander Szczęsny, "Naród i rodzina," *Bluszcz* 53, no. 14 (6 April 1918): 105–6; Mieczysław Smolarski, "O zdrowie społeczeństwa," *Bluszcz* 53, no. 26 (29 June 1918): 190.

10. Dr. Władysław Chodecki, "Małżeństwo i wojna," *Bluszcz* 53, nos. 33–34 (17/24 August 1918): 242.

11. Kazimiera Neronowiczowa, "Nowe prawa - nowe obowiązki," *Bluszcz* 53, no. 52 (28 December 1918): 391; Henryk Sienkiewicz, quoted in Matka-Polska, "Gdzież są?" *Bluszcz* 53, no. 30 (27 July 1918): 216.

12. See Michał Pietrzak, "Sytuacja prawna kobiet w II Rzeczypospolitej," in Żarnowska, *Równe prawa,* 77–91; Roman Wapiński, "Kobiety i życie publiczne—przemiany pokoleniowe," in Żarnowska, *Równe prawa,* 35–36; Andrzej Chojnowski, "Aktywność kobiet w życiu politycznym," in Żarnowska, *Równe prawa,* 39.

13. Janina Habernówna, "Na ślubnym kobiercu," *Moja Przyjaciółka* 6, no. 1 (10 January 1939): 4–5; "Na dzień Matki," *Moja Przyjaciółka* 3, no. 10 (25 May 1936): 180; Marian Obertyński, "Rodzina w świetle Wiary," *Rycerz Niepokalanej* 16, no. 1 (January 1937): 6–8.

14. Konstancja Hojnacka, "Kobieta w roli żony towarzyszki życia," *Moja Przyjaciółka* 6, no. 12 (26 June 1939): 337; Uczestnicy Diecezjalnego Kongresu Eucharystycznego w Łodzi, "Rezolucje diecezjalnego Kongresu Eucharystycznego w Łodzi," *Rycerz Niepokalanej* 7, no. 9 (September 1928): 259. Articles admonished women to act so as to keep men from seeking sexual partners outside the home. Similarly, if daughters "went bad," the mother was at fault.

15. Maria Warychówna, "Zadanie obecnej kobiety," *Moja Przyjaciółka* 3, no. 6 (25 March 1936): 92.

16. Wacława Dobrzyńska, "Kobiety polskie w służbie ojczyzny," *Moja Przyjaciółka* 6, no. 12 (26 June 1939): 339; Dr. E. R., "Cel pracy kobiecej," *Bluszcz* 54, no. 1 (15 October 1921): 2.

17. "Na dzień Matki," *Moja Przyjaciółka* 3, no. 10 (25 May 1936): 180.

18. Redakcja, "Żądamy praw," *Bluszcz* 53, no. 42 (19 October 1918): 310. The authors refer to Piłsudski's Legions of 1914–17, formed to fight for Poland's independence.

Aleksander Szczęsny, "Naród i rodzina," *Bluszcz* 53, no. 14 (6 April 1918): 105; Matka-Polska, "Gdzież są?" *Bluszcz* 53, no. 31 (30 July 1918): 216; Aleksandra Łapińska-Leśniewska, "Pierworodni," *Bluszcz* 53, no. 50 (14 December 1918): 375

19. Section I, Article One, no. 2, "Ustawa Konstytucyjna z dnia 23 kwietnia 1935 r.," *Dziennik Ustaw Rzeczypospolitej Polskiej* no. 30 (24 April 1935), 7; League of Nations, Nationality of Women. Second Report of the Secretary-General on the Information Obtained in the Execution of the Resolutions of the Assembly and the Council, Series of League of Nations Publications, V, Legal (Geneva: League of Nations, 1935), 3–5.

20. Walczewska, *Damy,* 23–26.

21. Janusz Rohoziński, "O nurcie kobiecym w literaturze polskiej XX wieku," *Kobiety Polskie. Praca zbiorowa,* ed. Jadwiga Biędrzycka (Warsaw: Książka i Wiedza,

1986), 291; Gabriela Zapolska, *Moralność Pani Dulskiej* (Wrocław: Zakład Narodowy im. Ossolinskich, 1966), 36. Written in 1906, the play was frequently staged in the interwar period, enjoying popular success and sustained attention from critics; Maria Pawlikowska-Jasnorzewska, "Egipska pszenica," and "Zalotnica niebieska," *Dramaty,* vol. 1 (Warsaw: Czytelnik, 1986), 429–556, 681–809. See Maria Kuncewiczowa, *Przymierze z dzieckiem* (Warsaw, 1927), *Cudzoziemka* (Warsaw: Roj, 1939).

22. Karol Irzykowski, *Recenzje teatralne. Wybór* (Warsaw: Państwowy Instytut Wydawniczy, 1965), 212.

23. J. N. Miller, cited in Karol Irzykowski, "Dramat," *Rocznik literacki za rok 1934* (1935): 65; Irzykowski, "Dramat," 65; Stanisław Żak, *Maria Kuncewiczowa* (Kraków: Polska Akademia Nauk, 1971), 5; Rozwiązłe obyczaje," *Rycerz Niepokalanej* 15, no. 5 (May 1936): 141.

24. Huntingdon, *Unsettled Account,* 18.

25. Data from Główny Urząd Statystyczny Rzeczypospolitej Polskiej, *Małżenstwa, urodzenia i zgony: 1927, 1928* (Warsaw, 1934), 28–29, 92–95; *1929, 1930* (Warsaw, 1937), 40–43, 134–37; *1931, 1932* (Warsaw, 1939), 62–65, 200–3. Regina Renz, "Kobiety a planowanie rodziny w latach międzywojennych (w świetle Źródeł kościelnych z Kielecczyzny)," in Żarnowska, *Kobieta i kultura życia codziennego,* 119; Katarzyna Sierakowska, "Matka i dziecko w życiu codziennym rodziny inteligenckiej w Polsce międzywojennej—wzorce stare i nowe," in Żarnowska, *Kobieta i kultura życia codziennego,* 112; Tadeusz Boy-Żelenski, "Piekło kobiet i zaułki paragrafów," *Reflektorem w mrok. Wybór publicystyki* (Warsaw: Państwowy Instytut Wydawniczy, 1978), 260.

26. Renz, "Kobiety a planowanie rodziny," in Żarnowska, *Kobieta i kultura życia codziennego,* 118; Tomasz Weiss, "Wstęp," in Zapolska, *Moralność,* iv–v; Zofia Nałkowska, *Dzienniki 1918–1929* (Warsaw: Czytelnik, 1980), passim.

27. Mary Poovey, *Uneven Developments: The Ideological Work of Gender in Mid-Victorian England* (Chicago: University of Chicago Press, 1988), 3.

28. Edmund Jankowski, *Eliza Orzeszkowa* (Warsaw: Państwowy Instytut Wydawniczy, 1964), 599.

29. M. Naturska, "Znak czasu," *Moja Przyjaciółka* 3, no. 1 (10 January 1936): 3.

30. AC, box 53, vol. 34, no. R6856; box 53, vol. 34, no. R7148.

31. AC, box 48, vol. 21, no. R2233; box 48, vol. 21, no. R1992.

32. AC, box 54, vol. 35, no. R7218. See also AC, box 48, vol. 20, no. R1893; box 36, vol. 3, no. 2199.

33. AC, box 38, vol. 5, no. 6083.

34. AC, box 54, vol. 35, no. R7158; box 54, vol. 35, no. R7391.

35. AC, box 45, vol. 14, no. 14301; AMB, box 33, teczka A, tom 3, Jadwiga Mateuszak.

36. AC, box 45, vol. 15, no. 14459. See also AC, box 42, vol. 10, no. 11528; box 43, vol. 10, no. 11945.

37. AC, box 45, vol. 14, no. 14321. See also AC, box 44, vol. 13, no. 14010; box 45, vol. 14, no. 14279.

38. I. A. Serov, "Regarding the Manner of Conducting the Deportation of the Anti-Soviet Elements from Lithuania, Latvia and Estonia. Strictly Secret," in *An Appeal to Fellow Americans on Behalf of the Baltic States,* United Organizations of

Americans of Lithuanian, Latvian and Estonian Descent (New York: Lithuanian American Information Center, 1944), 31–37.

39. AC, box 45, vol. 14, no. 14282; box 54, vol. 36, no. R7609.

40. AC, box 42, vol. 10, no. 11658; box 41, vol. 8, no. 10623; box 42, vol. 10, no. 11318.

41. See AC, box 41, vol. 8, no. 10689; box 56, vol. 40, no. R9089; box 35, vol. 1, no. 358; box 35, vol. 1, no. 1248; box 41, vol. 8, no. 9995; See AC, box 51, vol. 28, no. R4924; box 37, vol. 3, no. 3494; box 61, vol. 53, no. R14674.

42. MID, box 2, folder 4, "The Situation in Soviet-Occupied Poland."

43. See AC, box 35, vol. 1, no. 1037; box 41, vol. 7, no. 9678.

44. "Without fathers," see AC, box 57, vol. 43, no. R10054; also AC, box 36, vol. 3, no. 2217; box 44, vol. 13, no. 14023.

AC, box 45, vol. 14, no. 14325; box 45, vol. 13, no. 14191; box 42, vol. 10, no. 11653. These are the prisons that initially housed the Polish officers executed by the NKVD in 1940.

45. AC, box 45, vol. 13, no. 14196; box 43, vol. 10, no. 11931; box 43, vol. 11, no. 12507.

46. AC, box 36, vol. 2, no. 1976; box 45, vol. 14, no. 14448. See also AC, box 45, vol. 15, no. 14466.

47. AC, box 43, vol. 10, no. 11942; box 36, vol. 3, no. 2265.

48. AC, box 48, vol. 20, no. R1563.

49. Marian Obertyński, "Rodzina w świetle Wiary," *Rycerz Niepokalanej* 16, no. 1 (January 1937): 6–8; AC, box 45, vol. 14, no. 14317.

50. AC, box 45, vol. 14, no. 14336. See also AC, box 45, vol. 14, no. 14307; box 45, vol. 15, no. 14468.

51. Crying women appear almost as stock characters in men's descriptions. See AC, box 37, vol. 4, no. 3765; box 66, vol. 71, no. 16063; box 53, vol. 32, no. R6331.

52. AC, box 51, vol. 28, no. R4986. See also AC, box 41, vol. 8, no. 10172; box 51, vol. 27, no. R4522.

53. AC, box 36, vol. 2, no. 1907; box 44, vol. 13, no. 14005; box 41, vol. 8, no. 10691.

54. AC, box 37, vol. 4, no. 4238; box 48, vol. 19, no. R1355. See also AC, box 62, vol. 56, no. R15637; box 36, vol. 2, no. 1717; box 54, vol. 37, no. R7911; box 35, vol. 1, no. 1253.

55. AC, box 53, vol. 32, no. R6336. See also AC, box 39, vol. 6, no. 7556; box 44, vol. 13, no. 14007.

56. AC, box 45, vol. 14, no. 14367; box 45, vol. 13, no. 14194; box 56, vol. 41, no. R9233.

57. AC, box 44, vol. 12, no. 12627. See also AC, box 46, vol. 16, no. R00150.

58. AC, box 42, vol. 9, no. 10753; MID, box 198, folder 5, Anonymous, "I Am Forced To Leave My Country."

59. AC, box 45, vol. 14, no. 14291; box 45, vol. 14, no. 14301.

60. See AC, box 53, vol. 33, no. R6813; box 41, vol. 8, no. 9946.

61. AC, box 39, vol. 5, no. 7408. See also AC, box 59, vol. 49, no. R12586; box 37, vol. 4, no. 4264.

62. AC, box 46, vol. 16, no. R00150; box 44, vol. 12, no. 12697. In a piece notable for its frankness, a writer called attention to this reality in an interwar journal:

"In current times the entire burden of raising the young falls on women as mothers. The role of the father—in theory superior and leading, in practice amounts to zero." "Wielki ciężar spada na barki współczesnej matki," *Moja Przyjaciółka* no. 13 (10 July 1936): 262.

63. AC, box 36, vol. 3, no. 2217; box 42, vol. 10, no. 11656; box 46, vol. 15, no. 15527.

64. AC, box 42, vol. 10, no. 11528; box 42, vol. 9, no. 10756; box 45, vol. 14, no. 14317.

65. AC, box 44, vol. 13, no. 13970. See also AC, box 42, vol. 9, no. 10754.

66. AC, box 53, vol. 32, no. R6485; box 36, vol. 2, no. 1717; box 39, vol. 5, no. 6586.

67. See AC, box 51, vol. 29, no. R5159; box 62, vol. 56, no. 15289.

68. AC, box 41, vol. 8, no. 10691; AMB, box 33, teczka A, tom 3, Maria Bogusławska.

69. AC, box 48, vol. 20, no. R1874; box 42, vol. 10, no. 11652; box 43, vol. 10, no. 11690.

70. AC, box 42, vol. 9, no. 10753; box 39, vol. 5, no. 6810; box 42, vol. 10, no. 11676.

71. AC, box 41, vol. 8, no. 10691.

72. AC, box 36, vol. 2, no. 1561; box 39, vol. 5, no. 7355; box 41, vol. 8, no. 10623.

73. AC, box 45, vol. 13, no. 14175; box 43, vol. 10, no. 11942.

74. Goldman, *Women*, 11–12. See Alexandra Kollantai, *Communism and the Family* (London: Pluto Press, 1971).

75. Goldman, *Women*, 316–17, 333.

76. Norman M. Naimark, "The Deportation of the Chechens-Ingush (1944): Ethnic Cleansing in the Soviet Context" (Unpublished manuscript, 1998), 14.

77. Ronald G. Suny, *The Revenge of the Past. Nationalism, Revolution, and the Collapse of the Soviet Union* (Stanford, Calif.: Stanford University Press, 1993), 106.

78. AC, box 55, vol. 38, no. R8405. See also AC, box 41, vol. 8, no. 10052.

79. AC, box 42, vol. 9, no. 10753; box 42, vol. 10, no. 11330; box 42, vol. 9, no. 10753.

80. MID, box 198, folder 5, Anonymous, "I Am Forced To Leave My Country"; AC, box 40, vol. 7, no. 8994; AMB, box 33, teczka A, tom 3, Paulina Rzehaków.

81. AC, box 42, vol. 9, no. 10753; box 43, vol. 11, no. 12507; MID, box 98, folder 7, no. 25.91.

82. U.S. Department of State, *Records of the Department of State Relating to the Internal Affairs of Poland, 1916–1944*, reel 73, 860c.48/706 (Washington, D.C.: National Archives and Record Services, General Services Administration, 1981), letters, 6.

83. AC, box 43, vol. 10, no. 11946.

84. Gross, *Revolution*, 133–34.

85. AMB, box 33, teczka A, tom 3, Anna Szwedko.

86. See AC, box 39, vol. 6, no. 8100; box 43, vol. 10, no. 11902.

87. AC, box 45, vol. 14, no. 14318. See also AC, box 43, vol. 10, no. 11906; box 43, vol. 10, no. 11908.

88. AC, box 40, vol. 7, no. 9067; AMB, box 33, teczka A, tom 3, Bronisława Bartoszowa; Maria Stawowczykowa.

89. AC, box 52, vol. 31, no. R6104; AMB, box 33, teczka A, tom 3, Genowefa Wrzos.

90. AC, box 48, vol. 21, no. R1930; box 41, vol. 9, no. 10721.

91. AC, box 44, vol. 12, no. 12621; box 38, vol. 5, no. 6106.

92. AC, box 43, vol. 10, no. 11945. *Moskale* is a derogatory term used by Poles for Russians.

93. MIK, box 18, folder "November–December 1941," Zajawlenie, "Do Opieki Społecznej przy Ambasadzie w Kujbyszewie."

94. AC, box 48, vol. 21, no. R2258.

95. *Dark Side of the Moon*, 200.

96. AC, box 42, vol. 10, no. 11330.

97. AMB, box 33, teczka A, tom 3, Genowefa Wrzos.

98. AC, box 45, vol. 13, no. 14209.

99. Quoted in Giżejewska, "Deportacje obywateli polskich," in Strzembosz, *Studia z dziejów okupacji Sowieckiej*, 102.

100. See AMB, box 33, teczka A, tom 3, Maria Stawowczykowa; AC, box 40, vol. 7, no. 8994.

101. AC, box 36, vol. 2, no. 1933. I have found no comparable descriptions, in detail or emotional intensity, of the death of a child in men's statements. They typically relate such deaths factually, giving the name, perhaps the date or cause, revealing none of their own feelings. See AC, box 37, vol. 4, no. 3765; box 47, vol. 17, no. R614.

102. See AC, box 42, vol. 10, no. 11638; MID, box 91, folder 12, L. Besiadowska, "A Prisoner's Tale."

103. AC, box 63, letter, 20 December 1941; box 59, vol. 49, no. R12399.

104. AC, box 42, vol. 10, no. 11322.

105. See note 101, this chapter.

106. See AC, box 43, vol. 10, no. 11738; box 45, vol. 14, no. 14326; box 45, vol. 13, no. 14194; box 45, vol. 13, no. 14175.

107. AC, box 43, vol. 10, no. 11937; box 52, vol. 31, no. R6104.

108. AC, box 52, vol. 31, no. R6091; box 46, vol. 15, no. 15527; MID, box 198, folder 5, Anonymous, "I Am Forced To Leave My Country."

109. MIK, box 18, folder "September–November 1941," letter, Matki Polki rejonu Parabiel obl. Nowosybirskiej, to Poselstwa Polskiego w Moskwie; box 18, folder "November–December 1941," Zajawlenie, "Do Opieki Społecznej przy Ambasadzie w Kujbyszewie."

110. AC, box 43, vol. 11, no. 12394.

111. MIK, box 18, folder, "January–August 1942," letter, Dalomea Nieznańska to Kochani Rodacy; 22 March 1942.

112. AC, box 36, vol. 3, no. 2253; box 41, vol. 8, no. 10052.

113. AC, box 41, vol. 8, no. 10691; box 48, vol. 21, no. R2172.

114. AC, box 36, vol. 2, no. 1907. See also AC, box 36, vol. 2, no. 1858; box 48, vol. 21, no. R1965.

115. AC, box 52, vol. 31, no. R6098. See also AC, box 42, vol. 10, no. 11638; box 36, vol. 2, no. 1576.

116. AC, box 42, vol. 10, no. 11639; MID, box 91, folder, 12, Besiadowska; AC, box 44, vol. 13, no. 14008.

117. AC, box 48, vol. 20, no. R1595.

118. AC, box 54, vol. 35, no. R7182; box 45, vol. 15, no. 14459. See also AC, box 39, vol. 5, no. 7179; box 43, vol. 10, no. 11941.

119. AC, box 53, vol. 34, no. R7132; box 48, vol. 21, no. R2242.

120. AC, box 42, vol. 9, no. 10751; box 43, vol. 10, no. 11685.

121. In one instance this "family" numbered 700 deportees. AC, box 42, vol. 10, no. 11676.

122. AC, box 54, vol. 35, no. R7374; box 54, vol. 35, no. R7271; box 48, vol. 20, no. R1567.

123. AC, box 48, vol. 21, no. R1942; box 42, vol. 10, no. 11638; box 52, vol. 30, no. R5632.

124. AC, box 36, vol. 2, no. 1987; box 48, vol. 20, no. R1872.

125. AC, box 48, vol. 21, no. R2010. See also AC, box 56, vol. 42, no. R10021.

126. AC, box 48, vol. 21, no. R2136; box 67, vol. 74, no. 18066; box 46, vol. 16, no. R00150.

127. AC, box 41, vol. 7, no. 9672.

128. AC, box 40, vol. 6, no. 8600. See also AC, box 38, vol. 4, no. 5387; box 37, vol. 4, no. 3661.

129. AC, box 48, vol. 20, no. R1854. See also AC, box 67, vol. 74, no. 17948; box 41, vol. 8, no. 10704.

130. AC, box 47, vol. 18, no. R883; box 56, vol. 41, no. R9400.

131. See AC, box 52, vol. 30, no. R5664; box 67, vol. 74, no. 17983; box 48, vol. 21, no. R1854.

132. AC, box 61, vol. 53, no. R14614; box 39, vol. 6, no. 7556; box 67, vol. 74, no. 17967.

133. See Sybil Milton, "Women and the Holocaust: The Case of German and German-Jewish Women," in *When Biology Became Destiny: Women in Weimar and Nazi Germany,* ed. Renate Bridenthal (New York: Monthly Review Press, 1984), 297–333; Joan Ringelheim, "The Unethical and the Unspeakable: Women and the Holocaust," *Simon Wiesenthal Annual* no. 1 (1984): 69–87; Marlene Heinemann, *Gender and Destiny: Writers and the Holocaust* (Westport, Conn: Greenwood, 1986), 107.

134. AC, box 47, vol. 19, no. R1231.

135. AC, box 45, vol. 14, no. 14341; box 48, vol. 20, no. R1573.

136. AC, box 38, vol. 5, no. 6080. See also AC, box 38, vol. 5, no. 6106; box 48, vol. 21, no. R1949.

137. AC, box 46, vol. 15, no. 15544; box 36, vol. 2, no. 1615; box 48, vol. 21, no. R2179.

138. AC, box 48, vol. 20, no. R1575; box 48, vol. 20, no. R1872.

139. AC, box 37, vol. 3, no. 2401; box 61, vol. 53, no. R14666. See also AC, box 57, vol. 43, no. R10139.

140. AC, box 53, vol. 32, no. R6515; box 37, vol. 4, no. 4238; box 36, vol. 2, no. 1670. See also AC, box 54, vol. 37, no. R7911; box 40, vol. 7, no. 9427.

141. AC, box 52, vol. 30, no. R5664; box 53, vol. 32, no. R6515.

142. AC, box 39, vol. 5, no. 6586.

143. AC, box 58, vol. 47, no. R11774; box 40, vol. 7, no. 8795; box 41, vol. 9, no. 10719.

144. AC, box 44, vol. 12, no. 12697; box 61, vol. 53, no. R14590.

145. AC, box 36, vol. 3, no. 2253; box 45, vol. 15, no. 14455; MID, box 91, folder 12, Besiadowska.

146. AC, box 35, vol. 1, no. 78; box 36, vol. 2, no. 1933. See also AC, box 41, vol. 9, no. 10743; box 53, vol. 33, no. R6811.

147. AC, box 53, vol. 34, no. R7148.

148. AC, box 40, vol. 7, no. 8759; box 41, vol. 8, no. 10687.

149. AC, box 45, vol. 14, no. 14283. See also AC, box 45, vol. 14, no. 14266; box 53, vol. 34, no. R7128.

150. AC, box 45, vol. 13, no. 14189. See also AC, box 38, vol. 5, no. 6335; box 45, vol. 14, no. 14247.

151. MID, box 198, folder 5, Anonymous, "I Am Forced To Leave My Country." The hallmark of nineteenth-century Polish romanticism, this idea was popularized by the national poet Adam Mickiewicz. See Mickiewicz, *Księgi narodu polskiego.*

152. AC, box 39, vol. 5, no. 7127.

153. Maurycy Mochnacki, *Powstanie narodu polskiego w roku 1830 i 1831* vol. 1 (Warsaw, 1984), 217.

Chapter 5

1. The title of this chapter is from Serbian psychotherapist and activist, Lepa Mladjenovic. Cited in Rhonda Copelon, "Surfacing Gender: Reconceptualizing Crimes against Women in Times of War," in *Mass Rape: The War against Women in Bosnia-Herzegovina,* ed. Alexandra Stiglmayer (Lincoln: University of Nebraska Press, 1994), 202.

2. I take this phrase from Regenia Gagnier, *Subjectivities: A History of Self-Representation in Britain, 1832–1920* (New York: Oxford University Press, 1991), 59.

3. AC, box 36, vol. 2, no. 1554. See also AC, box 42, vol. 10, no. 11320; box 43, vol. 10, no. 11705.

4. AC, box 39, vol. 6, no. 8113; box 43, vol. 10, no. 11896; box 43, vol. 11, no. 12173. See also AC, box 36, vol. 2, no. 1557; box 39, vol. 5, no. 7252.

5. AC, box 68, no. 62c, Bohdan Podoski, "Polskie Wschodnie w 1939–1940," 14. Wielhorski calculated the yearly death rate at 20 percent among the deportees and 30 percent among those in the Gulag. Wielhorski, *Los Polaków,* 17–21. Siedlecki, however, states that by late 1941 the number of Polish dead reached 760,000. He claims that by the end of 1942, approximately 50 percent of the exiled Poles had died. Siedlecki, *Losy Polaków,* 47, 135. Sword refers to estimations of the mortality rate of 20 to 30 percent. Sword, *Deportation and Exile,* vii, 27. For new research, see Hryciuk, "Deportacje," in Ciesielski, *Masowe deportacje,* 61; Paczkowski, "Poland," in Courtois, *Black Book,* 372.

6. V. N. Zemskov, "GULAG (Istoriko-sotsiologicheskii aspekt)," *Sotsiologich-eskie issledovaniia* no. 6 (1991): 14–15.

7. AC, box 36, vol. 2, no. 1904; box 36, vol. 2, no. 1914; box 36, vol. 3, no. 2167.

8. AMB, box 33, teczka A, tom 3, Zofia Jurewiczowa; MID, box 98, folder 7, no. 21.19; AC, box 36, vol. 3, no. 2199.

9. AC, box 48, vol. 20, no. R1568.

10. AC, box 48, vol. 20, no. R1583.

11. See AC, box 53, vol. 34, no. R7094; box 39, vol. 6, no. 7628; box 38, vol. 5, no. 6281.

12. AC, box 38, vol. 5, no. 6080.

13. AC, box 38, vol. 5, no. 5638; box 39, vol. 5, no. 6918. On the "conveyer belt," see Conquest, *Great Terror*, 123–24; Evgeniia Semienovna Ginzburg, *Krutoi marshrut. Khronika vremen kul'ta lichnosti* (Milan: Arnoldo Mondadore Editore, 1967), 98–103.

14. AC, box 41, vol. 8, no. 10685.

15. AC, box 36, vol. 2, no. 1969; box 36, vol. 2, no. 1948; box 42, vol. 9, no. 11190.

16. AC, box 40, vol. 7, no. 8995; box 53, vol. 34, no. R6918; box 36, vol. 3, no. 2163.

17. AC, box 41, vol. 8, no. 10623; box 36, vol. 2, no. 1586.

18. AC, box 38, vol. 5, no. 6082; box 44, vol. 13, no. 14008.

19. AC, box 52, vol. 31, no. R6115; MID, box 142, folder 1, Maria Hojak. See also box 36, vol. 2, no. 1969; box 36, vol. 3, no. 2232.

20. AC, box 40, vol. 7, no. 9590. See also AC, box 36, vol. 3, no. 2208; box 44, vol. 13, no. 14005.

21. AC, box 36, vol. 2, no. 1858; box 36, vol. 2, no. 1561; box 45, vol. 13, no. 14189. See also AC, box 43, vol. 10, no. 11698; MID, box 91, folder 1, Anonymous, "The Deportation of Poles to Siberia."

22. AC, box 41, vol. 8, no. 10059.

23. AC, box 36, vol. 2, no. 1950.

24. AC, box 52, vol. 31, no. R6098; box 36, vol. 2, no. 1570.

25. AC, box 48, vol. 21, no. R1955. See also AC, box 43, vol. 11, no. 12164; box 42, vol. 10, no. 11223.

26. AC, box 38, vol. 5, no. 6310. Prisoners were not allowed to sleep during the day, nor to laugh, cry, sew, or write. While reading was not forbidden, the only available material was Communist propaganda, in Russian.

27. AC, box 44, vol. 13, no. 14005; box 48, vol. 21, no. R2172.

28. See AC, box 53, vol. 33, no. R6589; box 46, vol. 16, no. R164; box 38, vol. 5, no. 6111.

29. AC, box 36, vol. 2, no. 1610. See also AC, box 42, vol. 10, no. 11638; box 36, vol. 2, no. 1570.

30. Georges Vigarello, *Concepts of Cleanliness: Changing Attitudes in France Since the Middle Ages*, trans. Jean Birell (Cambridge: Cambridge University Press, 1988), 216.

31. Barbara Duden, *The Woman beneath the Skin: A Doctor's Patients in Eighteenth-Century Germany*, trans. Thomas Dunlap (Cambridge: Harvard University Press, 1991), 15.

32. Vigarello, *Concepts of Cleanliness*, 229–30.

33. Alain Corbin, "Backstage: The Secret of the Individual," in *A History of Private Life*, ed. Michelle Perrot, vol. IV, *From the Fires of Revolution to the Great War*, trans. Arthur Goldhammer (Cambridge: Harvard University Press, 1990), 482.

34. AC, box 43, vol. 10, no. 11944; box 41, vol. 8, no. 10059.

35. AC, box 48, vol. 21, no. R2270; box 42, vol. 9, no. 10745. See also AC, box 35, vol. 1, no. 353; box 43, vol. 10, no. 11710.

36. AC, box 36, vol. 2, no. 1933. See also AC, box 54, vol. 35, no. R7271.

37. Margarete Buber-Neumann, *Under Two Dictators* (New York: Dodd, Mead & Co., 1949), 115.

38. AC, box 36, vol. 2, no. 1545. See also AC, box 50, vol. 26, no. R4353; box 35, vol. 1, no. 52.

39. AC, box 35, vol. 1, no. 835. See also box 41, vol. 8, no. 10693; box 66, vol. 71, no. 16071.

40. This violation often first occurred when the NKVD arrived at the women's homes in Poland. Most people were asleep when the security officers arrived, and many women write that they were forced to dress in the presence of the officers, the first of many similar humiliations. See AC, box 38, vol. 5, no. 6107; box 43, vol. 10, no. 11932.

41. AC, box 54, vol. 35, no. R7190. See also AC, box 48, vol. 21, no. R2172; box 53, vol. 32, no. R6336.

42. AC, box 41, vol. 8, no. 10052; box 48, vol. 20, no. R1593; box 62, vol. 56, no. R15637.

43. AC, box 39, vol. 5, no. 7348; box 43, vol. 10, no. 11711; box 53, vol. 34, no. R7111.

44. AC, box 42, vol. 10, no. 11673. See also AC, box 39, vol. 5, no. 7138; box 48, vol. 21, no. R1950.

45. AC, box 50, vol. 25, no. R3589; box 41, vol. 9, no. 10741.

46. AC, box 39, vol. 5, no. 7109; box 42, vol. 10, no. 11377.

47. See AC, box 36, vol. 2, no. 1587; box 41, vol. 8, no. 9968; AMB, box 33, teczka A, tom 3, Małgorzata Utnik.

48. AC, box 42, vol. 10, no. 11330; box 41, vol. 8, no. 9966; box 35, vol. 1, no. 607.

49. The isolation of the female body from the traditional undefined one occured as part of the creation of the modern body that began in the late eighteenth century. See Duden, *Woman beneath the Skin*, 17–41.

50. AC, box 35, vol. 1, no. 482. See also AC, box 36, vol. 2, no. 1397; box 44, vol. 12, no. 12673.

51. AC, box 35, vol. 1, no. 537; box 41, vol. 8, no. 10693; box 65, vol. 70, no. 15876.

52. AC, box 44, vol. 12, no. 12583.

53. AC, box 38, vol. 4, no. 5339; box 64, vol. 66, no. R15704.

54. AC, box 37, vol. 3, no. 2701; box 38, vol. 5, no. 5723; box 43, vol. 11, no. 12578; box 45, vol. 15, no. 15052.

55. AC, box 41, vol. 8, no. 10623; MID, box 91, folder 12, Besiadowska; AC, box 41, vol. 8, no. 10691.

56. See AC, box 45, vol. 15, no. 14473; box 52, vol. 31, no. R6100; box 53, vol. 34, no. R7109.

57. MID, box 91, folder 12, Besiadowska; AC, box 42, vol. 9, no. 10754.

58. MID, box 91, folder 12, Besiadowska; AC, box 43, vol. 10, no. 11686; box 41, vol. 8, no. 10623.

59. Margaret Miles, *Carnal Knowing: Female Nakedness and Religious Meaning in the Christian West* (Boston: Beacon Press, 1989), 13.

60. Gérard Vincent, "A History of Secrets?" in *A History of Private Life*, ed. Antoine Prost and Gérard Vincent, vol. V, *Riddles of Identity in Modern Times*, trans. Arthur Goldhammer (Cambridge: Harvard University Press, 1991), 171.

61. "Biskupi przeciw dekoltom," *Rycerz Niepokalanej* 5, no. 9 (September

1926): 275; "Krótkie sukienki i tańce powodem gruźlicy," *Rycerz Niepokalanej* 7, no. 3 (March 1928): 78.

62. A. K., "Przykre, ale konieczne. . . ," *Rycerz Niepokalanej* 7, no. 10 (1928): 294. According to a characteristic article, the loss of the feeling of shame preceded mental illness. J., "Ważne słowa lekarzy," *Rycerz Niepokalanej* 6, no. 10 (October 1927): 308. One woman recalls attending a Catholic boarding school for girls in Warsaw in the 1930s, where the nuns required the girls to wear slips while bathing, considering it "sinful to look at one's own body." Christine Zamoyska-Panek, *Have You Forgotten? A Memoir of Poland 1939–1945* (New York: Doubleday, 1989), 16.

63. Uczestnicy Diecezjalnego Kongresu Eucharystycznego w Łodzi, "Rezolucje diecezjalnego Kongresu Eucharystycznego w Łodzi," *Rycerz Niepokalanej* 7, no. 9 (September 1928): 259.

64. AC, box 41, vol. 9, no. 10743; box 41, vol. 9, no. 10722.

65. AC, box 41, vol. 8, no. 10691; box 38, vol. 5, no. 6080. See also AC, box 36, vol. 3, no. 2186; box 55, vol. 39, no. R8585.

66. AC, box 42, vol. 9, no. 10756; box 53, vol. 34, no. R7094. Deportees report having aspersions cast on their chastity due to the socioeconomic position of male relatives. Elżbieta and Janina Kaliga both note that when the NKVD came to deport them, the agents called them "unclean" women because they were the daughters of a policeman and sisters of an officer. MID, box 142, folder 1, Tarnopol, nos. 8134 and 8135.

67. AC, box 39, vol. 6, no. 7628; box 38, vol. 5, no. 6281. Men, too, were called "bitch" and "prostitute" by their Russian guards and interrogators, whose favorite epithet seemed to be "fuck your mother." AC, box 49, vol. 24, no. R3165; box 41, vol. 7, no. 9690.

68. AC, box 53, vol. 34, no. R6915; box 36, vol. 3, no. 2186.

69. AC, box 36, vol. 2, no. 1555; box 48, vol. 21, no. R1980; box 53, vol. 32, no. R6336.

70. AMB, box 33, tom 3, Eugenia Pióro.

71. AC, box 40, vol. 7, no. 9590. See also AC, box 39, vol. 5, no. 7109; box 42, vol. 10, no. 11638. It is unclear if this practice represented a deliberate attempt to humiliate Polish women. Contrary to Polish accounts, women of other nationalities report that only female guards searched women. See Buber-Neumann, *Under Two Dictators,* 27; Ginzburg, *Krutoi marshrut,* 266; Elinor Lipper, *Eleven Years in Soviet Prisons* (Chicago: Henry Regnery Co., 1951), 6, 205.

72. AC, box 41, vol. 8, no. 10691.

73. AC, box 38, vol. 5, no. 6335; box 53, vol. 32, no. R6337. See also AC, box 36, vol. 2, no. 1884; box 43, vol. 10, no. 11698.

74. See AC, box 36, vol. 2, no. 2126; box 41, vol. 8, no. 10687.

75. AC, box 35, vol. 1, no. 537; box 41, vol. 8, no. 10696. See also AC, box 40, vol. 6, no. 8600; box 39, vol. 5, no. 6900.

76. AC, box 35, vol. 1, no. 835. See also AC, box 41, vol. 8, no. 10172. One man recalls being "startled and embarrassed" by an anal inspection. Janusz Bardach and Kathleen Gleeson, *Man Is Wolf to Man: Surviving the Gulag* (Berkeley: University of California Press, 1999), 198.

77. See AC, box 64, vol. 66, no. R15704; box 66, vol. 71, no. 16068.

78. AC, box 36, vol. 2, no. 1884.

79. MID, box 91, folder 12, Besiadowska; AC, box 42, vol. 9, no. 10756.

80. AC, box 43, vol. 10, no. 11942; box 41, vol. 8, no. 10623; box 41, vol. 8, no. 10059; MID, box 91, folder 12, Besiadowska; AC, box 53, vol. 34, no. R7094.

81. Lipper, *Eleven Years*, 150, 95, 157. See also Hilda Vitzthum, *Torn Out by the Roots: The Recollections of a Former Communist* (Lincoln: University of Nebraska Press, 1993), 172.

82. Valery Chalidze, *Criminal Russia: Essays on Crime in the Soviet Union*, trans. P. S. Falla (New York: Random House, 1977), 64. See also Conquest, *Great Terror*, 315.

83. AC, box 44, vol. 12, no. 12598.

84. AC, box 44, vol. 13, no. 13971.

85. Chalidze, *Criminal Russia*, 70. See Buber-Neumann, *Under Two Dictators*, 72; Lipper, *Eleven Years*, 93, 148.

86. AC, box 44, vol. 12, no. 12598.

87. Vitzhum, *Torn Out*, 134; Lipper, *Eleven Years*, 118–19, 159–61; *Dark Side of the Moon*, 155; Gustaw Herling-Grudziński, *Inny świat. Zapiski sowieckie* (Warsaw: Czytelnik, 1991), 45–49; Aleksandr I. Solzhenitsyn, *The Gulag Archipelago, 1918–1956. An Experiment in Literary Investigation*, Part III, 1st ed., trans. Thomas P. Whitney (New York: Harper & Row Publishers, 1975), 229–34.

88. AC, box 43, vol. 10, no. 11698.

89. AC, box 44, vol. 12, no. 12598. See also AC, box 46, vol. 16, no. R164.

90. MID, box 91, folder 12, Besiadowska; AC, box 42, vol. 10, no. 11658.

91. AC, box 43, vol. 10, no. 11698.

92. AC, box 38, vol. 5, no. 6103; box 48, vol. 20, no. R1617.

93. One woman writes that she reported a night raid on her hut by a band of local Kazakhs to the police but was charged with making a false report. AMB, box 33, teczka A, tom 3, Janina Dukjetowa.

94. AC, box 41, vol. 8, no. 9966; box 53, vol. 34, no. R7104.

95. MID, box 91, folder 12, Besiadowska. See also AC, box 40, vol. 6, no. 8413.

96. MID, box 198, folder 8, Halpern. See also AC, box 43, vol. 10, no. 11940; box 48, vol. 20, no. R1898.

97. MID, box 91, folder 12, Besiadowska; AC, box 43, vol. 10, no. 11941.

98. Chalidze, *Criminal Russia*, 198.

99. Ciesielski, *Polacy w Kazachstanie*, 72.

100. AC, box 48, vol. 21, no. R1914; box 44, vol. 13, no. 13971.

101. Jane Schultz, "Mute Fury: Southern Women's Diaries of Sherman's March to the Sea, 1864–1865," in *Arms and the Woman: War, Gender and Literary Representation*, ed. Helen Cooper, Adrienne Ruslander Munich, and Susan Merrill Squier (Chapel Hill: University of North Carolina Press, 1989), 60.

102. Vera Folnegovic-Smalc, "Psychiatric Aspects of the Rapes in the War against the Republics of Croatia and Bosnia-Herzegovinia," in Stiglmayer, *Mass Rape*, 176. See also Alexandra Stiglmayer, "The Rapes in Bosnia-Herzegovinia," in Stiglmayer, *Mass Rape*, 83, 101, 133.

103. AC, box 41, vol. 8, no. 10691.

104. AC, box 48, vol. 20, no. R1617; box 42, vol. 10, no. 11637.

105. AC, box 41, vol. 8, no. 10059; box 42, vol. 10, no. 11658; MID, box 91, folder 12, Besiadowska. See also AC, box 36, vol. 2, no. 1610; box 40, vol. 6, no. 8413.

106. AC, box 43, vol. 10, no. 11705.

107. Klaus Theweleit, "The Bomb's Womb and the Gender of War (War Goes

on Preventing Women from Becoming the Mothers of Invention)," in Cooke, *Gendering War Talk,* 308.

108. AC, box 43, vol. 10, no. 11898.

109. Schultz, "Mute Fury," in Cooper, *Arms and the Woman,* 72.

110. Copelon, "Surfacing Gender," in Stiglmayer, *Mass Rape,* 200.

111. Appendix C, Document no. 43, in *The Other Balkan Wars: A 1913 Carnegie Endowment Inquiry in Retrospect* (New York: Carnegie Endowment for International Peace, 1993), 304–5.

112. Norman M. Naimark, *The Russians in Germany: A History of the Soviet Zone of Occupation, 1945–1949* (Cambridge: Harvard University Press, 1995), 86, 81.

113. Slavenka Drakulic, "Women Hide behind a Wall of Silence: Mass Rape in Bosnia," *Nation* 256, no. 8 (1 March 1993): 271.

114. AC, box 38, vol. 5, no. 6082; box 39, vol. 5, no. 7365. Similar reports come from earlier occupations. Zofia Nowosielska, for example, writes that during WWI she, as a Polish woman, rejected all advances and courtesies from German and Russian officers; as a matter of patriotism and honor, flirting with the enemy was incomprehensible. Zofia Nowosielska, *In the Hurricane of War. Memoirs of a Woman Soldier* (n.p.: The Author, 1929), 37, 40, 44.

115. AC, box 37, vol. 3, no. 2555; box 35, vol. 1, no. 482.

116. Cited in Wierzbicki, "Stosunki polsko-białoruskie," in Strzembosz, *Studia z dziejów okupacji Sowieckiej,* 33.

117. AC, box 41, vol. 8, no. 10687.

118. See AC, box 36, vol. 2, no. 1393; box 44, vol. 12, no. 12583; box 45, vol. 15, no. 15051. I have not seen any reports of the sexual abuse of men in the testimonies. One man from Poland, originally forced into the Red Army and then imprisoned in the Gulag, writes about the rape of men in his memoir, published in 1999. He makes it clear that such rapes were common. Bardach, *Man Is Wolf,* 125, 293–94.

119. MID, box 98, folder 6, Świaniewicz, 16; AC, box 52, vol. 29, no. R5337.

120. Theweleit, "The Bomb's Womb," in Cooke, *Gendering War Talk,* 307. Emphasis in original.

121. Ruth Seifert, "War and Rape: A Preliminary Analysis," in Stiglmayer, *Mass Rape,* 68.

122. Annemarie Tröger, "Between Rape and Prostitution: Survival Strategies and Chances of Emancipation for Berlin Women after World War II," in *Women in Culture and Politics: A Century of Change,* ed. Judith Friedlander et al. (Bloomington: Indiana University Press, 1986), 97. Tröger demonstrates the normalization, during this chaotic period, of sexual relations that ordinarily would have been considered illegitimate and shameful, a phenomenon also found by historians of the Holocaust. See Milton, "Women and the Holocaust," in Bridenthal, *When Biology Became Destiny,* 315–16.

123. Tröger, "Between Rape and Prostitution," in Friedlander, *Women in Culture,* 111. The topic of sexual violation was so taboo among the Poles that it may have precluded the recognition of bonds between women. A deporteee who endured an attempted rape in Kazakhstan notes that she revealed her experience to no one—not even her best female friend in the settlement; she was only able to write about it forty years later. Huntingdon, *Unsettled Account,* 107.

124. Atina Grossmann, "A Question of Silence: The Rape of German Women by Occupation Soldiers," *October* 72 (spring 1995): 62.

125. This idea comes from Margaret Miles, who writes that adequate self-representation requires two conditions: public space and collective voice. Miles, *Carnal Knowing*, 84.

126. Published wartime memoirs by Polish women suggest that the fear and danger of rape were ubiquitous. Ida Kasprzak, an officer in the Home Army, relates encountering several drunken Polish men in the sewers of Warsaw; as soon as she spotted them, she was convinced they would try to rape her. "Uprising in Poland, 1939–1945," in Shelley Saywell, *Women in War* (Markham, Ontario: Viking, 1985), 113. Wanda Półtawska recalls several harrowing incidents after her release from the Ravensbrück concentration camp in which men of various nationalities tried to rape her. Wanda Półtawska, *I boję się snów* (Warsaw: Czytelnik, 1962), 154–64. Both women report escaping from these situations.

127. Seifert, "War and Rape," in Stiglmayer, *Mass Rape*, 55.

128. AC, box 39, vol. 5, no. 6710; box 41, vol. 8, no. 10689.

129. AC, box 41, vol. 8, no. 10691; MID, box 91, folder 12, Besiadowska.

130. Heinemann, *Gender and Destiny*, 18–21.

131. AC, box 47, vol. 19, no. R1231.

132. See Dominik Lasok, ed., *Polish Civil Law* vol. 1 (Leiden: A. W. Sijthoff, 1973).

133. Tadeusz Boy-Żeleński, *Piekło Kobiet. Jak skończyć z piekłem kobiet?* (Warsaw: Państwowy Instytut Wydawniczy, 1960), 170–71. The paragraph alluded to stipulated stringent penalties for abortion. See also Wanda Krahelska-Mackiewiczowa, "Pracy należy się szacunek," *Moja Przyjaciółka* 6, no. 14 (25 July 1939): 412.

134. Dobrochna Kałwa, "Głosy kobiet w sprawie planowania rodziny w świetle prasy z lat 1929–1932," in Żarnowska, *Kobieta i kultura życia codziennego*, 128.

135. Walczewska, *Damy*, 137.

136. AC, box 54, vol. 35, no. R7391; box 43, vol. 11, no. 12149; MID, box 142, folder 1, Maria Hojak; AMB, box 33, teczka A, tom 3, Janina Bilińska, Paulina Rzehaków.

137. See A. K., "Kult Niepokalanej jako potrzeba obecnej chwili," *Rycerz Niepokalanej* 6, no. 12 (December 1927): 344–45; Rr., "Niepokalana a dzisiejsza niewiasta Polska," *Rycerz Niepokalanej* 15, no. 12 (December 1936): 351–53.

138. The admission of an active sexual life, even socially "illegitimate," appears possible with the passage of a great deal of time. For example, Adina Blady Szwajger, a Polish Jew, writes openly about the sex lives of young Jews in hiding during WW II, including her own pregnancy and abortion. Significantly, she writes her account in 1990 when facing death. Adina Blady Szwajger, *I więcej nic nie pamiętam* (Warsaw: Volumen, 1994), 84, 113–14, 7. Another admission of an illicit sexual relationship (both parties were married) comes from Hilda Vitzhum, who wrote of her experiences in the Gulag only in 1993. Vitzthum, *Torn Out*, 190–223.

139. Walczewska, *Damy*, 136.

140. MID, box 91, folder 9, "Deportations from Soviet-Occupied Polish Territories," 7.

141. Półtawska, *I boję się snów*, 97–98; HIA, Stefania Lotocka, "Those Who Obeyed Orders," typescript memoir, 1966, 110.

142. Kathleen Canning, "Feminist History after the Linguistic Turn: Historicizing Discourse and Experience," *Signs: Journal of Women in Culture and Society* 19, no. 2 (winter 1994): 393.

Part III

1. Eley and Suny, "Introduction," in Eley, *Becoming National*, 19.
2. AC, box 35, vol. 1, no. 353.
3. See AC, box 39, vol. 5, no. 7482; box 48, vol. 20, no. R1617.
4. Only a few individuals report that Poles constituted the majority of the prison or camp populations in which they resided. See AC, box 38, vol. 5, no. 6094; box 52, vol. 30, no. R5644.
5. AC, box 39, vol. 5, no. 7481; box 44, vol. 13, no. 14008; box 38, vol. 5, no. 6084.
6. J. Arch Getty, Gabor Rittersporn, and Viktor Zemskov, "Victims of the Soviet Penal System in the Pre-war Years: A First Approach on the Basis of Archival Evidence," *American Historical Review* 98, no. 4 (1993): 1028–29.
7. See AC, box 46, vol. 15, no. 15544; box 48, vol. 20, no. R1878; box 48, vol. 21, no. R1944.
8. According to recent estimates, 1,802,392 alleged kulaks and their families were exiled from the central districts in 1930–1931. Getty, Rittersporn, and Zemskov, "Victims of the Soviet Penal System," 1024.
9. The signing of the Treaty of Riga in 1921, which established the Polish-Soviet border, left between 1 and 1.5 million Poles on Soviet territory, mostly in Ukraine and Belorussia. After 1934, they were subjected to severe repression, and from 1934–1938 approximately 50,000 Soviet Poles were deported to Kazakhstan. See John Lowell Armstrong, "Policy toward the Polish Minority in the Soviet Union, 1923–89," *Polish Review* 35, no. 1 (1990): 51–65; Iwanów, *Pierwszy naród ukarany*; Stanisław Ciesielski and Antoni Kuczyński, eds., *Polacy w Kazachstanie. Historia i współczesność* (Wrocław, Poland: Wydawnictwo Uniwersytetu Wrocławskiego, 1996).
10. Nira Yuval-Davies and Floya Anthias, "Introduction," in *Woman-Nation-State*, ed. Nira Yuval-Davies and Floya Anthias (London: Macmillan, 1989), 7.

Chapter 6

1. I take this term from Judith Butler, *Gender Trouble: Feminism and the Subversion of Identity* (New York: Routledge, 1990), 16–25.
2. The remaining 5 percent included Germans, Lithuanians, Russians, Czechs, and those who called themselves "local." Data from *Drugi Powszechny Spis,* 15. Doubting the accuracy of government figures, particularly regarding the Slavic minorities in the east, Jerzy Tomaszewski offers revised figures: Poles 65 percent, Ukrainians 16 percent, Jews 10 percent, and Belorussians 6 percent. Jerzy Tomaszewski, *Rzeczpospolita wielu narodów* (Warsaw: Czytelnik, 1985), 35.
3. "Ustawa z dnia 17 marca 1921 roku Konstytucja Rzeczypospolitej Polskiej," *Dziennik ustaw Rzeczypospolitej Polskiej,* no. 44 (1 June 1921): 650.
4. The "Piast Concept" of Poland, associated with Roman Dmowski and the peasantist and nationalist camps, stood for an ethnically pure Poland, strongly allied to Roman Catholicism. The opposing "Jagiellonian Concept," linked with Józef Piłsudski and more liberal thinkers, advocated the reunification of Poland and Lithuania, forming a federation of the border nations. It stressed the unity of different nationalities within one state. See Piotr Wandycz, "Poland's Place in Europe

in the Concepts of Pilsudski and Dmowski," *East European Politics and Society* 4, no. 3 (1990): 451–68.

5. Porter, *When Nationalism*, 6.

6. On Polish political romanticism (1830–48), see Walicki, *Philosophy and Romantic Nationalism.*

7. Porter, *When Nationalism*, 38.

8. Jedlicki, *Suburb of Europe*, 221; Porter, *When Nationalism*, 50.

9. Porter, *When Nationalism*, 158.

10. Theodore Weeks, *Nation and State in Late Imperial Russia: Nationalism and Russification on the Western Frontier, 1863–1914* (Dekalb: Northern Illinois University Press, 1996), 116. Prior to the 1880s, anti-Semitism, though certainly present, was not part of the Polish patriotic tradition.

11. William Hagen, "Before the 'Final Solution': Toward a Comparative Analysis of Political Anti-Semitism in Interwar Germany and Poland," *Journal of Modern History* 68, no. 2 (June 1996): 368. On national relations in Poland between the wars see Aleksandra Bergman, *Sprawy Białoruskie w II Rzeczypospolitej* (Warsaw: PAN, 1984); Andrzej Chojnowski, *Koncepcje polityki narodowościowej rządów polskich w latach 1921–1939* (Wrocław: Nakład Narodowy im. Ossolińskich, 1979); Wrzesiński, *Między Polską;* Tomaszewski, *Rzeczpospolita.*

12. The final 3 percent included Lithuanians, Russians, and Germans. In 1931, the population of the eight provinces of eastern Poland totaled approximately 13 million.

13. Jerzy Tomaszewski, "Kresy Wschodnie w polskiej myśli politycznej XIX i XX wiekach," in Wrzesiński, *Między Polską,* 101–5.

14. Hagen, "Before the 'Final Solution,'" 379. The literature on interwar Polish-Jewish relations is large and growing. See for example, Chimen Abramsky, Maciej Jachimczyk, and Antony Polonsky, eds., *The Jews in Poland* (London: Basil Blackwell, 1986); Władysław Bartoszewski, *Ethnocentrism: Beliefs and Stereotypes. A Study of Polish-Jewish Relations in the Early Twentieth Century* (Cambridge: University of Cambridge, 1984); Jerzy Tomaszewski, *Najnowsze dzieje Żydów w Polsce* (Warsaw: PWN, 1993).

15. Tomaszewski, *Rzeczpospolita,* 40.

16. See Roman Wapiński, "Kresy: alternatywa czy zależność?" in Wrzesiński, *Między Polską,* 10–11; Jacek Kolbuszewski, "Legenda kresów w literaturze Polskiej XIX i XX w.," in Wrzesiński, *Między Polską,* 47–95.

17. Jan Słomka, *From Serfdom to Self-Government: Memoirs of a Polish Village Mayor 1842–1927*, trans. William John Rose (London: Minerva Publishing Co., 1941), 171.

18. Juliusz Bardach, "O świadomości narodowej Polaków na Litwie i Białorusi w XIX–XX w.," in Wrzesiński, *Między Polską,* 268.

19. Both the Polish and Soviet governments hoped that their Ukrainian and Belorussian populations would attract discontented "ethnic brethren" from across the border. Martin, "Origins," 830–31, 842–46.

20. See Walicki, *Enlightenment and Birth;* Wielhorski is discussed in Bardach, "O świadomości narodowej," 237–38; Hobsbawm, *Nations and Nationalisms,* 93.

21. Czesław Miłosz, *Native Realm: A Search for Self-Definition*, trans. Catherine Leach (Garden City, NY: Doubleday & Co., 1968), 24. To this mélange should also be added Belorussian blood.

22. Quoted in Bardach, "O świadomości narodowej," in Wrzesiński, *Między Polską*, 258.

23. Władysław Bartoszewski, *The Convent at Auschwitz* (London: Bowerdean Press, 1990), 60. In the 1921 census, 26 percent of the people recording themselves as Jews by religion claimed their nationality as Polish. See Mendelsohn, *Jews of East Central Europe*, 29.

24. Joseph Lichten, "Jewish Assimilation in Poland, 1863–1943," in Abramsky, *Jews in Poland*, 124.

25. Tomaszewski, *Rzeczpospolita*, 35. Intermarriage provides evidence of this. In 1927, for example, 16.2 percent of the total marriages in Eastern Galicia took place between Poles and Ukrainians. Stanisław Skrzypek, *The Problem of Galicia* (London: Polish Association for the South Eastern Provinces, 1948), 23.

26. Żarnowski, *Społeczeństwo*, 373. See also Tomaszewski, *Rzeczpospolita*, 125–26; Orest Subtelny, *Ukraine: A History* (Toronto: University of Toronto Press, 1994), 428.

27. Wapiński, "Kresy," in Wrzesiński, *Między Polską*, 10. Bardach expresses the same opinion. Bardach, "O świadomości narodowej," in Wrzesiński, *Między Polską*, 268.

28. Mendelsohn, *Jews of East Central Europe*, 21.

29. Grudzińska-Gross, *War through Children's Eyes*, 6.

30. Pawel Korzec and Jean-Charles Szurek, "Jews and Poles under Soviet Occupation (1939–1941): Conflicting Interests," *Polin* 4 (1989): 217.

31. Gross, *Revolution*, 29.

32. Aleksander Smolar, "Jews as a Polish Problem," *Daedalus* (spring 1987): 38.

33. Report excerpted in Korzec, "Jews and Poles," 206. One of the first messengers to carry word of the brutal treatment of Jews in Poland by the Nazis, Karski cannot be dismissed as a biased Polish patriot. His reports contain sympathetic accounts of the Jews, as well as criticism of ethnic Poles.

34. Quoted in Tadeusz Piotrowski, *Poland's Holocaust* (Jefferson, N.C.: McFarland & Co., 1998), 50. See also Smolar, "Jews as a Polish Problem," 39; Aleksander Wat, *Mój wiek. Pamiętnik mówiony*, vol. 1 (London: Polonia Book Fund, 1977), 298. Jan Gross disputes the claim that Jews joined the new administration in large numbers and benefited from the establishment of Communist rule, concluding, "The Jewish community suffered probably the heaviest adverse impact of Sovietization." Jan Gross, "A Tangled Web: Confronting Stereotypes Concerning Relations between Poles, Germans, Jews, and Communists," in *The Politics of Retribution in Europe: World War II and Its Aftermath*, ed., Istvan Deak, Jan Gross, and Tony Judt (Princeton, N.J.: Princeton University Press, 2000), 103. See also Jan Gross, *Neighbors: The Destruction of the Jewish Community in Jedwabne, Poland* (Princeton, N.J.: Princeton University Press, 2001), 41–53.

35. According to Jaff Schatz, in interwar Poland never less than 22 percent of Communist Party members were Jews. In cities, they typically made up 50–60 percent of the Communists, reaching a peak of 65 percent in Warsaw in 1937. Also, the proportion of Jewish members of the Communist youth organizations exceeded 50 percent. Jaff Schatz, *The Generation: The Rise and Fall of the Jewish Communists of Poland* (Berkeley: University of California Press, 1991), 96–97. Despite the overrepresentation of Jews in the Communist Party, Schatz calculates that only 5 percent of all Jewish voters felt sympathetic to Communist ideals.

36. Karski adds, "Their attitude seems to me quite understandable." Korzec, "Jews and Poles," 207. In similar fashion, writing in 1957 another Pole blames anti-Semitism for Jewish support of the invaders: "The welcome extended to the Bolsheviks was above all a demonstration of a separate identity, of being different from those against whom the Soviets were waging war—from the Poles—a refusal to be identified with the Polish state. We must not pretend that we do not realize this, or fail to admit that it was a result of our own policies and of our anti-Semitism." Adam Uziembło, quoted in Smolar, "Jews as a Polish Problem," 39.

37. Korzec, "Jews and Poles," 214.

38. Korzec, "Jews and Poles," 220.

39. Smolar, "Jews as a Polish Problem," 38; Gross, *Revolution*, 31; Subtelny, *Ukraine*, 453–55.

40. Grudzińska-Gross, *War through Children's Eyes*, 9–10, 18–19.

41. Grudzińska-Gross, *War through Children's Eyes*, 6–7, 14; Mikołaj Iwanow, "The Belorussians of Eastern Poland under Soviet Occupation, 1939–41," in Sword, *Soviet Takeover*, 258–59; Gross, *Revolution*, 31.

42. Grudzińska-Gross, *War through Children's Eyes*, 9–10, 18–19; Wierzbicki, "Stosunki polsko-białoruskie," in Strzembosz, *Studia z dziejów okupacji Sowieckiej*, 7–10, 39.

43. Korzec, "Jews and Poles," 207.

44. Gross argues forcefully against the claim that Polish violence against the Jews under the German occupation was merely retributive. Gross, "Tangled Web," in Deak et al., *Politics of Retribution*, 74–116.

45. AC, box 76, AWBD, "Notatka Służbowa" 080543, 8 May 1943.

46. Siemaszko, "Mass Deportations," in Sword, *Soviet Takeover*, 231. According to research based on NKVD documents, among the deportees 63 percent were Poles, 22 percent Jews, 8 percent Ukrainians, 6 percent Belorussians, and the final 1 percent "others." Hryciuk, "Deportacje," in Ciesielski, *Masowe deportacje*, 68.

47. See Yosef Litvak, "The Plight of the Refugees from the German-Occupied Territories," in Sword, *Soviet Takeover*, 57–70. Ironically, deportation probably saved these Jews from a worse fate under the Nazis.

48. See AC, box 36, vol. 93, no. 2208; box 40, vol. 7, no. 8995. For a sympathetic attitude toward the plight of the Jews, see AC, box 41, vol. 9, no. 10721.

49. AC, box 36, vol. 2, no. 1871; box 42, vol. 9, no. 10756; box 36, vol. 2, no. 1555; box 36, vol. 3, no. 2163.

50. AC, box 46, vol. 15, no. 15544.

51. AC, box 48, vol. 21, no. R1984; box 52, vol. 30, no. R5654; box 41, vol. 8, no. 10068.

52. AC, box 36, vol. 2, no. 1610; box 44, vol. 12, no. 12598.

53. Historian Joachim Lelewel, for example, wrote in 1836: "Already for centuries the Ruthenian, Polish and Lithuanian languages have been brothers; they constitute no national division among themselves." Quoted in Brock, "Polish Nationalism," in Sugar, *Nationalism in Eastern Europe*, 322.

54. AC, box 38, vol. 5, no. 6106.

55. AC, box 39, vol. 5, no. 7481; box 44, vol. 12, no. 12624; box 48, vol. 21, no. R1940; box 48, vol. 21, no. R1946.

56. AC, box 38, vol. 5, no. 5638. See also AC, box 43, vol. 10, no. 11918; box 36, vol. 2, no. 1570.

57. AC, box 75, AWBD, no. D1267, Helena Antonewicza, "To co wiedziałam i przeżyłam w Rosji sowieckiej w latach 1940–1942."

58. AC, box 36, vol. 2, no 1555.

59. AC, box 38, vol. 5, no. 6106. The word *pan* in the Polish language is a polite form of address, like the English "Sir," used in everyday speech. The Soviets commonly used it to jeer at the Poles. In this pejorative sense, it would best translate as "lord."

60. AC, box 48, vol. 20, no. R1565; box 36, vol. 2, no. 1561.

61. AC, box 36, vol. 2, no. 1610.

62. AC, box 75, AWBD, no. D1267. Poles also accuse Ukrainians of being two-faced, supporting the other enemy of the Poles, the Germans. See AC, box 48, vol. 20, no. R1565; box 53, vol. 34, no. R6922.

63. Ola Watowa, *Wszystko co najważniejsze: rozmowy z Jackiem Trznadlem* (London: Puls Publications, 1984), 85–92.

64. AC, box 54, vol. 36, no. R7842; box 36, vol. 3, no. 2163; box 41, vol. 8, no. 10623; box 39, vol. 5, no. 6812.

65. On Jews, see AC, box 41, vol. 8, no. 10052; box 44, vol. 12, no. 12598. On Belorussians, see AC, box 36, vol. 2, no. 1871; box 54, vol. 35, no. R7347. On Ukrainians, see AC, box 48, vol. 21, no. R1914; box 55, vol. 37, no. R8078.

66. AMB, box 33, teczka A, tom 3, Antonina Siemińska.

67. See AC, box 41, vol. 8, no. 10074; box 52, vol. 30, no. R5632; box 54, vol. 37, no. R8073.

68. AC, box 44, vol. 12, no. 12627; box 39, vol. 6, no. 8128.

69. AC, box 52, vol. 30, no. R5654; box 48, vol. 20, no. R1868; box 38, vol. 5, no. 6094.

70. AC, box 44, vol. 13, no. 13970.

71. See AC, box 36, vol. 2, no. 1610; box 41, vol. 8, no. 10623.

72. AC, box 41, vol. 8, no. 10623. See also AC, box 44, vol. 12, no. 12621; box 44, vol. 12, no. 12701; box 54, vol. 35, no. R7184.

73. AC, box 41, vol. 8, no. 10052; box 48, vol. 20, no. R1874.

74. AC, box 48, vol. 21, no. R1965. See also AC, box 48, vol. 21, no. R1996; box 52, vol. 31, no. R6091.

75. AC, box 38, vol. 5, no. 5638; box 52, vol. 30, no. R5646; box 48, vol. 20, no. R1868.

76. Aleksandrs Birznieks, "I Was Twenty-One," in *We Sang through Tears: Stories of Survival in Siberia* (Riga: Janis Roze Publishers, 1999), 303.

77. Wat, *Mój wiek*, vol. 1, 335–36.

78. Julianne Burton, "Don (Juanito) Duck and the Imperial-Patriarchal Unconscious: Disney Studios, the Good Neighbor Policy, and the Packaging of Latin America," in Parker, *Nationalisms & Sexualities*, 32–33.

79. AC, box 54, vol. 35, no. R7184. See also AC, box 39, vol. 5, no. 7365; box 52, vol. 31, no. R6091.

80. AC, box 41, vol. 8, no. 10052. A rare comment on men of other nationalities appears in this connection. One woman reports with disdain that, in contrast to the Polish women, the imprisoned men—mostly Jews—did not "bring themselves to the point of protesting" the beatings. AC, box 39, vol. 5, no. 7481.

81. AC, box 48, vol. 20, no. R1880; box 41, vol. 8, no. 10056; box 48, vol. 21, no. R2200.

82. See AC, box 41, vol. 8, no. 10623; box 42, vol. 10, no. 11245; box 43, vol. 10, no. 11922; box 44, vol. 12, no. 12699.

83. AC, box 43, vol. 10, no. 11942; box 44, vol. 12, no. 12698; box 41, vol. 8, no. 10439; box 65, vol. 69, no. 15797. See also AC, box 45, vol. 14, no. 14442; box 45, vol. 15, no. 14470.

84. AC, box 39, vol. 5, no. 7365.

85. AC, box 44, vol. 12, no. 12598.

86. AC, box 41, vol. 8, no. 10052; box 44, vol. 12, no. 12629.

87. Zamoyska-Panek, *Have You Forgotten?* 186.

88. Miłosz, *Native Realm*, 28.

89. Geraldine Heng and Janadas Devan, "State Fatherhood: The Politics of Nationalism, Sexuality and Race in Singapore," in Parker, *Nationalisms & Sexualities,* 353.

90. Quoted in Abraham Brumberg, "Murder Most Foul," *Times Literary Supplement* (2 March 2001). On the issue of Polish wartime collaboration, see Gross, *Neighbors,* 152–63.

91. Bartoszewski, *Convent at Auschwitz,* 17.

92. AC, box 39, vol. 6, no. 7900.

93. AC box 52, vol. 30, no. R5640; box 54, vol. 35, no. R7167; box 44, vol. 12, no. 12627.

94. AC, box 67, vol. 74, no. 17948; box 40, vol. 6, no. 8600; box 38, vol. 5, no. 5532; box 48, vol. 20, no. R1854. See also AC, box 62, vol. 56, no. R15289; box 41, vol. 8, no. 10687; box 47, vol. 18, no. R1236.

95. A few examples will suffice. According to Czesław Spaczyński, the Jews considered the Soviet occupation heaven on earth. Cezary Makarewicz recounts paying a Ukrainian guide to secret him out of Poland, who turned him over to the NKVD at the border. The Belorussians, a teacher notes, taunted the Poles, jeering, "Your rule is over." AC, box 45, vol. 14, no. 14333; box 48, vol. 22, no. R2437; box 42, vol. 9, no. 10942.

96. AC, box 55, vol. 40, no. R8808. See also AC, box 48, vol. 20, no. R1854.

97. AC, box 37, vol. 4, no. 4502; box 41, vol. 8, no. 10696. See also AC, box 48, vol. 21, no. R2019; box 49, vol. 22, no. R2584.

98. AC, box 38, vol. 5, no. 5532; box 35, vol. 1, no. 459.

99. Wat, *Mój wiek,* vol. 1, 347, 349.

100. AC, box 39, vol. 6, no. 7829; box 41, vol. 8, no. 10623.

101. AC, box 41, vol. 8, no. 10056; box 36, vol. 2, no. 1610. See also AC, box 38, vol. 5, no. 6084; box 48, vol. 21, no. R1950.

102. AC, box 43, vol. 10, no. 11949; box 43, vol. 10, no. 11914; box 42, vol. 9, no. 10745.

103. Eley and Suny, "Introduction," in Eley, *Becoming National,* 21.

Chapter 7

1. AC, box 39, vol. 5, no. 7127; box 45, vol. 13, no. 14220; box 42, vol. 9, no. 10754; box 45, vol. 14, no. 14323. For male reactions, see AC, box 35, vol. 1, no. 744; box 45, vol. 14, no. 14236.

2. AC, box 38, vol. 5, no. 5723.

3. Bronisław Zaleski, cited in Artur Kijas, *Polacy w Kazachstanie. Przeszłość i terażniejszość* (Poznań: Abos, 1993), 10.

4. George Fredrickson, *The Arrogance of Race: Historical Perspectives on Slavery, Racism and Social Inequality* (Middletown, Conn.: Wesleyan University Press, 1988), 207.

5. Kazakhs and Uzbeks composed 1.30 percent and 1.86 percent of the total Gulag population, respectively. Getty, Rittersporn, and Zemskov, "Victims of the Soviet Penal System," 1,028.

6. Ciesielski, *Polacy w Kazachstanie*, 45.

7. Cited in Kijas, *Polacy w Kazachstanie*, 58.

8. Piotr Żaroń, *Ludność polska w Związku Radzieckim w czasie II wojny światowej* (Warsaw: Państwowe Wydawnictwo Naukowe, 1990), 394.

9. In December 1941, General Sikorski and Stalin agreed to send 21,500 Poles from the Arkhangel'sk region and the Komi ASSR to Kazakhstan. Elżbieta Budakowska, "Polacy w Kazachstanie—Historia i Współczesność," *Przegląd Polonijny* 18, no. 4 (1992): 18.

10. See AC, box 39, vol. 5, no. 7482; box 52, vol. 31, no. R6110.

11. Kijas, *Polacy w Kazachstanie*, 53.

12. Most works from the nineteenth and early twentieth centuries do not delineate Kazakhstan and Central Asia from Siberia when discussing the experience of exile. Early memoirs with information on Poles in Central Asia include: Michał Janik, *Dzieje Polaków na Syberji* (Kraków, 1928); Adolf Januszkiewicz, *Żywot Adolfa Januszkiewicza i jego listy ze stepów kirgiskich'* 2nd ed. (Berlin, 1875); Szymon Tokarzewski, *Siedem lat katorgi. Pamiętniki 1846–1857* (Warsaw, 1907). A renewed interest in the subject of Poles in Kazakhstan since the fall of the Communist regimes has resulted in new studies and memoirs, including: *W stepie dalekim: Polacy w Kazachstanie* (Poznan & Almaty, 1997); Anna Sobota, *W stepach Kazachstanu. Wspomnienia z lat 1939–1946* (Warsaw-Wrocław, 1993).

13. See Gajrat Sapargalijew and Wladimir Djakow, *Polacy w Kazachstanie w XIX w* (Wrocław: Czytelnik, 1982), 13; Budakowska, "Polacy w Kazachstanie," 31.

14. Janik, *Dzieje Polaków*, 399.

15. Sapargalijew and Djakow, *Polacy w Kazachstanie*, inside cover.

16. Tokarzewski, *Siedem lat katorgi*, 179–80.

17. Sapargalijew and Djakow, *Polacy w Kazachstanie*, 306–7.

18. Budakowska, "Polacy w Kazachstanie," 8.

19. Contrasting the general attitude depicted here, several important Polish researchers spent time learning the native languages and studying the culture and territory of the nomadic peoples and came to highly appreciate them. This group includes Tomasz Zan, Jan Witkiewicz, and Adolf Januszkiewicz.

20. AC, box 41, vol. 8, no. 10717; box 48, vol. 21, no. R1923; box 44, vol. 13, no. 14009; box 42, vol. 10, no. 11330.

21. I have only read sympathetic portrayals of the peoples of Central Asia, or reports of good relations with them, in personal narratives published in the 1980s and 1990s. See Marian Papiński, Rodzina Małachowskich, and Lesława Domańska, *Tryptyk kazachstański* (Warsaw: Instytut Studiów Politycznych PAN, 1992), 90, 180–81, 257–60; Eugenia Huntingdon, *Unsettled Account*, 109, 118; Tęczarowska, *Deportacja w nieznane*, 36. Exceptions are rare in the wartime documents. In her

memoir, Ada Halpern names a particular Kazakh as helpful and kind—the only one like that, she adds. MID, box 198, folder 8, Halpern, 36.

22. AC, box 52, vol. 30, no. R5640; box 48, vol. 20, no. R1565; box 43, vol. 10, no. 11943; MID, box 198, folder 8, Halpern, 13.

23. MID, box 198, folder 2, Czarkowska-Golejewska, 50.

24. AC, box 36, vol. 2, no. 1615; box 42, vol. 9, no. 11195. See also AC, box 43, vol. 10, no. 11907; box 45, vol. 14, no. 14289. For men's comments, see AC, box 41, vol. 8, no. 10694; box 41, vol. 8, no. 10717.

25. Mary Douglas, *Purity and Danger: An Analysis of the Concepts of Pollution and Taboo* (New York: Routledge, 1966), 2.

26. MID, box 198, Anonymous, "At Exile in Kazakhstan," 11; AC, box 52, vol. 30, no. R5636; MID, box 198, folder 2, Czarkowska-Golejewska, 66.

27. AC, box 48, vol. 21, no. R2195; box 48, vol. 21, no. R1955; box 39, vol. 5, no. 6810. See also AC, box 45, vol. 14, no. 14346.

28. In a manuscript written in 1944, one woman notes that the Kazakhs, "if they had any belief were Mohamadens." But she adds that she "certainly never saw the slightest evidence that the Kazakhs retained the faintest vestige of religion of any sort." MID, box 198, folder 2, Czarkowska-Golojewska, 124. Halpern notes in her manuscript that she too learned that Kazakhs were Mohammedans. MID, box 198, folder 8, Halpern, 26.

29. She understands the term "Kirghiz" as a label meaning "insurgent." AC, box 45, vol. 15, no. 14466. While in the 15th and 16th centuries the forbears of the Kazakhs, Kirghiz, and Uzbeks were ethnically indistinguishable and ruled by a single khan, subsequent political divisions, economic differences, and particularities in local customs and Islamic practices gradually led to distinctions among them. Russians, too, called the Kazakhs "Kirghiz" until the early Bolshevik period; a separate Kazakh Republic was created only in 1925. See Martha Brill Olcott, *The Kazakhs* (Stanford, Calif.: Hoover Institution Press, 1987), xx. The Poles do not use the terms "Turkic" or "Muslim" when referring to the peoples of Soviet Central Asia.

30. See Robert Berkhofer, Jr., *The White Man's Indian. Images of the American Indian from Columbus to the Present* (New York: Vintage Books, 1979).

31. Anderson, *Imagined Communities*, 143.

32. Elizabeth Bacon, *Central Asians Under Russian Rule* (Ithaca, N.Y.: Cornell University Press, 1966), 171; Olcott, *Kazakhs*, 198.

33. On Soviet attempts to transform Muslim social roles, see Gregory Massell, *The Surrogate Proletariat: Moslem Women and Revolutionary Strategies in Soviet Central Asia, 1919–1929* (Princeton, N.J.: Princeton University Press, 1974).

34. Olcott, *Kazakhs*, 198, 188.

35. The female literacy rate in Kazakhstan reportedly rose from 25 percent in 1936 to 66 percent in 1939. Olcott, *Kazakhs*, 196. In Tadzikistan only 1 percent of the women were considered literate in 1926, but by 1939 the percentage had risen to 77 percent. Norton Dodge, *Women in the Soviet Economy* (Baltimore: Johns Hopkins University Press, 1966), 143.

36. AC, box 48, vol. 20, no. R1617.

37. One young man does mention the children of the Kazakh family with whom he lived. Never describing them as boys or girls, he refers to them as "brats." MID, box 198, "At Exile in Kazakhstan."

38. AC, box 35, vol. 1, no. 115; MID, box 198, folder 8, Halpern.

39. AC, box 41, vol. 9, no. 10721; box 42, vol. 10, no. 11669.

40. Similarly, a young man describes the Kazakh woman in whose hut he lived in such a grotesque manner that she appears more as a deformed, disgusting animal than a woman. MID, box 198, "At Exile in Kazakhstan."

41. Douglas, *Purity and Danger*, 160.

42. AC, box 45, vol. 14, no. 14283; box 45, vol. 14, no. 14282; box 45, vol. 14, no. 14238. See also AC, box 59, vol. 48, no. 11816; box 59, vol. 48, no. 11850.

43. AC, box 45, vol. 15, no. 14466.

44. AMB, box 33, teczka A, tom 3, Czesława Matusiak; Mieczysława Bak.

45. AC, box 43, vol. 10, no. 11897; box 48, vol. 21, no. R2250.

46. AMB, box 33, teczka A, tom 3, Paulina Rzehaków; Janina Dukjetowa.

47. AMB, box 33, teczka A, tom 3, Janina Dukjetowa; AC, box 40, vol. 6, no. 8413; box 45, vol. 14, no. 14421; MID, box 198, folder 2, Czarkowska-Golejewska, 56.

48. AC, box 36, vol. 3, no. 2276; box 43, vol. 10, no. 11699; MID, box 91, folder 3, letter, Pani Wojewódzka.

49. AC, box 45, vol. 14, no. 14237.

50. In his research on the Soviet occupation of Germany at the close of WWII, Norman Naimark found race to be a crucial factor in the German image of the Soviets, whom they viewed as "Asiatics." His work shows that the racial aspect made the threat and incidents of rape by soldiers of the Red Army much more terrifying to the Germans. Naimark, *Russians in Germany*, 110–11.

51. George Fredrickson, *The Black Image in the White Mind. The Debate on Afro-American Character and Destiny, 1817–1914* (New York: Harper Torchbooks, 1972), 256–82.

52. Budakowska, "Polacy w Kazachstanie," 24.

53. Shoshana Keller, "Trapped between State and Society: Women's Liberation and Islam in Soviet Uzbekistan, 1926–1941," *Journal of Women's History* 10, no. 1 (spring 1998): 32.

54. Keller, "Trapped between State," 28.

55. Massell, *Surrogate Proletariat*, 114.

56. Fredrickson, *Black Image*, 279.

57. John D'Emilio and Estelle Freedman, *Intimate Matters: A History of Sexuality in America* (New York: Harper & Row, 1988), 297.

58. MID, box 91, folder 12, Besiadowska.

59. AC, box 43, vol. 10, no. 11940; box 48, vol. 20, no. R1898.

60. Krystyna Niemczyk, "Długa droga do Polski," in *Polacy w Rosji mówią o sobie*, ed. Edward Walewander (Lublin: Katolicki Uniwersytet Lubelski, 1993), 231.

61. U.S. Department of State, *Records of the Department of State Relating to the Internal Affairs of Poland, 1916–1944*, reel 73, 860c.48/706 (Washington, D.C.: National Archives and Record Services, General Services Administration, 1981), letters, 6.

62. MID, box 91, folder 5, no. L.dz.1036/Tj.41, Defense Minister Kazimierz Sosnkowski to Minister Professor Stanisław Stroński, 4 April 1941. The note states that the officer to whom the letter was addressed was currently in an army division in Jerusalem.

63. U.S. Department of State, *Records of the Department of State*, reel 73, 860c.48/710, item 193.

64. I have not seen the originals of these letters. I reproduce them from reports

of the Polish army and government-in-exile. The possibility exists that the letters were embellished or even constructed for propaganda purposes, particularly given the similarity of the style and content and the absence of names and dates. It may also be the case that one incident, described in a letter that was intercepted and reported by one department, showed up later in the documents of others, in distorted form.

65. Ciesielski, *Polacy w Kazachstanie*, 273–74.

66. Massell, *Surrogate Proletariat*, 114.

67. Anne McClintock, "Family Feuds: Gender, Nationalism and the Family," *Feminist Review* 44 (summer 1993): 65.

68. Ruth Harris, "The 'Child of the Barbarian': Rape, Race and Nationalism in France during the First World War," *Past and Present* 141 (November 1993): 179, 170.

69. MID, box 2, folder 6, Dr. Zdzisław Łęcki, "Działalność Związku Sowieckiego na terenie okupowanych ziem Polski od dnia agresji 17.9.39 do lipca 1941," 10 March 1942, 57.

70. MID, box 91, folder 3, no. N4/2B, "Polacy na Syberii."

71. MID, box 91, folder 5, Defense Minister Kazimierz Sosnkowski to Minister Professor Stanisław Stroński, 4 April 1941.

72. MID, box 2, folder 1, no. S/40/2, "Short Outline of the Soviet Occupation."

73. Deborah Gaitskell and Elaine Unterhalter, "Mothers of the Nation: A Comparative Analysis of Nation, Race and Motherhood in Afrikaner Nationalism and the African National Congress," in Yuval-Davies, *Woman-Nation-State*, 61.

74. Stanisław Mikołajczyk, *The Rape of Poland* (New York: Whittlesey House, 1948). Mikołajczyk uses the metaphor frequently, calling the Molotov-Ribbentropp Pact and subsequent invasions the "Nazi-Red rape of Poland" (34), and the Soviet postwar "takeover" of Poland its "raping" (ix). He views the entire experience as Poland's "debasement" (viii).

75. Klaus Theweleit offers a thoughtful perspective on the prevalence of gendered differences in discussing pain and torture: "Male language doesn't care about the unspeakable. It feels itself powerful enough to speak about everything. It can do so by cutting the cord between the voice and the body." Theweleit, "The Bomb's Womb," in Cooke, *Gendering War Talk*, 312.

76. MID, box 2, folder 6, Łecki.

77. MID, box 91, folder 3, no. S/23/8, Pplk. Dypl. Gano, Zastępca Szefa Oddziału II Sztabu Naczelnego Wodza, Report to General Sosnkowski, Minister Kot, Minister Stroński, 21 September 1941.

78. MID, box 91, folder 5, K. Sosnkowski, 4 April 1941.

79. This interpretation of wartime rape comes largely from Susan Brownmiller, *Against Our Will: Men, Women and Rape* (New York: Bantam Books, 1975), 23–87.

80. Christine Obbo, "Sexuality and Economic Development in Uganda," in Yuval-Davies, *Woman-Nation-State*, 85.

81. Julia Watson and Sidonie Smith, "De/Colonization and the Politics of Discourse in Women's Autobiographical Practices," in *De/Colonizing the Subject: The Politics of Gender in Women's Autobiography*, ed. Julia Watson and Sidonie Smith (Minneapolis: University of Minnesota Press, 1992), xvii.

82. Chandra Talpade Mohanty, quoted in Watson and Smith, "De/Colonization," xvi.

83. AC, box 42, vol. 10, no. 11330.

Chapter 8

1. Aleksander Wat, *Mój wiek. Pamiętnik mówiony*, vol. 2 (Warsaw: Czytelnik, 1990), 28.

2. Herling-Grudziński, *Inny świat (A World Apart)*, trans. Andrzej Ciozkosz (New York: Arbor House, 1951).

3. AC, box 67, vol. 74, no. 18077. See also AC, box 60, vol. 50, no. R12882; box 37, vol. 4, no. 3686.

4. Norman Davies, *Heart of Europe: A Short History of Poland* (Oxford: Oxford University Press, 1984), 345.

5. Polish Information Center, *Polish Facts and Figures* no. 2 (25 March 1944): 12.

6. Polish Information Center, *Polish Facts and Figures* no. 4 (25 April 1944): 1.

7. Jan Kucharzewski, *Od białego caratu do czerwonego* 7 vols. (Warsaw: Wydawnictwo Kasy im. J. Mianowskiego, 1923–35).

8. Quoted in Piotr Wandycz, *Soviet-Polish Relations, 1917–1921* (Cambridge: Harvard University Press, 1969), 98.

9. Wat, *Mój wiek*, vol. 1, 143.

10. Wandycz, *Soviet-Polish Relations*, 1–14, 287.

11. Wacław Lednicki, *Russia, Poland and the West: Essays in Literary and Cultural History* (London: Hutchinson, 1954), 14. See also Wacław Lednicki, *Russian-Polish Relations: Their Historical, Cultural and Political Background* (Chicago: Polish National Alliance Educational Department, n.d.).

12. AC, box 42, vol. 9, no. 10742; MIK, box 15, letter, Lola, 12 April 1940. The documents contain no accusations of rape made against soldiers of the Red Army. On the contrary, several women state that the Soviets "behaved well." See AC, box 41, vol. 9, no. 10741.

13. Wat, *Mój wiek*, vol. 1, 262.

14. Huntingdon, *Unsettled Account*, 33. See also MID, box 142, folder Tarnopol–1, no. 4681.

15. Davies, *Heart of Europe*, 344.

16. Zamoyska-Panek, *Have You Forgotten?* 105.

17. Douglas, *Purity and Danger*, 36, 160.

18. See AC, box 42, vol. 10, no. 11646; box 43, vol. 10, no. 11698.

19. AC, box 65, vol. 68, no. 15774; box 42, vol. 10, no. 11682; box 42, vol. 10, no. 11660; box 41, vol. 9, no. 10742; box 44, vol. 13, no. 14008.

20. Lipper, *Eleven Years*, v.

21. See AC, box 38, vol. 5, no. 5532; box 42, vol. 9, no. 10751.

22. AC, box 48, vol. 21, no. R2007. See also AC, box 50, vol. 25, no. R3862; box 38, vol. 5, no. 6113.

23. MID, box 198, folder 5, no. 01, Anonymous; AC, box 36, vol. 2, no. 1933. See also AC, box 45, vol. 13, no. 14180; box 35, vol. 1, no. 78.

24. AC, box 44, vol. 12, no. 12620; box 38, vol. 5, no. 5723; box 43, vol. 11, no. 12519.

25. AC, box 43, vol. 10, no. 11914.

26. Getty, Rittersporn, and Zemskov, "Victims of the Soviet Penal System," 1028.

27. AC, box 43, vol. 10, no. 11710.

28. See AC, box 35, vol. 1, no. 353; box 36, vol. 2, no. 1610. In contrast to the Polish depiction, a Latvian woman deported to the USSR as a child describes the Russians as "clean and religious." Elvira Sebre, "Serenity," in *We Sang through Tears*, 342–43. A Soviet woman arrested in 1937 describes the extreme discomfort she and other women felt at the conditions in prison and their own efforts to maintain personal cleanliness. Ginzburg, *Krutoi marshrut*, 233, 247, 356–57.

29. AC, box 38, vol. 5, no. 6103; box 54, vol. 37, no. R8071; box 36, vol. 2, no. 1906.

30. This derogatory term, which lacks an English equivalent, was used in convict slang to describe the most vicious of the female criminals in the Soviet labor camps. AC, box 42, vol. 10, no. 11669.

31. AC, box 44, vol. 12, no. 12629; box 44, vol. 13, no. 13970.

32. Getty, Rittersporn, and Zemskov, "Victims of the Soviet Penal System," 1022.

33. Robert Conquest states that while common criminals made up 10–15 percent of the total camp inmates, only about 5 percent of them were actually *urki*, the notoriously vicious professional criminals. Conquest, *Great Terror*, 313. Dallin and Nicolaevsky similarly report that only 12–15 percent of the camp population were common criminals: "The great majority—at least 85 percent—now comprised essentially honest men, sometimes men of outstanding moral integrity." Dallin and Nicolaevsky, *Forced Labor*, 232. Lipper also states that after 1937, most of the prisoners were sentenced as counterrevolutionaries. Lipper, *Eleven Years*, 105.

34. AC, box 49, vol. 24, no. R3386. See also AC, box 35, vol. 1, no. 71; box 44, vol. 12, no. 12696.

35. AC, box 55, vol. 37, no. R8060; box 38, vol. 5, no. 5723.

36. See AC, box 41, vol. 7, no. 9760; box 49, vol. 25, no. R3165; box 53, vol. 32, no. R6303.

37. AC, box 41, vol. 7, no. 9733; box 36, vol. 2, no. 1653.

38. AC, box 48, vol. 21, no. R1972; MID, box 91, folder 12, Besiadowska.

39. *Dark Side of the Moon*, 101.

40. AC, box 36, vol. 2, no. 1987.

41. AC, box 39, vol. 5, no. 7252.

42. Lipper, *Eleven Years*, 15.

43. AC, box 36, vol. 2, no. 1576; box 54, vol. 35, no. R7391; box 36, vol. 2, no. 1908.

44. AC, box 39, vol. 5, no. 7355. In Russian slang, "mat'" means swearing in general, and in particular, using the word "mother" in an obscene way. See Meyer Galler and Harlan Marquess, eds., *Soviet Prison Camp Speech: A Survivor's Glossary* (Madison: University of Wisconsin Press, 1972), 127–28.

45. AC, box 44, vol. 13, no. 13970; box 41, vol. 8, no. 10691; box 42, vol. 10, no. 11669.

46. MID, box 98, folder 6, Świaniewicz. See also AC, box 41, vol. 7, no. 9690; box 38, vol. 5, no. 5723.

47. MID, box 91, folder 12, Besiadowska; AC, box 44, vol. 13, no. 14005.

48. AC, box 41, vol. 8, no. 10059. I have not seen such comments from Polish men.

49. *Dark Side of the Moon*, 158.

50. AC, box 41, vol. 8, no. 10059; box 44, vol. 13, no. 13971; box 53, vol. 32, no. R6337. Such card games are widely reported in the literature on the camps. See Conquest, *Great Terror*, 314; Varlam Shalamov, *Kolyma Tales*, trans. John Glad (New York: W. W. Norton, 1980), 107–12; Solzhenitsyn, *Gulag*, 441–42.

51. MID, box 91, folder 12, Besiadowska.

52. Joan Scott, "Rewriting History," in Higonnet, *Behind the Lines*, 27.

53. Anne Gorsuch, "'A Woman Is Not a Man': The Culture of Gender and Generation in Soviet Russia, 1921–1928," *Slavic Review* 55, no. 3 (fall 1996): 638.

54. Goldman, *Women*, 316. See also Pushkareva, *Women in Russian History*, 258–59.

55. Ginzburg, *Krutoi marshrut*, 450–51.

56. Goldman, *Women*, 310–13.

57. Choi Chatterjee, "Soviet Heroines and Public Identity, 1930–1939," *Carl Beck Papers* no. 1402 (October 1999): 4.

58. Quoted in Oja, "Krestianka," 9.

59. AC, box 75, AWBD, no. D1267.

60. MIK, box 18, folder "September–November 1941," Jaszkar, "Sprawozdanie o stosunkach panujących na osiedlu p. n. 'Czwarty Skład'/Maryjska ASSR posiołek nr. 13"; MIK, box 18, folder "November–December 1941," letter, 10 November 1941; MID, box 99, folder 9, "Poles in the Soviet Union: Recollections of an Ex-Prisoner," 8.

61. AC, box 76, AWBD, Ankieta Kobieca.

62. AC, box 63, vol. 2, no. 1653; box 43, vol. 10, no. 11946.

63. AC, box 42, vol. 10, no. 11646; box 43, vol. 10, no. 11914. A few women report that even Soviet women were unable to perform the required labor. See AC, box 42, vol. 10, no. 11652.

64. AC, box 36, vol. 2, no. 1610; box 45, vol. 14, no. 14439; box 42, vol. 10, no. 11638; box 58, vol. 46, no. R11399.

65. AC, box 44, vol. 13, no. 13970.

66. Siegelbaum, *Stakhanovism*, 170–80.

67. MID, box 196, folder 3, Anna Szwaglisówna; box 198, folder 2, Czarkowska-Golejewska, 96.

68. MID, box 196, folder 4, Halina Borowik; box 196, folder 3, Anna Szwaglisówna; box 198, folder 7, "At Exile in Kazakhstan," 25.

69. AC, box 42, vol. 10, no. 11652.

70. AC, box 41, vol. 8, no. 10689.

71. AC, box 42, vol. 9, no. 10745; box 43, vol. 11, no. 12149; box 58, vol. 46, no. R11399; box 42, vol. 10, no. 11668; box 41, vol. 9, no. 10741.

72. Quoted in Goldman, *Women*, 5.

73. Goldman, *Women*, 106, 297.

74. Alan Ball, *And Now My Soul Is Hardened: Abandoned Children in Soviet Russia, 1918–1930* (Berkeley: University of California Press, 1994), 13–14.

75. Goldman, *Women*, 70–7.

76. Goldman, *Women*, 327.

77. Mary Buckley, *Women and Ideology in the Soviet Union* (Ann Arbor: University of Michigan Press, 1989), 129, 131–32.

78. AC, box 42, vol. 9, no. 10745; box 38, vol. 5, no. 6112; box 54, vol. 37, no. R7909; box, 41, vol. 8, no. 10052.

79. AC, box 42, vol. 10, no. 11668.

80. AC, box 45, vol. 14, no. 14445; box 41, vol. 9, no. 10742.

81. AC, box 42, vol. 9, no. 10748; box 66, vol. 71, no. 16063.

82. AC, box 43, vol. 10, no. 11710; box 45, vol. 13, no. 14217.

83. AC, box 45, vol. 13, no. 14178; box 41, vol. 9, no. 10742.

84. See MID, box 91, folder 12, Besiadowska; AC, box 41, vol. 9, no. 19742.

85. AC, box 42, vol. 9, no. 10745; box 41, vol. 9, no. 19742; box 43, vol. 10, no. 11710.

86. MID, box 91, folder 12, Besiadowska.

87. AC, box 42, vol. 9, no. 10745.

88. AC, box 42, vol. 9, no. 10745; box 42, vol. 10, no. 11652.

89. Yuval-Davies and Anthias, "Introduction," in Yuval-Davies, *Woman-Nation-State,* 10.

90. Quoted in Goldman, *Women,* 7.

91. Goldman, *Women,* 49–52, 255.

92. Goldman, *Women,* 109.

93. S. Ravich, quoted in Goldman, *Women,* 109.

94. See Ginzburg, *Krutoi marshrut,* 401–2.

95. Ball, *And Now My Soul,* 57, 195. In the early 1930s the Stalinist government forbade investigations into and articles about the *besprizornye,* not wanting to air any social problems that could be blamed on the government.

96. Ball, *And Now My Soul,* 79, 125, 196.

97. AC, box 36, vol. 2, no. 1908.

98. See AC, box 36, vol. 2, no. 1569; box 38, vol. 5, no. 6085; box 39, vol. 5, no. 7355.

99. AC, box 48, vol. 20, no. R1595; box 36, vol. 2, no. 1596.

100. AC, box 39, vol. 5, no. 7127; box 41, vol. 8, no. 10052.

101. AC, box 35, vol. 1, no. 353; box 39, vol. 5, no. 7252. See also AC, box 44, vol. 12, no. 12629.

102. AC, box 44, vol. 12, no. 12598; box 59, vol. 49, no. R12455; box 44, vol. 13, no. 14005.

103. Solzhenitsyn, *Gulag,* 233.

104. AC, box 38, vol. 5, no. 6112; box 36, vol. 2, no. 1570; box 42, vol. 10, no. 11660; MID, box 91, folder 12, Besiadowska. See also AC, box 36, vol. 2, no. 1576.

105. MID, box 91, folder 12, Besiadowska. Similarly, Solzhenitsyn states that among lesbians, "The women of a cruder type became the 'men.'" Solzhenitsyn, *Gulag,* 249.

106. AC, box 41, vol. 8, no. 10052; box 44, vol. 12, no. 12598; box 48, vol. 20, no. R1890. See also AC, box 36, vol. 2, no. 1966; box 38, vol. 5, no. 6335.

107. AC, box 54, vol. 35, no. R7314; box 41, vol. 8, no. 10059.

108. AC, box 42, vol. 10, no. 11662; box 38, vol. 5, no. 6111.

109. MID, box 91, folder 12, Besiadowska; AC, box 44, vol. 12, no. 12598.

110. AC, box 41, vol. 9, no. 10741. See also AC, box 38, vol. 5, no. 6082.

111. See MID, box 98, folder 6, Świaniewicz; Dallin and Nicolaevsky, *Forced Labor,* 187; Buber-Neumann, *Under Two Dictators,* 69, 82; Herling-Grudziński, *Inny świat,* 45–49; Lipper, *Eleven Years,* 159–61; Solzhenitsyn, *Gulag,* 229–34; Ginzburg, *Krutoi marshrut,* 414, 426, 429–30; 434–35; 472.

112. Solzhenitsyn, *Gulag,* 228.

113. Buber-Neumann, *Under Two Dictators,* 198.

114. Lipper, *Eleven Years,* 147. See also the Latvian account, Birznieks, "I Was Twenty-One," in *We Sang through Tears,* 303.

115. Wanda Kapuścińska represents one exception. She treats the issue of prostitution in the USSR with rare compassion for the women involved. While she neither applauds their mode of existence nor expresses any particular warmth for them, she attributes the source of their deviant behavior to the nature of men in general, and the Soviet system in particular. AC, box 41, vol. 9, no. 10742.

116. AC, box 38, vol. 5, no. 5723; box 41, vol. 8, no. 10687.

117. Bardach, *Man Is Wolf,* 125, 293.

118. MID, box 198, "At Exile in Kazakhstan," 9.

Conclusion

1. Sword, *Deportation and Exile,* 174–75. Approximately 50,000 Polish men who took part in the Soviet drive to Berlin also returned to Poland when the war ended, and an additional 100,000 to 200,000 Poles fled westward in 1943–1944 to escape violence at the hands of Ukrainians.

2. Groups of evacuees moved to Palestine, India, Uganda, Tanganyika, Kenya, South Africa, Northern and Southern Rhodesia, Mexico, and New Zealand. Many of them eventually settled in Great Britain, Canada, and the United States. See Elżbieta Wróbel and Janusz Wróbel, *Rozproszeni po świecie. Obozy i osiedla uchodżców polskich ze Związku Sowieckiego 1942–1950* (Chicago: The Authors, 1992).

3. Sword, *Deportation and Exile,* 195–97.

4. Małgorzata Fidelis, "Equality through Protection: The Politics of Women's Employment in Postwar Poland, 1945–1956" (Unpublished manuscript, 2001), 35–39.

Selected Bibliography

Archival Sources

Hoover Institution Archives, Stanford, California:

Anders, Władysław, Papers, 1939–1946

Karski, Jan, Papers, 1939–2000

Lotocka, Stefania, "Those Who Obeyed Orders," Typescript memoir, 1966

Mikołajczyk, Stanisław, Papers, 1938–1966

Poland, Ambasada (Soviet Union), Records, 1941–1944

Poland, Ministerstwo Informacji i Dokumentacji, Records, 1939–1945

Poland, Ministerstwo Spraw Zagranicznych, Records, 1925–1945

Rosarkhiv/Hoover Archives Project, Fond 89

Periodicals and Newspapers

Bluszcz

Dziennik ustaw Rzeczypospolitej Polskiej

Izvestiia

Moja Przyjaciółka

Rycerz Niepokalanej

Published Primary Sources

Bardach, Janusz, and Kathleen Gleeson. *Man Is Wolf to Man: Surviving the Gulag.* Berkeley: University of California Press, 1998.

Buber-Neumann, Margarete. *Under Two Dictators.* Translated by Edward Fitzgerald. New York: Dodd, Mead & Co., 1949.

Bugai, Nikolaj, ed. "'Specjalna Teczka Stalina': Deportacje i Reemigracja Polaków." *Zeszyty Historyczne* 107 (1994): 76–140.

Carnegie Endowment for International Peace. *The Other Balkan Wars: A 1913 Carnegie Endowment Inquiry in Retrospect.* New York: Carnegie Endowment for International Peace, 1993.

Dark Side of the Moon. London: Faber & Faber, 1946.

Documents on Polish-Soviet Relations, 1939–1945. London: Heinemann, 1961.

Drugi Powszechny Spis Ludności z dnia 9.XII.1931 roku. Mieszkania i gospodarstwadomowe. Ludność. Stosunki zawodowe. Polska. Vol. 7. Statystyka Polski, Series C, no. 62. Warsaw: Główny Urząd Statystyczny Rzeczypospolitej Polskiej, 1937.

Ginzburg, Evgeniia Semienovna. *Krutoi marshrut. Khronika vremen kul'ta lichnosti.* Milan: Arnoldo Mondadore Editore, 1967.

Główny Urząd Statystyczny Rzeczypospolitej Polskiej. *Małżeństwa, urodzenia i zgony. 1927, 1928.* Series C, no. 102. Warsaw, 1934.

———. *Małżeństwa, urodzenia i zgony. 1929, 1930.* Series C, no. 45. Warsaw, 1937.

———. *Małżeństwa, urodzenia i zgony. 1931, 1932.* Series A, no. 27. Warsaw, 1939.

Grudzińska-Gross, Irena, and Jan Gross, eds. *War through Children's Eyes.* Stanford, Calif.: Hoover Institution Press, 1981.

Halpern, Ada. *Liberation, Russian Style.* London: Maxlowe Publishing Co., 1945.

Herling-Grudziński, Gustaw. *Inny świat. Zapiski sowieckie.* Warsaw: Czytelnik, 1991.

Huntingdon, Eugenia. *The Unsettled Account: An Autobiography.* London: Severn House, 1986.

Irzykowski, Karol. "Dramat." *Rocznik literacki za rok 1934* (1935): 60–79.

———. "Dramat w teatrze." *Rocznik literacki za rok 1933* (1934): 60–73.

———. *Recenzje teatralne. Wybór.* Warsaw: Państwowy Instytut Wydawniczy, 1965.

Januszkiewicz, Adolf. *Żywot Adolfa Januszkiewicza i jego listy ze stepów kirgiskich.* 2nd ed. Berlin: n.p., 1875.

Katyń. Dokumenty ludobójstwa. Dokumenty i materiały archiwalne przekazane Polsce 14 pażdziernika 1992 r. Warsaw: Instytut Studiów Politycznych Polskiej Akademii Nauk, 1992.

Kollontai, Alexandra. *Communism and the Family.* London: Pluto Press, 1971.

Kon, Feliks. *Pol'sha na sluzhbe imperializma.* Moscow: Gosudarstvennoe izd., 1927.

Kot, Stanisław. *Listy z Rosji do Generała Sikorskiego.* London: Jutro Polski, 1955.

———. *Rozmowy z Kremlem.* London: Jutro Polski, 1959.

Krockow, Christian. *Hour of the Women.* Translated by Krishna Winston. London: Faber & Faber, 1992.

Kuncewiczowa, Maria. *Cudzoziemka.* 4th ed. Warsaw: Roj, 1939.

———. *Przymierze z dzieckiem.* Warsaw, 1927.

League of Nations. *Nationality of Women. Second Report of the Secretary-General on the Information Obtained in the Execution of the Resolutions of the Assembly and the Council.* Geneva, 1935. C.310.M.163.1935.V.

———. *Publications. V. Legal.* Geneva, 1935. A.7.1935.V.

———. *Status of Women. Communications from Governments and Women's International Organizations.* Geneva, 1936. A.33.1936.V.

League of Nations, Documents of the 12th Assembly. *Nationality of Women. Second Report of the Secretary-General.* Geneva, 1931. A.19.

Lipper, Elinor. *Eleven Years in Soviet Prisons*. Translated by Richard and Clara Winston. Chicago: Henry Regnery Co., 1951.

Lista Katyńska. Jeńcy obozów Kozielsk, Ostaszków, Starobielsk zaginieni w Rosji Sowieckiej. Warsaw: Agencja Omnipress-Spółdzielnia Pracy Dziennikarzy i Polskie Towarzystwo Historyczne, 1989.

Mickiewicz, Adam. *Księgi narodu polskiego i pielgrzymstwa polskiego*. Kraków: Nakładem Krakowskiej spółki wydawniczej, 1924.

Mikołajczyk, Stanisław. *The Rape of Poland. Pattern of Soviet Aggression*. New York: Whittlesey House, 1948.

Miłosz, Czesław. *Native Realm: A Search for Self-Definition*. Translated by Catherine Leach. Garden City, N.Y.: Doubleday & Co., 1968.

Ministerstwo Pracy i Opieki Społecznej. *Instrukcja szczegółowa z dnia 20 czerwca 1929 r. o czynnościach i programie działalności w sprawach ochrony pracy kobiet i młodcianych*. Warsaw: Ministerstwo Pracy i Opieki Społecznej, 1929.

Nałkowska, Zofia. *Dzienniki 1918–1929*. Vol. 3. Warsaw: Czytelnik, 1980.

Norwid, Cyprian. *Pisma wszystkie*. Vol. 9. Warsaw: Państwowy Instytut Wydawniczy, 1971.

Nowosielska, Zofia. *In the Hurricane of War. Memoirs of a Woman Soldier*. N.p.: The Author, 1929.

"Obliczenia Klotza." *Karta* 12 (1994): 107–10.

Papiński, Marian, Rodzina Małachowskich, and Lesława Domańska. *Tryptyk kazach-stański*. Warsaw: Instytut Studiów Politycznych PAN, 1992.

Pawlikowska-Jasnorzewska, Maria. *Dramaty*. Vols. 1–2. Warsaw: Czytelnik, 1986.

Polish Information Center. *Polish Facts and Figures*. New York, 1944.

Polska w polityce międzynarodowej (1939–1945). Zbiór dokumentów. Vol. 1. Warsaw: PIW, 1989.

Półtawska, Wanda. *I boję się snów. . . .* Warsaw: Czytelnik, 1962.

Roszkowski,Wojciech, ed. *Konflikty Polsko-Sowieckie 1942–1944*, vol. 3. Warsaw: PAN, 1993.

Shalamov, Varlam. *Kolyma Tales*. Translated by John Glad. New York: W. W. Norton, 1980.

Sierpińska, Zofia. *Anatema*. Łódź: Klio, 1994.

Słomka, Jan. *From Serfdom to Self-Government: Memoirs of a Polish Village Mayor 1842–1927*. Translated by William John Rose. London: Minerva Publishing Co., 1941.

Sobota, Anna. *W stepach Kazachstanu. Wspomnienia z lat 1939–1946*. Wrocław, Poland: 1993.

Sosabowska, Krystyna. *The Bridges I Have Crossed. A Polish Woman's Reminiscences*. Edinburgh: Albyn Press, 1985.

Świaniewicz, Stanisław. *W cieniu Katynia*. Paris: Instytut Literacki, 1976.

Szwajger, Adina Blady. *I więcej nic nie pamiętam*. Warsaw: Volumen, 1994.

Tęczarowska, Danuta. *Deportacja w nieznane. Wspomnienia 1939–1945*. London: Veritas, 1981.

Tokarzewski, Szymon. *Siedem lat katorgi. Pamiętniki 1846–1857.* Warsaw, 1907.

United Organizations of Americans of Lithuanian, Latvian and Estonian Descent. *An Appeal to Fellow Americans on Behalf of the Baltic States.* New York: Lithuanian American Information Center, 1944.

United States, Department of State. *Records of the Department of State Relating to the Internal Affairs of Poland, 1916–1944.* Washington, D.C., 1981. Microfilm. Reel 73, 860c.48/706.

Vitzthum, Hilda. *Torn Out by the Roots: The Recollections of a Former Communist.* Lincoln: University of Nebraska Press, 1993.

Walewander, Edward, ed. *Polacy w Rosji mówią o sobie.* Lublin, Poland: Katolicki Uniwersytet Lubelski, 1993.

Wańkowicz, Melchior. *Dzieje rodziny Korzeniewskich.* Rome: Oddział kultury i prasy, 2 korpusu, 1945.

Wat, Aleksander. *Mój wiek. Pamiętnik mówiony.* Vol. 1. London: Polonia Book Fund, 1977.

———. *Mój wiek. Pamiętnik mówiony.* Vol. 2. Warsaw: Czytelnik, 1990.

Watowa, Ola. *Wszystko co najważniejsze: Rozmowy z Jackiem Trznadlem.* London: Puls Publications, 1984.

We Sang through Tears: Stories of Survival in Siberia. Riga: Janis Roze Publishers, 1999.

Zagadnienia demograficzne Polski. Ruch naturalny ludności w latach 1895–1935. Dokładność rejestracji urodzeń i zgonów. Urodzenia wielorakie. Statystyka Polski, Series C, no 41. Warsaw: Główny Urząd Statystyczny Rzeczypospolitej Polskiej, 1936.

Zamoyska-Panek, Christine. *Have You Forgotten? A Memoir of Poland, 1939–1945.* New York: Doubleday, 1989.

Zapolska, Gabriela. *Moralność Pani Dulskiej.* Wrocław, Poland: Zakład Narodowy im. Ossolinskich, 1966.

Żeleński, Tadeusz Boy. *Piekło Kobiet. Jak skończyć z piekłem kobiet?* Warsaw: Państwowy Instytut Wydawniczy, 1960.

———. *Reflektorem w mrok. Wybór publicystyki.* Warsaw: Państwowy Instytut Wydawniczy, 1978.

Secondary Sources

Abramsky, Chimen, Maciej Jachimczyk, and Antony Polonsky, eds. *The Jews in Poland.* London: Basil Blackwell, 1986.

Anderson, Benedict. *Imagined Communities: Reflections on the Origin and Spread of Nationalism.* London: Verso, 1991.

Andrle, Vladimir. *Workers in Stalin's Russia: Industrialization and Social Change in a Planned Economy.* New York: St. Martin's Press, 1988.

Armstrong, John Lowell. "Policy toward the Polish Minority in the Soviet Union, 1923–89." *Polish Review* 35, no. 1 (1990): 51–65.

Bacon, Elizabeth. *Central Asians under Russian Rule*. Ithaca: Cornell University Press, 1966.

Ball, Alan. *And Now My Soul Is Hardened: Abandoned Children in Soviet Russia, 1918–1930*. Berkeley: University of California Press, 1994.

Bartoszewski, Władysław. *The Convent at Auschwitz*. London: Bowerdean Press, 1990.

———. "Poles and Jews as the 'Other.'" *Polin* 4 (1989): 6–17.

Baxter, Janeen. "Is Husband's Class Enough? Class Location and Class Identity in the United States, Sweden, Norway, and Australia." *American Sociological Review* 59 (April 1994): 220–35.

Bergman, Aleksandra. *Sprawy Białoruskie w II Rzeczypospolitej*. Warsaw: PAN, 1984.

Berkhofer, Robert, Jr. *The White Man's Indian. Images of the American Indian from Columbus to the Present*. New York: Vintage Books, 1979.

Będrzycka, Jadwiga, ed. *Kobiety polskie. Praca zbiorowa*. Warsaw: Książka i Wiedza, 1986.

Bridenthal, Renate, Atina Grossmann, and Marion Kaplan, eds. *When Biology Became Destiny: Women in Weimar and Nazi Germany*. New York: Monthly Review Press, 1984.

Brownmiller, Susan. *Against Our Will: Men, Women and Rape*. New York: Bantam Books, 1975.

Brumberg, Abraham. "Murder Most Foul." *Times Literary Supplement*, 2 March 2001.

Buckley, Mary. *Women and Ideology in the Soviet Union*. Ann Arbor: University of Michigan Press, 1989.

Budakowska, Elżbieta. "Polacy w Kazachstanie—Historia i współczesność." *Przegląd Polonijny* 18, no. 4 (1992): 5–37.

Butler, Judith, and Joan Scott, eds. *Feminists Theorize the Political*. New York: Routledge, 1992.

Canning, Kathleen. "Feminist History after the Linguistic Turn: Historicizing Discourse and Experience." *Signs* 19, no. 2 (winter 1994): 368–404.

———. "Gender and the Politics of Class Formation." *American Historical Review* 97, no. 3 (June 1992): 736–68.

Chalidze, Valery. *Criminal Russia: Essays on Crime in the Soviet Union*. Translated by P. S. Falla. New York: Random House, 1977.

Chatterjee, Choi. "Soviet Heroines and Public Identity, 1930–1939." *Carl Beck Papers* No. 1402 (October 1999).

Chojnowski, Andrzej. *Koncepcje polityki narodowościowej rządów polskich w latach 1921–1939*. Wrocław, Poland: Nakład Narodowy im. Ossolińskich, 1979.

Ciesielski, Stanisław. *Polacy w Kazachstanie w latach 1940–1946. Zesłańcy lat wojny*. Wrocław, Poland: Wydawnictwo Uniwersytetu Wrocławskiego, 1996.

Ciesielski, Stanisław, Grzegorz Hryciuk, and A. Srebrakowski, eds. *Masowe deportacje radzieckie w okresie II wojny światowej*. 2nd ed. Wrocław, Poland: Instytut Historyczny Uniwersytetu Wrocławskiego, 1994.

Ciesielski, Stanisław, and Antoni Kuczyński, eds. *Polacy w Kazachstanie—Historia i współczesność.* Wrocław, Poland: Wydawnictwo Uniwersytetu Wrocławskiego, 1996.

Conquest, Robert. *The Great Terror: A Reassessment.* New York: Oxford University Press, 1990.

————. *Soviet Nationalities Policy in Practice.* New York: Frederick A. Praeger, 1967.

Cooke, Miriam, and Angela Woollacott, eds. *Gendering War Talk.* Princeton, N.J.: Princeton University Press, 1993.

Cooper, Helen, Adrienne Ruslander Munich, and Susan Merrill Squier, eds. *Arms and the Woman: War, Gender and Literary Representation.* Chapel Hill: University of North Carolina Press, 1989.

Courtois, Stéphane, et al., eds. *The Black Book of Communism: Crimes, Terror, Repression.* Translated by Jonathon Murphy and Mark Kramer. Cambridge: Harvard University Press, 1999.

Czapski, Joseph. *The Inhuman Land.* New York: Sheed & Ward, 1952.

D'Emilio, John, and Estelle Freedman. *Intimate Matters: A History of Sexuality in America.* New York: Harper & Row, 1988.

Dallin, David, and Boris Nicolaevsky. *Forced Labor in Soviet Russia.* New Haven, Conn.: Yale University Press, 1947.

Davies, Norman. *Heart of Europe: A Short History of Poland.* Oxford: Oxford University Press, 1984.

————. "Poles and Jews: An Exchange." *New York Review of Books,* 9 April 1987.

Deak, Istvan, Jan Gross, and Tony Judt, eds. *The Politics of Retribution in Europe: World War II and Its Aftermath.* Princeton, N. J.: Princeton University Press, 2000.

Dodge, Norton. *Women in the Soviet Economy.* Baltimore: Johns Hopkins University Press, 1966.

Douglas, Mary. *Purity and Danger: An Analysis of the Concepts of Pollution and Taboo.* New York: Routledge, 1966.

Drakulic, Slavenka. "Women Hide behind a Wall of Silence: Mass Rape in Bosnia." *Nation* 256, no. 8 (1 March 1993): 253, 268–72.

Duden, Barbara. *The Woman beneath the Skin: A Doctor's Patients in Eighteenth-Century Germany.* Translated by Thomas Dunlap. Cambridge: Harvard University Press, 1991.

Eley, Geoff, and Ronald Suny, eds. *Becoming National: A Reader.* New York: Oxford University Press, 1996.

Fidelis, Małgorzata. "Equality through Protection: The Politics of Women's Employment in Postwar Poland, 1945–1956." Unpublished manuscript, 2001.

Fredrickson, George. *The Arrogance of Race. Historical Perspectives on Slavery, Racism and Social Inequality.* Middletown, Conn.: Wesleyan University Press, 1988.

————. *The Black Image in the White Mind: The Debate on Afro-American Character and Destiny, 1817–1914.* New York: Harper Torchbooks, 1971.

Friedlander, Judith, and Blanche Wiesen Cook, eds. *Women in Culture and Politics: A Century of Change*. Bloomington: Indiana University Press, 1986.

Gagnier, Regenia. *Subjectivities: A History of Self-Representation in Britain, 1832–1920*. New York: Oxford University Press, 1991.

Getty, J. Arch, Gabor Rittersporn, and Viktor Zemskov. "Victims of the Soviet Penal System in the Pre-war Years: A First Approach on the Basis of Archival Evidence." *American Historical Review* 98, no. 4 (1993): 1017–49.

Głowacki, Albin. *Sowieci wobec Polaków na ziemiach wschodnich w II Rzeczypospolitej*. Łódź: Wydawnictwo Uniwersytetu Łódzkiego, 1997.

Goldman, Wendy. *Women, the State and Revolution: Soviet Family Policy and Social Life, 1917–1936*. Cambridge: Cambridge University Press, 1993.

Gomułka, Stanisław, and Antony Polonsky, eds. *Polish Paradoxes*. London: Routledge, 1990.

Gorsuch, Anne. "'A Woman Is Not a Man': The Culture of Gender and Generation in Soviet Russia, 1921–1928." *Slavic Review* 55, no. 3 (fall 1996): 636–60.

Gross, Jan T. *Neighbors: The Destruction of the Jewish Community in Jedwabne, Poland*. Princeton, N.J.: Princeton University Press, 2001.

———. *Revolution from Abroad: The Soviet Conquest of Poland's Western Ukraine and Western Belorussia*. Princeton, N.J.: Princeton University Press, 1988.

Grossmann, Atina. "A Question of Silence: The Rape of German Women by Occupation Soldiers." *October* 72 (spring 1995): 43–63.

Gurjanow, Aleksander. "Cztery deportacje 1940–41." *Karta* 12 (1994): 114–36.

Hagen, William. "Before the 'Final Solution': Toward a Comparative Analysis of Political Anti-Semitism in Interwar Germany and Poland." *Journal of Modern History* 68, no. 2 (June 1996): 351–81.

Harris, Ruth. "The 'Child of the Barbarian': Rape, Race and Nationalism in France During the First World War." *Past and Present* 141 (November 1993): 170–206.

Heinemann, Marlene. *Gender and Destiny: Writers and the Holocaust*. Westport, Conn.: Greenwood, 1986.

Higonnet, Margaret, et al., eds. *Behind the Lines: Gender and the Two World Wars*. New Haven, Conn.: Yale University Press, 1987.

Hobsbawm, E. J. *Nations and Nationalisms Since 1780: Programme, Myth, Reality*. Cambridge: Cambridge University Press, 1990.

Iwanów, Mikołaj. *Pierwszy naród ukarany. Polacy w Związku Radzieckim 1921–1939*. Warsaw-Wrocław, Poland: Państwowe Wydawnictwo Naukowe, 1991.

Janik, Michał. *Dzieje Polaków na Syberji*. Kraków, 1928.

Jankowski, Edmund. *Eliza Orzeszkowa*. Warsaw: Państwowy Instytut Wydawniczy, 1964.

Jasiewicz, Krzysztof. "Obywatele Polscy aresztowani na terytorium tzw. Zachodniej Białorusi w latach 1939–1941 w świetle dokumentacji NKWD/KGB." *Kwartalnik Historyczny* 101, no. 1 (1994): 105–34.

Jasnowski, Józef, and Edward Szczepanik, eds. *Napaść sowiecka i okupacja polskich ziem wschodnich. Wrzesień 1939*. London: Polska Fundacja Kulturalna, 1985.

Jaworski, Rudolf, and Bianka Pietrow-Ennker, eds. *Women in Polish Society*. New York: Columbia University Press, 1992.

Jedlicki, Jerzy. *A Suburb of Europe: Nineteenth-Century Polish Approaches to Western Civilization*. Budapest: Central European University Press, 1999.

Jędruszczak, Hanna. "Employment in Poland in 1930–60." *Acta Poloniae Historica* 18 (1968): 250–63.

Jedynak, Barbara, ed. *Kobieta w kulturze i społeczeństwie*. Lublin, Poland: Wydawnictwo Uniwersytetu Marii Curie-Skłodowskiej, 1990.

Jones, Gareth Stedman. *Languages of Class: Studies in English Working Class History, 1832–1982*. Cambridge: Cambridge University Press, 1983.

Kadziela, J., J. Kwiatkowski, and I. Wyczańska, eds. *Literatura Polska w okresie międzywojennym*. Vol. 2. Kraków: Wydawnictwo Literackie, 1979.

Keller, Shoshana. "Trapped between State and Society: Women's Liberation and Islam in Soviet Uzbekistan, 1926–1941." *Journal of Women's History* 10, no. 1 (spring 1998): 20–44.

Kijas, Artur. *Polacy w Kazachstanie. Przeszłość i teraźniejszość*. Poznań: Abos, 1993.

Korzec, Pawel, and Jean-Charles Szurek. "Jews and Poles under Soviet Occupation (1939–1941): Conflicting Interests." *Polin* 4 (1989): 204–25.

Krahelska, Halina. *Praca kobiet w przemyśle współczesnym*. Warsaw: n.p., 1932.

Kucharzewski, Jan. *Od białego caratu do czerwonego*. 7 vols. Warsaw: Wydawnictwo Kasy im. J. Mianowskiego, 1923–35.

Kuromiya, Hiroaki. *Stalin's Industrial Revolution: Politics and Workers, 1928–1932*. Cambridge: Cambridge University Press, 1989.

Kuśnierz, Bronisław. *Stalin and the Poles. An Indictment of the Soviet Leaders*. London: Hollis & Carter, 1949.

Lasok, David, ed. *Polish Civil Law*. Vol. 1. Leiden, Netherlands: A. W. Sijthoff, 1973.

Lednicki, Wacław. *Life and Culture of Poland as Reflected in Polish Literature*. New York: Roy Publishers, 1944.

———. *Russia, Poland and the West: Essays in Literary and Cultural History*. London: Hutchinson, 1954.

Lelewel, Joachim. *Polska, dzieje i rzeczy jej*. Poznań: Nakład księg. J. K. Zupańskiego, 1864.

Lewin, Moshe. "Society and the Stalinist State in the Period of the Five Year Plans." *Social History* 2 (May 1976): 139–75.

Litauer, Jan, and Walerjan Przedpelski, eds. *Prawo cywilne obowiązujące na obszarze b. Kongresowego Królestwa Polskiego*. Warsaw: Biblioteka Prawnicza, 1930.

Lorence-Kot, Bogna. *Child-Rearing and Reform: A Study of the Nobility in Eighteenth-Century Poland*. Westport, Conn.: Greenwood Press, 1985.

———. "Klementyna Tanska Hoffmanowa, Cultural Nationalism and a New Formula for Polish Womanhood." *History of European Ideas* 4–5 (1978): 435–50.

Martin, Terry. "The Origins of Soviet Ethnic Cleansing." *Journal of Modern History* 70, no. 4 (December 1998): 813–61.

Massell, Gregory. *The Surrogate Proletariat: Moslem Women and Revolutionary Strategies in Soviet Central Asia, 1919–1929.* Princeton, N.J.: Princeton University Press, 1974.

McClintock, Anne. "Family Feuds: Gender, Nationalism and the Family." *Feminist Review* 44 (summer 1993): 61–80.

Mendelsohn, Ezra. *The Jews of East Central Europe between the World Wars.* Bloomington: Indiana University Press, 1983.

Miles, Margaret. *Carnal Knowing: Female Nakedness and Religious Meaning in the Christian West.* Boston: Beacon Press, 1989.

Mochnacki, Maurycy. *Dzieła Maurycego Mochnackiego.* Poznań, Poland: Nakład księg. J. K. Zupańskiego, 1863.

Naimark, Norman M. "The Deportation of the Chechens-Ingush (1944): Ethnic Cleansing in the Soviet Context." Unpublished manuscript, 1998.

———. *The Russians in Germany: A History of the Soviet Zone of Occupation, 1945–1949.* Cambridge: Harvard University Press, 1995.

Oja, Matt. "From Krestianka to Udarnitsa: Rural Women and the Vydvizhenie Campaign, 1933–1941." *Carl Beck Papers* No. 1203 (July 1996).

Olcott, Martha Brill. *The Kazakhs.* Stanford, Calif.: Hoover Institution, 1987.

Paczkowski, Andrzej. *Prasa Polska.* Vol. 3, *1918–1939.* Warsaw: Państwowe Wydawnictwo Naukowe, 1980.

Parker, Andrew, Mary Russo, Doris Sommer, and Patricia Yaeger, eds. *Nationalisms & Sexualities.* New York: Routledge, 1992.

Parsadonova, V. S. "Deportatsiia naseleniia iz Zapadnoi Ukrainy i Zapadnoi Belorussii v 1939–1941 gg." *Novaia i noveishaia istoriia* 2 (1989): 26–44.

———. "Tragediia Pol'shi v 1939 g." *Novaia i noveishaia istoriia* 5 (1989): 11–44.

Perrot, Michelle, ed. *A History of Private Life.* Vol. 4, *From the Fires of Revolution to the Great War.* Translated by Arthur Goldhammer. Cambridge: Harvard University Press, 1990.

Piotrowski, Tadeusz. *Poland's Holocaust.* Jefferson, N.C.: McFarland & Co., 1998.

Polacy na Syberji. Szkic historyczny. Warsaw, 1928.

Poovey, Mary. *Uneven Developments: The Ideological Work of Gender in Mid-Victorian England.* Chicago: University of Chicago Press, 1988.

Porter, Brian. *When Nationalism Began to Hate: Imagining Modern Politics in Nineteenth-Century Poland.* New York: Oxford University Press, 2000.

Prost, Antoine, and Gérard Vincent, eds. *A History of Private Life.* Vol. 5, *Riddles of Identity in Modern Times.* Translated by Arthur Goldhammer. Cambridge: Harvard University Press, 1991.

Pushkareva, Natalia. *Women in Russian History: From the Tenth to the Twentieth Century.* Translated and edited by Ewe Levin. Armonk, N.Y.: M.E. Sharpe, 1997.

Ringelbaum, Emmanuel. *Polish-Jewish Relations during the Second World War.* New York: Howard Fertig, 1976.

Ringelheim, Joan. "The Unethical and the Unspeakable: Women and the Holocaust." *Simon Wiesenthal Annual* 1 (1984): 69–87.

Selected Bibliography

Roberts, Mary Louise. *Civilization Without Sexes: Reconstructing Gender in Postwar France, 1917–1927*. Chicago: University of Chicago Press, 1994.

Rossi, Zhak. *Spravochnik po Gulagu*. London: Overseas Publications Interchange, 1987.

Sapargalijew, Gajrat, and Wladimir Djakow. *Polacy w Kazachstanie w XIX w.* Wrocław, Poland: Czytelnik, 1982.

Schatz, Jaff. *The Generation: The Rise and Fall of the Jewish Communists of Poland.* Berkeley: University of California Press, 1991.

Scott, Joan. *Gender and the Politics of History.* New York: Columbia University Press, 1988.

———."The Woman Worker." In *A History of Women in the West.* Vol. 4, *Emerging Feminism from Revolution to World War.* Edited by Genevieve Fraisse and Michelle Perrot. Cambridge: Harvard University Press, 1993.

Siedlecki, Julian. *Losy Polaków w ZSRR w latach 1939–1986.* London: Gryf Publications, 1987.

Siegelbaum, Lewis. *Stakhanovism and the Politics of Productivity in the USSR, 1935–1941.* Cambridge: Cambridge University Press, 1988.

Siekierski, Maciej. "Hoover Institution's Polish Collections: An Overview and a Survey of Selected Materials on Polish-Soviet Relations." *Polish Review* 33, no. 3 (1988): 325–41.

Siemieńska, Renata. *Płeć, zawód, polityka. Kobiety w życiu publicznym w Polsce.* Warsaw: Uniwersytet Warszawski, Instytut Socjologii, 1990.

Skrzypek, Stanisław. *The Problem of Galicia.* London: Polish Association for the South Eastern Provinces, 1948.

Smolar, Aleksander. "Jews as a Polish Problem." *Daedalus* (spring 1987): 31–73.

Solzhenitsyn, Aleksandr. *The Gulag Archipelago, 1918–1956. An Experiment in Literary Investigation.* Translated by Thomas P. Whitney. New York: Harper & Row Publishers, 1975.

"Sprawozdanie z dyskusji dotyczącej liczby obywateli polskich wywiezionych do Związki Sowieckiego w latach 1939–1941." *Studia z dziejów Rosji i Europy Środkowo-Wschodniej* 31 (1996): 117–48.

Stegmann, Natali. "Von 'Müttern der Nation' und anderen Frauen: Zum Stand der historischen Frauenforschung in Polen." *Jahrbücher für Geschichte Osteuropas* 46 (1998): 269–75.

Stiglmayer, Alexandra, ed. *Mass Rape: The War against Women in Bosnia-Herzegovina.* Lincoln: University of Nebraska Press, 1994.

Strzembosz, Tomasz, ed. *Studia z dziejów okupacji Sowieckiej (1939–1941). Obywatele polscy na kresach północno-wschodnich II Rzeczypospolitej pod okupacją sowiecką w latach 1939–1941.* Warsaw: Biblioteka Ziem Wschodnich, 1997.

Subtelny, Orest. *Ukraine: A History.* Toronto: University of Toronto Press, 1994.

Sugar, Peter, and Ivo Lederer, eds. *Nationalism in Eastern Europe.* Seattle: University of Washington Press, 1969.

Sulek, Leon. "Wojenne losy Polaków żołnierzy Armii Czerwonej (1940–1945)." *Zeszyty Historyczne* 99 (1992): 30–39.

Suny, Ronald G. *The Revenge of the Past. Nationalism, Revolution, and the Collapse of the Soviet Union.* Stanford, Calif.: Stanford University Press, 1993.

Sword, Keith. *Deportation and Exile: Poles in the Soviet Union, 1939–1948.* New York: St. Martin's Press, 1994.

———, ed. *The Soviet Takeover of the Polish Eastern Provinces, 1939–41.* London: Macmillan, 1991.

Tomaszewski, Jerzy. *Najnowsze dzieje Żydów w Polsce.* Warsaw: PWN, 1993.

———. *Rzeczpospolita wielu narodów.* Warsaw: Czytelnik, 1985.

Tuszynski, Marek. "Soviet War Crimes against Poland during the Second World War and its Aftermath: A Review of the Factual Record and Outstanding Questions." *Polish Review* 44, no. 2 (1999): 183–211.

Vigarello, Georges. *Concepts of Cleanliness: Changing Attitudes in France Since the Middle Ages.* Translated by Jean Birell. Cambridge: Cambridge University Press, 1988.

Walczewska, Sławomira. *Damy, rycerzy, feministki: kobiecy dyskurs emancypacyjny w Polsce.* Kraków: Wydawnictwo eFKa, 1999.

———, ed. *Głos mają kobiety. Teksty feministyczne.* Kraków: Convivium, 1992.

Walicki, Andrzej. *The Enlightenment and the Birth of Modern Nationhood. Polish Political Thought from Noble Republicanism to Tadeusz Kościuszko.* Translated by Emma Harris. Notre Dame, Ind.: University of Notre Dame Press, 1989.

———. *Philosophy and Romantic Nationalism: The Case of Poland.* Oxford, England: Clarendon Press, 1982.

Wandycz, Piotr. "Poland's Place in Europe in the Concepts of Pilsudski and Dmowski." *East European Politics and Society* 4, no. 3 (1990): 451–68.

———. *Soviet-Polish Relations, 1917–1921.* Cambridge: Harvard University Press, 1969.

Wapiński, Roman. "The Endecja and the Jewish Question." *Polin* 12 (1999): 271–83.

Watson, Julia, and Sidonie Smith, eds. *De/Colonizing the Subject: The Politics of Gender in Women's Autobiography.* Minneapolis: University of Minnesota Press, 1992.

Weeks, Theodore. *Nation and State in Late Imperial Russia: Nationalism and Russification on the Western Frontier, 1863–1914.* Dekalb: Northern Illinois University Press, 1996.

———. "Poles, Jews, and Russians, 1863–1914: The Death of the Ideal of Assimilation in the Kingdom of Poland." *Polin* 12 (1999): 242–56.

Wielhorski, Władysław. *Los Polaków w niewoli sowieckiej.* London: Rada Ziem Wschodnich R.P., 1956.

Wiles, Timothy, ed. *Poland between the Wars: 1918–1939.* Bloomington: Indiana University Polish Studies Center, 1985.

Wróbel, Elżbieta, and Janusz Wróbel. *Rozproszeni po świecie. Obozy i osiedla uchodźców polskich ze Związku Sowieckiego 1942–1950.* Chicago: The Authors, 1992.

Wrzesiński, Wojciech, ed. *Między Polską etniczną a historyczną.* Wrocław, Poland: PAN, 1988.

Selected Bibliography

Yuval-Davies, Nira, and Floya Anthias, eds. *Woman-Nation-State*. London: Macmillan, 1989.

Zamorski, Kazimierz. *Dwa tajne biura 2 Korpusu*. London: Poets and Painters Press, 1990.

Zawodny, Janusz Kazimierz. *Death in the Forest: The Story of the Katyn Forest Massacre*. Notre Dame, Ind.: Notre Dame University Press, 1962.

Zbrodnicza ewakuacja więzień i aresztów NKWD na kresach wschodnich II Rzeczypospolitej w czerwcu - lipcu 1941 roku. Materiały z sesji naukowej w 55. rocznicę więźniów NKWD w głąb ZSRR. Łódź, 10 czerwca 1996 r. Warsaw: Główna Komisja Badania Zbrodni Przeciwko Narodowi Polskiemu, 1997.

Zemskov, Viktor. "Spetspereselentsy: po dokumentatsii NKVD-MVD SSSR." *Sotsiologicheskie issledovaniia* 11 (1990): 3–17.

Żak, Stanisław. *Maria Kuncewiczowa*. Kraków: Polska Akademia Nauk, 1971.

Żarnowska, Anna, and Andrzej Szwarc, eds. *Kobieta i edukacja na ziemiach polskich w XIX i XX w.* 2 vols. Warsaw: Instytut Historyczny Uniwersytetu Warszawskiego, 1992.

———. *Kobieta i kultura życia codziennego wiek XIX i XX*. Warsaw: Wydawnictwo DiG, 1997.

———. *Kobieta i praca. Wiek XIX i XX*. Warsaw: Wydawnictwo DiG, 2000.

———. *Kobieta i społeczeństwo na ziemiach Polskich w XIX w.* Warsaw: Instytut Historyczny Uniwersytetu Warszawskiego, 1990.

———. *Kobieta i świat polityki w niepodległej Polsce 1918–1939*. Warsaw: Wydawnictwo Sejmowe, 1996.

———. *Równe prawa i nierówne szanse. Kobiety w Polsce międzywojennej*. Warsaw: Wydawnictwo DiG, 2000.

Żarnowski, Janusz. *Społeczeństwo Drugiej Rzeczypospolitej 1918–1939*. Warsaw: PWN, 1973.

Żaroń, Piotr. *Ludność polska w Związku Radzieckim w czasie II wojny światowej*. Warsaw: Państwowe Wydawnictwo Naukowe, 1990.

Index

abortion: in exile, 177; in Poland, 97, 177–78; in Russia, 264
absenteeism, 64–65
accidents, work, 143, 144
administrative exile *(administrativno-vysslanye)*, 15, 22, 23–24, 58
agriculture, 48–50, 61, 68
Altai *krai*, 34, 82, 217
amnesty, xiv–xv, 34; collective farm work after, 222; death rate after, 144; female's self-perceived helplessness after, 108; health care after, 41–42; living conditions after, 39–40; nationality of Polish minority after, 204; resettlement after, 222–23, 284, 334n2
Anders, Władysław, xiv, xvi–xvii
Anders army, xiv, xv, xvii–xviii, 106, 108, 117
anti-Semitism, 191, 192, 323n36
Arkhangel'sk *oblast'*, 34, 104, 201
arrests, mass, 6, 7
arrestees: estimated number of, 9, 291n23; female, 24–26, 34–35, 297n35; male, 12, 23, 26
Asia, Polish female dread of, 220–21, 230–31
AWBD. *See* Bureau of Documents of the Polish Army in the East

bathing facility, gender mixing at, 157–61, 164
Belorussia, 34
Belorussians: as dashing hopes of Polish females, 209; in deportation, 184, 199; in eastern borderlands, 191; as informers, 214; in interwar

Poland, 190, 320n2; minority status in pre–World War I Poland, 191; Polish female attitudes toward after exile, 199, 201–3; sexual morality of females, 212; and Soviet occupation, 196, 198; as treasonous, 204–6, 210, 218–19; violation to nation/community by, 206–8. *See also* minorities, in Poland
Beria, Lavrenti, 11, 14, 15, 17, 18, 38, 39, 57–58
besprizorniki (homeless youth), 257, 264, 269, 333n95
Białystok, 29, 45, 65, 77, 99, 296n24
birth control in Poland, 97, 177, 178
black work *(czarna robota)*, 77
Bluszcz (Ivy), 50, 94
body search, 161–64, 169–70, 176, 180, 316nn76
Bolsheviks, 67–68, 115, 249, 251, 252
border transgression as crime, 7, 24–25, 100, 257, 296n14
Boy-Żeleński, Tadeusz, 97, 177–80
bribes for labor quota, 74, 304n99
brickmaking, 62, 63, 66–67
bride price *(kalym)*, 237
brucellosis, 41, 42
Brześć-nad-Bugiem, 41, 263
Bureau of Documents of the Polish Army in the East (AWBD), xvi, 69–70, 82, 83, 199
burial in foreign soil, 125–26
Buzhenovskii state farm, 46
bytovichki (common criminals), 256–57, 269–70

camp husband *(lagernyi muzh)*, 166–67, 173, 174, 273–74
Catholic Church in Poland, 53, 89, 96, 97, 178, 269
Central Asia, Soviet: climate of, 39, 40, 62; exiles sent to, 33, 34, 222; families left in by fathers/husbands, 109; historical exile of Poles to, 223–24, 235; mortality rate in, 223; national composition of population in, 184, 185; Polish perception of as monolithic, 221, 224, 227. *See also* labor camps; Muslim females; Turkic males; Turkic peoples
Central Committee (Communist Party), 16, 58
childbirth, 116, 128–29, 177, 178
children, Polish: death of, xix, 19, 27, 122–26, 144–45, 311n101; as deportees, 12, 26, 293–94n42; difficulty for working mothers to care for, 117–18; effect of Kazakhs on, 233; reeducation of, 118, 119–20; separated from mothers, 100–103, 112–13; in Soviet orphanage, xx, 109, 116, 120–23
Ciesielski, Stanisław, 168, 237
cleanliness: and female identity, 150, 151, 167; gendered ideas about, 152–53; and national identity, 151–52; Western cultural notion of, 150–52
climate extreme, in exile, 39–40, 62
collective farm *(kolkhoz);* hunger at, 110; lack of gendered division of labor at, 70; living conditions at, 38–39; national composition of population at, 38–39; percentage of deportees living at, 35; refusal to employ Poles at, 59; work at after amnesty, 222
Congress Kingdom of Poland, 47–48, 53, 191
Constitution (1921), 190
Constitution (1935), 95
convict laborer *(katorżnik)*, 59

Council of People's Commissars. *See* Sovnarkom
criminals: common, 165, 166, 256–57, 269–70, 331n33; hardened *(urki)*, 165, 169, 331n33
Criminal Code, 24, 25
cult of Virgin Mary, 178
czarna robota (black work), 77

day nursery, Soviet, 118
death: among exiles, 19, 41, 108, 144, 315n5; attributed to climate, 39; attributed to disease, 42; increase in, after amnesty, 144; of Polish children, 27, 123–26, 144–45, 311n101; on transports, 19, 101, 144. *See also* execution
denouncement, 9, 132, 206
deportations, 9–10; estimated numbers in, 13, 291nn23–24, 292n26, 293n35; national groups in, 184, 199; number of persons in each, 295n3; pregnant females in, 178. *See also* first deportation; fourth deportation; second deportation; third deportation
deportees, civilian: death rate of, 144, 313n5; elderly, 27, 144; estimated number of, 9, 222, 291n23; as primarily female/child, 12, 235, 293–94n42; reasons for, 12, 13–14, 21, 99; voluntary, 292n32. *See also* administrative exile; special settlement
depression, 135, 136
Det-Domy (Children's Homes), 119–20
disease, 41–42, 123–24, 240, 270–73
divorce in USSR, 264–65
Dmowski, Roman, 190, 191, 320n4

education, 9, 49, 119–20
Egipska pszenica (Egyptian Wheat), 96
employment of Polish females, 47–48, 92
enemy class, Polish nation as, 77–78, 86

Estonians, in deportation, 184
ethnic Poles: as exiles, 22–23, 199, 295n4, 296n6; as traitorous, 214
European Russia, northern, 33, 34, 61
evacuation of Poles from USSR: circumstances of, xv, xvii; numbers in, xvii
execution of male prisoners, xi, xii, xiii, xv, 15, 287nn1–2
exiles: estimated numbers of, 291n23; prevalence of disease in, 41–42
exiles, characteristics of typical female: age, 26–27; ethnic Poles as, 22–23, 295n4, 296n6; final destination of, 33–35; occupation of, 29–32; place of origin, 27–28, 29; socioeconomic status, 27–29
exiled settlers (ssyl'no-poselentsy), 16

family: relationships and female identity, 140, 238; relationships as reason for deportation, 98–100; Soviet exploitation of, 111–13; surrogate, 129–31, 134–35, 140–41; in USSR, 115–16, 263–65, 267, 277. See also family, Polish; females, Polish; females, Russian
family, Polish, 268; division of during deportation/arrest, 100–104; duty of wife/mother in, 93–94; nineteenth-century exiles included in, 138; traditional, 87, 88. See also females, Polish
females, Polish: effect of hard labor on identity of, 45; elevation of maternal role of, 88–89; and emancipation, 90–91; family identity of, 100, 140, 238; gender identity of, 281, 286; ideal of mother/wife, 89, 93–94, 95, 98; ideal Polish, 89, 93–94, 95, 98; identity and sexual honor, 173, 174; identity and cleanliness, 149, 150–51, 167; indirect attack on identity of, 280; maternal identity of, 80, 83, 126–27; national identity of,

113–15; Polish notion of nature of, 51–52, 67, 80; as professional women, 49; self-effacement of, 110–11; as sole economic providers, 7–8, 75; traditional duty of, 88, 89–90, 92, 93, 94, 116, 140; work identity of, 51–53. See also prostitution
females, Russian: ability of to fulfill norm, 261–62; aggression of, 258; and camp marriage, 272–73; cleanliness of, 253–54, 331n28; as common criminals, 254–57, 269–70; description of in Gulag, 254; lack of personal hygiene by, 253–54; lack of solidarity among, 254; lesbian, 272; and mixed bathing facility, 160–61; morality of, 255, 256, 268–69, 271–72, 275, 276; as mothers, 265, 267; non-Polish view of, 252, 275; physical labor by, 259, 260–63, 277; Polish compassion toward, 252–53; politicals, 254; sexual deviance of, 272–73, 276; swearing by, 257–58; view of equal rights of, 262–63; as "wives" in camps, 256. See also prostitution; Russians; Union of Soviet Socialist Republics
feminist as pejorative term, 96
first deportation (Feb. 1940), xv, 13, 14–15, 20, 22, 144, 288n15. See also special settler
flirting with enemy, 318n114
Flying University, 90
fourth deportation (May/June 1941), 13, 15–16, 22, 101–2, 296n5
free exile: in Central Asia, 222; gender mixing in, 155; living conditions of, 38; sexual exploitation during, 167–68; work requirements of, 58–59
Frontier Defense Corps (K.O.P.), 193

gendered view: about cleanliness, 152–53; of national identity, 136–37, 141; of Polish minority, 214–15;

rape: *(cont.)*
in USSR, 165, 269, 274; during
World War I, 239
Red Army, 4, 9, 11, 14, 195, 196, 198,
249–51, 293n38
reeducation, 116, 118, 119–20
refugees *(bezhentsy)*, 15
religion: and affiliation of exiles, 22;
and holiday observation, 134;
suppression of, 119, 120. *See also*
Jews; Muslim females
repatriation; of Jews to German partition, 15; of Poles, 284, 334n1
resistance, 25; through educating children as Poles, 120–21; through
preserving Polishness, 120–21,
133–34; against mixed bath facilities, 159, 160; against prison conditions, 128–29
Resolution no. 2122-617ss, 57–58
Romania, 4, 113, 290n2
Rusini, 201, 202
Russians: gendered view of, 255; percentage of workers in camps, 253;
Polish view of, 246–47, 251–52.
See also female, Russian; Gulag;
male, Russian; Siberia; Union of
Soviet Socialist Republics. *See
also* females, Russian
Russo-German war, 186, 228–29
*Rycerz Niepokalanej (The Knight of
the Virgin Mary)*, 52, 160, 301n23
Rychliński, Stanisław, 55

Scott, Joan, 47, 81, 85, 258–59
second deportation (April 1940), xv,
13, 15, 22, 26, 288n15. *See also* administrative exile
Second Polish Republic. *See* interwar
Poland
Sejm, 193
selective memory, 171, 174–75
self-depiction, by Polish females,
103–5. *See also* females, Polish
Semipalatynsk *oblast'*, 34
sexual division of labor: in interwar
Poland, 47, 49, 53; Marxist view

of, 67; Polish female view of,
66–71, 75, 77, 79–80, 84; Polish
government view of, 80–81;
Polish male view of, 69; Soviet
view of, 46, 67–68, 70, 77, 79, 85,
87
sexual exploitation, xix; during interrogation, 164–65, 169–70; of men,
318n118; as taboo subject,
169–72, 175, 177, 181, 237,
238–39, 318n123. *See also* rape
sexuality, as taboo subject, 178–79
sexually transmitted diseases, 240,
270–73
shame, 157, 316n63, 318n122
shock worker, 68, 73, 260, 303n78
Siberia, 28, 38, 270–71; climate in, 39,
62; death in, 41; as final destination for exile, 33, 34, 185; lack of
sanitation in, 151; sexual exploitation in, 170–71; types of labor
performed in, 61. *See also* females, Russian; Russians; Union
of Soviet Socialist Republics
single motherhood in Poland, 97
social class: identity, xxii, 53–56; of
Poles in USSR: leveling of, 81–85,
183; tensions in after amnesty, 83;
working class in interwar Poland,
54
socioeconomic order, Polish: disruption of, 71–72; in interwar period,
70, 71, 76
solidarity: among Polish females,
128–31, 134–35, 160, 208–9, 254;
among Polish males, 131–32;
among Polish minorities, 209;
lack of among Poles, 132–33; lack
of among Russian females, 254;
lack of among/within Polish minorities, 208, 209
Sosnkowski, Kazimierz (Soviet of
People's Commissars), 57–58, 240
Soviet Slavic minorities, 216–17
Sovietization: of children, 118–20, 122;
of occupied Poland, 6–9
Sovnarkom, 14–16

special settlement, percentage of deportees in, 35
special settlers *(spetspereselentsy-osadniki)*, 14, 57–58, 155–56, 222
special settlers-refugees *(spetspereselentsy-bezhentsy)*, 15
Stakhanovite, 69–70, 73, 74, 262, 303–4*n*85, 304*n*94
Stalin, Joseph, xv, 39, 56, 260
state farm *(sovkhoz)*, 35, 40; at Buzhenovskii, 46; national composition of population at, 35; in Northern Kazakhstan, 224–25; in Uzbekistan, 236
suicide, 19, 123, 135, 136, 173
Sukhobezvodna. *See* labor camps
support network, gendered differences in, 133
surrogate family, 129–31, 134–35, 140–41
Sverdlovsk *oblast'*, 210–11, 262–63

tardiness at work, punishment for, 64–65
Tadzikistan, female literacy in, 327*n*35
teachers, Polish, 120, 132, 156, 185
Temnikov. *See* labor camps
textile industry, 47, 49
third deportation (June 1940), 13, 15, 22, 27, 144, 295*n*5. *See also* special settlers
torture: emotional, 113; of female Poles, 107, 113–14; during interrogation, 111, 135, 145–47; of male Poles, 107, 128, 135
traitorous behavior, 132–33, 136
transport: conditions during, xix, 17–19, 144, 179–80; death on, 19, 101, 144; gender mixing during, 154, 155, 156–57
Treaty of Riga (1921), 320*n*9
tuberculosis, 41
Turkic males: description of, 233–34, 243; fear of, 236–37; as rapist, 234–35. *See also* Turkic peoples
Turkic peoples: as animal-like, 231; crimes against females, 235–36;

description of, 276; relative silence on children of, 230; relative silence on individuals, 211–12, 228–32, 243–44, 282; stereotype of, 224–26, 234–36. *See also* Kazakh; Kirghiz; Muslim women; Turkic males; Uzbek
tutejszy (locals), 193

Ukraine, as final destination for exile, 34
Ukrainian Nationalist Organization (O.U.N.), 192
Ukrainian SSR (USSR), 58–59, 303*n*78
Ukrainians: in deportation, 184, 199; in eastern borderlands, 191; hope for future by, 209; as informers, 214; in interwar Poland, 190, 320*n*2; minority status in preWorld War I Poland, 191; nationalism among, 192; Polish female attitude toward after exile, 199, 201–3; and Soviet occupation, 196, 198, 200; as treasonous, 204–6, 210, 211, 214, 218–19; violation to nation/community by, 206–7. *See also* minorities
Union of Soviet Socialist Republics (USSR): abortion in, 264; children in, 264–67; day nursery in, 118; family in, 115–16, 263–67, 277; homeless youth in, 257, 264, 269, 333*n*95; industrialization/modernization in, 56–57, 67–68, 77–78, 228–29, 259–60; infanticide in, 265; invasion of Poland by, 4–9, 192, 195, 249–50, 277–78, 279; males in, 265–66; marriage/divorce in, 263–65, 269; orphanages in, xx, 109, 116, 120–23, 266, 267; prostitution in, 254, 255, 263, 334*n*115; rape in, 165, 269, 274; schools in, 118; similarity of people of to Poles, 245, 276; unemployment/labor shortage in, 57. *See also* females, Russian; Gulag; males, Russian; Russians; Siberia